Digital Capitalism in the New Media Era

Çiçek Topçu
Antalya Belek University, Turkey

IGI Global
PUBLISHER of TIMELY KNOWLEDGE

A volume in the Advances in Finance, Accounting, and Economics (AFAE) Book Series

Published in the United States of America by
IGI Global
Information Science Reference (an imprint of IGI Global)
701 E. Chocolate Avenue
Hershey PA, USA 17033
Tel: 717-533-8845
Fax: 717-533-8661
E-mail: cust@igi-global.com
Web site: http://www.igi-global.com

Library of Congress Cataloging-in-Publication Data

Names: Topçu, Çiçek, 1993- editor.
Title: Digital capitalism in the new media era / Çiçek Topçu.
Description: Hershey, PA : Information Science Reference, [2024] | Includes bibliographical references and index. | Summary: "The structure of the media-society relationship, which is revealed in the political economy of the traditional media, continues to be discussed in the light of new technologies. The possibilities and limitations of new media under digital capitalism are determined within its political economy context"-- Provided by publisher.
Identifiers: LCCN 2023046100 (print) | LCCN 2023046101 (ebook) | ISBN 9798369311820 (hardcover) | ISBN 9798369311837 (ebook)
Subjects: LCSH: Digital media--Economic aspects. | Digital media--Social aspects. | Capitalism. | Information society.
Classification: LCC HM851 .D5163 2024 (print) | LCC HM851 (ebook) | DDC 302.23/1--dc23/eng/20240110
LC record available at https://lccn.loc.gov/2023046100
LC ebook record available at https://lccn.loc.gov/2023046101

This book is published in the IGI Global book series Advances in Finance, Accounting, and Economics (AFAE) (ISSN: 2327-5677; eISSN: 2327-5685)

British Cataloguing in Publication Data
A Cataloguing in Publication record for this book is available from the British Library.

For electronic access to this publication, please contact: eresources@igi-global.com.

Advances in Finance, Accounting, and Economics (AFAE) Book Series

ISSN:2327-5677
EISSN:2327-5685

Editor-in-Chief: Ahmed Driouchi, Al Akhawayn University, Morocco

MISSION

In our changing economic and business environment, it is important to consider the financial changes occurring internationally as well as within individual organizations and business environments. Understanding these changes as well as the factors that influence them is crucial in preparing for our financial future and ensuring economic sustainability and growth.

The **Advances in Finance, Accounting, and Economics (AFAE)** book series aims to publish comprehensive and informative titles in all areas of economics and economic theory, finance, and accounting to assist in advancing the available knowledge and providing for further research development in these dynamic fields.

COVERAGE

- Investments and Derivatives
- Wages and Employment
- Economics of Innovation and Knowledge
- Economic Indices and Quantitative Economic Methods
- E-Accounting
- Comparative Accounting Systems
- Risk Analysis and Management
- Economic Policy
- Bankruptcy
- Field Research

IGI Global is currently accepting manuscripts for publication within this series. To submit a proposal for a volume in this series, please contact our Acquisition Editors at Acquisitions@igi-global.com or visit: http://www.igi-global.com/publish/.

The Advances in Finance, Accounting, and Economics (AFAE) Book Series (ISSN 2327-5677) is published by IGI Global, 701 E. Chocolate Avenue, Hershey, PA 17033-1240, USA, www.igi-global.com. This series is composed of titles available for purchase individually; each title is edited to be contextually exclusive from any other title within the series. For pricing and ordering information please visit http://www.igi-global.com/book-series/advances-finance-accounting-economics/73685. Postmaster: Send all address changes to above address.

Titles in this Series

For a list of additional titles in this series, please visit:
www.igi-global.com/book-series/advances-finance-accounting-economics/73685

Digital Currency Assets and Challenges to Financial System Stability
Adekunle Alexander Balogun (University of Ibadan, Nigeria) and Yusuf Olatunji Oyedeko (Federal University Oye-Ekiti, Nigeria)
Business Science Reference • copyright 2024 • 227pp • H/C (ISBN: 9798369307700) • US $275.00 (our price)

Democratization of Africa and Its Impact on the Global Economy
Ndwakhulu Tshishonga (University of KwaZulu-Natal, South Africa) and Icarbord Tshabangu (Leeds Trinity University, UK)
Information Science Reference • copyright 2024 • 320pp • H/C (ISBN: 9798369304778) • US $240.00 (our price)

Algorithmic Approaches to Financial Technology Forecasting, Trading, and Optimization
Amandeep Singh (Chitkara Business School, Chitkara University, India) Sanjay Taneja (Graphic Era University (Deemed), India) and Pawan Kumar (Chandigarh University, India)
Business Science Reference • copyright 2024 • 266pp • H/C (ISBN: 9798369317464) • US $275.00 (our price)

Econometric Analyses on Global Finance and Economic Development
Yekeen Oku Abdul-Maliq (University of Abuja, Nigeria)
Business Science Reference • copyright 2024 • 300pp • H/C (ISBN: 9798369316108) • US $265.00 (our price)

Fintech Applications in Islamic Finance AI, Machine Learning, and Blockchain Techniques
Mohammad Irfan (Business School, NSB Academy, Bangalore, India) Seifedine Kadry (Noroff University College, Norway) Muhammad Sharif (Department of CS, COMSATS University Islamabad, Wah Cantt, Pakistan) and Habib Ullah Khan (Qatar University, Qatar)
Business Science Reference • copyright 2024 • 334pp • H/C (ISBN: 9798369310380) • US $265.00 (our price)

For an entire list of titles in this series, please visit:
www.igi-global.com/book-series/advances-finance-accounting-economics/73685

IGI Global
PUBLISHER of TIMELY KNOWLEDGE

701 East Chocolate Avenue, Hershey, PA 17033, USA
Tel: 717-533-8845 x100 • Fax: 717-533-8661
E-Mail: cust@igi-global.com • www.igi-global.com

Table of Contents

Detailed Table of Contents

There are emerging new paradigms based on cognitive IoT services. By fusing industrial assets with the newest and most advanced methods and technologies, this paradigm change is communicated. Despite this, there are a number of difficulties confronting modern industrial systems. Accordingly, the researchers held that the current IoT-based systems significantly lack cognitive intelligence, which means they cannot satisfy the requirements for industrial services. After that, the authors looked at the research obstacles and unresolved problems to speed up knowledge creation in the cognitive internet of things (CIoT) related to industrial systems.

The chapter compares and analyzes the cost and profit efficiency of India's public sector banks (PSBs). The information was obtained and examined between 1995 and 2017, or from the start of the post-liberalization era until the big State Bank of India merger in 2017. For each PSB in India, the average profit efficiency (PE) and cost efficiency (CE) ratings were examined year by year. Using non-parametric Friedman's two-way Annova and Wilcoxon signed rank tests, the distribution and median of efficiency scores in two subperiods were also evaluated. The findings showed that PSBs in the chosen time period had profit inefficiencies. PE scores are lower than CE scores for the whole time period. The results also showed significant variances amongst public sector banks between 1995 and 2022. In addition, since India's 1991 banking sector reform, the PE of PSBs has been falling.

Today, with the rapid development of technology, the number and importance of people operating in digital fields are increasing. Digital labor includes the processes of producing, creating, and distributing information using the internet, computers, and digital technologies. Digital labor is a concept that brings the concept of traditional business to digital fields. Studies on the internet, social media, blogs, video platforms, and other digital media are examples of digital labor. This type of labor includes a variety of skills and may require expertise in areas such as creative thought, digital marketing, content production, written and visual communication. This study discusses what digital labor is, its role in content production, and its current importance.

In the post-COVID-19 era, digital empowerment has become significant, especially with reference to media messages and communication technologies being used to financially empower citizens. As past histories of media are leaving behind a legacy of analog and archaic forms of media content creation, new technologies are building the 'media archaeology' of past traditions, heritages, epistemologies to generate meanings, and dialogue for new means of storytelling, thereby preserving heritage in 'digital formats'. The study has some broader mission and objectives

only recently became a member of the 2030 Agenda for Global Development and accepted the Paris Agreement. You may consider both triumphs as occurring at the same time. India just assumed two major new global obligations. The main topic of discussion in these talks is how to move toward diverse and environmentally conscious economies. India just made promises to the world. The primary objective of both agreements is to ensure that everyone lives a cozy, healthful, and ecologically responsible life. There is a common objective among these agreements. Achieving sustainable growth—a prerequisite for a green economy—requires us to expand our economies in ways that advance social justice, the environment, and equality. The lack of sustainable economic development makes the establishment of a green economy more challenging.

Chapter 7
Review of Internet Addiction and Internet Use Habits of Canakkale People.... 124
Merve Erdoğan, Çanakkale Onsekiz Mart Üniversitesi, Turkey

With technological advancements, the internet, a global communication tool, has become part of our lives. More and more demand has been placed on the internet, which quickly and easily meets people's needs, such as information, entertainment, communications, and so on. But the widespread use of the internet has brought negative consequences. This study will therefore address the concept of internet dependency, one of the negative consequences of the internet. The research was done to determine the internet addiction and internet usage habits of Çanakkale people. Two hundred eleven people aged 18-46 participated in the study using the general scan model. The study using the random sampling technique uses the descriptive statistical technique. The findings found that most participants were using the internet to inform and research and were angry when the internet was disconnected or slowed down. In addition, it has been found that most participants are happy and peaceful when they use the internet, and that using the internet comforts them when they feel anxious or troubled.

Chapter 8
The Reflections of the Digital Nomad Community on Social Media: A Case Study on Twitter.. 141
Burak Ili, Iğdır University, Turkey

Digital nomads, who can be defined as individuals capable of conducting all their work digitally and frequently traveling without being tied to a fixed home or workplace, are pursuing a lifestyle characterized by flexibility and freedom. This research aims to uncover how the concept is defined on the Twitter social network, specifically within the context of the #digitalnomad hashtag. Designed as a qualitative study, content analysis was employed as the data analysis strategy. The obtained data were subjected to analysis using the qualitative analysis software MAXQDA.

According to the findings, the most frequently used hashtags alongside #digitalnomad were found to be #workfromhome, #remotework, #remotejob, #workanywhere, #workfromanywhere, #freelance, #passiveincome, #entrepreneur, #travel, and #coworking. This indicates that the concept of digital nomadism is predominantly associated with financial freedom and promises individuals a more flexible lifestyle.

In the intricate domain of digital capitalism, we are at a crossroads where promise and complexity intersect. This transition into the digital era necessitates a comprehensive comprehension of the difficulties and opportunities presented by new media technologies. The insights shared in this chapter provide a foundation for envisioning policies, strategies, and collaborations that can propel us toward a future where digital capitalism catalyzes profound social transformation. This envisioned future is one in which the digital landscape becomes a powerful instrument for dismantling profoundly ingrained gender biases, fostering inclusivity, and making gender equality a concrete reality. It represents a world in which the digital domain is not just a place to fantasize about equality but a platform where equality thrives. We can utilize the potential of technology to dismantle existing gender biases, thereby creating a digital world that fosters equality. This promises endless chances and gender equality for everybody.

The aim of this study is to examine Netflix's film What Happened, Miss Simone, which is an example of a biographical documentary, with sociologist Erving Goffman's concept of self-presentation and performance, and to reveal the roles in the star's life. The details of individual identity, group relations, the impact of the environment, and the action and interactive meaning of information, which Goffman deals with with a micro-sociological analysis, constitute the scope of the study. The documentary tells the life of civil rights activist and American singer Nina Simone during the turmoil of the 1960s. Goffman's approach to the mode of presentation used by the actor and its meaning in the wider social context appears to offer a new perspective on the nature of social interaction and the psychology of the individual in documentary film.

Preface

Greetings to all enthusiasts and scholars of the evolving landscape of media, technology, and society!

Digital Capitalism in the New Media Era beckons you to explore the vibrant tapestry of our digital existence, where the fusion of media and technology has revolutionized our global landscape. This meticulously crafted reference book is more than just an assembly of ideas; it's a clarion call to decipher the intricacies of our digital epoch.

Dive into a comprehensive exploration of the nexus between traditional media's political economy and the disruptive force of emerging technologies. Witness how our world has metamorphosed into a unified global marketplace, intertwined with the influence of big tech conglomerates, personalized advertisements, and the omnipresent algorithms shaping our digital realities.

Embark on an intellectual odyssey delving into the evolution of digital capitalism within the larger context of capitalist history. This book acts as a beacon, illuminating the paths traversed by our society under the dynamic influence of cutting-edge communication technologies.

Venture forth to unravel the potential and limitations nestled within the bosom of new media, operating under the auspices of digital capitalism. Engage with diverse perspectives that challenge preconceived notions, presenting a kaleidoscope of ideas curated by esteemed scholars and visionaries.

This compendium doesn't merely inform; it ignites discourse, painting a vivid picture of our current system while introducing avant-garde perspectives that shed light on the intricate tapestry of our digital realm.

Designed for seekers of knowledge, researchers, astute sociologists, media professionals, communication scientists, and passionate learners alike, the book's themes span a wide spectrum of crucial subjects:

- Open science
- Gender and social gender equality
- Digital capitalism

- Informational capitalism
- Surveillance Capitalism
- Access to technology challenges
- International news monopoly
- Inequality of opportunity in digital education
- Digital labor
- Digital surveillance
- Digital divide
- Subaltern studies
- The post-truth era
- Algorithms
- Microtargeting
- Digital trace tracking
- Personal data
- Knowledge gap
- Political knowledge gap

Join us in this exhilarating expedition through the labyrinthine corridors of digital capitalism in the new media era. Engage with its complexities, unravel its mysteries, and emerge enlightened, armed with a deeper understanding of our ever-evolving digital terrain.

CHAPTER OVERVIEWS

Chapter 1: Cognitive Computing for Smart Environments, Survey, Technologies, and Research Challenges

In this chapter, Suriyan, Nagarajan, and Guruprasath unveil the emerging paradigms within cognitive IoT services. They highlight the paradigm shift in industrial systems, emphasizing the pressing need for cognitive intelligence to meet the requirements of modern industrial services. The researchers delve into the challenges hindering the evolution of the Cognitive Internet of Things (CIoT) within industrial systems, emphasizing unresolved issues and research obstacles that impede the rapid advancement of knowledge in this domain.

Chapter 2: Comparison of Indian Public Sector Banks' Cost and Profit Efficiencies in the Post-Reform Period

Magar, Shrivastava, Rajput, Sahu, Kumar, Pramanik, and Pandey meticulously analyze the cost and profit efficiencies of India's Public Sector Banks (PSBs) post the 1991 banking sector reforms. Through a comprehensive study spanning 1995 to 2017, they scrutinize the efficiency ratings, employing statistical tests to uncover patterns. The chapter underscores the profit inefficiencies within PSBs during the period, delineating the declining trend in profit efficiency post the banking sector reform, offering insights into the banking sector's performance over time.

Chapter 3: Digital Labor Business Power of the New Period

Dölkeles sheds light on the burgeoning landscape of digital labor, elucidating its significance amidst rapid technological advancements. The chapter navigates through the domains of digital production, creation, and distribution of information via various digital platforms, illustrating the integration of traditional business concepts into the digital realm. It delves into the multifaceted nature of digital labor, encompassing diverse skill sets and expertise in digital fields like marketing, content creation, and communication, accentuating its pivotal role in contemporary content production.

Chapter 4: Digitally Empowering Women Through Community Radio and Mobile Storytelling in India

Jha, Redhu, Pande, and Bolesnikov explore the post-COVID digital empowerment sphere, particularly focusing on media messages and technologies fostering financial empowerment. The study delves into the convergence of past media traditions with new storytelling technologies, emphasizing the preservation of heritage in digital formats. With specific research queries, it probes into digital literacy among community radio practitioners, the empowering relationship between women content creators and consumers, and the tools of digital empowerment.

Chapter 5: Evaluating Strategies of Activist-Public Relations From a Mainstream to Digital Activism Perspective

Güzeloglu, Erten, and Atak dissect the evolving landscape of activist-public relations, probing the intersection between activism and public relations strategies. Examining the convergence and divergence of corporate and social perspectives, the chapter illuminates the tools and methodologies employed in activist-public relations. Highlighting primary strategies like framing issues, networking, message crafting, and effectiveness measurement, it underscores the growing awareness and responsibilities among diverse actors and movements.

Chapter 6: Green Economy and Sustainable Development in India

Dhabliya, Gupta, Dari, Dhabliya, Dhablia, Sakhare, and Pramanik delve into India's journey towards sustainable development amidst recent global commitments. Examining India's role in the 2030 agenda and the Paris Agreement, the chapter elucidates the challenges and objectives in transitioning towards environmentally conscious economies. It emphasizes the need for sustainable growth and the challenges in establishing a green economy within an environment that lacks sustainable economic development.

Chapter 7: Review of Internet Addiction and Internet Use Habits of Çanakkale People

Erdogan scrutinizes the concept of internet addiction and usage habits among Çanakkale residents. Through a comprehensive study involving participants aged 18-46, the chapter reveals patterns in internet usage, emotions associated with internet connectivity, and the impact of internet use on participants' emotional well-being. It highlights the varied purposes of internet usage, uncovering emotional responses and dependencies associated with internet access.

Chapter 8: The Reflections of the Digital Nomad Community on Social Media – A Case Study on Twitter

Ili investigates the portrayal of digital nomadism on Twitter, aiming to discern perceptions and representations associated with the #digitalnomad hashtag. Employing content analysis, the chapter unravels the association of digital nomadism with financial freedom and a flexible lifestyle. It highlights the predominant themes, hashtags, and implications associated with the digital nomad community's discourse on Twitter.

Chapter 9: Unveiling Gender Dynamics in Digital Capitalism – Navigating the Path to Social Gender Equality

Singha outlines the intricate landscape of gender dynamics within digital capitalism, envisioning a future where technology catalyzes social transformation. Emphasizing the potential for technology to dismantle gender biases, the chapter envisions a digital domain fostering inclusivity and equality. It explores policies and strategies to leverage technology for gender equality, aiming to create an egalitarian digital world.

Chapter 10: Biographical Documentaries on Digital Platforms as a Self-Presentation – *What Happened, Miss Simone?* Performance and Pain in the Documentary

CANTAS scrutinizes the biographical documentary "What Happened, Miss Simone?" through sociologist Goffman's concept of self-presentation and performance. Analyzing the documentary's portrayal of Nina Simone's life during the 1960s, the chapter uncovers the nuances of individual identity, social interactions, and the impact of information in documentary filmmaking. It provides a fresh perspective on the social psychology of individuals depicted in documentary films.

These chapters collectively illuminate diverse facets of the evolving digital landscape, offering unique insights into technological advancements, societal implications, and the intersection of media, technology, and human behaviors.

As we draw the curtain on this captivating journey through "Digital Capitalism in the New Media Era," we stand at the threshold of a dynamic, ever-evolving landscape where media, technology, and society intersect. The chapters within this compendium are not merely disparate pieces of information but rather threads intricately woven into the fabric of our digital epoch.

From the emergence of cognitive IoT services to the intricate analyses of Indian Public Sector Banks' efficiencies post-reform, from unraveling the multifaceted landscape of digital labor to exploring gender dynamics within digital capitalism, each chapter unravels a distinct facet of our digital reality. These chapters serve as beacons illuminating the path through the labyrinthine corridors of digital capitalism and its ramifications on our societal fabric.

The intricate nexus between traditional media's political economy and the disruptive force of emerging technologies forms the crux of our exploration. The fusion of media and technology has not only reshaped our global landscape but has also necessitated a deeper understanding of the intricate mechanisms at play.

Our expedition through the realms of digital labor, internet addiction, empowerment through community radio, and gender dynamics within digital capitalism exposes us to the complexities and nuances inherent in our digitally driven world. From the portrayal of digital nomadism on social media to the examination of biographical documentaries through sociological perspectives, each chapter offers a distinct lens to scrutinize our digital reality.

This compendium doesn't just present insights; it catalyzes discourse, inviting scholars, enthusiasts, and learners alike to engage deeply, challenging established notions and embracing avant-garde perspectives. The diverse array of subjects covered within these chapters spans a wide spectrum, encapsulating the intricacies of our digital terrain.

We extend our deepest gratitude to the esteemed contributors whose scholarly endeavors have enriched this compendium, inviting readers to traverse through the multifaceted domains of digital capitalism. As we bid adieu to this intellectual odyssey, we do so with the hope that the insights gleaned from these chapters propel us forward into a future where knowledge, inclusivity, and technological advancements converge to shape a more informed, equitable, and empowered digital society.

With warm regards,

Çiçek Topçu
Antalya Belek University, Turkey

Chapter 1
Cognitive Computing for Smart Environments:
Survey, Technologies, and Research Challenges

Kannadhasan Suriyan
https://orcid.org/0000-0001-6443-9993
Study World College of Engineering, India

R. Nagarajan
https://orcid.org/0000-0002-4990-5869
Gnanamani College of Technology, India

R. Guruprasath
Gnanamani College of Technology, India

ABSTRACT

There are emerging new paradigms based on cognitive IoT services. By fusing industrial assets with the newest and most advanced methods and technologies, this paradigm change is communicated. Despite this, there are a number of difficulties confronting modern industrial systems. Accordingly, the researchers held that the current IoT-based systems significantly lack cognitive intelligence, which means they cannot satisfy the requirements for industrial services. After that, the authors looked at the research obstacles and unresolved problems to speed up knowledge creation in the cognitive internet of things (CIoT) related to industrial systems.

DOI: 10.4018/979-8-3693-1182-0.ch001

INTRODUCTION

In order to develop new applications and services and accomplish shared objectives, physical, virtual, and digital worlds are coming together to build smart environments that improve the intelligence of cities, transportation, energy, and many other domains. IoT plays a significant role in making equipment accessible that was previously locked away in well-designed silos in production processes. Such development could enable IoT or ICT to penetrate more advanced industrial systems that are digitalized or smarter. The Internet of Things (IoT) will link the industrial unit to a vast array of cutting-edge applications that are used throughout the production. Starting with connecting the workplace to the smart grid, diffusion of facilities in the production service, and/or allowing for more agility and flexibility inside the manufacturing organisations themselves are all possible options. Automation, operations information, and sophisticated analytics are three crucial productivity variables that are integrated in smart Manufacturing, an example of a smart environment. Some of these elements, like tools and machines operating on open platforms and with the ability to "think," lead to the creation of organisations that may be able to collaborate with one another, analyse data to predict disasters, organise themselves, and adjust to changes in the industrial practise itself. By improving perception and appropriate use of contextual information related to processes and goods, it is hoped to boost throughput in a process and ultimately across the whole pricing chain. This will allow real people to get correct information at the right moment. Most organisations and several industry studies indicate that smart industrial systems are not yet ready to be implemented. Furthermore, according to the studies, technology by itself is insufficient for smart or cognitive manufacturing systems to succeed and must instead be incorporated into more comprehensive strategic design, planning, and management procedures. In addition, additional factors, such as architectural paradigms, frameworks, and models, are necessary for a productive manufacturing system, whether it is intelligent or cognitive. In light of this, the architectural design of CIoT-based systems, including cognitive manufacturing systems, is concerned with architecture styles, networking and communication, cooperative data processing and security, smart things, services of the web with corresponding applications, business models with their corresponding processes, etc.

Technology-wise, the architectural design of the Internet of Things, for instance, should take into account scalability, modularity, extensibility, and interoperability across heterogeneous devices. Alternatively, the installed base for the Internet of Objects will increase to roughly 212 billion items by 2020, including over thirty billion linked things or gadgets, predicts industry research company IDC. IDC acknowledges that this development is primarily driven by intelligent systems that will be installed and collecting data from both consumer and business applications.

Prior literature was methodically read while keeping an eye on the manufacturing instances, and numerous alternative methods were looked at. One of the goals of this investigation is to assess what cognitive IoT-based technology, architectural frameworks, and alternative approaches are available and why they are needed. Another goal is to determine how cognitive capability was developed in order to achieve more practical, acceptable, and unstoppable smart or cognitive manufacturing.

As is well known, cognitive computing refers to the development of computer systems that are designed after the human brain and have the capacity to understand natural language, learn from the past, organically collaborate with people, and aid in decision-making. Researchers looked at how quickly advancing computers outpaced the human brain around the turn of the century and with the resurgence of cognitive computing. Additionally, researchers started to utilise the phrase cognitive computing, a new word that combines technology and biology, in an effort to reengineer the brain, one of the most powerful and efficient computers in the world. The majority of industrial systems are becoming into learning systems thanks to cognitive computing. As a result, they include embedded data analytics, automated management, and data-centric designs, where storage, memory, switching, and processing are all relocating closer to the data. They do not analyse vast amounts of data in a linear or predictable manner. With this in mind, the paper's main objective is to familiarise readers with the "CIoT" paradigm, which essentially deals without human intervention with how common items function as proxies and interact with the physical world and/or social networks. In order to achieve this, several research projects have been carried out to empower and integrate IoT with smart settings in order to generate the cognitive capabilities. This has been made possible at this time by the fast growth of IoT and the creation of new and improved technologies (Clarke, 2012; Iarovyi, 2016). After conducting a thorough investigation into the discrepancies between the offering and requirement, the researchers came to the conclusion that existing IoT has sufficient intelligence, which suggests that it cannot deliver the anticipated performance increases. IoT has been widely used in smart settings, such as smart homes, cities, buildings, transportation, health care, and industries.

However, the existing IoT-based systems notably lack cognitive intelligence in the sphere of contemporary intelligent services and cannot satisfy the industrial application need. Therefore, generic objects in IoT-based systems must have the capacity for independent learning, thought, and comprehension of the physical and social worlds. By supporting, guiding, and expanding human skills, substantial advancements in cognitive science will greatly boost human productivity. For instance provide detailed descriptions of some of the new cognitive engineering systems, such as Cognitive Materials, Cognitive (smart) Cameras, Cognitive Production Systems, and other cognitive infrastructures. Furthermore, despite the fact that the corpus of literature on the topic of smart manufacturing and industry is expanding quickly, there is currently no widely accepted definition of what makes a manufacturing system "smart" in academia (Shayan, 2015; Mekki, 2019). A lot of smart and—more recently—cognitive literature has attempted to define Smart manufacturing with regard to the integration of technologies, techniques, and related items in order to establish a succinct standard definition for the use of Cognitive/ smart manufacturing. For instance, additive manufacturing, digital manufacturing, smart factories and Industry 4.0 are mostly employed on situation by few researchers SM and other intelligent systems advanced industries.

Additionally, in fundamental concepts for defining smart systems are highlighted, including IoT, SoS, service-oriented SoA, autonomous units, large data analysis, complex event processing, adaptive and predictive control, or anticipating composite circumstances. In this context, the terms "smart" and "environment" allude to the capacity to acquire and apply information on one's own. Therefore, intelligent environments are those that can learn and use that information to adapt to the demands of its inhabitants to improve that residents' experience of that environment. When the term "Smart Manufacturing" is used, it means that manufacturing operations and systems are elevated to a novel level of openness, connectivity, and intelligence and is defined as: "Smart Manufacturing is the endeavour to design, deploy, and manage enterprise manufacturing operations and systems that enable proactive management of the manufacturing enterprise through in-depth analytics." Advanced information, communication, and manufacturing process technologies are used to build new and/or expanded versions of existing manufacturing systems, which are then synergistically integrated to produce new or expanded versions of manufacturing systems with the desired level of advanced automation, analysis, and integration capabilities. Additionally, from an engineering and technological perspective, SM advances beyond so-called "smart" technologies while maintaining intelligence and reasoning. It is a stage in the development of production system control that uses computers (Samuel, 2016; Desouza, 2019). Smart industry thus refers to the excessive application of sophisticated intelligent systems that enable rapid industrialization of innovative yields, energetic response to invention request, immediate optimization of industrial fabrication and resource sequence networks, and attachment of all manufacturing phases, from the consumption of new resources to the distribution of completed yields to the market.

COGNITIVE COMPUTING

The third age of computing is cognitive computing. The idea of a programmable computer was initially developed in the first period (19th century) by Charles Babbage, commonly regarded as the "father of the computer." His computer was designed to tabulate polynomial functions for use in navigation calculations. In the second period (1950), digital programming machines like the ENIAC ushered in a new age of programmable systems and modern computing. And now we come to cognitive computing, which uses big data analytics and deep learning algorithms to provide insights. As a result, the neural network, which is the basic idea underpinning deep learning, functions as the brain of a cognitive system. The neural network is a hardware and software system designed to emulate the human central nervous system in order to estimate functions that rely on a vast number of unidentified inputs.

An artificial intelligence that functions and thinks like a human brain? With the technological innovation that never ceases to amaze us, nothing is impossible! Today, one may "give eyes and a brain to his computer," making him capable of taking the place of people for monotonous work and greatly enhancing our everyday lives! Today, this idea is referred regarded as "cognitive computing." Computers may not have cognitive capacities, yet they are nonetheless able to do tasks that only depend on human perception. Any work requiring cognitive abilities may benefit from the use of automation; computers are capable of doing tasks like handwriting recognition, facial recognition, and behavioural pattern detection.

Since the invention of the computer, artificial intelligence has been a distant objective of computing, but new cognitive computing models suggest that we may be closer than ever. The studies of the human brain's structure and function, cognitive science, and computer science have been combined to create cognitive computing. Today, scientists are creating new technologies that combine the brain's highly complex functions with a computer's enormous data storage. Cognitive computing is built on self-learning systems that use machine learning methods to carry out certain activities that resemble those carried out by intelligent humans. To imitate human mental processes using a digital model is the aim of cognitive computing. The computer may imitate how the human brain functions by using self-learning algorithms that employ data mining, pattern recognition, and natural language processing. Some claim that cognitive computing is the third age of computing, after programmable systems in the 1950s and computers that could tabulate sums in the 1900s.

Enterprise IT infrastructure is strengthened by cognitive technologies. Business companies are thus better able to save costs by assuring improved efficiency and faster operational processes. Cognitive computing, according to Deloitte, is "more comprehensive than the conventional, limited notion of artificial intelligence." In fact, he claims, the term "AI" has mostly been used to characterise systems capable of carrying out activities that would typically need human intellect. A branch of computer science called cognitive technology uses techniques like natural language processing, data mining, and pattern recognition to simulate how the human brain works. In the next years, it is anticipated to have a significant impact on how people

Figure 1. IoT cognitive computing

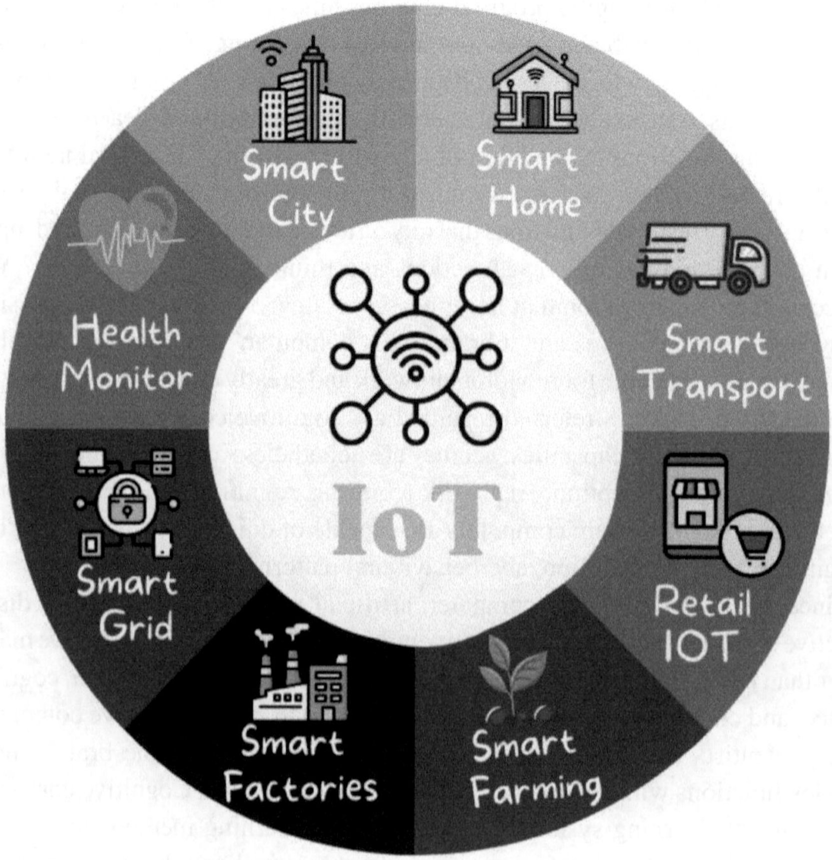

engage with technology, especially in the areas of automation, machine learning, and information technology.

The larger area of artificial intelligence, which includes cognitive technologies, may be thought of as a subset of biomimetics. Although research on artificial intelligence has been ongoing for a very long time, cognitive technology mostly emerged from the internet (particularly the web and the cloud). Science of the mind In essence, cognitive science is the study of thinking. It is a general word for the study of the structure and operation of the brain. However, specialists have developed more precise concrete definitions of cognitive science, such as the junction of languages, anthropology, neurology, philosophy, psychology, and, last but not least, artificial intelligence. There are many different subfields of cognitive science, including psychology and philosophy. An undertaking in cognitive science may include brain imaging. The same is true for a study that focuses on behavioural patterns supported by data. Projects involving language processing may also have a significant cognitive science element is shown in Figure 1.

Prior to the dawn of the twenty-first century, cognitive science was mostly regarded as an academic discipline associated with human biology. This has changed significantly in recent years, and one of the major shifts has to do with technology. All of that has altered in light of recent advances in artificial intelligence. A cognitive science project nowadays is equally as likely to use networks and other artificial intelligence techniques to mimic biological cognitive function. The field of cognitive science as well as some of its subfields, such as neuroscience, is being drastically altered by this. For instance, whereas previous neuroscience projects were limited to studying the human brain through biological research and some data modelling, current neuroscience projects can now concentrate on learning about the human brain through looking at artificial intelligence as well. In essence, cognitive science has grown and advanced with the advancement of artificial intelligence. With the study of technology, it has merged and linked.

CHALLENGES OF COGNITIVE COMPUTING

The goal of cognitive computing (COC) is to incorporate human cognition into digital models. The nature of Cognitive Computing is not, however, categorised in a scientific way. Information Systems (IS), in contrast to the medical and computer science sectors, has done relatively little study on COC. Although there is a lot of room for significant research advancements in this field, we contend that the absence of a consistent definition of what counts as COC has resulted in subpar COC research in IS. Therefore, in order to identify and direct potential study topics in IS, we must first properly define COC as a phenomena. The published literature on COC research is analysed thematically using a phenomenological method in this study. Then, we go through how IS could influence the creation of design science artefacts covered by the COC. In addition, by demonstrating how IS researchers may make significant contributions to this developing field, the work poses crucial issues for future research.

Even though artificial intelligence (AI) is not a new concept, the degree of interest in it recently is amazing. Massive media attention has been generated by a mix of vendor marketing, worries about job losses, and even speculation of "robot overlords." Behind the fanfare, there is a lot of substance as well. Cognitive technologies have the potential to boost productivity, improve knowledge-based consumer interactions, and tackle issues that are too difficult for human brains to handle. Despite the fact that there have been a number of "AI winters" and "AI springs" over the previous 50 years, there is cause to believe that this AI spring's blossoming will permanently alter the garden. However, enterprises must quickly transition from curiosity to acceptance in order to benefit from this outstanding collection of technologies. In many instances, the technology is already usable and several major, well-known businesses are pushing forward with production applications. The current name for AI is "cognitive technology," which denotes a seeing and learning capacity that is comparable to, and sometimes even surpasses, that of humans. Although there are still certain barriers standing in the way of cognitive technologies taking their rightful position at the head of the technological table, tenacious enterprises can get around them. It's unclear when or if cognitive technologies will ever develop to the point of "artificial general intelligence," commonly referred to as "The Singularity," when they would be superior to humans at every kind of thinking we do. However, technology is already dramatically altering companies and organisations for the better.

What are the effects of this sudden rise in awareness and interest in cognitive technologies? Why has it happened? This tendency is influenced by variables related to supply and demand. There are strategic, tactical, and operational elements to the demand side. Strategically, businesses usually want profitable expansion, and boosting productivity is a popular means of doing so. A typical human approach to analytics and decision-making is now impractical in many circumstances on the demand side as well. For people to use their own brains to make these judgements, there is just too much information to consider and not enough time to do so. Without some kind of cognitive technology, it would be hard to successfully operate in many areas of business today, including digital advertising, medical diagnostics, predictive maintenance of industrial equipment, and many more. Finally, although human labour has numerous advantages over robots in terms of the basic operational characteristics of demand, it is nevertheless costly and challenging to manage. Of course, clever people and smart robots will often collaborate at work, and that is often the most effective arrangement. But there's no denying that automation's seductive song is advancing cognitive technologies. Software with cognitive capabilities is readily accessible, and these features are progressively being integrated into other forms of software. IBM has staked a lot on Watson as a stand-alone software solution, even if it can also be used in conjunction with other programmes thanks to a number of APIs (application programming interfaces). For instance, neural networks have been around since the 1950s. However, modern variations of these, some of which are referred to as "deep learning." A growing class of computing infrastructures meshes together many processors to support the application of sophisticated cognitive algorithms. Applications are expanded when performance improves It's simple to locate instances of cognitive technologies' achievements. The field of computer vision has advanced quickly as well. According to a common benchmark used by computer vision researchers, the accuracy of picture categorization increased by a factor of four between 2010 and 2014. In a peer-reviewed publication, Facebook claimed that its Deep Face technology can now accurately identify faces 97% of the time. Prior to its infamous Jeopardy! triumph in 2011, IBM was able to double the accuracy of Watson's responses. The business now claims that its technology is 2,400% "smarter" than it was on the day of that victory. For a variety of industries and job tasks, "several businesses are attempting to customise and bundle cognitive technologies, making them simpler to acquire and easier to implement." The range of applications for a technology increases as performance increases. For instance, speech recognition systems found use in specialist fields like medical dictation but did not find widespread acceptance since they needed tedious training and could only function properly with regulated vocabularies. Not other cognitive technologies are advancing as quickly. The development of machine translation has slowed down. For example, professional translators often use machine translation to boost productivity by automating repetitive translation jobs so they can concentrate on the more difficult ones.

Enterprises leverage employee knowledge, data from machines, and information that has been made actionable by leveraging all available data or pertinent expertise to intelligently automate business activities. Cognitive decision-making techniques are brought by several processes at one location. Cognitive Computing employs Affective Computing systems to design an architecture that automates business operations, while Affective Computing used to research and develop systems and devices that can identify, interpret, process, and imitate human impacts. Systems for cognitive computing are a subset of wider computing, which combines a variety of system operations and tools to improve the effectiveness, accuracy, relevance, and dependability of business operations. There are several possibilities and problems that must be the focus when implementing a Cognitive Computing system in a company. How various Cognitive Computing elements may be used to handle unstructured data in corporate systems. Some of the difficulties in deploying Enterprise Cognitive Computing (ECC) systems may be overcome using semantic technology. How the ECC system uses techniques from semantic technology to reduce its difficulties.

computational thinking: Artificial intelligence and signal processing have a scientific bent thanks to the technical approach known as cognitive computing. That essentially includes technologies such as dialogue and story synthesis, machine learning, reasoning, natural language processing, voice recognition, object recognition, and human-computer interaction. With the aid of its encompassing technologies, cognitive computing systems imitate human mental processes in a digital model in a manner similar to how the human brain operates.

As of right now, we can assert that any application may use semantic technology tools and its languages to harness the outcomes and processing processes in business cognitive computing systems. After learning that unstructured data difficulties in business cognitive computing applications may be resolved by semantic technology, the next step in this process will be to identify the semantic technology tools that can be used to construct enterprise cognitive computing systems.

As we all know, fault tolerance refers to a system's or software's capacity to recognise an issue in the system's operation and either overlook it or fix it before it worsens and causes the system to break down or crash. Fault tolerance has evolved into a crucial development criteria in this age of quick-moving and rapid development of software and systems. Because of this, this idea has emerged as one of the most crucial and challenging elements for developers. On the bright side, high-performance systems and software exist because of fault tolerance and related principles. Cognitive computing and deep learning is a significant area in computer science. The practise of employing human reasoning abilities to create an algorithm that may result in the artificial duplicate of the same computer process is known as cognitive computing. The development of a better algorithm that aids in a highly effective system for fault tolerance may be done using these two huge computer science principles.

In the system, cognitive computing solely addresses these two processes. The chemical reaction that takes place simply produces "yes" or "no," just as in a brain cell. This process is used in deep learning to create the algorithm that will carry out the tolerant service. Here, the perceptron theory may be used. As we already mentioned, the outcome of the neuron's process is either yes or no; therefore, in this instance, scientists have created a virtual machine called a perceptron that performs the same function as a neuron but with a bias as the weights of the quantities to which we compare and decide if something is true or false, as in the case of the perceptron, it's "case 1 or case 2." The perceptron is a notion derived from the human brain that functions very similarly to a neuron. The deep learning method, which is completely dependent on perception, has one of the greatest implementations to date. The algorithm's only concern is the system's development in order to be able to provide us with the best option from the algorithm's previously studied scenarios. In the implementation and development of our algorithm, we are employing this idea.

So, the first thing that comes to mind is how and, more importantly, where this abstract idea may be put into practise. Fault tolerance, along with cognitive computing and deep learning, is a broad idea of development and mistake correction in this area of software development. In this instance, we create a deep learning algorithm to examine the system, analyse the implementation, and provide us the best system solution. Let's imagine algorithm A was developed using the same principles as previously; it now has access to the system software implementation and examines the code or the user experience to look for defects and problems. This also only occurs during system application since system design is only completed during system application and not at all during system implementation. When it comes across faults or mistakes, it alerts the user right away and requests login in order to process the issue or error and provide a fix.

Fault tolerance refers to the idea of attempting to accept or overlook the problem, or, if that is not feasible, to fix it. After processing the mistake, the algorithm offers the user a choice between removing the implementation and continuing with the code component. We must introduce mistakes into the algorithm throughout development in order for it to learn at a specified pace and be able to rectify and identify systemic flaws. As was already established, the perceptron notion contains two scenarios, with bias in each case dependent on prior supervised learning of the algorithm. We offer two scenarios to illustrate the mistake detection and rectification issue. One is to identify the mistake, although given its gravity, it may be disregarded or allowed. Case number two is when the algorithm determines that the mistake or defect cannot be corrected by a typical user and must be quickly eliminated or quarantined to avoid major errors. The issue now is, to what degree is this method effective now that we have used the algorithm? The implementation itself holds the key to the solution. The algorithm has a comprehensive thorough description of the system in the form of a database that it generates, as we have said that it goes through all the previous faults of the system that arise in the development stage and also keeps track of all the operations that are occurring in the system. This fault tolerance scenario will include every possible mistake type and its associated severity. Additionally, this approach may be used to resolve inconsistencies of mistakes that may arise in the real-time application of the code system.

CONCLUSION

The deep learning algorithm's efficiency is thus quite high and well regarded in this sector of technological sciences, even if we are not yet at the point where we can provide specific statistics. If necessary, Deep Learning may be improved utilising a variety of accelerator algorithms to provide much superior algorithmic results. However, the method itself is quite effective and can be in this fault-tolerant situation. It is not yet possible to put this method into practise. But. This idea can be applied in large businesses since it primarily focuses on the value of fault tolerance and how to combine it with deep learning algorithms. Additionally, it may be used to the most extent possible by optimising the output of the perceptron utilising a variety of acceleration techniques. In addition, the method is widely known among scientists, and our approach simply requires minor adjustments and modifications to the current code. This implementation's scope is superb. As was previously said, fault tolerance is a crucial element of development systems and cannot always be disregarded as a whole. Therefore, this implementation may assist programmers in coming up with innovative approaches to improve the way we think about fault tolerance, aid in the development of improved high-performance systems, and spur new developments in the fields of deep learning and cognitive computing.

REFERENCES

Al-Sarawi, S., Anbar, M., Alieyan, K., & Alzubaidi, M. (2017). Internet of Things (IoT) communication protocols: Review. *Proceedings of the ICIT 2017—8th International Conference on Information Technology*, 685–690.

Baldini, G. (2011). A Cognitive Framework for Realizing and Exploiting the Internet of Things Concept. In *27th WWRF Meeting*, Dusseldorf, Germany

Clarke, J., Castro, R., Sharma, A., Lopez, J., & Suri, N. (2012). Trust & security RTD in the internet of things: Opportunities for international cooperation. *Proc. 1st Int. Conf. Security of Internet of Things*, 172-178. 10.1145/2490428.2490452

de Souza, J. T., de Francisco, A. C., Piekarski, C. M., & do Prado, G. F. (2019). Data mining and machine learning to promote smart cities: A systematic review from 2000 to 2018. *Sustainability (Basel)*, *11*(4), 1077. doi:10.3390/su11041077

Hammi, B., Khatoun, R., Zeadally, S., Fayad, A., & Khoukhi, L. (2018). IoT technologies for smart cities. *IET Networks*, *2018*(7), 1–13. doi:10.1049/iet-net.2017.0163

Iarovyi, P. (2016). *From artificial cognitive systems and open architectures to cognitive manufacturing systems.* Academic Press.

Kuppusamy, P., Muthuraj, S., & Gopinath, S. (2016). Survey and challenges of Li-Fi with comparison of Wi-Fi. *Proceedings of the 2016 International Conference on Wireless Communications, Signal Processing and Networking (WiSPNET)*, 896–899. 10.1109/WiSPNET.2016.7566262

Kuzlu, M., & Pipattanasomporn, M. (2013). Assessment of communication technologies and network requirements for different smart grid applications. *Proceedings of the 2013 IEEE PES Innovative Smart Grid Technologies Conference, ISGT 2013*, 1–6. 10.1109/ISGT.2013.6497873

Li, F., Jin, C., Jing, Y., Wilamowska-Korsak, M., & Bi, Z. (2013). A rough programming model based on the greatest compatible classes and synthesis effect. *Systems Research and Behavioral Science*, *30*(3), 229–243. doi:10.1002/sres.2175

Mekki, K., Bajic, E., Chaxel, F., & Meyer, F. (2019). A comparative study of LPWAN technologies for large-scale IoT deployment. *ICT Express, 5*(1), 1–7. doi:10.1016/j.icte.2017.12.005

Nagorny, K., Lima-Monteiro, P., Barata, J., & Colombo, A. W. (2017). "Big Data Analysis in Smart Manufacturing": A Review. *International Journal of Communications, Network and Systems Sciences, 10*(3), 31–58. doi:10.4236/ijcns.2017.103003

Samuel, S. S. I. (2016). A review of connectivity challenges in IoT-smart home. *Proceedings of the 2016 3rd MEC International Conference on Big Data and Smart City, ICBDSC 2016*, 364–367. 10.1109/ICBDSC.2016.7460395

Shayan, N. (2015). A survey on Internet of Things: applications and challenges. *Second International Congress on Technology, Communication and Knowledge)-Mashhad Branch, Islamic Azad University, Mashhad, Iran,* 165-169.

Wu, H. (2014). Developing Vehicular Data Cloud Services in the IoT Environment. *IEEE Transactions on Industrial Informatics, 10*(2), 1587–1595. doi:10.1109/TII.2014.2299233

Wuest, T. (2016). Machine learning in manufacturing: advantages, challenges, and application. *Production & Manufacturing Research: An Open Access Journal, 4*(1), 23-45. http://dx.doi.org/ doi:10.1080/21693277.2016.119251

Xu, L. (2013). Introduction: Systems science in industrial sectors. *Systems Research and Behavioral Science, 30*(3), 211–213. doi:10.1002/sres.2186

Chapter 2
Comparison of Indian Public Sector Banks' Cost and Profit Efficiencies in the Post-Reform Period

Anshuman Vijay Magar
https://orcid.org/0000-0002-7349-5011
Lexicon Management Institute of Leadership and Excellence, India

Gitanjali Shrivastava
Symbiosis Law School, Symbiosis International University, India

Namita Rajput
Sri Aurobindo College, University of Delhi, India

Aradhana Sahu
Rungta College of Engineering and Technology, India

Bhupendra Kumar
https://orcid.org/0000-0002-9609-2311
Galgotias University, India

Sabyasachi Pramanik
https://orcid.org/0000-0002-9431-8751
Haldia Institute of Technology, India

Digvijay Pandey
https://orcid.org/0000-0003-0353-174X
Government of Uttar Pradesh, India

ABSTRACT

The chapter compares and analyzes the cost and profit efficiency of India's public sector banks (PSBs). The information was obtained and examined between 1995 and 2017, or from the start of the post-liberalization era until the big State Bank of India merger in 2017. For each PSB in India, the average profit efficiency (PE) and cost efficiency (CE) ratings were examined year by year. Using non-parametric Friedman's two-way Annova and Wilcoxon signed rank tests, the distribution and

DOI: 10.4018/979-8-3693-1182-0.ch002

median of efficiency scores in two subperiods were also evaluated. The findings showed that PSBs in the chosen time period had profit inefficiencies. PE scores are lower than CE scores for the whole time period. The results also showed significant variances amongst public sector banks between 1995 and 2022. In addition, since India's 1991 banking sector reform, the PE of PSBs has been falling.

INTRODUCTION

Being the lifeblood of the economy, banks significantly contribute to the country's GDP growth, infrastructure investment, and the development of rural regions. Because of their financial services' multiplier effects on the whole economy and long-term sustainability, banks have a particularly important responsibility when it comes to sustainable development. Commercial banks were created to generate profits for their shareholders and are similar to other businesses in that (a) they have a sizable branch network and generate significant revenues, making them one of the largest enterprises in the nation, and (b) they are publicly traded on stock exchanges. The society that supports the banks by using their goods and services has a duty to them as well.

BACKGROUND

A healthy financial system that supports both the economy and society is necessary for a nation to prosper. Therefore, banks nowadays are essential to the social and economic health of the country. In 1991 and 1998, respectively, the Narshimham Committee's recommendations led to changes in the Indian banking industry. Cooperative banks and Scheduled Commercial Banks (SCBs) (Ray, A. M. et al, 2023) make up the Indian banking system. The SCBs are further broken down into four categories: PSBs (Public Sector Banks), PSBs (Private Sector Banks), Foreign Banks, and Regional Rural Banks. PSBs include the State Bank of India, its subsidiaries, and Nationalized Banks. In 1955, 1969, and 1980, respectively, three stages of public ownership of banks were completed. The Reserve Bank of India (RBI) and the Ministry of Finance both has regulatory authority over PSBs. With their numerous branches and sizable rural presence, PSBs in India provide the majority of job chances to the populace.

EFFICIENCY OF PUBLIC SECTOR BANKS IN TERMS OF COST AND PROFIT

The efficacy of the financial system is connected with economic efficiency. The PSBs in the Indian economy are being consolidated or privatized due to a lack of efficiency. The operating issues among PSBs became more severe in the wake of COVID 19 (Pandey, D. et al. 2021). Apart from the growing NPAs, the mandated social responsibility standards of PSBs also put a strain on banks. It is now required to determine the efficiency (or lack thereof) of each PSB and consider prospective growth areas. Due to PSBs' deteriorating performance, it is also critical to assess their effectiveness. Given this, the present research uses Data Envelopment Analysis (DEA) (Pramanik, S. et al. 2022) to examine the Cost Efficiency (CE) and Profit Efficiency (PE) of PSBs in India. The Indian banking system is a desirable case study due to a number of factors:

(i) It categorizes "best practices" and "worst practices" involved in efficiency score calculations and aids in improving PSB performance in India;
(ii) Examining the dynamics of efficiency based on bank ownership is useful for policymakers in an economy.

Although there is a wealth of information on assessing the technical efficiency of commercial banks throughout the years, there is little information on measuring and examining the cost and profit efficiency (Samanta, D. et al. 2021) of PSBs in India. The majority of the relevant research focuses on utilizing financial ratios to measure and analyze banks' profitability. These financial measures don't account for all aspects of a corporation and have issues estimating competitive advantage. There are six parts in this chapter, including: The study is introduced in part 1, and previous investigations are covered in section 2. With data descriptions and criteria for choosing inputs and outputs, Section 3 describes the DEA technique for computing the CE and PE of PSBs. Section 4 discusses the main results, Section 5 brings the study to a close, and Section 6 discusses the ramifications.

A REVIEW OF PREVIOUS STUDIES

Table 1. The following is a survey of the literature related to the measurement and causes of efficiency in the banking sector:

Table 1.

Authors	Resident	Period of Time	Significant Findings
Isik and Hassan (2002)	Turkey	Particular Years 1992, 1996, and 1998	1.The average cost and profit efficiency for banks was 90% and 84%, respectively. 2. Turkish banks managed expenses more skillfully.
Maudos et al (2003)	Many nations	1993 to 2000	1. Banks' high cost and low profit efficiencies proved that the inefficiencies were on the revenue side. 2. The countries with the greatest revenues and the lowest cost-efficiency were Portugal and the United Kingdom.
Postor and Maudos, 2003	Germany	1955–2002	1. For cost efficiency, savings and commercial banks received scores of 90.9% and 80.2%, respectively. 2. The average profit efficiency of commercial banks was 66.5%, compared to 47.2% for saving banks. 3. In the alternative profit efficiency area, commercial banks scored 52.9%, compared to savings banks' 34.7%.
Das et al(2008)	India	1998-2011	1. The findings showed that the majority of banks had strong cost-efficiency rankings. 2. From 2001 to 2003, the profitability of PVBs, FBs, and PSBs improved.
Kasram and Yildirim (2006)	Sweden	1998–2015	1. The average cost-efficiency (Jayasingh, R. et al. 2022) rating for international banks was 0.207%. 2. Estonia had the lowest cost inefficiency, at 17.4%. 3. The country with the highest cost-efficiency rating was the Czech Republic (21,3%). 4. Throughout the study period, Lithuania and the Czech Republic were the most lucrative countries.
SemihYildirim and Philippatos (2007)	France	1993–2000	1. According to DFA, the cost effectiveness of banks ranged from 45% to 66%. 2. The cost efficiency for the 12 CEE countries was, on average, 77% based on the SFA data. 3. The two countries that produced the most were Poland and Slovenia.
Ariff and Can (2008)	China	1999 to 2012	1. In China, banks' profit efficiency was lower than their cost efficiency. 2. The cost efficiency and profit efficiency of Chinese banks were 79.8% and 50.5%, respectively. 3. In China, the PSBs were the least effective banks, while the commercial banks that were jointly run were the most effective.
Kamaruddin et al (2008)	Muslim Nations	1999- 2009	1. Each bank received a grade for cost efficiency of 69.5% and profit efficiency of 62%. 2. With a score of 70.8% compared to 63.6%, domestic banks outperformed foreign banks in terms of cost efficiency. 3. The profit efficiency of domestic Islamic banks was 73.7% as opposed to 57.9% for international Islamic banks.
Das and Ghosh (2009)	India	1998-2010	1. During the chosen time period, the profit efficiency of Indian banks was under 50%. 2. The PSBs outperformed other Indian banks in terms of profit efficiency.
Ghosh (2009)	South Africa	2000-2009	a. PSBs obtained cost efficiency ratings of above 85% from 1992 to 2004. b. For the majority of the years, banks' profit efficiency ranges between 40.04% and 70.63%. c. When compared to other banks, PSBs had superior profitability efficiency.
Ray and Das (2010)	Sri Lanka	2000-2012	1. Compared to other banks, State Bank of India and its affiliates were more cost-effective. 2. In terms of profit efficiency rankings, private banks performed the least effectively, while state banks excelled.
Jayaraman and Srinivasan (2019)	Bangladesh	2008-2016	1.During the research period, there was a correlation between the chosen banks' cost and profit efficiency. The findings also showed that the banks were profitable provided they were cost-efficient. 2. In India, the most effective metric for distinguishing between performing and non-performing banks was profit efficiency.
Parikshit (2022)	Canada	2005-2009	1. In India, banks demonstrated better levels of cost, revenue, and profit efficiency. 2. Compared to other banks, PSBs had lower costs.

Source: Explanation by the author

Figure 1. Cost-efficiency

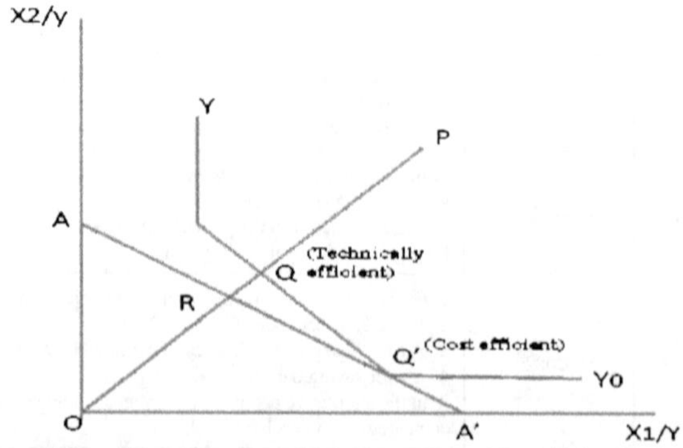

Data Envelope Modeling

DEA (Chandan, R. R. et al. 2023) employs the non-parametric frontier approach of linear programming. With inputs and outputs, Farrell (1957) pioneered productivity measurement. The highest efficiency for each chosen unit in relation to the optimal border is stated by the DEA's frontier approach. The Decision-Making Units (DMUs) (Omrani, H., et al. 2023) created with DEA either reside on the efficient frontier or are engulfed by it. DMUs that are located on the efficient border have a score of 1, whereas DMUs that are engulfed by it have values between 0 and 1. The following procedures are necessary for the DEA application on the data:In the first step, the inputs and outputs of DMUs (Banks) are selected.In the second step, efficiency ratings for DMUs are estimated by dividing outputs (weighted total) by inputs (weighted sum) (Pramanik, S. 2023).

CREDIT AFFINITY

Cost Efficiency (CE) (Naidu, G. T. et al. 2023) measures how closely a bank's expenses adhere to the frontier of best practices given certain outcomes. Cost efficiency calculations need the goal function and input prices, as shown in Figure 1.

In order to construct Y, the bank uses the inputs X1 and X2, as indicated in the picture. The efficient unit isoquant YYo was also represented by the production frontier of the bank y = f (X1, X2), which showed consistent returns to scale. Technically speaking, the bank will be successful if the business (Pramanik, S. et al. 2020) uses YYO output since (OR/OP) = (OR/OQ) X (OQ/OP)

A linear combination connects bank (i) to all other banks, where yi is the output vector and Wi is the input price vector. According to the constant returns to scale

Figure 2. Profitability (diagrammatic)

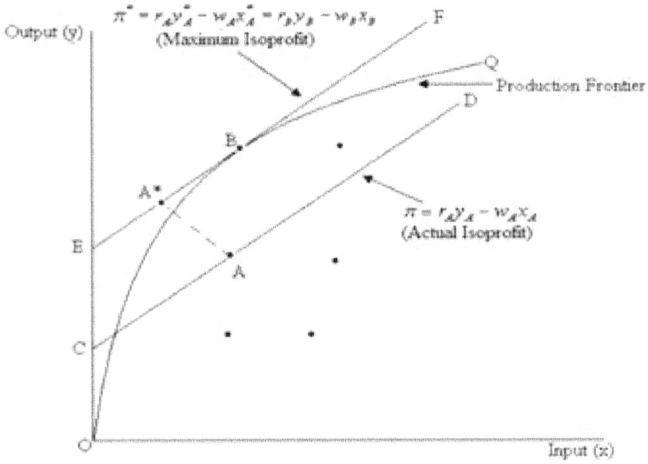

method, the optimal input combination vector xi under CRS is the only input necessary. To determine the minimal cost Wi'Xi CRS, the minimum and observed costs Wi'Xi of bank (i) are compared. The following cost effectiveness is the result: $WiXi^{CRS} / WiXi = CEi^{CRS}$

REVENUE EFFICIENCY

In the current environment, the bank's proximity to the standard border (bank) is a sign of profit efficiency. By dividing the maximum earnings by the actual profits, which are shown as follows:

The OQ curve represents the boundary of production possibility, according to graph 1. The combination of Bank A's input and output is shown at real level at location (A) with (xA, yA). The profits made by Bank A are shown by the equation qAyA - wAxA. The combinations of Bank B's inputs and outputs with respect to x and y, inputs and outputs, respectively, are * disclosing the highest normalized (Ahamad, S. et al. 2023) profits. The iso-profit line crossing EF at which profits equal Bank B as follows: *= qA y*A -wAx*A =qByB -wBxB is the greatest profit line that bank A can attain.

The efficiencies (Mondal, D. et al. 2023) permitting both an increase and a reduction in inputs and outputs with the current market prices in an economy were estimated using a non-oriented DEA model. Let's assume that an economy with n banks (B = 1,.... c) generating a vector of s outputs O=(o1,....., os) sold at a price p= (p1..., qp) vector is used for i inputs. With the use of linear programming formulae, Fare et al. (1997) and Fare and Grosskopf (1997) calculated profit efficiency as follows:

$$\text{Max} \sum_{r=1}^{s} q^{a}_{ry_{ra}} - \sum_{i=1}^{c} p^{a}_{i} x^{D}_{ia}$$

With respect to:

$$\sum_{j=1}^{c} \lambda_B x^{D}_{iB} \leq x^{D}_{ia}, \text{ i = 1,.....,c}$$

$$\sum_{j=1}^{c} \lambda_B x^{QF}_{KB} \leq x^{QF}_{ka}, \text{ k=1,......1}$$

$$\sum_{j=1}^{c} \lambda_B y^{1}_{rB} \leq y_{ro}, \text{r =1......s}$$

$$x_{ia} \geq x^{D}_{ia}$$

$$y_{ro} \leq y_{ro}$$

$$\lambda_B \geq 0,$$

B = 1...., c

The maximum profits can be computed as $\sum_{r=1}^{s} q^{a}_{r} y_{ra} - \sum_{r=1}^{s} p^{a}_{i} x_{ia}$. The profit efficiency of Bank "a" is then determined by dividing the actual profit by the maximum standard bank profit.

The computed profit efficiency scores can only go up to a maximum of 1, and they are also restricted above that number. The profit efficiency is between (-∞,1). Additionally, low-profit efficiency with negative values is a possibility.

SELECTION OF INPUTS AND OUTPUTS

Most academics, researchers, and scholars struggle with deciding the inputs and outputs to utilize to quantify banking efficiency. Humphrey (1985) addressed the production approach and the intermediation approach as two methods for choosing the inputs and outputs of banks. Under the production model, the number of accounts for deposits and loans was seen as an output, designating DMU (bank) as a service provider to banks' clients. On the other hand, banks' inputs include physical capital and its cost. According to the intermediation strategy, DMU is a producer of assets that uses client deposits to create assets for banks. This approach allows banks to offer intermediation services by estimating monetary outputs and total costs, which include interest payments and operating expenses. Both of these approaches use the traditional microeconomic theory to apply to the banking industry as a whole, with the exception of how the activities of banks are stated. The inputs and outputs of the present study are handled using a modified version of the intermediation approach rather than the production strategy, in accordance with the empirical research for Banks. The following is a description of the input and output vectors:

The following variables are part of the input vector:

1. Capital: Fixed Assets (in millions of Rupees)
2. Total number of bank employees
3. Deposits and Borrowings from the Bank (in Millions of Rupees)

The following variables are part of the output vector:

1. Bank loan advances include those made to Indian borrowers (term loans, discounted and purchased bills, cash credits, etc.) as well as overseas borrowers (in millions of rupees).
2. Bank investments include those made both domestically (in government securities and other assets that have been approved, etc.) and internationally (in rupees).
3. Other sources of income include commissions, exchange, brokerage, and other forms of sales revenue, as well as net profits or losses from the sale of real estate and other assets, other revenues, and net exchange operations profits (in millions of rupees).
4. Equity in terms of capital: capital + bank reserves (in millions of rupees) (quasi-fixed input variable).

The following inputs' prices were included:

1. The cost of capital, which is the sum of all expenses (such as electricity, taxes, rent, office supplies, printing, depreciation on assets, insurance, repairs, and maintenance), divided by the capital.
2. The cost of hiring bank personnel divided by total labor yields is the payment to labor.
3. The following formula is used to determine how much banks charge for loan able funds: Divided by the total of interest on deposits, interest on loans from other institutions, and interest on borrowing from the RBI.

The following outputs' prices are included:

1. The cost of bank loans is calculated by dividing the total advances by the interest and discounts on bills and loans.
2. Investment Price is calculated as (Income from Investments)/total Investments.
3. The price of non-interest income is one (when seen as a constant).
4. It is expected that the price of equity will never change.

The bank's net profits from lending money and investing in both government and non-government securities are referred to as variable non-interest income. The term "non-interest income" refers to the revenue that banks get through commission, exchange, and brokerage activities that are not shown on their balance sheet. Non-interest revenue is taken into consideration when calculating efficiency ratings in order to take into account changes in the production services offered by PSBs in addition to their traditional banking.

The chapter's sample size was selected as a general rule of thumb based on the related literature since the sample size of the study affects the DEA calculated efficiency findings. The study found the following recommendations:

N must be greater than equal to max $\{a \times b; 3(a + b)\}$,

where:

n = DMUs (number)

a = inputs (number)

b = outputs (number)

The number of DMUs used in the present study was 27, exceeding the ideal sample size recommended by the rule of thumb (Avikiran, 1999b) when $a = 3$ and $b = 2$.

The information for the present research's inputs and outputs was gathered from the RBI website. To get the actual values, the nominal data that was obtained from the RBI was deflated. With the exception of bank employees, the research used actual numbers calculated using the implicit GDP price deflator at factor cost (base 2014-2015=100).

By dividing the input and output variables by the number of branches each bank had for each year, the input and output variables for efficiency estimates were normalized. To reduce the random noise brought on by measurement error in the selected inputs and outputs, the researchers normalized the data.

FINDINGS

In accordance with the research of Pasiorus et al. (2007), the chapter makes use of distinct bank-wise efficiency boundaries for each year. According to Isik and Hassan (2002), there are two benefits to calculating a separate annual border: (i) Because it is flexible, it is more suitable than creating a strict multi-year restriction for PSBs. ii) It lessens the problem of random errors in DEA by allowing an efficient bank to become inefficient in a later year. It is based on the hypothesis that data inaccuracies do not persist over time. Additionally, efficiency predictions derived from the grand frontier are typically exaggerated since they are affected by broad technical advancement in the industry. As a result, it is believed that year-by-year computation efficiency frontiers are more dependable and precise than the grand frontier efficiency model.

The following are the key conclusions of cost efficiency scores, as shown in table 1: In the first sub-period, the relative mean cost efficiency ratings were rather high. The bulk of PSBs in this time frame are situated close to the benchmark cost border. The average cost-inefficiency of PSBs between 1995 and 2004 was found to be less than 9%.In the second sub-period, the bulk of PSBs have low levels of relative mean cost efficiency ratings and are located far from the benchmark cost frontier. The average cost-inefficiency of PSBs was found to be below 60% in 2012; by 2013, it had fallen to below 40%. It showed how less technically and allocationally efficient PSBs were in India. Because of this, PSBs were unable to control the input-mix in a way that would meet their competing requirements and avoid underutilizing resources.To put it another way, PSBs in India demonstrated both a high degree of technical and locative efficiency. As a consequence, PSBs were successful in controlling the waste and underutilization of input resources and, for the most part, choosing the appropriate input-mix when balancing conflicting demands. As a consequence, PSBs are able to limit resource underutilization and regulate the input-mix in proportion to their competing requirements.

We discuss the efficiency scores as follows:

1. Profit efficiency ratings among public sector banks indicate significant differences. With the exception of 2004, when PSBs were profit inefficient, PSBs were particularly inside the efficient profit frontier throughout the first

Table 2. Cost efficiency on average

Years	Cost Efficiency		
	Average		STDEV
1995	0.965418		0.065478
1996	0.954872		0.075632
1997	0.954730		0.021457
1998	0.978034		0.056874
1999	0.925783		0.065413
2000	0.958741		0.089543
2001	0.922367		0.078521
2002	0.942581		0.075304
2003	0.987453		0.064132
2004	0.902458		0.078025
2005	0.654789		0.132587
2006	0.923574		0.085204
2007	0.859874		0.156217
2008	0.723654		0.143347
2009	0.966587		0.175237
2010	0.821733		0.257483
2011	0.858741		0.269781
2012	0.465321		0.187452
2013	0.598754		0.232587
2014	0.858741		0.269871
2015	0.823654		0.266478
2016	0.823105		0.223781
2017	0.582154		0.389254
2018	0.785462		0.225871
2019	0.856324		0.354781
2020	0.987452		0.452377
2021	0.854247		0.235485
2022	0.543216		0.324782
Average	0.839928		0.147974
Grand Mean			
Entire Period (1995-2022)		0.836981	0.156237
First Sub-Period (1995-2008)		0.956321	0.078531
Second Sub-Period (2008-2022)		0.778523	0.236587

Source: Calculation by the author

subperiod. In 1995, 1997, 1999, 2001, 2002, and 2003, PSBs' profit efficiency was more than 100%. Furthermore, a considerable and persistent standard deviation (Talukdar, V. et al. 2023) in terms of profit efficiency made the influence of the reforms of 1991 clear in the convergence of PSBs performance throughout the first sub-period.

2. Notable variability in profit efficiency ratings was seen among PSBs during the second sub-period. Banks' profitability was inefficient during 2008 to 2011 as a result of the global financial crisis, and banks were located within the benchmark frontier. As PSBs fought to decrease input resource waste and underutilization and, to a great degree, succeeded in selecting the right input mix in response to conflicting demands in the second half of the sub-period, the performance of banks was very near to the benchmark. These findings indicated deterioration in market dominance in price fixing as well as a variation in the output quality of banks as shown by variations in input costs. High and stable standard deviations indicated that convergence was a result of the second-generation reforms.
3. These findings were in line with studies that indicate banks are ineffective at turning a profit. The interbank changes in the output-mix have a substantial influence on the PSBs' capacity to calculate their input prices given the relative factor prices in the policy environment. Through proper credit management, investment selection, and investment mix, this presents several chances for greater profitability and efficiency. The results are in line with Humphrey's (1998) study, which discovered that (Cost) X-inefficiency is a key factor in financial institutions' underperformance. The PSBs in India are less efficient, which is reflected in the lower profit efficiency.

ANALYSIS OF COST AND PROFITABILITY

The performance of PSBs is broken down into two sub-periods for the full period (1995 to 2017): 1995 to 2004 (the period immediately after the liberalization and globalization reforms) and 2005 to 2017 (the period starting with the introduction of social control rules in 2005 until the significant merger of SBI in 2017). The research also shows that profit efficiency is lower than cost efficiency scores in both sub-periods, with the second sub-period showing substantially worse profit efficiency, as seen in Figures 3 and 4.

Figure 3. Compares profit and cost effectiveness from 1995 to 2004 graphically

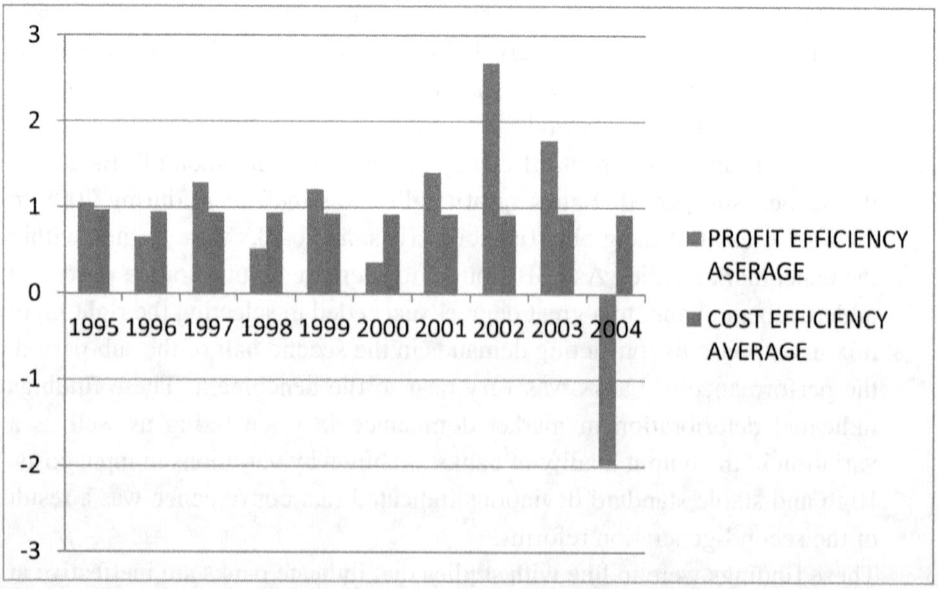

Figure 4. Profit and cost efficiency from 2005 to 2017 are compared graphically

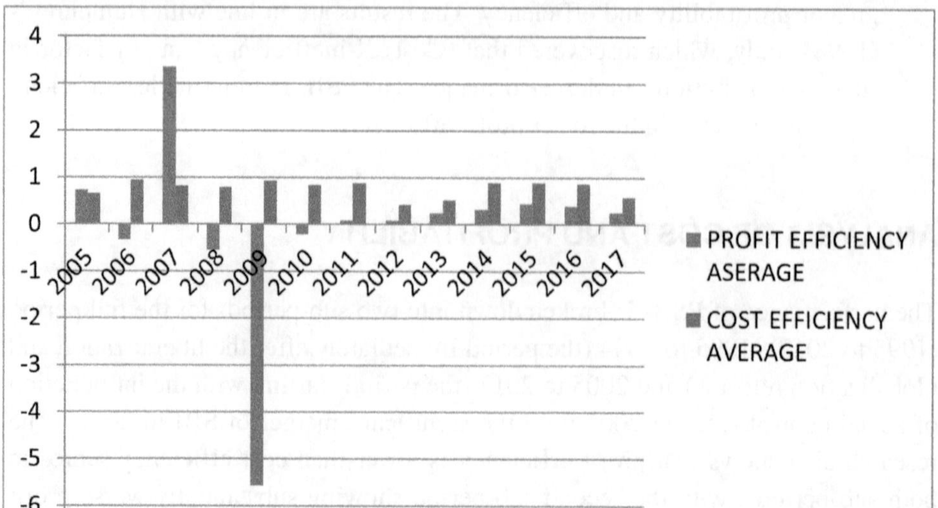

PROBABILITY TESTING

The two non-parametric techniques for testing hypotheses, the Friedman Annova and Wilcoxon Signed rank tests, were used to confirm the hypotheses.

Wilcoxon's tests track the variance in medians between the two periods, while Friedman's tests highlight changes in the distribution of the two specified periods. Additionally, both the median efficiency score from 2005 to 2017 and the median efficiency score from 1995 to 2004 are 0 (i.e., the same). The efficiency value distribution from 1995 to 2004 and the efficiency value distribution from 2004 to 2017 are both the same. The findings of both non-parametric hypothesis tests are 00, rejecting the null hypothesis, according to which banks' cost and profit efficiency in two sub-periods is comparable.

CONCLUSION

The majority of the literature on bank efficiency that is currently accessible focused on technology efficiency and dismissed the idea of possible inefficiencies on the cost and revenue sides. According to the presently known studies on profit efficiency, profit inefficiency is worse than cost inefficiency. Using a non-parametric approach, the profitability and cost-effectiveness of PSBs in India were investigated in the context of this chapter from 1995 to 2017. The findings indicate that:

1. PSBs are very inefficient in terms of expenses and revenue. In the chosen time frame, profit efficiency is less effective than cost efficiency.
2. The null hypothesis was rejected by the considerable variations in the distribution and median of profit and cost efficiency throughout the two sub-periods, 1995 to 2004 and 2005 to 2017.
3. From 1995 to 2017, Public Sector Banks had considerable fluctuations. Additionally, compared to cost efficiency, profit efficiency for PSBs is dropping.

IMPLICATIONS

PSBs should operate well to avoid using up too much of the government's financial resources. The government, which supplies them with their capital, expects them to provide value. To boost their profit efficiency, banks should increase their return on assets, broaden their net interest margins, improve the quality of their assets by lowering their NPAs, and lower the cost of deposits. Additionally, it's important to pinpoint the inefficiencies in banks, which may be related to (i) a lack of management and technical expertise, (ii) the hiring of inexperienced workers, (iii) an undeveloped socioeconomic environment, etc. To increase profit efficiency and save expenses, banks should refresh their banking models throughout this moment of transition. As a result, the government may use these resources to raise money for its social goals. Some of that money may also be used to encourage banks to behave responsibly toward society without harming their bottom line.

SUMMARY OF FUTURE RESEARCH DIRECTIONS

The technique may be used with a non-parametric approach in future study. Future research in this area should examine the relationship between bank profitability and efficiency.

REFERENCES

Ahamad, S., Veeraiah, V., Ramesh, J. V. N., Rajadevi, R., Reeja, S. R., Pramanik, S., & Gupta, A. (2023). *Deep Learning based Cancer Detection Technique, Thrust Technologies' Effect on Image Processing*. IGI Global.

Chandan, R. R., Soni, S., Raj, A., Veeraiah, V., Dhabliya, D., Pramanik, S., & Gupta, A. (2023). Genetic Algorithm and Machine Learning. In Advanced Bioinspiration Methods for Healthcare Standards, Policies, and Reform. IGI Global. doi:10.4018/978-1-6684-5656-9

Ihsan & Kabir Hassan. (2002). Technical, scale and allocative efficiencies of Turkish banking industry. *Journal of Banking & Finance, 26*(4), 719-766. doi:10.1016/S0378-4266(01)00167-4

Jayasingh, R., & Kumar, J. (2022). Speckle noise removal by SORAMA segmentation in Digital Image Processing to facilitate precise robotic surgery. *International Journal of Reliable and Quality E-Healthcare, 11*(1), 1–19. Advance online publication. doi:10.4018/IJRQEH.295083

Karaman, Özen, & Yildirim. (2006). Structure and Operation of AtaNesA Object Warehouse. *Education and Science, 31*(140). http://213.14.10.181/index.php/EB/article/view/5005

Maudos, J., & Pastor, J. M. (2003). Cost and profit efficiency in the Spanish banking sector (1985–1996): A non-parametric approach. *Applied Financial Economics, 13*(1), 1–12. doi:10.1080/09603100110086087

Mohamed, A. R. I. F. F., & Luc, C. A. N. (2008). Cost and profit efficiency of Chinese banks: A non-parametric analysis. *China Economic Review, 19*(2), 260-273. doi:10.1016/j.chieco.2007.04.001

Mondal, D., Ratnaparkhi, A., Deshpande, A., Deshpande, V., Kshirsagar, A. P., & Pramanik, S. (2023). Applications, Modern Trends and Challenges of Multiscale Modelling in Smart Cities. In *Data-Driven Mathematical Modeling in Smart Cities*. IGI Global. doi:10.4018/978-1-6684-6408-3.ch001

Omrani, H., Shamsi, M., & Emrouznejad, A. (2023). Evaluating sustainable efficiency of decision-making units considering undesirable outputs: An application to airline using integrated multi-objective DEA-TOPSIS. *Environment, Development and Sustainability, 25*(7), 5899–5930. doi:10.1007/s10668-022-02285-8 PMID:35370449

Pandey, D., Ogunmola, G. A., Enbeyle, W., Abdullahi, M., Pandey, B. K., & Pramanik, S. (2021). *Covid-19: A Framework for Effective Delivering of Online Classes during Lockdown.* Human Arenas. doi:10.1007/s42087-020-00175-x

Pramanik, S. (2022). Carpooling Solutions using Machine Learning Tools. In *Handbook of Research on Evolving Designs and Innovation in ICT and Intelligent Systems for Real-World Applications*. IGI Global. doi:10.4018/978-1-7998-9795-8.ch002

Pramanik, S. (2023). A Novel Data Hiding Locating Approach in Image Steganography. *Multimedia Tools and Applications*. Advance online publication. doi:10.1007/s11042-023-16762-3

Pramanik, S., Ghosh, R., Ghonge, M., Narayan, V., Sinha, M., Pandey, D., & Samanta, D. (2020). A Novel Approach using Steganography and Cryptography in Business Intelligence. In A. Azevedo & M. F. Santos (Eds.), *Integration Challenges for Analytics, Business Intelligence and Data Mining* (pp. 192–217). IGI Global.

Ray, A. M., Pramanik, S., Das, B., Khanna, A. (2023). Hybrid Cryptography and Steganography Method to Provide Safe Data Transmission in IoT. *ICDAM 2023*.

Samanta, D., Dutta, S., Galety, M. G., & Pramanik, S. (2021). A Novel Approach for Web Mining Taxonomy for High-Performance Computing. *The 4th International Conference of Computer Science and Renewable Energies (ICCSRE'2021)*. 10.1051/e3sconf/202129701073

Semih Yildirim, H., & Philippatos, G. C. (2007). Efficiency of Banks: Recent Evidence from the Transition Economies of Europe, 1993–2000. *European Journal of Finance, 13*(2), 123–143. doi:10.1080/13518470600763687

Talukdar, V., Kurniullah, A. Z., Keshwani, P., Khan, H., Pramanik, S., Gupta, A., & Pandey, D. (2023). *Load Balancing Techniques in Cloud Computing, Emerging Trends in Cloud Computing. In Analytics, Scalability, and Service Models*. IGI Global.

Taviti Naidu, G., & Ganesh, K. V. B. (2023). Technological Innovation Driven by Big Data. In Advanced Bioinspiration Methods for Healthcare Standards, Policies, and Reform. IGI Global. doi:10.4018/978-1-6684-5656-9

Chapter 3
Digital Labor:
Business Power of the New Period

Gülce Dölkeleş
https://orcid.org/0000-0002-2747-7648
Antalya Belek University, Turkey

ABSTRACT

Today, with the rapid development of technology, the number and importance of people operating in digital fields are increasing. Digital labor includes the processes of producing, creating, and distributing information using the internet, computers, and digital technologies. Digital labor is a concept that brings the concept of traditional business to digital fields. Studies on the internet, social media, blogs, video platforms, and other digital media are examples of digital labor. This type of labor includes a variety of skills and may require expertise in areas such as creative thought, digital marketing, content production, written and visual communication. This study discusses what digital labor is, its role in content production, and its current importance.

Humanity has undergone many changes and transformations from its existence on the world to this day. It has undergone psychological, sociological, and biological transfiguration in the historical process, and some of them have lost their effects until today, leaving it open to new forms of change. Today, digitalization is the main transformation tool that sometimes supports past movements and sometimes stands against them and takes humanity on a global scale.

Digitalization is a phenomenon that circulates all areas of life. Digitization, which accelerates its supply and transmission by digitizing information, makes it invisible among individuals, societies and nations. However, digitalization plays a styling role

DOI: 10.4018/979-8-3693-1182-0.ch003

in the social, economic, and political relations of humanity and the ways in which it perceives the world. Although digitalization is a phenomenon that has recently increased influence and has gained widespread globally, its basis is based on the knowledge they have gained as a result of the historical periods of humanity. The information society that is the result of the accumulation of knowledge in question; It is shaped by the contributions of individuals to the nations of the primitive society and the agricultural and industrial societies on a global scale. The person, who is a hunter and gatherer in the primitive society, has moved to the producer position in the agricultural society, and in the industrial society, he reinforced this producer identity through the machines. In the information society after the industrial society; it continues some of its habits in previous community periods to address its basic needs. By today, there has been no break from agriculture or industry, but since information is a new element of capital, it has become a supervisory mechanism in the context of these two concepts, both by changing the semantics of labor.

With the fact that information is in such a strong position, it is of great role to be able to effectively store and spread in gaining a decisive position on production relations. Existing information that crosses borders and reaches the world faster than any agricultural or industrial product is a phenomenon that will be produced unlimitedly as long as it is its shareholder. The sharing and dissemination of information has been historically with the feature of communication, which has changed its place in human life and has increased in different forms. People needed to receive information and share information, effective and accurate communication has been a need for people for centuries (Bayçu, 2013: 127). In order to overcome this requirement, the person turned to the search for solutions and included the communication tools in his life with the conditions imposed by everyday life. The person who conveyed his knowledge to the present day by drawing pictures on the cave walls in the early ages, invented the article and recorded his knowledge, with the help of technology, the newspaper, It produced a one-way communication flow by producing tools such as radio and television (Yengin ve Bayrak, 2017: 377). These tools that people need to communicate and exchange information have undergone change and transformation in historical and social processes. Technical, economic and social advances played an active role in the transformation of communication tools (İnuğu, 1993: 15-16).

It is now routine in the daily routine with the use of digital environments as a versatile adaptation process in life rather than imperative. There is a digital life integrated into the entire living space of individuals. A life without digitalization, digital tools have not been in our age, cannot be imagined. Almost everything is digitalized today. It has become almost impossible to perform the necessary activities in both everyday life and business life without the support of digital media. Individuals, institutions, developing relationships with other individuals and institutions use these tools to enter different exchanges.

Today, with the rapid development of technology, the number and importance of people operating in digital fields are increasing. Digital labor includes the processes of producing, creating and distributing information using the internet, computers and digital technologies.

Digital labor is a concept that brings the concept of traditional business to digital fields. Studies on the Internet, social media, blogs, video platforms and other digital media are examples of digital labor. This type of labor includes a variety of skills and may require expertise in areas such as creative thought, digital marketing, content production, written and visual communication. This study discusses what digital labor is, its role in content production and its current importance.

DIGITAL LABOR AND FEATURES

This section describes what the concept of digital labor is and what features it has.

The term "digital" signifies "pertaining to numbers" in a broad sense, and its Turkish counterpart is "numeric." The specific numerical aspect being referred to corresponds to a binary system comprised of the numbers 1 and 0 within the realm of information technologies literature. Hence, this binary system, serving as the foundation for all data-driven technologies and their associated elements, is distinguished by its inherent digital nature.

Digital labor theory is a concept stemming from Marxist ideology. It emerged from the inquiry into whether social media users should be deemed productive labor. To what degree do social media users contribute to the capital accumulation processes of social media corporations? In the era of information technologies, the productivity facet of labor within the digital economy, along with this novel context, is starting to come under scrutiny. One of the prominent theorists of digital labor, Fuchs (2015), has defined digital labor as the paid or unpaid engagement in the creation, utilization, distribution, and reproduction of content within the realm of social media.

Digital labor is a concept that emerged in our age when modern technologies and the internet were widely used. Basically, digital labor refers to the labor of people working in computer-based jobs and producing over digital platforms. Digital labor is concerned with the examination of unpaid user labor and other types of labor that are essential for the accumulation of capital in the realm of information and communication Technologies (Fuchs, 2016: 92). While numerous scholars characterize digital labor as the unpaid efforts of social media users, Fuchs unveils a specific manifestation of digital labor-that of the consuming producer within the realms of social media. Stressing that this manifestation is intricately tied to and interconnected with various other forms of global exploitative systems comprising the fabric of digital media existence, Fuchs endeavors to elucidate the labor processes within this domain.

This concept is an important element that affects employees and ways of doing business in various sectors. Digital laborers are professionals who usually run their business on computers and the internet. The realm of digital labor encompasses various specialized roles, including computer programmers, web designers, software engineers, digital marketing experts, data analysts, content producers, and freelancers. This modern form of work has revolutionized the traditional work structure, enabling remote work and eliminating the necessity for physical office spaces. Working from home or working remotely has become a key characteristic of digital labor. Internet-based platforms act as bridges connecting digital laborers with potential employers. These platforms serve as marketplaces where job seekers can find suitable projects, and employers can discover talented individuals with specific expertise. Notable examples of such self-employment platforms include Upwork, Freelancer, and Fiverr. Unlike conventional employment, digital labor provides job opportunities that are accessible to a global audience. However, this advancement comes with a challenge known as digital inequality. People lacking proper internet infrastructure and digital skills may face difficulties accessing digital labor opportunities, resulting in exclusion.

Digital labor allows employers and customers to monitor and interact with online employees easily. Through time tracking tools and digital analytics, employers can measure the effectiveness and efficiency of their remote workers. While this level of oversight can be beneficial for businesses, it may also lead to a sense of intense surveillance among employees. As technology continues to advance, digital labor will undoubtedly play an increasingly pivotal role in the business world. Hence, understanding the dynamics and impacts of digital labor is crucial in establishing equitable and sustainable relationships between employers and employees.

Digital labor represents a novel mode of work resulting from the convergence of traditional business practices and technological progress. Digital laborers are individuals proficient in various specialties, utilizing computers and internet technologies. These experts often specialize in areas requiring digital skills, such as software development, mobile application design, digital marketing, content production, graphic design, and translation. Additionally, freelancers working remotely are a prominent part of the digital labor force, contributing to diverse projects independently. Emphasizing flexibility, digital labor opens up remote work opportunities for both employers and employees. Workers can efficiently perform their tasks from home or remote locations, breaking free from the constraints of physical offices. This arrangement allows employers to access a global talent pool and fosters improved work-life balance for employees.

Digital labor's essence lies in internet-based marketplaces that simplify the process of connecting employers with skilled freelancers. Employers can effortlessly publish projects and identify digital laborers with relevant expertise and experience. These platforms also facilitate seamless payment and efficient business processes between parties. Nonetheless, digital labor's advancements risk exacerbating disparities due to limited internet access and insufficient digital skills in certain regions or communities. Addressing these inequalities necessitates efforts to enhance digital literacy through training and equitable policies.

Unlike traditional job structures, digital labor can introduce uncertainties for workers. Project-based work and self-employment arrangements may result in irregular income streams, creating financial insecurity. Consequently, finding ways to mitigate these uncertainties becomes crucial for sustaining a thriving digital labor ecosystem.

It is important to develop regulations and protective policies on issues such as social rights, insurance and retirement. Digital labor allows employers to measure employee effectiveness and efficiency more precisely. Technologies such as applications, time monitoring tools and performance analytics can continuously monitor employees' activities. This can create an intense sense of oversight among employees and affect the working environment.

Digital labor plays an important role in the rapidly changing workforce world of our time, and its impact will increase in the future. Hence, it is important to comprehend and tackle the problems and possibilities presented by digital labor to enhance working relationships and business conditions.

DIGITAL LABOR AND CONTENT PRODUCTION

In this section, information about digital labor, content production and digital platforms formed in this context will be given and their effects on the practices of doing business today will be transferred.

An important aspect of digital labor is content production. It can be in content, text, visual, audio or video format and aims to provide information that will attract users. Content production plays a key role in being on digital platforms and attracting the target audience. Content production on the Internet has gained momentum, especially with the rise of social media platforms. Users can create their own personal brand by producing content in different formats such as blog posts, video content, podcasts and visual media (Jenkins, 2006: 20). It includes various areas such as content production, blogging, video production, podcast preparation, graphic design and social media management. Each requires different skills and abilities. For example, a blogger should produce understandable and engaging content, and a video maker should have impressive visual expression and editing skills. However, digital labor and content production bring some controversy. In particular, whether content producers are fairly compensated and copyright issues are often raised. If a content becomes viral, the content maker may sometimes not receive sufficient payments or be unauthorized users of the content (Gillespie, 2018: 50). Today, studies on digital labor, content production and digital platforms are becoming increasingly important. Growth in areas such as the spread of the Internet, the power of social media platforms, e-commerce and digital marketing has revealed digital labor as a business and profession. Blog Writing and Digital Journalism: An important aspect of digital labor is content production activities such as blogging and digital journalism. Bloggers share their knowledge and experience as a specialist in a particular field. Topic expertise, sectoral analysis, and content that enables interaction with the target audience are key elements of blogging. For example, a person specializing in health can share health advice, nutritional advice and exercise programs by opening a personal blog. Video production is the process of preparing video content professionally. Producing quality videos for digital platforms, creating visually and audibly impressive content is another area of digital labor.

Digital journalism refers to an area that brings traditional journalism to digital platforms. Digital journalism plays an important role in the news industry, thanks to its advantages such as being able to publish news instantly, preparing interactive content and interacting with readers instantly. YouTuber and Video Production: With the popularization of video platforms, YouTubers are one of the most remarkable elements of digital labor. YouTubers provide entertainment, education, information and guidance by preparing videos. For example, a travel enthusiast can create a YouTube channel that promotes the places it travels and gives travel tips. Social Media Management and Digital Marketing: Social media play a critical role in creating digital assets and reaching their target audiences today. Social media management involves processes of creating content, enabling follower interaction and increasing brand awareness by effectively using brands' social media accounts. Digital marketing is a discipline that carries out brand promotion, advertising and marketing activities through digital platforms. Search engine optimization (SEO), creating content marketing, email, and advertising on social media are distinct approaches within the realm of digital marketing. Graphic Design and Digital Art: Graphic design creates a creative aspect of digital labor. Preparing visual content for digital platforms, designing logos, banners, brochures and other promotional materials are one of the core activities of graphic design. In addition, digital artists create artistic works in digital environments and exhibit their work through digital art galleries. Podcast Making and Audiobooks: Podcasts have become an important component of digital media consumption. By opening the podcast channel, speech programs, interviews, storytelling and educational content can be presented. In addition, the popularity of audiobooks has increased and has created new business opportunities for voice actors.

Digital labor, content production and digital platforms have become an integral part of business and social life today. Areas such as blogging, video creation, social media marketing, graphic design and digital art are concrete examples of digital labor. Digital labor and content production also changed the concept of traditional work. Especially for freelancers, opportunities to do business through digital platforms have increased without being connected to a physical office. This can increase the flexibility of the workforce while at the same time bringing uncertainties.

As a result, digital labor and content production play an increasingly larger role. Thanks to the global access of the Internet, individuals can demonstrate their own abilities and earn income, while the regulation of these processes and fair compensation remain important. With the developing technology and the spread of the internet, the impact and importance of digital labor will continue in the future.

DIGITAL LABOR AND LIBERTY

The purpose of this section is to examine the concept of freedom that digital labor offers in traditional business models.

Digital labor provides employees with greater freedom and flexibility compared to traditional business models. It offers flexibility and freedom in different areas such as the proliferation of the Internet and digital technologies, the possibility of working remotely, freelance and content production. Employees can benefit from remote work and manage their jobs from where they wish, without being dependent on traditional office environments. This is an attractive advantage especially for digital workers. Those who want to start their own business can work freely by creating their own content over digital platforms.

Digital labor helps employees to balance work and life by offering remote work opportunities. Many employers now allow their employees to work outside the office. In this way, while traffic stress and waste of time are reduced, employees can also run their jobs from home, cafes or places where they travel. For example, software developers, graphic designers or digital marketing experts focus on their projects and can be more efficient using the advantage of working remotely.

Digital labor also contributed to the spread of the self-study model. Thanks to the Internet, it is possible to connect with employers or customers anywhere in the world. Freelancers can choose jobs that fit their abilities and have more control by setting their own working hours. For example, a content writer can work freely to write articles on different topics and work at any time.

Digital labor also provides freedom in content production and personal brand creation. Bloggers, YouTubers, podcast makers and other content producers can make their own voices heard by creating their own content. In addition to creating personal brands, these content also offers a chance to get different business opportunities and sponsorships. Digital labor creates lower cost and risky business opportunities for entrepreneurship. Digital business models allow businesses to be set up and grow on digital platforms, rather than opening physical stores or offices. For example, opening an e-commerce store and selling products online is a popular option for entrepreneurs using digital labor.

However, there are some difficulties that digital labor brings with these freedoms. Producing content continuously and presenting remarkable materials can be challenging in the digital world where competition is intense. Also, the instability of revenues compared to traditional jobs may raise concerns about financial assurance for some employees.

DIGITAL SOCIETY

In this section, the important effects of digitalization on social structures and the resulting digital society are focused on creating a new order in social, economic, political and cultural fields. In this context, the concepts of society and digital society are discussed in detail.

The concept of society, which has been studied in many ways and studied in many ways, is a structuring that man has developed in order to survive, lead an easier and more satisfying life. Person has organized social structures as the ideal way of life, using his mind, which is his strongest aspect. Considering the social development stages of human history, we basically face four periods. These periods; It is possible to classify as primitive society, agricultural society, industrial society and information society (Aktan ve Tunç, 1998: 119).

The Primitive Society period, the first of which is accepted from the different stages of socioeconomic development of societies, is trying to discover the possibilities of nature that humanity is at the beginning of everything and that it strives to live, it refers to a stage where collective consciousness and social memory have not yet been fully formed, where most of them experience it through trial and error.

B.C. with the agricultural revolution that occurred in 5000, humanity left behind the primitive society phase and moved to the Agricultural Society stage (Dursun, 1998: 154). The Agricultural Society symbolizes a structure in which humanity has managed to tame the land and not be content with what nature has given it to it and to direct it to give what it wants. Humanity has started to live in a more stable, less risky and more comfortable life by moving to established life where there are fertile lands that it can mow. With the development of knowledge about domestication of animals, the processing of household soil, individuals have become more than they consume.

Industrial Society, which emerged after 1750 with the application of information to processes, products and tools, the use of technological innovations, political, economic, took its place as a process that included its reflection in social and cultural fields (Drucker, 1994: 33-34). The Industrial Society, which emerged with the discovery of steam power and its use in production environments, the phenomenon of mass production and consumption is included in human life, and urbanization has become evident, It is the social structure in which new class structures such as bourgeois and working class come to the agenda. The industrialization movement has improved greatly since the second half of the 18th century, in this process the machines have been replaced by the soil and the designation of the society has been mechanical Technologies (Aktan ve Tunç, 1998: 119). As a result of this situation, the agricultural community structure has begun to lose its former importance.

Besides the cheapness of information technology, the structure that lifts the borders from the wood brought the production to the global dimension (Fukuyama, 2000: 13). The sectoral separation information sector consisting of agriculture, industry and service branches was also included. Information The capital of the society is human. In the information age, labor and capital are also human-sourced and human-owned. The fact that information is taken to the center by the individual and the fulfillment of the requirements of the age is not equal in every person, they did not enter the age in which they were in different societies in the same time period. It is clear that although there are temporal differences between them in terms of transforming societies into information society, it is not as intermittent as in other ages. The biggest share of the masses worldwide in reaching the information age at close intervals is the developing cheapening and widely used technology and its natural consequence digitalization.

Digitalization, which has significant effects on social structures and almost creates a digital society, and builds a brand new order in social, economic, political and cultural fields, is very popular. The biggest share in the spread of technology globally is the computer that has become the symbol of the information society (Karaman, 1998: 241). Internet technologies, the most important building block of the network society, are also important (Özkaya, 2013: 159). With the introduction of internet into social life in the years 1990, it has revealed that nothing will be the same. The Internet has also caused change and transformation on social relationships with ease of use, speed of interaction and time, eliminating space constraints. Thus, a new human model emerged with technology. The digital society has become a global audience living on the axis of the rules and habits it produces. People who would not be able to come side by side under normal conditions were in interaction thanks to the platforms. There is also a danger of losing the characteristic features that people who are so close are socially carrying. Digital lives are increasingly similar. Virtual communities are where this change and resemblance situation can be best observed. It consists of virtual communities of people who come together around certain common points. Masses formed on social media are at the head of these virtual communities. With virtual masses formed as a fan community or a nurse community, people have united around common ideas, leaving their personal differences aside. The Internet has continued the development of technology, enabling the emergence of a culture that has effects on living beyond virtual, to become widespread and fast in everyday life. With digitalization, no culture has become able to fully preserve its essence. Intercultural interaction is experienced very quickly. Digitalization, which enters human life with the information society, creates new types of professions, jobs and jobs. International economic activities can be done easily, meetings and events can be organized. People's tolerance, interactions and relationships to each other have changed. Virtual communities, digital activity formations, relationships over social media, etc. all of them are situations that come with digitalization. The reactions or behaviors that people give them are socially and psychologically decisive in their lives.

DIGITAL LABOR AND SOCIAL CHANGE

In this section, we talk about the change in the social structure shaped by digital labor, the new business models and interaction that emerge.

Digital labor is an important force that triggers and shapes social change. With the proliferation of internet and digital technologies, transformations have occurred in different areas of society and new business models, communication methods and forms of social interaction have emerged.

Digital labor has led to a revolutionary change in communication and information access. Thanks to the Internet, it is possible to reach information quickly and easily. For example, a news event is instantly shared on digital news sites and social media, people anywhere in the world are instantly informed. This has deeply influenced the way societies receive news, information and react to world events.

Digital labor has brought a big change in the field of education and learning. Digital platforms offer online training opportunities and create distance learning opportunities. For example, thanks to Mass Online Courses, people around the world can access the courses of world-famous universities for free and learn new skills.

Digital labor has also caused a significant change in the business world. Thanks to the Internet, the processes of job search and job postings have been digitized, and online business platforms have emerged. In addition, digital labor has contributed to the spread of the self-study business model. Opportunities such as working remotely from the Internet and producing digital content offer wider business opportunities and eliminate borders.

It has also transformed the digital labor, entertainment and art sectors. Digital platforms make access to content such as music, movies, TV series and games easier. For example, musicians can reach a wider audience by publishing their own music on digital platforms and can pursue a career independently. Digital art galleries create a new space where digital artists can showcase their works.

Digital labor has increased the power of social activism and social movements. Social media and digital communication allow mass media to be announced and social change demanded. For example, many social movements and protests are organized on digital platforms and bring voice worldwide.

Digital labor has triggered an effective change in many areas in society. Thanks to the internet and digital technologies, transportation to information has increased, education and learning processes have transformed and cultural expression forms have changed. In addition, communication, entertainment and information activities with content made on digital platforms have become easier. Digital labor has also made a significant impact in the business sphere. The ascent of digital media has revolutionized conventional media and advertising industries, resulting in fresh business prospects. Digital marketing and content creation have empowered small enterprises to access a broader audience.

Numerous facets of society have undergone substantial transformations owing to the utilization of digital labor. Communication, information retrieval, education, employment, entertainment, art, and social activism are domains where digital technologies and digital labor exhibit unmistakable influence. The future is poised to sustain this momentum due to ongoing social shifts, rapid technological advancements, and the continued prominence of digital labor. To effectively adapt to these social changes and transformations, it is vital to consider the impacts and repercussions of the digital realm.

One of the new technologies that has an impact on societies and that has frequently mentioned its name today is artificial intelligence. It was discovered by McCarthy in 1955 (Aydın and Değirmenci, 2018: 15). Artificial intelligence, which meets an unnatural being with the ability to evaluate and make choices, is also an important position in terms of social dynamics beyond its impact on technologies.

Artificial intelligence has the ability to interpret data correctly, learn from data in action, and apply what it learns. Artificial intelligence is the field of science and engineering that involves the development of systems that exhibit properties that can be associated with intelligence, such as perception of human behavior, natural language processing, problem solving, planning and learning. Its main goal is; to understand the principles that enable intelligent behavior in animals and artificial factors in humans (Tecuci, 2012: 168).

Perceptors have experienced three research phases of artificial intelligence with the aim of researching theories that can perform tasks requiring biological or human intelligence through functions such as decision making, recognition and control, and developing computer systems (Fan & others, 2012: 1-2). The first of these; processing power of computers with limited computational capacity. The second is; the development of artificial neural networks and the third is deep learning, similar to the human brain and computers with better computing capacity.

Augmented reality, developed in the late 1950's as well as artificial intelligence, gaining prevalence in 1990's and expressing the creation of real-world perception with digital data with the help of computers (Kılıç, 2017: 91) and holography, which is a boat to a modern image (Işık, 2013: 212) technologies such as digitalization can be observed otherwise in social life. Thanks to these technologies, it is envisaged that there will be changes in the way societies perceive and make sense of the world. Increased interaction of artificial intelligence with different objects, such as wearable devices, vehicles, industrial sensors, smartphones or security cameras, it is suggested that the development of innovative services for societies and organizations will play a binding role. Because smart technologies are needed to facilitate and support innovation, sustainability, and competition in order to deal with the changes brought by fast-moving digital Technologies (Sharma & others, 2020: 1).

The realization of the significant effects of artificial intelligence on social life is a result of technological developments, social change, and transformation. New systems are produced that are effective and functional in every field, including transportation, trade, agriculture, manufacturing, public administration, health, and education. In the realm of emerging technological ecosystems, artificial intelligence manifests in various forms, including AI robots assuming decision-making roles in meetings, smart city applications, vision systems incorporating augmented reality, 3D printed manufacturing systems, and driverless vehicles. The progress of technology, particularly artificial intelligence, is steering advancements towards the creation of a knowledge-based society. This is achieved by channeling the scientific community's focus towards critical elements such as thinking, imagination, learning, creativity, and invention, fostering effective competition in innovation. The advent of artificial intelligence is anticipated to bring about shifts in the nature of jobs and professions, a phenomenon already beginning to manifest its effects today. In many countries, professions such as information engineering, process engineering, performance engineering, data analysis, database specialization, 3D modeling technology, personal training guidance, and hologram design have already been integrated into educational systems. The social and technological transformation in the world continues at a high pace. It is important not to be indifferent to technological developments, especially artificial intelligence, but to adapt to the elimination of all operations in the system as a whole.

Time will undoubtedly show how all these current and possible technologies, digitalization and social transformation will draw the roadmap and what opportunities or threats will be present on the marked paths.

CONCLUSION

The information society is a social structure that emerges with the emergence of information and communication technologies, especially computers. The spread of information technologies from business to private life to life brought with it radical changes and transformations. In this process, economic, social and cultural elements got their right without digitalization. Individuals benefit from digitalization in business forms, economic relations and many efforts brought by social life. This situation is expected to increase gradually in the future. Making machines and digital systems a part of his life, man can incorporate digitalization into his life to an unpredictable extent in the coming years. These transformations have influenced relational processes more than business adhesion forms affect business processes. With the globalization, the world has become a global village with the words of Marshall Mcluhan. Nothing is as far or as close as it is now thought. It is a fact that individuals change and transform today, but not all are at the same level. The basis of this level difference between individuals and societies; It dates back to the first periods of history. Individuals societies have not been able to have new technologies and ideas all over the world. While the agricultural revolution in a geography at the same time could not fully show itself, it was seen that industrialization steps were taken in other regions. These level differences continue today, but thanks to digitalization, its impact has decreased. While the agricultural revolution in a geography at the same time could not fully show itself, it was seen that industrialization steps were taken in other regions. These level differences continue today, but thanks to digitalization, its impact has decreased. Individuals and societies can now practically witness the development of the era, whether they adapt or not. The provider of this situation is the developments in information and communication technologies.

The notion of digital labor is gaining increasing significance in today's world. Content production stands as a pivotal component of digital labor, facilitating the exchange of information and interaction across digital platforms. While digital labor generates novel business models and opportunities by offering autonomy and adaptability, it can also introduce challenges and heightened competition. Socially, digital labor contributes to social change and contributes significantly to the shaping of the new-term workforce in the business world.

The change created by digital technologies also leads to significant changes in working life. More qualified workforce is needed in the new period. At the same time, while many professions disappear, new professions are born instead. The fact that many jobs will be done by robots with artificial intelligence constitutes the perception that demand for the workforce will decrease. In contrast, there are new professions to emerge and employees have a chance to close this gap on the basis of these professions. While the new working order offers opportunities for some, it also carries great risks for some.

Technological developments are also thought to be devastating for the labor markets and digital labor will replace human labor.

Digitization causes automation of jobs and tasks that require low-level, routine skills. But digitalization causes many jobs to disappear, but it also creates new business opportunities. This process is against low-skilled workers working in routine professions, while favoring highly skilled workers. In line with the professions whose demand is falling and the demand is increasing, there is a need for digital skills that will adapt individuals to these new professions. While these new professions increase the demand for new skills, they also create new opportunities for education and training.

The skills needed for new professions are as follows; analytical thinking, endurance, stress tolerance, learning strategies, reasoning, problem solving, generating ideas, emotional intelligence, critical thinking and analysis, troubleshooting and user experience, creativity, originality, leadership and social impact, system analysis and evaluation, technology use monitoring and control, persuasion and discussion, technology design and programming.

As of 2030, most of the professions will turn into newly created professions, and these professions will undergo significant transformations in terms of content and skill. Employees who add additional skills to their current skills will progress faster and increase inequality among low-skilled people. This is likely to be inevitable, especially considering that digital technologies increase demand for high skills.

The professions of the future also require hunch. Individuals, companies and nations who are far from the digital age or technological transformation will be doomed to experience problems over time. Instead of reviving these new professions that emerge in this direction, there is a need for an education system, digital human resources and policies that can be integrated into the world that will enable the ability required by transformation. In this context, the private and public sector should master information communication technology and artificial intelligence terminology. The required infrastructure should be created and a budget should be allocated to this area.

Skill and competence training should be provided so that existing employees can adapt to digital technologies during the transition to new jobs. The skills that employers need to move their companies to high value-added and innovative activities should be compatible with industry and skill policies. Digital technology has made it possible for individuals around the world to express their ideas more easily to the global market, which is why digital entrepreneurship opportunities should be increased. To promote digital entrepreneurship, it is important to provide incentives by opening courses and programs. In order for businesses to grow digital human resources, they should provide training compatible with digital technologies in university and company cooperation. In addition to receiving national level training to have digital professions and the digital skills required in the international arena, they should participate in training and receive certificates through digital platforms.

It can also be predicted that digital labor will expand the problems that exist today and cause new problems that may arise in the future. This situation requires new policies. The success of the measures to be taken will show whether the developments to be experienced will be justified or those who evaluate the digital transformation positively or negatively.

While it is difficult to make precise predictions about the future role of digital labor and content production, it is clear that with the rapid development of digital technologies, the impact of digital labor will continue. For this reason, it is important that those who want to operate in the digital field constantly improve themselves and follow new trends.

REFERENCES

Aktan, C. C., & Tunç, M. (1998). Bilgi Toplumu ve Türkiye. *Yeni Türkiye Dergisi*, *4*(19), 118–133.

Aydın, İ. H., & Değirmenci, C. H. (2018). *Yapay Zeka*. Girdap Kitap.

Bayçu, S. (2013). Halkla İlişkilerde Medya İlişkileri ve Uygulamaları. In Anadolu Üniversitesi Açıköğretim Fakültesi Yayınları. Eskişehir.

Drucker, P. F. (1994). Kapitalist Ötesi Toplum. İnkılap Kitapevi.

Fan, J., Fang, L., Wu, J., Guo, Y., & Dai, Q. (2020). From Brain Science to Artificial Intelligence. *Engineering (Beijing)*, *6*(3), 248–252. doi:10.1016/j.eng.2019.11.012

Fuchs, C. (2015). *Dijital Emek ve Karl Marx*. Notabene Yayınları.

Fuchs, C. (2016). Sosyal Medya: Eleştirel Bir Giriş. NotaBene Yayınları.

Fukuyama, F. (2000). Büyük Çözülme: İnsanın Doğası ve Toplumsal Düzenin Yeniden Oluşması. Sabah Kitapları.

Gillespie, T. (2018). *Custodians of the Internet: Platforms, content moderation, and the hidden decisions that shape social media*. Yale University Press.

Işık, V. (2013). Holografik Sanat. *Elektronik Sosyal Bilimler Dergisi*, *12*(47), 212–231.

Jenkins, H. (2006). *Convergence culture: Where old and new media collide*. NYU Press.

Karaman, İ. (1998). Bilgi Toplumu Olmaya Süratle Yönelmeliyiz. *Yeni Türkiye Dergisi*, *4*(19), 239–250.

Kılıç, N. P. (2017). *Artırılmış Gerçeklik Uygulamalarının Halkla İlişkiler Açısından Olanak ve Sınırlılıkları. İletişim Araştırmaları*, *14*(2), 87–118.

Özkaya, B. (2013). *Yeni Medy'da Demokrasi: Sosyal Medya'ya Dair Araştırmalar*. Literatürk Yayınları.

Sharma, G. D., Yadav, A., & Chopra, R. (2020). Artificial Intellegence and Effective Governance: A Review, Critique and Research Agenda. *Sustainable Futures : An Applied Journal of Technology, Environment and Society*, 1–6.

Tecuci, G. (2012). Artificial Intelligence. *Wiley Interdisciplinary Reviews: Computational Statistics*, *4*(2), 168–180. doi:10.1002/wics.200

Yengin, D., & Bayrak, T. (2017). Sosyal Medyada Dijital Kamuoyu. *The Turkish Online Journal of Design, Art and Communication*, *7*(2), 376–386.

Chapter 4
Digitally Empowering Women Through Community Radio and Mobile Storytelling in India

Soumya Jha
Bennett University, India

Vishesh Redhu
Bennett University, India

Navodita Pande
https://orcid.org/0000-0001-5316-1527
Bennett University, India

Minja Bolesnikov
https://orcid.org/0000-0003-3735-602X
Swiss School of Business and Management, Serbia

ABSTRACT

In the post-COVID-19 era, digital empowerment has become significant, especially with reference to media messages and communication technologies being used to financially empower citizens. As past histories of media are leaving behind a legacy of analog and archaic forms of media content creation, new technologies are building the 'media archaeology' of past traditions, heritages, epistemologies to generate meanings, and dialogue for new means of storytelling, thereby preserving heritage in 'digital formats'. The study has some broader mission and objectives with more specific research questions: What are the key themes of digital literacy among community radio practitioners? Which theoretical frameworks can define digital literacy? What are the different tools of digital empowerment? Is there an emerging 'empowering relationship' among women content creators and consumers?

DOI: 10.4018/979-8-3693-1182-0.ch004

INTRODUCTION

In the post-Covid era, digital empowerment has become significant, especially with reference to media messages and communication technologies being used to financially empower citizens. As new age forms of technologies are increasingly being used to depict cultures, traditions and lifestyles, such online platforms are becoming tools to empower citizens and initiate a financial dialogue among its users and consumers. The study looks into the ways in which women are empowered through platforms like community radio in a 'digital way' and also investigates the methods and processes through which women are digitally empowered through different forms of 'storytelling' on YouTube as a mobile medium. This study, however, addresses the issue of the political economy of the internet and web 5.0 in the light of theoretical framework of technological determinism. Another aspect which is probed is the ability of the new media to generate a new methodology of studying and retaining culture, where it creates new databases as forms of 'media archaeology' (Ellis & Hall, 2019).

The study deals with information from content creators of community radio stations and YouTube channels to indicate that such platforms empower women and generate profiles based on participatory communication networks promoting culture and building a media archaeology around it. While the theory of technological determinism mentions the ways in which technology shapes and weaves knowledge and information around humans determining agendas, opinions and debates, hands-on approach or media archaeology validates the need for 'skills' and digital encounters affecting physical skills, literacy-levels, knowledge and views. It also leads one to believe that political economy of the internet can co-exist with 'financial empowerment' of users on platforms that have user-generated content like YouTube.

LITERATURE REVIEW

Haggart (2019) persuasively argues that the whole of our being (including mood and confidentiality of the personal) is now subject to collection, processing, deduction, and crucially marketization. In such a 'political economy' of digital platforms, community radio stations produce content that create a civic infrastructure (Horrigan & Schement, 2021) which empowers women by making them content producers and educating other women consumers in the process.

The study mentions that consumers' love for mobile devices, and viewing with privacy along with their glocal content are the main reasons they prefer digital platforms. Hence such digital platforms become the voice of several citizens indulging in participatory communication leading to positive social change and generating 'cultural meanings' that promote heritages and new paradigms in cultural theories.

Rodriguez (2001) proposes that such media is a form of 'citizens' media' where ordinary people gain control and stay immersed through continuous experiences of such environments of 'mediascape'. As past histories of media are leaving behind a legacy of analog and archaic forms of media content creation, new technologies are building the 'media archaeology' of past traditions, heritages, epistemologies to generate meanings and dialogue for new means of storytelling thereby preserving heritage in 'digital formats'.

The study has some broader mission and objectives with more specific research questions as discussed below.

TECHNOLOGICAL DETERMINISM

Ripp & Hauer (2017) are of the view that technological determinism forms the basis for society's transformation. Toffler understood technology to be a determinant of all of society's changes, he believed it still had the major impact on human psyche when he wrote about the 'shock of the future' (Toffler, 1980). Other theorists mention 'new media' as the field of computing, computer technologies, and associated data contents primarily applying to technology-determined (Ripp & Hauer, 2017). Manovich (2001) mentions five principles that determine the definition of new media-numerical representation, modularity, automatization, variability and transcoding. Levy (1988) argues that while technology determines the nature of society, it is also a product of society and culture. This goes on to tell us that technology and new media is a cause and effect of the society and culture we see around us.

The concept around technology initiates a discussion around digital literacies (media literacies, information and communication technology literacies) also grouped as new literacies. Creativity and innovation, and competence in the use of digital technologies and media is one of the pillars of modern-day education and adult literacy education (Ripp & Hauer, 2017). Tilley (2011) mentions that in the world of technology, professional ethics must work in close association with expectations of society in which various professions are practiced.

MEDIA ARCHAEOLOGY

While media archaeology mentions that histories and cultures are preserved on digital and online platforms leading to creation of digital content in a hands-on way (Ellis & Hall, 2019), it is also interested in the specific effects of abandoned media technologies (Huhtamo & Parikka, 2011). The move from analog to digital has been significant in this regard (*ibid).* The approach focuses on the relationship between people and technologies. The relationship, authors argue, is one of mutual adaptation (Ellis & Hall, 2020).

The method, often used to study the evolving relationship between machine and man, highlights a process of documentation of the work of skilled workers on diverse online platforms as a form of 'knowledge bank' (Ellis & Hall, 2020). The hands-on approach thus focusses on audio-visual recordings as a form of knowledge-creation generated by 'physical immersion' of researchers in analog and digital processes. Latour (1999) argues his case regarding the coming together of human and tool by providing an analogy of the gunman- the responsibility lies in the way the two, gun and individual, come together to construct a new hybrid agent- the gunman. Just as the act of killing or not killing is the responsibility of the gunman, the socio-technical network created by humans and machines in the coming together on digital platforms is one of ethical responsibility towards society and culture.

Malafouris (2013) mentions a 'material engagement theory' arguing that the way humans think is determined by 'extracranial bodily processes and material artifacts'. Hence human cognition comprises element in the immediate material environment and surroundings.

POLITICAL ECONOMY OF WEB 5.0

It is thus argued that creation of new literacies and technological frameworks gives rise to a 'political economy' of the internet. Salgues (2018) argues that political economy of the internet gives rise to a society which can be called society 5.0. This society is determined by innovations, industry and cybernics. It employs information and communication technologies and humanity both at its centre.

Gavalda & Ribera-Fumaz (2012) highlight the importance of trasitioning of societies from knowledge to smartness which has been made possible through the internet and the sustainability effort of countries to adapt to new technologies with a socio-political framework in Barcelona, Spain. Due to technology and internet, there is better use of industry, talent, innovation and engineering solutions to transition to a 'resilient structure' due to the political economy of the internet.

However, a question arises whether such 'smart concepts' are sustainable, catering equally to all citizens in society, incorporating the problem of 'digital divide' or simply growing and transforming on an 'uneven scale'?

The concepts that are studied include digital empowerment (within the framework of technology, digital literacies, media archaeology), mobile storytelling (that lead to innovation, new literacies and skillsets for learners) and engaging in community radio and YouTube as tools for the study (giving rise to participatory communication and financial inclusion).

RESEARCH GAPS

As the current research indicates, gaps exist in determining how current skillsets works to empower women through digital forms of storytelling, including community radio stations that enhance financial and digital inclusion of women into the mainstream. In such a role, media works to promote equal participation, which is under-studied. In India, the top YouTubers need to be studied and efforts need to be made to understand the use of community radio and YouTube in India as a form of storytelling that leads to empowerment of women and their active participation.

Mission

Informed by prior studies, this study has as its primary mission:

- Observe such media histories
- Analyse such media content
- Inquire into content creators and their engagement in storytelling
- Critically examine traditional and folk heritages leading to financial goals for women
- Encourage histories to tell stories of digitally empowered future for women

The broader objectives of the research are to look into:

- Practices of content creators
- Highlight key agendas of digital curators
- Observe participatory ways of communication among women
- Study the groups and communities engaging in financial dialogue

This brings us to the specific research questions which are:

Research Questions

RQ1: What are the key themes of digital literacy among community radio practitioners?
RQ2: Which theoretical frameworks can define digital literacy?
RQ3: What are the different ways, techniques, tools of digital empowerment through mobile storytelling?

RQ4: Is there an emerging 'empowering relationship' among women content creators and consumers?

RQ5: Are new media platforms leading to an empowered 'media archaeology' of ancient cultures and traditions?

The research methodology used is in-depth interviews of community radio practitioners and YouTubers and also analysing the content of top ten female YouTubers in India. Both the methods were adopted to generate data to study the answers to the questions mentioned above. Thematic coding was used to analyse the interviews (format attached) and content of YouTube platform.

RESULTS

Community radio is a form of radio broadcasting that involves public broadcasting which is participatory and usually engages communities where it is run or broadcast. It is different from a commercial radio station and usually does not run for a profit or for business purposes.

Fraser & Restrepo-Estrada () argue that it is managed by the community and usually and its operated mainly by the community's own resources. Its principal functions are- reflect and promote local identity, create diversity of voices and opinions, encourage open dialogue and democratic process, promote social change and development and promote good governance and civil society.

In the context of the study here, community radio stations in India are run either by government bodies or non-government organizations, educational institutions, rural and suburban communities. Under the official body of advertising and publicity in India, DAVP (Directorate of Advertising and Visual Publicity), more than 40 community radio stations are functional along with those in ministries of health and family welfare, consumer affairs, science and technology, Panchayati Raj and women and child development.

Here community radio stations in the state of Bihar are studied.

Radio Mandakini Ki Aawaz

Radio Mandakini Ki Aawaz is a community radio based in Rudraprayag district of Uttarakhand. The persons interviewed are Manvendra Negi (male) and Poonam Rawat (female), the two radio jockeys. They are of ages 40 years and 30 years, respectively. Several questions were posed to them to which their responses are indicated below. They are both graduates and work full-time for the radio station.

Key Themes of Digital Literacy

Question: Do you have a show/name on Digital literacy?

Answer: Tech Sakhi

Question: Is the show targeted at men, women, youth or children?

Answer: Women in the age-group of 40-50 years and college-going girls around the age of 18.

Question: What is the content of the show?

Answer: Online safety

Question: What is the duration and frequency of the show?

Answer: Twice a week, each episode being fresh and sometimes a repeat broadcast.

Question: Does the show help listeners in better digital participation?

Answer: Yes

Question: In which ways are listeners enabled to have a digital life and awareness?

Answer: Women started sharing their stories on phone and in community meetings

Question: Does the show encourage listeners to take digital decisions?

Answer: Yes

Question: What are the digital ways that listeners use after the show?

Answer: They don't share things easily on social media and are discreet about their information thus being more conscious about safeguarding their online privacy. They often use passwords and frequently change the passwords from time to time. They use the social media account safely. They call for help. They question if something is wrong.

Emerging 'Empowering Relationship' Among Women Content Creators and Consumers

Question: Do you have any shows on feedback from listeners**?**

Answer: Yes

Question: How do you get feedback from the listener?

Answer: Primarily from phone calls and community engagement or messages

Question: How many and what kind of feedback you get from the listener?

Answer: We have received 5 calls immediately after the show. Later we received a total no of 60 calls in three months.

Question: How many such shows are run by women?

Answer: Only one show is run by three women presenters; all of whom are community radio practitioners

Question: How many listeners among them are women?

Answer: All our calls are from women listeners only; 50 to 60 calls of women alone

Question: Do any women talk about how the shows that informed them?

Answer: Yes, they confirmed that the programme was very useful in helping them discern unwanted from wanted messages on online platforms; for example, they don't use Instagram but used to get random WhatsApp video call and messages on Instagram. Most of them don't have smart phones as their kids grab it but they were satisfied they are acquiring knowledge for their kids. They were also facing intrusions from fake social media account of strangers who used to bully them and harass them.

Question: Is there any survey done on how has the show impacted the women?

Answer: No, not exactly a survey

Question: Has the show made the women take control in decisions 'digitally'?

Answer: Yes, of course, now they are demanding more shows on women issues and problems and engaging in dialogue and discussion.

Question: How long was your show on air?

Answer: It was on-air for three months; the show duration was of fifteen minutes; broadcast twice a week.

Question: How do you gauge the popularity of the show ?

Answer: The phone-in calls during the show and after the show

Question: Any last suggestions and comments on the topic?

Answer: Digital safety is very necessary so we are creating digital awareness.

Radio Mayur

Radio Mayur is a community radio station in Chhapra district of Bihar. The community radio practitioner is Abhishek Arun (male), who is 30 years old and holds a Masters degree. He works full-time in the community radio station which is his primary profession.

The show being done on this platform is the same as the previous one, namely Tech Sakhi. Responses are repetitive, hence not included here. However, the theme, respondent said, was much needed for the community as young generation girls used smartphones and were not aware about digital scams and frauds. They had applied online for college admissions through online forms. Therefore, digital safety is very necessary, so that digital awareness is created. Almost one and a half lakh people were active listeners to the show.

Radio Ghazipur

Amitesh Singh, a resident of Ghazipur is 43 years old and a regular contributor to this community radio station where he is a full-time practitioner. The radio station was active for about five to six years from 2017-2023. There was no show, however, based on women or run by women. There were shows that worked to promote financial literacy for women, especially those in the farming and agricultural sector. All shows were primarily targeted towards farming practices and how to make them more productive for the farmers, informing them of diverse government schemes and policies targeted at the farmer. Women farm laborers and agriculturalists benefitted from such techniques that made them aware about how to work better for an increased output.

The respondent believed that more steps need to be taken to improve financial inclusion of women from all socio-economic backgrounds. More programmes need to be created and generated so that women are granted agency, control over their decision-making processes in personal and professional lives.

Youtuber Profile

Agreya Sharma, a sixteen-year old student of Delhi Public School, Kanpur, runs his own YouTube channel, The Wrestling Stand. He earns an income of INR 10, 000 per month based on his videos which he edits and uploads on his channel. This is his only source of income as a young student. He has made an effort to initiate girls, his classmates, into this process but the girls seemed less interested in earning an income out of this. His gaming episodes not only provided entertainment to subscribers and millions of viewers but also were a platform to network, create and share with his classmates and friends. He has made an effort to inform and educate other women and help them start their own YouTube channels.

The YouTuber feels more steps need to be taken to encourage and assimilate women into the ‘financial fold’ of YouTube. Financial literacy, he said, is an important and crucial step towards digital empowerment, besides information and communication literacies.

YouTube has become the largest and most visited video-sharing platform (Snelson, 2011). It is now a common form of media on the web. It provides diverse experiences to users in the fields of politics, science, research, lifestyle, and other themes. It is a form of experiential learning with lots of do-it-yourself steps to make personal and professional lives easier.

Chad Hurley, Steve Chen and Jawed Karim founded YouTube in 2004 as a post to share and upload video material. It has been defined in different ways by different researchers. While Miles (2013) calls it a video-sharing site, social networking and advertising and marketing site, Miller (2012) contends it is a free, public online video archive focusing on sharing knowledge for users’ diverse interests, Snickars & Vondereau (2009) place it in the wider category of ‘platform’ for various ‘cultural institutions’ being hypothesized as a library, archive, audio-visual medium, and a digital laboratory.

For the purpose of the study, few influencers and YouTube creators with their own personal channels were chosen. Each one had a huge set of fans. Their profiles were listed and content was analysed keeping in mind the research questions discussed above- how is YouTube as a platform for mobile storytelling empowering women in a digital way.

YouTube Creators

Another step towards digital empowerment and its study is done by content analysing profiles of top ten YouTubers of India (female). The following results were generated:

These are the women who are not only empowered and financially literate but also empowering others in the process of creating content for their YouTube channels. The nature and profile of each channel was studied to indicate and generate findings which showcased 'digital empowerment' through online tools.

In the table above subscribers, playlists, channels and shorts give an indication on how popular are their channels and how good are they at the community level. Their community is either large or small dependent upon the number of user comments to the posts showcased on their community channel. For example, user 11, Vidya Vox, is an Indian-American and has a large community catering to audience which is culturally diverse, but primarily Indian.

Similarly, the results of coding categories are indicated below:

Table 1. List of sample YouTubers

1.	#PuneetKaur	@KaurBeauty
2.	#PayalJain	@thepaayaljain
3.	#PoojaLuthra	@poojaluthra
4.	#AnishaDixit	@rickshawali
5.	#SonaliBhadauria	@LiveToDanceWithSonali
6.	#ScherezadeShroff	@SherryShroff
7.	#SurbhiBagga	@SurbhiBagga
8.	#ShrutiArjunAnand	@ShrutiArjunAnand
9.	#PragatiVerma	@PragatiVermaa
10.	#NatashaNoel	@NatashaNoel001
11.	#VidyaVox	@VidyaVox

Table 2. User profiles of YouTubers

Users	Foundation Year	Subscribers	Videos	Channels	Playlists	Community	Shorts
1.	2016	3.04 million	54	3 (Paayal Tena Short Videos, Tena Jaiin Vlogs, Paayal Vlogs)	0	Large	0
2.	2020	2, 73, 000	0	0	0	Small	0
3.	2012	7.52 million	4, 800	0	117	Large	124
4.	2013	3.14 million	564	2 (Anisha Dixit Shorts, Simply Anisha Dixit)	17	Large	84
5.	2016	3.01 million	391	0	8	Large	163
6.	2013	3, 32, 000	1000	2 (Coupling, GottaDoIndia)	62	Large	110
7.	2016	3, 16, 000	78	1 (The Overthink Tank With Surbhi)	10	Large	13
8.	2010	10.1 million	837	5 (Anaysa, Toy Stars, DIY Queen, Anaysa Shorts, Shruti Shorts)	19	Large	171
9.	2018	6.17 Million	218	3 (Pragati Verma Shorts, Pragati Verma Vlogs, Tripti Verma)	12	Large	0
10.	2013	7, 48, 000	186	0	18	Large	18
11.	2014	7.63 million	89	1 (Shankar Tucker)	8	Large	31

Table 3. Results of coding categories

Users	Element of Culture	Element of Information and Literacy	Element of Women Empowerment and Agency	Element of Entertainment
1.	No	No	Yes	Yes
2.	No	No	No	No
3.	No	Yes	Yes	No
4.	No	No	No	Yes
5.	No	Yes	Yes	Yes
6.	No	Yes	Yes	Yes
7.	No	No	Yes	Yes
8.	No	No	Yes	Yes
9.	No	No	Yes	Yes
10.	No	No	Yes	Yes
11.	Yes	Yes	Yes	Yes

FINDINGS AND ANALYSIS

Digital Literacy by Community Radio Practitioners

The results have indicated how community radio practitioners, along with their colleagues, generate a dialogue with audiences giving rise to various form of empowerment and literacy through mobile storytelling (on mobile) and digital narratives (on laptops and computers). As pointed out by Shaw et al (2021) community radio practitioners almost function as social workers engaging with narrative inquiry where audience is at the centre of the stories giving them a sense of control and agency in their own lives. Through the interviews above, Tech Sakhi, the show for women, engaged women in dialogues and narratives related to their lives and online identities, how they need to guard their privacy and work on cybersecurity. While the radio jockeys interacted with women audience a narrative was created where the women shared their lives, their digital actions, giving rise to storytelling that made sense of the events and decisions they took on the digital platforms (Riessman & Quinney, 2005). Women were informed about how and in which ways they need to create and interact with persons on social media platforms thus making them aware of their digital rights. Digital literacy also gives rise to digital forms of storytelling, narratives, cultures where art, culture, lifestyle is used as a catalyst for social change (Wehbi et al, 2017; Wehbi et al, 2018) and visual documentation and photo voices are used as significant creators of change and empowerment (Brotman et al, 2019).

Participatory Communication

The theoretical framework used to indicate digital literacy in this regard is one of participatory communication whereby groups and communities of women engage, create, nurture and recreate dialogues, photos, audio and video files in the process of learning through mobile storytelling. Asuman & Subeshini (2023) argue that community radio has the power to generate participation in communities resulting in inclusion and horizontal management practices which would not have been possible in business-oriented commercial radio stations. They also argue that through women-led radio projects, community radio can be used to implement bottom-up development approaches and serve to influence government policies and developmental agendas of ruling governments (Myers, 2008). Milan (2009) argues that such radio stations provide platforms for women and girls to share their stories and express their opinions and get their voices heard (Offor, 2002). Harvey et al (2012) argue that participatory action research with community radio broadcasters in Ghana showcases how power relations and opportunities for sustainable actions are related to climate impacts. There is thus a participatory form of development where the audience, too, engages in community development and promotion of beneficial outcomes.

Digital Empowerment in New Media

The user-generated content of YouTube creators goes on to indicate that empowerment takes place at the digital level for women who have such accounts. Different elements of culture, information and communication literacy (including media literacy), women empowerment and agency are all studied which generates data from the sample about how does YouTube create narratives around empowerment for women.

Petit (2010) argues that citizens' media and communication are poorly understood in the content of developmental policy due to the lack of coherent grasp of social, cultural and political processes that should make them transformative. While for YouTube content generators, such platforms may prove to be empowering, the nature of its strength is left to be viewed in the perspective of 'digital empowerment' for users and citizens. It is reiterated that at the local level such forms of citizen participation allow people to shape their spaces and control their lives through self-expression*(ibid).*

Empowering Relationships on Mobile Platforms

The engagement of various YouTube users with their audiences generates dialogue and participatory communication which creates awareness and satisfies needs of such users by either granting them information or simply even by entertaining them.

Such forms of broadcast (through community radio) is also called as new media, or alternative media, which 'is concerned as much with its sociocultural context as with its subject matter' (Atton, 2015). It is empowering for the audience is mostly the content creator as well. While the fundamental process is that of participation (Bailey et al, 2008; Waltz, 2005), which is unique for any developing society as that is a basic human right for developing societies and crucial in making them inclusive and participatory (Bailey et al, 2008). Such platforms generate inputs from ordinary people putting them at the centrestage of economic and social development encouraging 'maximalist forms of participation' (Carpentier, 2011) nurturing individual and representative structures associated with radical democracies. Makinen (2006) argues that empowerment essentially means increased control over life and coping skills which gets nurtured by participatory forms of content on mobile (radio or user-generated platforms). A pertinent question, however, arises whether such forms of participation and empowerment are 'asymmetrical' giving rise to unequal knowledge societies (Mansell, 2015). They assimilate and give rise to cultures which are directed in multiple directions at a digital level.

Media Archaeology

Due to the multiplicity of communication among creators and users, a historical and cultural perspective shows that media archaeology is generated which leads to a new form of 'media consumption' (Hockenberry & LaRiviere, 2020). As is indicated through the findings above, community radio practitioners and YouTubers are dealing with online and mobile forms of engagement which is a level up above the outdated forms of technology. Thus 'media archaeology' has often been termed as 'media assemblage', where media is 'resurrected to new uses' (Hertz & Parikka, 2012). As one studies the 'network reality', format theory of media requires an explanation about the changing formations of media and the 'contexts of their receptions', 'conjectures that shaped their sensual characteristics', questioning the 'institutional politics in which such digital formats are enmeshed' (Sterne, 2015). While this raises debates and discussions around 'digital curation' of content, citizen curation also became popular with such newage technologies. The *Pebble Mill Project* by the BBC (Jackson, 2020) through their social media pages showcases collaborative online histories putting to light the role of archives in stimulating memory, crowd-sourcing in a nonlinear fashion and collectively building a multi-authored, multimedia repository of citizens' content.

DISCUSSION

Digital Capitalism

Fuchs & Mosco (2016) argue that digital capitalism is back with the revival of Marxian concept of the internet and 'digital democracy'. It essentially refers to the use of media tools and techniques in ways that result in domination of media technology infrastructures by the economically and politically powerful elites. This tends to give rise to a hegemony of such structures that may often result in subjugation of the marginalized groups living on the periphery of developing societies. In the context of community radio and mobile storytelling, such hegemonic structures are diluted and more engagement and participation leads to outcomes that benefit communities living on the edge. Digital platforms work to bridge the divide between those who are equipped with advanced technologies and the ones who work with not-so-developed outdated systems giving rise to a culture that is global, unique, less dominating. Marxian concept of media technologies functions more with respect to commercial and for-profit structures and less with forms of participatory communication.

With respect to the media, Marx (Mosco & McKercher, 2009) has highlighted the following attributes in the media sector:

- Media technology as rationalization technology in the media sector
- Process of capital concentration and centralization in media sector
- Production of media capital, knowledge workers as wage laborers in production houses and media organizations
- Communication technologies as means for spatial expansion of capitalist production
- Transmission technologies as means of accumulating media infrastructure capital
- Media as carriers of advertisements
- Media as means and outcomes of globalization of world trade
- Media as carriers and circulators of ideologies
- Alternative media that functions as means of class struggle and means of circulation of critical ideas

This leads to cultures that are barely understood but need a discussion below.

Digital Cultures

Sadowski (2020) argues that digital capitalism is not just leading to smart technology but also giving rise to data which is redefining the way lives are lived, technological society is created and is beginning to control lives beyond the human measure. Betancourt (2015) argues that there is a 'colonization of social relations' by digital technology. As each radio functions and becomes accessible to locals within the frequency of the community radio, audiences get driven by the content and generate cultures which belong to them and to others. A YouTube creator engages audience and generates data that is not only providing information but even being used for play, gaming, entertainment which may not be directly empowering but the consumption of such content leads to satisfaction, and user comments lead to further content generation. As digital content is consumed and re-used, a 'digital aura' is generated giving rise to effective immortality of digital media, creating a potential for endless 'replication' (*ibid).* Barassi (2015) argues that digital capitalism also gives rise to media anthropology which showcased a 'cultural turn' in the media viewed in the larger context of social and cultural processes it initiates in the process of content curation and generation. It essentially deals with (Askew & Wilk, 2002):

- How people negotiate with communication technologies
- Scholars' willingness to understand media as everyday practices
- Challenging ethno-centric and techno-deterministic of media impacts by understanding the larger cultural variations

Thus these cultures are giving rise to newage technologies that still need exploration.

New Age Technologies

The new age technologies discussed above are primarily community radio platforms accessed by audiences through mobile devices and user-generated platforms like YouTube accessed and assimilated through mobile devices as well. Tsiatsis et al (2020) argue that newage technologies like the media form a part of IoT (internet of things), which have innovative business models that generate new content, structures and forms of governance. Gupta et al (2020) argue that such newage media technologies are targeting customers and engaging them across platforms through data analytics where consumer insights are generated. In the case of media, the numbers of subscribers, likes, emojis in comments sections, user comments all add on to the popularity and social likeability of the YouTube creators leading to positive outcomes for the YouTubers at this digital platform. Bacon (2012) adds that newage technologies have given rise to a new age of participation where there is collaborative work as the basis of communication, leading to an art of community-building and sharing. Chetty et al (2018) further add to this argument around newage technologies (contextualizing their study around G20 nations) indicating that the 'digital divide' is a problem one needs to deal with in the age of new media, particularly between men and women. This is likely to continue due to the effects of unemployment, poverty, inequality and poorly developed digital skills and sociocultural norms. Women, it is argued, particularly get left behind as they do not get equal access to digital services. The authors (*ibid*) generate a three-pronged strategy to get out of the 'digital divide trap'- monitor digital skills, incorporate holistic digital skills strategy in educational programmes, contextualize digital skills in sociocultural norms that shape outcomes of digital skilling programmes.

Media Perspectives

The debates around community radio and its role in empowerment of women through online platforms generates ideas of revisiting government policies, taking a fresh look at media policies, working on digital upskilling of citizens, particularly girls and women who are considered 'marginalized' depending upon the existing socio-cultural norms of the country. While female YouTubers are empowered by their mere presence on digital platforms, an empowering dialogue is generated among women through them where profiles are created, shared and consumed.

The narratives around mobile forms of storytelling are indicative of dialogues and 'consumer culture' around user-generated content that creates insights of customers and content creators. This is made possible through 'digital curation', collaboration, assimilation of content, thereby empowering those who create and those who consume simultaneously. This dual nature of online participatory form of communication nurtures newage technologies, archives dialogues, saves content for future generations, bridges 'digital divide' between low and high-income groups, financially empowers women, provides entertainment, information and awareness in a post-digital world. Digital capitalism enables such intense activity with high frequency and increased duration of engagement on online modes of entertainment, leading to a renewed debate around alternative media and its role in radical democracy. The debate around whether media infrastructures are being used and exploited by the bourgeoise to control the proletariat is open to debate as net neutrality and easy accessibility of the internet is widely seen across developing and the developed world.

CONCLUSION

The study considers the larger theme of digital platforms- specifically dealing with community radio stations and mobile storytelling like YouTube videos and channels. However, it not only creates a 'political economy' of such platforms but also informs and empowers women, thereby empowering community and society through engagement, archaeology, legacy, history and digital media. The collaborative nature of such platforms is discussed as debates around socio-cultural norms, marginalization of communities in 'digital divide trap', women-engagement on digital platforms is subject for future research. Alternative media revolutionizes the media landscape in making it more participatory and accessible, yet faces challenges of sustainability, financial security and radical user-generated comments that question societies and forms of governance. Future researchers may look into Marxian study of communication as the world gets increasingly digitalized. The study may inform future studies on 'digital divide'. Community radio stations are important forms of communication and broadcasting and work to promote participation, coherence, cohesion and togetherness within a community. These platforms provide practitioners an opportunity to engage in dialogue and become a part of solutions that have long-term impacts on communities in developing and empowering them. When such engagement is through engagement on the mobile ways, accessibility and reach of the community radio increases manifold.

REFERENCES

Askew, K., & Wilk, R. (Eds.). (2002). *The Anthropology of Media: A Reader*. Blackwell.

Asuman, M. K. A., & Subeshini, M. (2023). 17 Women's Participation in Indigenous Language Media An Analysis of Five Community Radio Stations in Northern Ghana. *African Language Media*, 12.

Atton, C. (Ed.). (2015). *The Routledge companion to alternative and community media*. Routledge. doi:10.4324/9781315717241

Bacon, J. (2012). *The art of community: Building the new age of participation*. O'Reilly Media, Inc.

Barassi, V. (2015). *Activism on the web: Everyday struggles against digital capitalism*. Routledge. doi:10.4324/9781315870991

Betancourt, M. (2015). *The critique of digital capitalism: An analysis of the political economy of digital culture and technology*. Punctum Books.

Brotman, S., Ferrer, I., & Koehn, S. (2019). Situating the life story narratives of aging immigrants within a structural context: The intersectional life course perspective as research praxis. *Qualitative Research, 20*(4), 465–484. doi:10.1177/1468794119880746

Carpentier, N. (2011). *Media and participation: A site of ideological-democratic struggle*. Intellect. doi:10.26530/OAPEN_606390

Chetty, K., Aneja, U., Mishra, V., Gcora, N., & Josie, J. (2018). Bridging the digital divide in the G20: Skills for the new age. *Economics*, *12*(1), 20180024. doi:10.5018/economics-ejournal.ja.2018-24

Ellis, J., & Hall, N. (2019). Introduction: What is hands on media history? In Hands on Media History (pp. 1-8). Routledge.

Fraser, C., & Estrada, S. R. (2001). *Community radio handbook*. Unesco.

Fuchs, C., & Mosco, V. (2016). Introduction: Marx is back–the importance of Marxist theory and research for critical communication studies today. In Marx in the age of digital capitalism (pp. 1-21). Brill.

Gavaldà, J., & Ribera-Fumaz, R. (2012). Barcelona 5.0: from knowledge to smartness? *IN3 Working Paper Series*.

Guedes, B. O., Bart, C., & Nico, C. (2008). *Understanding Alternative Media*. Open University Press.

Gupta, S., Kumar, V., & Karam, E. (2020). New-age technologies-driven social innovation: What, how, where, and why? *Industrial Marketing Management*, *89*, 499–516. doi:10.1016/j.indmarman.2019.09.009

Haggart, B. (2019). The age of surveillance capitalism: The fight for a human future at the new frontier of power. *Journal of Digital Media & Policy*, *10*(2), 229-243.

Hall, N., & Ellis, J. (2020). *Hands on media history: A new methodology in the humanities and social sciences*. Taylor & Francis.

Harvey, B., Burns, D., & Oswald, K. (2012). Linking community, radio, and action research on climate change: Reflections on a systemic approach. *IDS Bulletin*, *43*(3), 101–117. doi:10.1111/j.1759-5436.2012.00326.x

Hertz, G., & Parikka, J. (2012). Zombie Media: Circuit Bending Media Archaeology into an Art Method. *Leonardo*, *45*(5), 424–420. doi:10.1162/LEON_a_00438

Hockenberry, M., & LaRiviere, J. (Eds.). (2020). Hands on media history: A new methodology in the humanities and social sciences. Taylor & Francis.

Horrigan, J. B., & Schement, J. R. (2021). *Broadband as civic infrastructure: community empowerment, equity, and a Digital New Deal*. German Marshall Fund of the United States.

Huhtamo, E., & Parikka, J. (2011). *Media Archaeologies: Approaches, Applications, and Implications*. University of California Press. doi:10.1525/9780520948518

Jackson, V. (Ed.). (2020). Hands on media history: A new methodology in the humanities and social sciences. Taylor & Francis.

Latour, B. (1999). *Pandora's Hope: Essays on the Reality of Science Studies*. Harvard University Press.

Levy, S. J. (1988). *Information technologies in universities: An institutional case study*. Northern Arizona University.

Mäkinen, M. (2006). Digital empowerment as a process for enhancing citizens' participation. *E-Learning and Digital Media*, *3*(3), 381–395. doi:10.2304/elea.2006.3.3.381

Malafouris, L. (2013). *How Things Shape the Mind: A Theory of Material Engagement*. MIT Press. doi:10.7551/mitpress/9476.001.0001

Manovich, L. (2001). What is new media. *The Language of New Media, 6*, 1-15.

Manovich, L. (2001). Post-media aesthetics. *Transmedia frictions, the digital, the arts, and the humanities, 416*.

Mansell, R. (2015). Futures of knowledge societies–destabilization in whose interest? *Information Communication and Society*, *18*(6), 627–643. doi:10.1080/1369118X.2014.979215

Milan, S. (2009). Four steps to community media as a development tool. *Development in Practice*, *19*(4-5), 598–609. doi:10.1080/09614520902866421

Miles, J. (2013). *YouTube marketing power: How to use video to find more prospects, launch your products, and reach a massive audience*. McGraw-Hill.

Miller, K. (2012). *Playing along: Digital games, YouTube, and virtual performance*. Oxford University Press. doi:10.1093/acprof:oso/9780199753451.001.0001

Mosco, V., & McKercher, C. (2009). *The laboring of communication: Will knowledge workers of the world unite?* Rowman & Littlefield.

Myers, M. (2008). *Radio and development in Africa*. A concept paper prepared for the International Development Research Centre (IDRC) of Canada.

Offor, J. O. (2002). *Community radio and its influence in the society. The case of the Enugu State, Nigeria*. IKO-Verlag fur Interkulturelle Kommunikation.

Petit, E., Ferrari, S., Mekni, M. M., & Rouillon, S. (2010). Citizen participation in the steps for emisssion permits: economic efficiency and ethical questions. *VertigO- La Revue Electronique en Sciences de l'Environment, 10*(1).

Riessman, C., & Quinney, L. (2005). Narrative in social work. *Qualitative Social Work: Research and Practice, 4*(4), 391–412. doi:10.1177/1473325005058643

Ripp, M., & Hauer, S. (2017). Communication model for built heritage assets going from knowing to identification. *Built Heritage, 1*(4), 1–10. doi:10.1186/BF03545653

Rodriguez, C. (2001). *Fissures in the mediascape: An international study of citizens' media*. No Title.

Sadowski, J. (2020). The internet of landlords: Digital platforms and new mechanisms of rentier capitalism. *Antipode, 52*(2), 562–580. doi:10.1111/anti.12595

Salgues, B. (2018). *Society 5.0: industry of the future, technologies, methods and tools*. John Wiley & Sons. doi:10.1002/9781119507314

Shaw, J., Ferrer, I., & Lorenzetti, L. (2021). Ethical Storytelling and Digital Narratives: Lessons Learned in Student-led Podcasts and Community Radio Partnerships. *International Journal of Social Work Values & Ethics, 18*(1).

Snelson, C. (2011). YouTube across the disciplines: A review of the literature. *Journal of Online Learning and Teaching*.

Snickars, P., & Vondereau, P. (2009). *The YouTube reader*. National Library of Sweden.

Sterne, J. (2015). Compression: A Loose History. In L. Parks & N. Starosielski (Eds.), *Signal Traffic: Critical Studies of Media Infrastructures*. University of Illinois Press.

Tilley, E. (2011). *New Culture/Old Ethics: What Technological Determinism Can Teach Us About New Media. In The Ethics of Emerging Media: Information, Social Norms and New Media Technology*. The Continuum International Publishing Group.

Toffler, A. (1980). The third wave. Morrow.

Tsiatsis, V., Karnouskos, S., Holler, J., Boyle, D., & Mulligan, C. (2018). *Internet of Things: technologies and applications for a new age of intelligence*. Academic Press.

Waltz, M. (2005). *Alternative and activist media*. Edinburgh University Press. doi:10.1515/9780748626229

Wehbi, S., Cowell, A., Perreault-Laird, J., El-Lahib, Y., & Straka, S. (2017). Intersecting interests: Qualitative research synthesis on art in the social work classroom. *The Canadian Journal for the Scholarship of Teaching and Learning*, *8*(3), 1–15. doi:10.5206/cjsotl-rcacea.2017.3.6

Wehbi, S., El-Lahib, Y., Perreault-Laird, J., & Zakharova, G. (2018). Oasis in a concrete jungle: Arts-informed methods in social work classrooms. *Social Work Education*, *37*(5), 617–632. doi:10.1080/02615479.2018.1450372

KEY TERMS AND DEFINITIONS

Citizen Media: This refers to media that is used by citizens to exchange messages and create content which is further used by other citizens, essentially referring to social media platforms and user-generated content.

Digital Curation: This refers to digitally saving and curating content for further use by others. These maybe in the form of art, videos, audio files and other formats.

Digital Empowerment: This term denotes the empowerment of citizens through digital means and tools, either in the media or generally through the internet.

Media Archaeology: It refers to histories and outdated forms of media tools, equipment, techniques, production processes which are preserved on digital platforms generating a repository of new age digital media tools.

Mobile Storytelling: This refers to narratives which are created, generated and consumed on mobile devices remotely.

User-Generated Content: This refers to content on media platforms that is created and generated by users, where users are content creators and consumers simultaneously.

APPENDICES

Sample In-Depth Interview Guide

Introduction

I am Navodita Pande. The purpose of this interview is to get insights into the practices of a community radio station in empowering women and ways in which the interviewee conducts programmes to empower women digitally. The social value of the research is in generating knowledge about 'financial inclusion' of women.

Section I: Demographics

Q1. Name of the Community Radio/Frequency/City
Q2. Name of the interviewee/optional
Q3. Age of the interviewee

Section II: RQ1- Shows on financial literacy

Q4. Do you have a show on financial literacy?
Q5. Is the show targeted at men/women/youth/children?
Q6. What is the content of the show?
Q7. Does the show encourage listeners to take individual financial decisions?
Q8. Is there a /call in/ show where listeners have shared their experiences?
Q9. What has been the feedback of listeners?
Q10. What does financial literacy mean to you?

Section III: RQ4- Content creators and consumers

Q11. Do you have any shows on feedback from listeners?
Q12. How many such shows are run by women?
Q13. How many listeners among them are women?
Q14. Do any women talk about how the shows informed them?
Q15. Is there any survey done on how has the show impacted the women?
Q16. Has the show made the women take agency in 'decisions'?
Q17. Any last suggestions and comments on the topic

Chapter 5
Evaluating Strategies of Activist-Public Relations From a Mainstream to Digital Activism Perspective

Ebru Belkıs Güzeloğlu
Faculty of Communication, Ege University, Turkey

Elif Üstündağlı Erten
https://orcid.org/0000-0001-5111-927X
Faculty of Economics and Administrative Sciences, Ege University, Turkey

Zümrüt Atak
https://orcid.org/0009-0000-2489-7535
Social Sciences Institute, Ege University, Turkey

ABSTRACT

Public relations, which has traditionally been used by corporations, is now being observed as a strategy within the activist realm. Activist organizations employ public relations (PR) strategies while advocating for a cause, while institutions utilize PR research to manage their interactions with activists. Hence, the precise definition, extent, and limitations of activist public relations remain ambiguous. This study examines activism as a social movement in relation to public relations (PR) to represent the convergence and divergence of interactions between corporate and social perspectives, as well as the reciprocal development of activism and PR. The study revealed that legitimacy and visibility, framing the issue, networking, crafting the message, resource enhancement, actions and implementations, communication media and tools, transformation and restructuring, and measuring effectiveness are the primary public relations tools that are effective for including different actors and movements with increasing awareness and responsibility.
DOI: 10.4018/979-8-3693-1182-0.ch005

1. INTRODUCTION

The development of Public Relations and the methods and tools utilized by social movements have contributed to the foundations (Coombs & Holladay, 2012b; Roberson, 2020) and progression of this concept. Social movement, especially activism, studies from a communication perspective provide references regarding the role of interaction in social change. The activism concept refers to a bridge between public relations and social movements that aims to address issues such as social justice, economic disparity, environmental degradation, and globalization by bringing attention to these issues and encouraging change through various cultural mediums (F. V. Harrison, 2004). Activists also use creative methods, such as artistic activism through drama performances, to increase public awareness of environmental issues and effect positive change in society (Rodriguez-Labajos, 2022). When individuals hold convictions, they engage in activism by attending events and financially supporting groups (Leonidou et al., 2022). As an example, women's environmental activist movements have brought attention to the traditional taboos and legal restrictions that make it hard for women to access and manage environmental resources and take part in production systems (F. V. Harrison, 2004). Activists have a role in fighting corporate control of food production systems and questioning institutional racism that prevents black and indigenous populations from accessing good food, hence emphasizing food justice (Alkon & Norgaard, 2009).

It is crucial for businesses to understand activism in order to effectively communicate with customers about their initiatives (Nassani et al., 2013). In contemporary business world, some CEOs are taking part in what is known as "CEO activism," in which they try to affect social concerns that aren't directly related to their company's operations (Chatterji & Toffel, 2017). As CEO speeches grab media attention and form public discourses that have the capacity to impact public policy, these actions could be seen as camouflage (Jabareen, 2008). However, they are also raising the visibility of social movements (Chatterji & Toffel, 2017). Generally, activists identify 'social problem' concerns that they own and issues requiring change, but mainstream organizations view these issues as 'topics or situations' that can be disregarded within the status quo, do not require change, or should not be changed. When activist organizations have a clear goal of changing social problems, they seek ways to communicate with the parties involved in the problem. However, when the change or transformation is important and involves a lengthy process, structured communication is required for issues in which diverse parties, or governmental or private organizations take countermeasures. When communication shifts from interaction to relationship structuring, it can be observed that inside movement actions, strategic methods, and tactics of public relations become significant, and communication tools are employed more consciously and systematically. This study focuses on activism as a social movement in connection to public relations (PR) to reflect the convergence and divergence of contacts between corporate and social perspectives, as well as the reciprocal evolution of activism and PR. Despite the fact that public relations are a strategic tool for businesses (Edwards, 2018), activism has altered public relations to show how social movements and business operations are related.

2. MATERIALS AND METHODS

This study used the systematic literature review (Chalmers & Altman, 1995; Kitchenham, 2004) method to fill the gap in the literature, as previous studies have only covered the interaction of PR and activism from a narrow perspective. The method of collecting all the literature on public relations and activism allows for a systematic assessment of the literature, which is important for drawing a comprehensive inference.

Public relations' premier scholarly publications are under the review's purview. This study's goals necessitated the identification of databases housing the periodicals that would be used for a systematic literature review. By searching Scopus, Business Source Complete (EBSCOhost), Sage Journals, Science Direct, and Web of Science for the terms "activism" and "public relations" in the title, abstract, and keywords fields of English-language publications, a total of 121 relevant articles were retrieved for analysis. Eight articles' sources were inaccessible, and eighteen articles were omitted from the study because they did not represent the relationship between public relations and activism. The selected material from the bibliography reflects 95 articles and related interactions published between 1992 and 2019. Following a comprehensive literature study, the discovered articles were subjected to both content analysis and thematic analysis. With an emphasis on the concerns of public relations and activism that were raised in the literature, content analysis was utilized to comprehend, illuminate, and develop ideas from multiple perspectives. Attempts were made to minimize the number of cited articles and relate the subject's settings and consequences. First, the collected texts were reviewed multiple times, and information of significance was underlined. The excluded parts were then reevaluated, and the meaning units were open-coded. The open codes were then put into groups based on the themes using both inductive and deductive methods (Bengtsson, 2016). In line with the goals of the study, the framework of activist public relations and the PR strategies of activist and mainstream groups were compared. After figuring out how well the themes went with the coded quotes, a theme map was developed and evaluated. Each theme is defined and titled independently (Vaismoradi et al., 2013). Two authors separately reviewed the papers to generate their own collection of conceptual concepts as a proven process. Three authors iteratively compared, contrasted, and discussed convergences and divergences with regard to these lists (Tranfield et al., 2003). The study includes the reactions of the immediate target of the activist movement and the techniques that evolved, as well as the case-specific data from the articles.

3. RESULTS

3.1. Decisions and Actions Points From the Street to Digital Activism

In the literature, activist movement cases predominate, with the reactions of mainstream organizations (primarily private enterprises) also cited as the intended target. Corporate social responsibility (CSR) literature focuses primarily on the agency positions of businesses regarding a social issue. With techniques such as organizational activism and corporate leadership, corporations have emerged in recent literature as action initiators.

3.1.1. Legitimacy and Visibility

Many activist efforts begin with making the topic or problem apparent, becoming visible, and raising awareness that individuals produce "voices" relating to the subject. Public visibility serves first and foremost as a means of organizing and legitimizing the topic (Ali et al., 2016; D. S. Anderson, 1992; W. B. Anderson, 2017; Brooks et al., 2018; Doan & Toledano, 2018; Hallahan, 2001; Woods, 2019). Organization is the process of assembling alliances, linked public offices, volunteers, and others in order to make the issue prominent (Hallahan, 2001). But what establishes a group's legitimacy is its ability to recognize a problem when it sees one or to sketch out a plan of action for dealing with a challenging scenario. The people at the heart of most activist groups are justifiable in the eyes of the general public because they are directly impacted by or have created the situation at hand (Brooks et al., 2018; Bullert, 2000; Ciszek, 2017b; Curtin, 2016). Occasionally, it may be necessary to exert additional effort in order to awaken and stimulate a slumbering audience and to form a network or alliance with the goal of identifying a topic or event as an issue (Ali et al., 2016; W. B. Anderson, 2017; Curtin, 2016; De Moya & Bravo, 2016; Dimitrov, 2008; Doan & Toledano, 2018; Hallahan, 2001). In circumstances where the organization is already visible, greater emphasis is placed on the topic's visibility and the organization's ability to own and defend the topic; this generates a driving force (D. S. Anderson, 1992; Coombs & Holladay, 2012a; Honda, 2016;

Niesen, 2015; Rome, 2019; Wolf, 2018). Leadership is another aspect of visibility and legitimacy.

There may be natural leaders in the conflict as the problem's victims, or there may be leaders inside interest groups. Activist groups have used the "expert" effect, particularly when the general public is unaware of scientific topics (Avenell, 2016; Prescott, 2019). During the movement-structuring process, professional activist leaders might supplant those who define the problem at the helm (Hallahan, 2001).

3.1.2. Framing the Issue

The key aspect of the theme is bringing awareness to the situation. Visibility is related to identifying it as a problem in the eyes of the public, its legitimacy, and the urgency with which it is being fought, as well as making it visible by 'warning' inactive publics (Hallahan, 2001).

In order to understand the visibility of a social issue, it is essential to know how its agency situation was triggered. Major attention-grabbing triggers include a sensation, a shocking or remarkable incident or tale, discourse or action causing a crisis that victimizes or offends a certain group of people, a risk-inducing incident for the public, or incident patterns. The greater the number of victims and the amount of public support, the greater the likelihood that a cause will become a movement. It establishes a foundation for the growth of the movement when victims and/or profiles of the incident are ordinary and innocent (Curtin, 2016), when other heroes are recognized, or when the incident is sensational and extraordinary (D. S. Anderson, 1992; Ciszek, 2017b; Curtin, 2016; De Moya & Bravo, 2016; Denisova & O'Brien, 2019; Dimitrov, 2008).

The presentation of undeniable real-world indications, events, and experiences in a public forum generates facts even in the absence of a precipitating circumstance. A problem's context can be identified and exposed through the use of accumulated cases, the development of events, the life stage of victims, and the impact on social life by activists. There has been a long history of campaigning by activists and interest groups, but a recent incident has brought the problem into sharp focus. The discourse has been reignited by a recent action or event (Avenell, 2016; Benecke & Oksiutycz, 2015; Burns et al., 2018; Ciszek, 2017b, 2017a; Henderson, 2005; Jackson & Foucault Welles, 2015). Generally, activists attempt to raise their exposure by establishing a library or data bank, collecting information, monitoring, and reporting (Rome, 2019; White, 2012).

When bringing an issue to the public's attention, it is evident that how the issue is presented to the public is decided. In this decision-making process, the framework of the issue in terms of what level, which aspects, and how it will be presented in the eyes of the public is outlined. Two frameworks emerge from the analysis of how the topic is presented: with or without media. These frameworks resemble the legitimacy methods stated by Wood (2019) about activists.

3.1.2.1. Framing Situations and Conditions. As the number of incidents and victims rises, the pervasiveness and frequency of the problem become an indication of its significance and severity. To increase the perception of the significance of society during the process of visibility, situational framing employs real-world indicators. In this type of framing, in addition to its severity, the issue's dimension, and organic connections with related issues or problems, arguments for why now is the time to intervene, solution examples, evaluations, and recommendations for the desired change are presented (D. S. Anderson, 1992; W. B. Anderson, 2017, 2019; Benecke & Oksiutycz, 2015; Ciszek, 2017b; De Moya & Bravo, 2016; Demetrious, 2008).

3.1.2.2. Framing on Values. Within the scope of an issue established by activists, it is also required to express a point of view to mobilize groups, institutions, and the general populace. Along with the overall severity, rates, or numbers, the issue is presented in terms of different points of view, meanings, and values. Building awareness and values that unite and activate in the perception of the area of conflict is accomplished by adding meaning and emotions to the issue, sharing these meanings and emotions, and connecting them with values (Ali et al., 2016; D. S. Anderson, 1992; Brooks et al., 2018; Ciszek, 2017b, 2017a; Coombs & Holladay, 2012a; De Moya & Bravo, 2016; Dimitrov, 2008; Moscato, 2019; Ortiz Juarez-Paz, 2017; Prescott, 2019).

In addition to the public interest, it is encouraging that the mainstream media and governmental institutions are engaged in the solution while social, cultural, national, or religious values are used to address the problems (W. B. Anderson, 2019; Dimitrov, 2008; Doan & Toledano, 2018; Han & Zhang, 2009; Henderson, 2005; Weaver, 2010). Due to the dominant social structure, cultural, national, or religious values, as well as dominant or divided political ideas, there is a possibility of the existence of opposing organizations or the emergence of such groups (Ciszek, 2016, 2017a; Prescott, 2019). As a result, it can be observed that a greater emphasis is placed on universal principles to provide a more unified representation of certain societal issues. This also provides the foundation for the movement to become more multinational and to transcend politics.

3.1.3. Networking

To bring about critical social change and gain momentum, the activists must garner the most support possible. Involving people and motivating them to act are two of the most crucial aspects of effective framing. Ali et al. (2016) discover in their examination of case studies involving gender-based violence that activists have profited from victims' narratives that are rich in language, statistics, values, and emotions as a framing strategy. Public relations products use frames to selectively emphasize certain parts of the world. In other words, even though it was evident at the beginning of the movement, the issue frame's boundaries are reproduced with the aid of the growing community.

In the literature, activists, activist groups, and institutions are the only common aspects of the definition of activist PR. Because activist PR relates to change-initiating activists, the reactions of institutions to these efforts are also considered activist PR actions. It's not subject-independent (Sancar, 2017, pp. 4–5). Besides these themes, many people, institutions, and structures can be parties to forming a community. In community development, parties must be analyzed for social change targeting and positioning. In the analysis, three parties become significant for activists in the action process: the network community, alliances, and agents of change. Depending on variables such as the subject framework, the success of the actions, and the initial positions of the parties (particularly those of the targeted groups), they may shift during the conflict.

3.1.3.1. The Community in the Network. Community development in the network ensures that these groups are in ongoing contact with individuals and organizations interested in or capable of addressing the social problem, who will start the movement, provide financial and social support for its growth, and raise questions. The formation of a network requires the participation of crucial activists and active citizens. The continuity of interaction is essential for quickly forming groups. Over time, additional audiences are invited to participate. Participation in a network is stimulated and encouraged by the exchange of narratives that develop the framework based on a variety of experiences and problems.

An additional important aspect is that the activists contact the impacted local populations and spread the movement with their participation. This is an incentive to involve locals who share a similar culture and way of life, individuals who are familiar with the region, and institutions that serve the community (W. B. Anderson, 2017; Bullert, 2000; Coombs & Holladay, 2012a; Dhir, 2007; Guiniven, 2002; Han & Zhang, 2009; Kwak, 2018; Moscato, 2019; Wakefield, 2007; Whitehead, 1987; Wolf, 2019).

Activists' actions are also driven by politics. In activist ties with institutions, political structures remain an invisible objective or component (Avenell, 2016; Demetrious, 2008; Henderson, 2005; Robertson, 2011; Sejrup, 2014). When movements pursue change, they anticipate that bureaucratic institutions will activate legal processes, auditing, legal enforcement, legal restrictions, and incentives for implementations, policy shifts, and progress. A discourse, action, or project can target bureaucratic institutions directly (Weaver, 2010; Wolf, 2019).

3.1.3.2. Alliances and Change Agents. Following analyses, activists encourage institutions, organizations, groups, and individuals to participate in networking, as well as other organizations and civil initiatives linked to the issue. Alliances are created to complete a project or to create permanent, continuous collaboration. According to the findings, this scenario is viewed independently from the movement's dominant group since it develops by uniting forces, obtaining assistance for knowledge and competencies, penetrating additional bases, and/or building a special unity. Even though it's the same social problem, multiple structures with different identities, missions, and visions need a shared meaning and solution method (W. B. Anderson, 2017).

Key individuals and groups supporting the movement can be included in the networks, both for the movement's expansion and for the issue's reflection in daily life. These individuals and organizations, functioning as change agents, primarily due to their positions, experiences, and access, play crucial roles in making the subject visible, increasing visibility, generating pressure, and enabling the essential change to be reflected in daily life. Participation by change agents improves public justification of conflict by removing the occasion from the conflict between activists and corporations (Ross, 2008). It is possible to contribute to national vision with the participation, expertise, and support of international organizations, bureaucratic structures and representatives, chambers of profession, schools, universities, students, scientists, science institutes and associations, celebrities, opinion leaders, journalists and media program producers, writers, religious representatives, business leaders, and labor unions (W. B. Anderson, 2017, 2019; Ciszek, 2017b, 2017a; De Moya & Bravo, 2016; A. Harrison & Scorse, 2006; Honda, 2016; Kovacs, 2001; Maxwell & Miller, 2016; Moscato, 2019; Prescott, 2019; Robertson, 2011; E. J. Sommerfeldt & Yang, 2017; Weaver, 2010).

3.1.4. Building the Message

In addition to the subject framework, the messaging strategy relates to how the subject is presented to the public. In the message, together with the emotion and motion generated by a shared meaning and value, the transformation and the promise of a solution are mirrored by the abstract vision of the desired future. Style and tone of communication are also components of message strategy. In the communication of movements conducted as campaigns, slogans are usually employed as the name and/or rhetoric of the campaigns. The use of scientifically-based determinations, approaches to reasoning with evidence, examples from real life, evidence or findings, and/or ironic, striking, humorous, parody, and satirical contrasts is appropriate in areas where the issue is not marked as a problem by a large group or where awareness is low (Bullert, 2000; Jackson & Foucault Welles, 2015; Ortiz Juarez-Paz, 2017; Stokes & Atkins-Sayre, 2018; Tombleson & Wolf, 2017).

Activists' message methods can vary based on movements. Attractive factors such as stimulus, irony, and contrast support emotions including fear, drama, excitement, and enthusiasm. In addition, positive messages are disseminated to increase confidence that a solution to the problem may be discovered with the assistance of the network's leader and to encourage participation (Doan & Toledano, 2018). In certain instances, the drama of stories inspired by real events is utilized (Ortiz Juarez-Paz, 2017; Rome, 2019).

To imprint concepts and emotion frameworks in perception and memory, adjectives, symbols, icons, and symbols are used in visual, auditory, and written texts. Symbolization is carried out occasionally through people (Denisova & O'Brien, 2019; Dhir, 2007) and occasionally through abstract or physical objects (Dimitrov, 2008). With symbolization, creating the face or symbol of the campaign (for instance, visuals of the heroes of the stories, visuals of protestors with attractive and contrasting characteristics, objects such as colorful ribbons, sleeve bands, special clothing or accessories, etc.) can provide an advantage to attract media attention and remain on the agenda. There are also audio symbols like solidarity songs, music made for the campaign, and melodies (Dhir, 2007; Moscato, 2019).

3.1.5. Resource Enhancement

It is important for activists to create opportunities and raise funds in order to broaden the scope of their movement (Ali et al., 2016; Seo et al., 2009). Networking is the primary means by which needs are fulfilled and assistance is offered (Ciszek, 2017a; Doan & Toledano, 2018).

International organizations also provide funds and incentives to assist activist structures. While financing programs foster capacity building, activists, non-governmental groups, platforms, networks, civil initiatives, and various other structures do the same. However, this could lead to contentious circumstances, such as the structure of motions being constrained, controlled, or "tamed."

3.1.6. Actions and Implementations

3.1.6.1. Activist Actions. Within its expansive scope, activist PR encompasses the tactics of dissent and protest (Adi, 2018; Moloney et al., 2013). According to Moloney et al. (2013) (p. 3), dissenting PR ignites a debate to draw attention to a problem and activates the views of knowledgeable individuals. Public speeches, publications such as letters, bulletins, declarations, press conferences, briefings, participation in programs and presentations, and organized programs such as debates, party meetings, and visits are examples of dissent PR actions (Adi, 2018; Ali et al., 2016; D. S. Anderson, 1992; W. B. Anderson, 2019; Avenell, 2016; Benecke &

Oksiutycz, 2015; Brooks et al., 2018; Bullert, 2000; Ciszek, 2017b; Curtin, 2016; Demetrious, 2008; Doan & Toledano, 2018; Henderson, 2005; Knight & Greenberg, 2002; Toledano, 2016). Opposition is the basis of protest PR, and their views, behaviors, and policies include persuasive actions (Adi, 2018; D. S. Anderson, 1992; Avenell, 2016; Burns et al., 2018; Dhir, 2007; Hou, 2021; Hung, 2003; Knight & Greenberg, 2002; Rentschler, 2015). These actions demonstrate the issue's gravity and the groups' willingness to implement solutions (Dhir, 2007). According to the Einstein Institute, there are 198 types of nonviolent dissent or protest actions (198 Methods of Nonviolent Action, 2014). As digital technology evolved, several types of activism emerged. Even though a portion of digital methods are modifications of previous PR efforts, the introduction of distinct and newly developed approaches has broadened the scope of action.

3.1.6.2. Special Activities. Wearing, carrying, and sharing movement symbols on a designated day, as well as planning and promoting special events for that day, are all actions that keep the issue vivid in the minds of the public and the media (W. B. Anderson, 2019; Benecke & Oksiutycz, 2015; Hung, 2003). Protest public relations involve strategies of non-collaboration and highlight resistance by organizing sit-in protests, protest demonstrations, camping, strikes, marches, meetings, and concerts.

Different public, private, and government groups can also take part in local, national, and international competitions, conferences, meetings, fairs, and marketplace activities. In the actions of the movement, its alliances, and the structures they target, public speeches, gatherings, concerts, performances, exhibitions, opening stands, and mobile scanning-consulting services may be included.

3.1.6.3. Training, Rehabilitation, and Solidarity Programs. Activists use long-term, counter-institutional strategies, including training and solidarity programs, to increase awareness, consciousness, and the transformation of lifestyles that sustain the status quo. Actions taken throughout the movement or to accommodate or mirror the resulting changes in everyday life (W. B. Anderson, 2019; Ciszek, 2015, 2017a; Dimitrov, 2008; Sejrup, 2014).

3.1.6.4. Lobbying. Alliances are formed to exert pressure on bureaucratic institutions and political actors, with activities like negotiations, meetings, and visits aimed at enacting legal mechanisms and providing incentives for improving legal auditing and regulations. The involvement of bureaucratic institutions or actors can occur naturally (Han & Zhang, 2009) or with the help of the actions of the movement's representatives, depending on the nature of the issue at hand (Burns et al., 2018; Ciszek, 2015; Henderson, 2005). Within the movement, if there is a position belonging to the ruling government or a policy supported by them, a project, a person, a group, or a position against them, then lobbying is performed to create opposition within the ruling power or to get the support of existing political opposition to participate in the movement (Avenell, 2016; Hung, 2003). Throughout the movement process, ongoing lobbying is essential for keeping the change once the movement's aims have been attained, and case studies demonstrate that this is done with the aid of legal regulations (Dimitrov, 2008; Henderson, 2005; Stückelberger, 2009).

3.1.7. Communication Media and Tools

Important parameters for the use of mass media power include the quality of the subject or issue, how the issue frame is constructed, the quality of supporters and opponents of the subject or issue, the intensity and sensationalism of the related incident, the potential to enter the media agenda, and the alliance or collaboration status of media organizations or representatives with the movement. Movement strategists and the mainstream media evaluate these characteristics when making media decisions. In the case study publications, virtually every action engaged the media. There are cases and examples in which mainstream institutions and/or representatives with a role as an alliance or change agent join the movement (Curtin, 2016; Doan & Toledano, 2018; Moscato, 2019; White, 2012) and ignore or disregard it (D. S. Anderson, 1992; Rome, 2019). Following the success of digital alternatives and social media, the aim is to attract the attention of mainstream media (Han & Zhang, 2009; Moscato, 2019; Tombleson & Wolf, 2017). In terms of public attention, mainstream media is still in a prestigious position in terms of story framing (Seo et al., 2009). The most prevalent actions are reported in the news and media via news bulletins, press conferences, media reports, letters, program participations, and documentaries (Benecke & Oksiutycz, 2015; Ragas, 2013; Reber et al., 2010; Reber & Berger, 2005; Rentschler, 2015).

Moreover, activists are the earliest adopters of internet-based communication tools (Coombs & Holladay, 2012b). When mainstream media ignore the actions of the movement or do not provide sufficient coverage of the action, or when organizations and their networks want to develop highly interactive contact points with related publics, they create media for their own community or the general public. Social media platforms can also serve as change agents for movements or assume movement leadership (Tombleson & Wolf, 2017; Uysal & Yang, 2013). Common examples of digital media include the personal social media accounts of new activists, the social profile of a targeted company, the organization's website, groups and platforms created simultaneously with social media accounts, general or issue-specific online forums, and alternative news websites. In addition to texts and comments, individual and chain e-mails, online bulletins, E-library domains, research and report announcements, E-petition, and hashtags are used to convey personal messages (Ciszek, 2016; Honda, 2016; Madden et al., 2018; E. Sommerfeldt, 2011; E. J. Sommerfeldt et al., 2012; Uysal & Yang, 2013; Veil et al., 2015).

According to Castells (2013, p. 15), the activist movement has a communicative character because of the tools and methods it employs for communicating. On the other hand, activists may deliberately use social media to disturb integrity, prolong arguments, market misinformation, or misuse media in order to ruin harmony and split (Kutoglu Kuruç & Opiyo, 2019). Another study indicated that non-governmental organization members are wary of social media due to the ease with which they can be manipulated (Seo et al., 2009).

3.1.8. Transformation and Restructuring

Generally, the termination of movements is the result of an agreement between the negotiating parties. When the targeted party accepts the activists' requests, the movement enters a new phase. This new phase includes the negotiation and agreement between parties on the change of direction. Activists primarily seek completion of projects and actions (D. S. Anderson, 1992; Han & Zhang, 2009; Stokes & Atkins-Sayre, 2018), regulations in supply and production processes (Coombs & Holladay, 2012a; Veil et al., 2015; Zoller & Tener, 2010), employment rights, union rights, economic empowerment, developed infrastructure, and starting programs providing regular income (Dhir, 2007; A. Harrison & Scorse, 2006; Knight & Greenberg, 2002; Ross, 2008, 2008; Stückelberger, 2009), support for local and national public services (Dhir, 2007), agreement on policy making and audited activities (D. S. Anderson, 1992; Dhir, 2007; Dimitrov, 2008; Henderson, 2005; Niesen, 2015; Stokes & Atkins-Sayre, 2018; Stückelberger, 2009; Weaver, 2010). During the negotiation process, when companies are expected to undergo significant change, they may request extra time or refrain from making any adjustments for a while if they stick to the plan (Coombs & Holladay, 2012a). Under these conditions, monitoring becomes very important.

3.1.9. Measuring Effectiveness

In case studies about assessment and evaluation, there are few specifics regarding the behavior patterns of activist movements. However, some researchers who discuss the impact of actions mention the absence of measurement of audience attitudes (W. B. Anderson, 2019) or the absence of an integrated reporting system (Benecke & Oksiutycz, 2015). The development of digital resources has enabled monitoring, analysis, and data visualization, which facilitates the measurement of the issue, actions, and impact of participation.

When examining the example cases, we can observe the monitoring of the relevant subjects, the primary assessment, and the evaluation of movements. Independent audits occasionally monitor, report, and share their data with the public. From the perspective of corporate accountability, monitoring and reporting focus primarily on the company's own operations (Hallahan, 2001). The success of relationship management and corporate social responsibility initiatives can be quantified in terms of their impact on reputation, which can then be factored into issue management. However, there is no public tracking of developments in the issue's or subject's resolution. Budgeting and priority are given to consumer research in marketing and purchasing to ascertain monitoring and trends.

3.2. From a Mainstream Perspective: Activism Effects and Transforming PR

The relationship between activism and public relations has been studied primarily through examples of activist movements in literature. As a definition, "activist PR" refers to strategies, methods, and techniques employed by activists primarily for protest and dissent. The purpose of activist communication actions is to establish connections between social issues and related processes. Through communication actions, the processes of "emergence of the issue," "real effect size and definition of the issue," "inclusion of all parties and their involvement with the issue," "distribution of shares in the issue and solution," and "assumption of responsibility and building the change" are realized and interconnected. When the themes that emerged from the analysis are placed into these processes, a flow pattern resembling the planning phases of strategic communication management can be observed. This is hardly surprising given the notion that social movements are the origin of PR (Coombs & Holladay, 2012b; Roberson, 2020). Nonetheless, because each movement is unique in terms of its structure, partners, timing, and context, in each initiative scenario, none of the processes indicated by the listed themes can develop in an orderly and regulated manner. Furthermore, activists do not want to maintain all processes under control and in order. However, these processes progress in a more linear and sequential manner within the communication of the firms. Because they have a pattern of actions that they are accustomed to and confident will benefit them within the system of economic connections. They have a tendency to chain together all the processes in the system of social relations in order to maintain control over both the processes and the relationships. In a continual, antagonistic relationship with activists, processes can be broken and readily harmed.

The first conflict-related problem that can be addressed is the refusal to recognize the legitimacy of activists. Many examples of heightened conflict have seen responses such as ignoring, not engaging, or ridiculing activists and their actions, as well as degrading, silencing, or dodging the subject (Coombs & Holladay, 2012a; Hung, 2003; Knight & Greenberg, 2002; Stokes & Atkins-Sayre, 2018; Wakefield, 2007). When reactions reach a point where they cannot be ignored, the process to improve the relationship with the activists must first be regulated and then managed. If it is not possible to avoid action and divert attention, corporations typically exhibit a defensive response (Hallahan, 2001). Activists view the company's activities, in addition to its tactics, as an indication of its stance and attitude toward structures and circumstances that are significant to the system of social interactions.

3.2.1. Pressure of Corporate Social Responsibility (CSR) Criticism

Analysis suggests that a corporate social responsibility strategy beginning with mandatory rules in the institutional and economic domains is one of the most divisive issues in the social element of mainstream public relations in times when the government cannot stay unresponsive to activist influences. The controversial aspect of the CSR approach adopted by companies in order to demonstrate to the public that they willingly accept their social responsibilities has been framed by veiled financial value, marketing, and persuasive implicit goals (Aronczyk, 2018; Bodkin et al., 2015; Coombs & Holladay, 2012a; Demetrious, 2008; Elms, 2006; Knight & Greenberg, 2002; Stokes & Atkins-Sayre, 2018, p. 7). On the other side, activities such as cover-up, washing, and spinning that demonstrate the incompatibility of discourse and action were observed and prompted activist responses (Bodkin et al., 2015; Knight & Greenberg, 2002; Rome, 2019; Stokes & Atkins-Sayre, 2018).

3.2.2. Institutional Solutions to Social Issues

In a social system rife with difficulties, companies' attempts to construct social value with the priority of commercial value indicate that they do not internalize the responsibility. From the perspective of the public, when expectations evolve into demands for evidence of a balance between financial and social worth, the methods and tools utilized by businesses for relationship management are standard paperwork, labels, and institutional reports. As a result of activist efforts, strategies are implemented to mitigate adverse reactions with little collateral damage, and they are portrayed to the public as institutional openness and accountability.

As social issues are stated, activist reactions produce a wider public, which diminishes the likelihood of firms dismissing the problems and converts into an understanding where the company's perspective on social issues is defined and voluntary adjustments are made (Stokes & Atkins-Sayre, 2018; Stokes & Rubin, 2010). However, this perspective is criticized due to its narrow focus on issue management and damage reduction, when businesses seek to identify the issue's potential relevance to the company's goals and eliminate it (Wolf, 2018). Communication with the public in this process is mostly about understanding the public interest by financially supporting society, making institutional contributions to public issues, engaging in practices such as agenda support, and using bureaucratic mechanisms (Aronczyk, 2018).

3.2.3. Dialogue, Negotiation, and Consensus

As businesses move from an asymmetrical to a symmetrical relationship with the activist public, institutional sympathy toward activism is demonstrated through support for some groups that are more receptive to collaboration in the eyes of the public. As measures of cooperation and common sense for the public's benefit, mainstream relationship dynamics are given. In a case analysis (Uysal & Yang, 2013), the functional approach asserts that activists employ a symmetrical or asymmetrical strategy and engage with corporations in order to reach a potential agreement (p. 459). As the most active institution in the social change process, activists encourage firms to take on their own decision-making perspectives and direct company policy. However, in another instance, it is evident that for some businesses, activist-mainstream conflict has been portrayed to the public as the refusal of assistance (Demetrious, 2008). Company messaging in this case emphasizes the value of open dialogue aimed at finding mutually beneficial solutions to problems. It is evident that the pressure to cooperate comes from the firms themselves.

3.2.4. Proactivity and Volunteering

The proactivity approach has been at the forefront of the communication process and activities with activists, as views on companies' ability to identify problems before they become crises and realize activist transformation within themselves have come to the fore (Veil et al., 2015; Zoller & Tener, 2010). To the extent that a company takes affirmative and willing steps to alter its practices, it demonstrates its dedication to satisfying public expectations and meeting legal requirements (Zoller & Tener, 2010). When a problem arises, the company at issue applies the application that is predicted to receive public support or approval based on surveys and PR claims of collaboration with the public (Stokes & Rubin, 2010). In the proactive strategy, there are strategic steps such as analyzing threats and opportunities, influencing favorable external events, and aligning company demands with their objectives (Zoller & Tener, 2010). Paradoxically, the company's reactive and defensive activity is concealed as a voluntary move, despite the fact that it has not yet become obvious (Zoller & Tener, 2010). It is not realistic to state that every example of a proactive approach is an internalized activity that attempts to meet the needs of the public sphere or provide support for a solution. Activists may also define proactivity as an endeavor to control demands, responses, and actions.

3.2.5. The Rise of Activism

The data reveals that firms primarily react to activist movement responses. However, there are a few instances in literature where companies and activism overlap. This trend is addressed on a narrow line between corporate participation in civic engagement and conflict resolution processes and the adoption of a new strategy for mainstream activism against movement reactions (Berger, 2005; Coombs & Holladay, 2012a; Lan et al., 2020; Thompson, 2016). In one case study, despite their initial commercial goal, activist public relations efforts can benefit society in both corporate social responsibility and social action (Thompson, 2018). Participating in public discussions on recent social issues without any obligation to announce their responsibility and involvement, developing leading policies, exerting pressure on legal authorities, mechanisms, and sectors, and soliciting participation are examples of actions seen in mainstream activist movement practice, regardless of whether companies have had conflicts with activists in the past or not (De Moya & Bravo, 2016; Lan et al., 2020; Maxwell & Miller, 2016). New strategies and technologies developed by activist groups are also accessible to the mainstream (Kiyan, 2019). In this method, which legitimizes the stance of corporations as defenders in the social and political sphere, the duty of representing opposing viewpoints within or outside the organization is assigned to a PR practitioner appointed from within or outside the organization (Henderson, 2005; Holtzhausen & Voto, 2002; Lan et al., 2020; Roberson, 2020; Wolf, 2019). It is stated that the combination of activism and public relations can perform functions such as exerting pressure on organizations, initiating power shifts in dominant coalitions, and providing open support for beliefs and values (Hou, 2021).

4. CONCLUSION

Western worlds have adhered to the economic principles of neoliberalism, emphasizing personal accountability, free markets, and enterprise. As nations become more conscious of the social and environmental hazards brought by economic expansion, this discourse is now being challenged (Roper, 2012). It's not enough to save the environment; we must also alter the system (Hart et al., 2021; O'Brien et al., 2018). Especially the COVID-19 pandemic, which reveals substantial shifts in how individuals view their responsibility to protect the environment. This is especially putting pressure on corporations and society because of their production and consumption activities. The degrowth movement, as an example, began as a response to the continued expansion of the economy, with the goal of achieving voluntary reductions in production and consumption that are compatible with social and environmental sustainability (O'Brien et al., 2018). Strong sustainability demands a new form of corporate, government, and societal collaboration (Mäkelä & Olkkonen, 2021; Roper, 2012). Activists protest pollution and other misbehavior by companies. Companies were both targets and activists, advocating for environmental sustainability and employee rights. This contradicts the traditional notion of activism as a push between NGOs and firms, as companies can use activism to improve their businesses and industries (Mäkelä & Olkkonen, 2021). Thus, activism is a productive method of opposition and a new path (Müller, 2021; Pink, 2015).

Activist movements' use of mainstream channels and tools has developed with the help of various skills and possibilities regarding face-to-face communication between people or mediated by an opinion leader, the distribution and dissemination of posters, brochures, or bulletins, the ability to buy space or time on high-cost media, the ability to cover media by eluding gatekeepers, and the ability to contact the public and/or media. Because activists can only expand their weak coverage area by employing multiple communication channels (Kiyan, 2019), numerous items or spaces like people, clothes, walls, or public buildings or areas are transformed into creative communication channels or instruments. With the growth of digital communication technologies, more people now have access to popular mass communication tools with limited skills and potential, making them more powerful and able to reach more people.

Utilizing social media effectively in public relations strategies can create conversions. Digital storytelling is utilized in social media advertising in a way that is both immersive and compelling and supports many kinds of content sharing (Allagui & Breslow, 2016). This research demonstrates the expanding scope of activist public relations as it pertains to both activist organizations and corporations. The activist perspective on PR's social component is growing in tandem with the rise of activist structures' use of PR for their own ends. This circumstance also contributed to the social aspect of the mainstream perspective's turn towards activism.

Relationship conflict has shaped and developed PR. The social dimension of PR is based on both activism-based PR and mainstream social relations. Social change movements involve all parties, directly or indirectly. Social movement groups have developed strategic communication plans over time, and mainstream structures have adopted activist methods. When it comes to the relationship between activism and public relations, finding patterns and approaches in how parties act can help define activist PR. This view can show the future direction and development of PR's social dimension in a crisis-filled future. According to Smith (1995, pp. 45–50), structures were interconnected, followed one another, and co-created the driving force of change by passing through one another. Activist-company tensions have increased historically as a result of the corporations' "stance" toward the social problem, their attempt to "control" the relationship or the process, and their "profit-seeking" posture in their actions. The claim of activism compels businesses to recognize all types of social problems, regardless of whether they affect them. In some instances, the organization may need to oppose all structures that oppose social progress. Furthermore, activism must not only be viewed as a strategic type of public relations, but it must also be owned by all parties inside the organization. Based on the theories of Pierre Bourdieu, an activist's job is not to persuade society to follow but to ask questions, challenge conventions, and urge others to do the same (Wolf, 2018). The abilities of a PR practitioner to ask questions, collect data, and encourage others increase his or her activism potential (Ciszek, 2018). Focusing on the public benefit priority and the consensus strategy that embraces disputes can bring the two parties together at the point of starting debates on topics and establishing social discourse (Ciszek, 2016; Roberson, 2020).

Keeping the social dialogue environment separate from financial interactions, like in the case of LeadSA (Benecke & Oksiutycz, 2015), appears to be a structural prerequisite for the activist PR of corporations. According to Verhoeven et al. (2018, p. 472), the future of hypermodern culture is replete with paradoxes that make connections challenging, particularly for organizations and communicators. In such a future, firms are encouraged to promote their own ideals by participating in social conversations and influencing social values, as opposed to only responding to the demands of critical publics.

REFERENCES

Adi, A. (2018). *Protest Public Relations: Communicating dissent and activism.* Routledge. doi:10.4324/9781351173605

Ali, H. M., Boddy, J., O'Leary, P., & Ewart, J. (2016). *Exploring the use of public relations in organising activism: Implications for addressing gender-based violence in the developing world.* Academic Press.

Alkon, A., & Norgaard, K. M. (2009). Breaking the food chains: An investigation of food justice activism. *Sociological Inquiry, 79*(3), 289–305. doi:10.1111/j.1475-682X.2009.00291.x

Allagui, I., & Breslow, H. (2016). Social media for public relations: Lessons from four effective cases. *Public Relations Review, 42*(1), 20–30. doi:10.1016/j.pubrev.2015.12.001

Anderson, D. S. (1992). Identifying and responding to activist publics: A case study. *Journal of Public Relations Research, 4*(3), 151–165. doi:10.1207/s1532754xjprr0403_02

Anderson, W. B. (2017). Social movements and public relations in the early twentieth century: How one group used public relations to curtail venereal disease rates. *Journal of Public Relations Research*, *29*(1), 3–15. doi:10.1080/1062726X.2017.1281135

Anderson, W. B. (2019). How to keep Rosie the riveter from contracting VD: A case study of how U.S. social reformers used public relations during World War II. *Public Relations Review*, *45*(5), 101787. doi:10.1016/j.pubrev.2019.05.008

Aronczyk, M. (2018). Public relations, issue management, and the transformation of american environmentalism, 1948–1992. *Enterprise and Society*, *19*(4), 836–863. doi:10.1017/eso.2017.69

Avenell, S. (2016). Antinuclear radicals: Scientific experts and antinuclear activism in Japan. *Science, Technology & Society*, *21*(1), 88–109. doi:10.1177/0971721815622742

Benecke, D. R., & Oksiutycz, A. (2015). Changing conversation and dialogue through LeadSA: An example of public relations activism in South Africa. *Public Relations Review*, *41*(5), 816–824. doi:10.1016/j.pubrev.2015.06.003

Berger, B. K. (2005). Power Over, Power With, and Power to Relations: Critical Reflections on Public Relations, the Dominant Coalition, and Activism. *Journal of Public Relations Research*, *17*(1), 5–28. doi:10.1207/s1532754xjprr1701_3

Bodkin, C. D., Amato, L. H., & Amato, C. H. (2015). The influence of green advertising during a corporate disaster. *Corporate Communications*, *20*(3), 256–275. doi:10.1108/CCIJ-08-2014-0055

Brooks, K. J., Wakefield, R. I., & Plowman, K. D. (2018). Activism, prosocial public relations and negotiation: The case of St Vincent de Paul. *Corporate Communications*, *23*(1), 139–150. doi:10.1108/CCIJ-10-2016-0072

Bullert, B. J. (2000). Progressive Public Relations, Sweatshops, and the Net. *Political Communication*, *17*(4), 403–407. doi:10.1080/10584600050179022

Burns, J. P., Green, C. D., & Nolan, J. (2018). New genealogies and the courage of truth: Toward an ethics of adversarial public educational scholarship and policy activism. *Education Policy Analysis Archives*, *26*, 151–151. doi:10.14507/epaa.26.3397

Castells, M. (2013). *Communication Power*. OUP Oxford.

Chalmers, I., & Altman, D. G. (1995). *Systematic reviews*. BMJ Publishing.

Chatterji, A. K., & Toffel, M. W. (2017). Can CEO Activism Spark Sustainability Transitions? Evidence from a Field Experiment. Harvard Business School.

Ciszek, E. L. (2015). Bridging the gap: Mapping the relationship between activism and public relations. *Public Relations Review, 41*(4), 447–455. doi:10.1016/j.pubrev.2015.05.016

Ciszek, E. L. (2016). Digital activism: How social media and dissensus inform theory and practice. *Public Relations Review, 42*(2), 314–321. doi:10.1016/j.pubrev.2016.02.002

Ciszek, E. L. (2017a). Activist Strategic Communication for Social Change: A Transnational Case Study of Lesbian, Gay, Bisexual, and Transgender Activism. *Journal of Communication, 67*(5), 702–718. doi:10.1111/jcom.12319

Ciszek, E. L. (2017b). Public relations, activism and identity: A cultural-economic examination of contemporary LGBT activism. *Public Relations Review, 43*(4), 809–816. doi:10.1016/j.pubrev.2017.01.005

Ciszek, E. L. (2018). Queering PR: Directions in theory and research for public relations scholarship. *Journal of Public Relations Research, 30*(4), 134–145. doi:10.1080/1062726X.2018.1440354

Coombs, W. T., & Holladay, S. J. (2012a). Fringe public relations: How activism moves critical pr toward the mainstream. *Public Relations Review, 38*(5), 880–887. doi:10.1016/j.pubrev.2012.02.008

Coombs, W. T., & Holladay, S. J. (2012b). Privileging an activist vs. A corporate view of public relations history in the U.S. *Public Relations Review, 38*(3), 347–353. doi:10.1016/j.pubrev.2011.11.010

Curtin, P. A. (2016). Exploring articulation in internal activism and public relations theory: A case study. *Journal of Public Relations Research, 28*(1), 19–34. doi:10.1080/1062726X.2015.1131696

De Moya, M., & Bravo, V. (2016). The role of public relations in ethnic advocacy and activism: A proposed research agenda. *Public Relations Inquiry, 5*(3), 233–251. doi:10.1177/2046147X16635225

Demetrious, K. (2008). Corporate social responsibility, new activism and public relations. *Social Responsibility Journal, 4*(1/2), 104–119. doi:10.1108/17471110810856875

Denisova, A., & O'Brien, M. (2019). From High Visibility to High Vulnerability: Feminist, Postcolonial and Anti-Gentrification Activism at Risk. *Westminster Papers in Communication and Culture, 14*(1), 1. Advance online publication. doi:10.16997/wpcc.323

Dhir, K. S. (2007). Stakeholder activism through nonviolence. *Corporate Communications*, *12*(1), 75–93. doi:10.1108/13563280710723769

Dimitrov, R. (2008). Gender violence, fan activism and public relations in sport: The case of "Footy Fans Against Sexual Assault.". *Public Relations Review*, *34*(2), 90–98. doi:10.1016/j.pubrev.2008.03.002

Doan, M. A., & Toledano, M. (2018). Beyond organization-centred public relations: Collective action through a civic crowdfunding campaign. *Public Relations Review*, *44*(1), 37–46. doi:10.1016/j.pubrev.2017.10.001

Edwards, L. (2018). Public relations, voice and recognition: A case study. *Media Culture & Society*, *40*(3), 317–332. doi:10.1177/0163443717705000

Elms, H. (2006). Corporate (and stakeholder) responsibility in Central and Eastern Europe. *International Journal of Emerging Markets*, *1*(3), 203–211. doi:10.1108/17468800610674435

Guiniven, J. E. (2002). Dealing with activism in Canada: An ideal cultural fit for the two-way symmetrical public relations model. *Public Relations Review*, *28*(4), 393–402. doi:10.1016/S0363-8111(02)00162-5

Hallahan, K. (2001). The Dynamics of Issues Activation and Response: An Issues Processes Model. *Journal of Public Relations Research*, *13*(1), 27–59. doi:10.1207/S1532754XJPRR1301_3

Han, G., & Zhang, A. (2009). Starbucks is forbidden in the Forbidden City: Blog, circuit of culture and informal public relations campaign in China. *Public Relations Review*, *35*(4), 395–401. doi:10.1016/j.pubrev.2009.07.004

Harrison, A., & Scorse, J. (2006). Improving the conditions of workers? Minimum wage legislation and anti-sweatshop activism. *California Management Review*, *48*(2), 144–160. doi:10.2307/41166342

Harrison, F. V. (2004). Global Apartheid, Environmental Degradation, And Women's Activism For Sustainable Well-Being: A Conceptual And Theoretical Overview. *Urban Anthropology and Studies of Cultural Systems and World Economic Development*, *33*(1), 1–35.

Hart, E., Kuijpers, G., Laverack, G., & Scheele, F. (2021). The Process Leading to Physician Activism for Sustainable Change. *Sustainability (Basel)*, *13*(18), 18. Advance online publication. doi:10.3390/su131810003

Henderson, A. (2005). Activism in "Paradise": Identity Management in a Public Relations Campaign Against Genetic Engineering. *Journal of Public Relations Research, 17*(2), 117–137. doi:10.1207/s1532754xjprr1702_4

Holtzhausen, D. R., & Voto, R. (2002). Resistance From the Margins: The Postmodern Public Relations Practitioner as Organizational Activist. *Journal of Public Relations Research, 14*(1), 57–84. doi:10.1207/S1532754XJPRR1401_3

Honda, L. P. (2016). Motivations for activists' participation in the 'It Gets Better Project.'. *Public Relations Inquiry, 5*(3), 253–276. doi:10.1177/2046147X15625710

Hou, J. Z. (2021). The articulation of 'agency': How can public relations scholarship and institutional theory enrich each other? *Public Relations Inquiry, 10*(1), 97–117. doi:10.1177/2046147X20932136

Hung, C. F. (2003). Relationship building, activism, and conflict resolution—A case study on the termination of licensed prostitution in Taipei City. *Asian Journal of Communication, 13*(2), 21–49. doi:10.1080/01292980309364837

Jabareen, Y. (2008). A New Conceptual Framework for Sustainable Development. *Environment, Development and Sustainability, 10*(2), 179–192. doi:10.1007/s10668-006-9058-z

Jackson, S. J., & Foucault Welles, B. (2015). Hijacking #MYNYPD: Social Media Dissent and Networked Counterpublics. *Journal of Communication, 65*(6), 932–952. doi:10.1111/jcom.12185

Kitchenham, B. (2004). *Procedures for performing systematic reviews* [Technical Report TR/SE-0401]. Keele University.

Kiyan, Z. (2019). İletişim Teknolojileri ve Toplumsal Hareketler: Sistematik Bir Literatür İncelemesi. *Gaziantep University Journal of Social Sciences, 18*(2), Article 2.

Knight, G., & Greenberg, J. (2002). Promotionalism and Subpolitics: Nike and Its Labor Critics. *Management Communication Quarterly, 15*(4), 541–570. doi:10.1177/0893318902154002

Kovacs, R. (2001). Relationship building as integral to British activism: Its impact on accountability in broadcasting. *Public Relations Review, 27*(4), 421–436. doi:10.1016/S0363-8111(01)00098-4

Kutoglu Kuruç, U., & Opiyo, B. (2019). Social media usage and activism by non-western budding PR professionals during crisis communication. *Corporate Communications, 25*(1), 98–112. doi:10.1108/CCIJ-07-2019-0082

Kwak, N. H. (2018). Anti-gentrification Campaigns and the Fight for Local Control in California Cities. *New Global Studies*, *12*(1), 9–20. doi:10.1515/ngs-2018-0008

Lan, X., Tarasevich, S., Proverbs, P., Myslik, B., & Kiousis, S. (2020). President Trump vs. CEOs: A comparison of presidential and corporate agenda building. *Journal of Public Relations Research*, *32*(1-2), 1–17. doi:10.1080/1062726X.2020.1719494

Leonidou, C. N., Gruber, V., & Schlegelmilch, B. B. (2022). Consumers' Environmental Sustainability Beliefs and Activism: A Cross-Cultural Examination. *Journal of International Marketing*, *30*(4), 78–104. doi:10.1177/1069031X221128786

Madden, S., Janoske, M., Winkler, R. B., & Harpole, Z. (2018). Who loves consent? Social media and the culture jamming of Victoria's Secret. *Public Relations Inquiry*, *7*(2), 171–186. doi:10.1177/2046147X18764216

Mäkelä, M., & Olkkonen, L. (2021). Sustainability activism: A review of the state of the art. Research Handbook of Sustainability Agency, 140–154.

Maxwell, R., & Miller, T. (2016). The Propaganda Machine Behind the Controversy Over Climate Science: Can You Spot the Lie in This Title? *The American Behavioral Scientist*, *60*(3), 288–304. doi:10.1177/0002764215613405

Methods of Nonviolent Action. (2014). Einstein Institute. https://www.aeinstein.org/wp-content/uploads/2014/12/198-Met hods.pdf

Moloney, K., McQueen, D., Surowiec, P., & Yaxley, H. (2013). *Dissent and Protest Public Relations*. Public Relations Research Group.

Moscato, D. (2019). The metanarrative of rural environmentalism: Rhetorical activism in Bold Nebraska's Harvest the Hope. *Public Relations Inquiry*, *8*(1), 23–47. doi:10.1177/2046147X18810733

Müller, N. (2021). *Corporate activism trends and public relations strategies for the UN sustainable development goals*. Academic Press.

Nassani, A. M., Khader, J. A., Moemen, M. A., & Ali, I. (2013). Consumer environmental activism, sustainable consumption behavior and satisfaction with life. *Life Science Journal*, *10*(2), 1000–1006.

Niesen, M. (2015). From Gray Panther to National Nanny: The Kidvid Crusade and the Eclipse of the U.S. Federal Trade Commission, 1977–1980. *Communication, Culture & Critique*, *8*(4), 576–593. doi:10.1111/cccr.12100

O'Brien, K., Selboe, E., & Hayward, B. M. (2018). Exploring youth activism on climate change: Dutiful, disruptive, and dangerous dissent. *Ecology and Society*, *23*(3), art42. doi:10.5751/ES-10287-230342

Ortiz Juarez-Paz, A. V. (2017). Undocumented identity storytelling:(Re) framing public relations. *International Journal of Media and Cultural Politics*, *13*(1–2), 165–178. doi:10.1386/macp.13.1-2.165_1

Pink, S. (2015). Ethnography, co-design and emergence: Slow activism for sustainable design. Global Media Journal: Australian Edition, 9(2), 1–10.

Prescott, H. M. (2019). We Must Not Allow a Contraception Gap: Planned Parenthood's Campaign for New Birth Control and Feminist Health Activism in the 1990s. *Technology and Culture*, *60*(3), 816–832. doi:10.1353/tech.2019.0074 PMID:31422967

Ragas, M. W. (2013). Agenda building during activist shareholder campaigns. *Public Relations Review*, *39*(3), 219–221. doi:10.1016/j.pubrev.2013.03.007

Reber, B. H., & Berger, B. K. (2005). Framing analysis of activist rhetoric: How the Sierra Club succeeds or fails at creating salient messages. *Public Relations Review*, *31*(2), 185–195. doi:10.1016/j.pubrev.2005.02.020

Reber, B. H., Pētersone, B., & Berger, B. K. (2010). Managing from the middle: The role of mid-level gatekeepers in mobilizing grassroots activism and encouraging facilitative relationships. *Journal of Communication Management (London)*, *14*(1), 32–46. doi:10.1108/13632541011017799

Rentschler, C. A. (2015). Distributed Activism: Domestic Violence and Feminist Media Infrastructure in the Fax Age. *Communication, Culture & Critique*, *8*(2), 182–198. doi:10.1111/cccr.12079

Roberson, T. (2020). On social change, agency, and public interest: What can science communication learn from public relations? *JCOM, Journal of Science Communication*, *19*(2), Y01. doi:10.22323/2.19020401

Robertson, K. (2011). Capitalist Cocktails and Moscow Mules: The Art World and Alter-globalization Protest. *Globalizations*, *8*(4), 473–486. doi:10.1080/14747731.2011.585849

Rodriguez-Labajos, B. (2022). Artistic activism promotes three major forms of sustainability transformation. *Current Opinion in Environmental Sustainability*, *57*, 101199. doi:10.1016/j.cosust.2022.101199

Rome, A. (2019). DuPont and the Limits of Corporate Environmentalism. *Business History Review*, *93*(1), 75–99. doi:10.1017/S0007680519000345

Roper, J. (2012). Environmental risk, sustainability discourses, and public relations. *Public Relations Inquiry*, *1*(1), 69–87. doi:10.1177/2046147X11422147

Ross, A. (2008). The quandaries of consumer-based labor activism: A low-wage case study. *Cultural Studies*, *22*(5), 770–787. doi:10.1080/09502380802246017

Sancar, G. A. (2017). Aktivist Halkla İlişkiler Bağlamında WWF Dünya Saati Kampanya Örneği. *Erciyes İletişim Dergisi*, *5*(1), 2–18. doi:10.17680/erciyesakademia.291883

Sejrup, J. (2014). Awakening the sufferers: Reflections on public relations, activism, and subalternity in postcolonial controversies between Taiwan and Japan. *Public Relations Inquiry*, *3*(1), 51–68. doi:10.1177/2046147X13519637

Seo, H., Kim, J. Y., & Yang, S.-U. (2009). Global activism and new media: A study of transnational NGOs' online public relations. *Public Relations Review*, *35*(2), 123–126. doi:10.1016/j.pubrev.2009.02.002

Smith, A. D. (1995). *Toplumsal Değişme Anlayışı (İşlevselci Toplumsal Değişme Kuramının Bir Eleştirisi)* (Ü. Oskay, Trans.). Gündoğan Yayınları.

Sommerfeldt, E. (2011). Activist online resource mobilization: Relationship building features that fulfill resource dependencies. *Public Relations Review*, *37*(4), 429–431. doi:10.1016/j.pubrev.2011.03.003

Sommerfeldt, E. J., Kent, M. L., & Taylor, M. (2012). Activist practitioner perspectives of website public relations: Why aren't activist websites fulfilling the dialogic promise? *Public Relations Review*, *38*(2), 303–312. doi:10.1016/j.pubrev.2012.01.001

Sommerfeldt, E. J., & Yang, A. (2017). Relationship networks as strategic issues management: An issue-stage framework of social movement organization network strategies. *Public Relations Review*, *43*(4), 829–839. doi:10.1016/j.pubrev.2017.06.012

Stokes, A. Q., & Atkins-Sayre, W. (2018). PETA, rhetorical fracture, and the power of digital activism. *Public Relations Inquiry*, *7*(2), 149–170. doi:10.1177/2046147X18770216

Stokes, A. Q., & Rubin, D. (2010). Activism and the Limits of Symmetry: The Public Relations Battle Between Colorado GASP and Philip Morris. *Journal of Public Relations Research*, *22*(1), 26–48. doi:10.1080/10627260903150268

Stückelberger, C. (2009). Dialogue Ethics: Ethical Criteria and Conditions for a Successful Dialogue Between Companies and Societal Actors. *Journal of Business Ethics*, *84*(3), 329–339. doi:10.1007/s10551-009-0201-2

Thompson, G. (2016). Towards a theory of rent-seeking in activist public relations. *Public Relations Inquiry*, *5*(3), 213–231. doi:10.1177/2046147X16644005

Thompson, G. (2018). Social gains from the public relations voice of activist investors: The case of Herbalife and Pershing Square Capital Management. *Public Relations Review*, *44*(4), 481–489. doi:10.1016/j.pubrev.2018.04.003

Toledano, M. (2016). Advocating for reconciliation: Public relations, activism, advocacy and dialogue. *Public Relations Inquiry*, *5*(3), 277–294. doi:10.1177/2046147X16666595

Tombleson, B., & Wolf, K. (2017). Rethinking the circuit of culture: How participatory culture has transformed cross-cultural communication. *Public Relations Review*, *43*(1), 14–25. doi:10.1016/j.pubrev.2016.10.017

Tranfield, D., Denyer, D., & Smart, P. (2003). Content analysis and thematic analysis: Implications for conducting a qualitative descriptive study. *British Journal of Management*, *14*, 207–222. doi:10.1111/1467-8551.00375

Uysal, N., & Yang, A. (2013). The power of activist networks in the mass self-communication era: A triangulation study of the impact of WikiLeaks on the stock value of Bank of America. *Public Relations Review*, *39*(5), 459–469. doi:10.1016/j.pubrev.2013.09.007

Vaismoradi, M., Turunen, H., & Bondas, T. (2013). *Content analysis and thematic analysis: Implications for conducting a qualitative descriptive study*. Academic Press.

Veil, S. R., Reno, J., Freihaut, R., & Oldham, J. (2015). Online activists vs. Kraft foods: A case of social media hijacking. *Public Relations Review*, *41*(1), 103–108. doi:10.1016/j.pubrev.2014.11.017

Verhoeven, P., Zerfass, A., Verčič, D., Tench, R., & Moreno, A. (2018). Public relations and the rise of hypermodern values: Exploring the profession in Europe. *Public Relations Review*, *44*(4), 471–480. doi:10.1016/j.pubrev.2018.06.001

Wakefield, R. I. (2007). Theory of International Public Relations, the Internet, and Activism: A Personal Reflection. *Journal of Public Relations Research*, *20*(1), 138–157. doi:10.1080/10627260701727069

Weaver, C. K. (2010). Carnivalesque activism as a public relations genre: A case study of the New Zealand group Mothers Against Genetic Engineering. *Public Relations Review*, *36*(1), 35–41. doi:10.1016/j.pubrev.2009.09.001

White, C. (2012). Activist efforts of the Center for Media and Democracy to affect FCC policy for video news releases. *Public Relations Review*, *38*(1), 76–82. doi:10.1016/j.pubrev.2011.12.001

Whitehead, C. A. (1987). Southampton versus Out-of-Town Shopping Centres. *Property Management*, *5*(4), 350–354. doi:10.1108/eb006672

Wolf, K. (2018). Power struggles: A sociological approach to activist communication. *Public Relations Review*, *44*(2), 308–316. doi:10.1016/j.pubrev.2018.03.004

Wolf, K. (2019). PRi special edition: The intersections between public relations and neoliberalism – The road to nowhere: Re-examining activists' role in civil societies. Public Relations Inquiry, 8(2), 167–188. doi:10.1177/2046147X19846578

Woods, C. L. (2019). From an "outside group" to a catalyst for corporate change: Examining activists' legitimation strategies. *Public Relations Review*, *45*(2), 332–347. doi:10.1016/j.pubrev.2019.02.001

Zoller, H. M., & Tener, M. (2010). Corporate Proactivity as a Discursive Fiction: Managing Environmental Health Activism and Regulation. *Management Communication Quarterly*, *24*(3), 391–418. doi:10.1177/0893318909354116

Chapter 6
Green Economy and Sustainable Development in India

Dharmesh Dhabliya
https://orcid.org/0000-0002-6340-2993
Vishwakarma Institute of Information Technology, India

Ankur Gupta
https://orcid.org/0000-0002-4651-5830
Vaish College of Engineering, India

Sukhvinder Singh Dari
https://orcid.org/0000-0002-6218-6600
Symbiosis International University, India

Ritika Dhabliya
Yashika Journal Publications Pvt. Ltd., India

Anishkumar Dhablia
Altimetrik India Pvt. Ltd., India

Nitin N. Sakhare
https://orcid.org/0000-0002-1748-799X
BRACT'S Vishwakarma Institute of Information Technology, India

Sabyasachi Pramanik
https://orcid.org/0000-0002-9431-8751
Haldia Institute of Technology, India

ABSTRACT

The ideal strategy for transitioning to economies that are inclusive and sustainable has long been a topic of discussion, both domestically and internationally. India only recently became a member of the 2030 Agenda for Global Development and accepted the Paris Agreement. You may consider both triumphs as occurring at the same time. India just assumed two major new global obligations. The main topic of discussion in these talks is how to move toward diverse and environmentally conscious economies. India just made promises to the world. The primary objective ofboth agreements is to ensure that everyone lives a cozy, healthful, and ecologically responsible life. There is a common objective among these agreements. Achieving sustainable growth—a prerequisite for a green economy—requires us to expand

DOI: 10.4018/979-8-3693-1182-0.ch006

our economies in ways that advance social justice, the environment, and equality. The lack of sustainable economic development makes the establishment of a green economy more challenging.

INTRODUCTION

In 1989, the UK government released a paper called "Blueprint for a Green Economy," which is probably where the term "green economy" originated worldwide. Prominent environmental economists collaborated to draft the paper, which was eventually published as a consequence of their work. Creating a "green economy" means developing an economic structure that prioritizes long-term development without compromising the environment while also reducing ecological dangers and resource depletion. This is the category of economic system that fits the description of "sustainable" or "eco-friendly" systems. According to the United Nations Environment Program (UNEP) "Green Economy Report," that in order for an economy to be green, it must not only be efficient, but it must also be fair." Finding the global and national dimensions of equality is especially important for facilitating a fair transition to a low-carbon, resource-efficient, and socially inclusive economy. This acknowledgement has to happen at the national and international levels.

This is because the characteristics of national and global equality have varying effects on different groups of people. Recognizing equitable features at the national and international levels is essential to achieving justice. It was described as follows by the Green Economy Coalition: "A green economy is one that results in improved human well-being and social equity while significantly reducing environmental risks and ecological scarcities." It's interesting to remember this definition. In addition, the dominant brown economy, which is given a high weighting in the equation, is strongly favored by and benefits from the enabling circumstances. This is a result of the brown economy's substantial weighting in the system. In the marketing sector, "green marketing" (Ahmed, R.R. et al. 2023) has been one of the most prominent topics of focus recently. This is probably because it may provide companies in the marketing industry an edge over their competitors. Investments are nevertheless critical to advancing technological capabilities, convincingly communicating the advantages to customers, and implementing any process changes that may be required.

LITERATURE REVIEW

Noteworthy research (Wang, W. et al. 2022) highlights the potential benefits of implementing gamification in the travel and hospitality business. According to (Dal-

Ré, R. et al. 2023), travelers are increasingly seeking distinctive experiences that entail engaging and stimulating several senses. There is a growing need to thoroughly examine the impact that gamification may have on the travel and hospitality industry. This work adds to the current knowledge of the phenomena by finding and analyzing the available literature on the issue. Concurrently, it emphasizes aspects that are not yet understood or ambiguous, offering valuable guidance for future investigations.

According to (Carvalho, I. et al. 2023), a literature review is often used to combine and analyze current research and data, with the aim of identifying and exploring areas that need more investigation. The SLR, or Systematic Literature Review, is a reliable and replicable scientific approach widely used in several social sciences, such as the T&H sector. It is known for its transparency and has been embraced by researchers in these fields (Ho, CL. Et al. 2023). Following (Choi, A. et al. 2023) ideas this systematic literature review (SLR) seeks to achieve "summarization" by using empirical data to draw conclusions about what is already known. This involves condensing several empirical examples into a more digestible collection of findings.

RESEARCH QUESTIONS

A considerable number of Indian businesses (Pramanik, S. et al. 2020) have recently started positioning themselves as environmentally conscious entities in response to certain government laws and a global trend in consumer demand. There is a global change in consumer demand that is evident.

However, little study has been done in India on green marketing, so it's unclear whether or not consumers are aware of the environmentally friendly items that they might buy. There is considerable debate to be had over the attitudes of Indian consumers toward eco-friendly items and the relationship between such attitudes and their purchasing choices. Since green marketing (Vargo, S.L. et al. 2023) differs from conventional marketing, how can marketers use it to their advantage? First, how can marketers make sure they understand the variables that influence consumers to purchase eco-friendly products? It is not necessary for traditional marketers to possess this information. By looking at a variety of consumer categories, this study seeks to address the research topic of what influences customers' decisions about whether or not to buy environmentally friendly things. The survey participants were already familiar with eco-friendly products and practices. The great majority of respondents, however, were unaware of the actions done by the federal, state, and local governments, as well as businesses and non-governmental organizations (NGOs) (Nguyen, H. 2023), to promote green marketing techniques in India.

METHODOLOGY

Digital Platforms

It is anticipated that digital platforms would revolutionize value generation and establish new economic ecosystems. They affect industrial value production in a variety of ways, including the transition transforming value chains into networks for the development of digital value. Through obtaining, organizing, and evaluating data, platforms bring together, for example, suppliers, partners, and consumers on a single platform advancing the interests of multiple participants. Digital platforms (Kaushik, D. et al. 2022) are often supposed to encourage creativity and teamwork by facilitating cooperation and communication amongst many stakeholders and partners. Additionally, consumers may be included in the process of creating value, for example, via open innovation competitions. Because platforms allow for the exploration of fresh viewpoints and novel means of communication, partnerships, they serve as the foundation for new business model development.

The report defines "digital platforms" as "items, services, and technology that are arranged according to a similar framework that allows a business to produce derivative goods, services, and technology". They thereby provide the framework on which outside businesses may add their goods, innovations, and offerings. In doing so, they open the door for new economic ecosystems such as well as fresh reasoning for generating value. Additionally, the paper makes advantage of the definition's expansion by (Veeraiah, V. et al. 2023), who state that "multi-sided platforms" have two central elements: These platforms must, first and foremost, allow for direct communication between two or more participants while, Secondly, every participant is linked to the platform. Thus, the digital platform meets the requirements of many client groups, merging their requirements to create synergies for a single business model (Trischler, M.F.G. et al. 2023) and additive outcomes. Digital platforms are not the same as conventional technological platforms in that regard. These technologies Platforms are often distinguished by their ability to provide several goods and services, supplier to its clientele. The amalgamation of many clientele segments, which might furthermore partly fulfill as suppliers of information for other clients, for example, and their real-time connectivity, is not seen on conventional digital platforms. Therefore, the technical prerequisites also as the fundamental theories guiding the production of value for consumers vary greatly throughout technologies digital as well as platform-wise.

For years, information technology firms have been creating these kinds of platforms, but the less work is done in this area by the more conventional industrial sector especially in the industrial In this regard, established businesses struggle to find collaborators to develop digital platforms and to create fresh, competitive company strategies. Furthermore, digital platforms need the creation lacking sufficient IT (Dhamodaran S. et al. 2023) skills, which do not constitute a fundamental capability of conventional industry producers. Furthermore, there are still unanswered questions about who owns the data, how to effectively manage the connections between participants on such platforms and how to regulate them. In spite of platforms' importance, particularly in the context of industry (Dhamodaran S. et al. 2023), there are very few academic researches looking at the management implications and impacts of digital platforms viewpoint or within a business setting. Furthermore, current study more closely relates to a certain comprehending or to certain parts rather than creating a comprehensive image (Pandey, B. K. et al. 2023). However, researchers should be interested in exploring how digital platforms might assist solve future difficulties. Within the framework of Industry 4.0 (Talukdar, V. et al. 2023), platforms are anticipated to support data-centric (Ngọc, T. H. et al. 2023) business models. Additionally, several writers provide instances of successful platform applications inside the framework of the Internet of Things.

Digital Format and Green Economy

The long-term objectives of innovation-oriented industrial advanced economies and rising markets, such as the USA, European Union, and Scandinavian countries, in some nations, like Japan and South Korea, the process of digitization and greening of the economy are seen as mutually reinforcing and beneficial, since they contribute to inclusive, socially responsible, and sustainable growth. The EU Commission's communication to the European Parliament has highlighted the importance of establishing digital green industrial ecosystems and attaining climate-neutral digital leadership in the industry. These objectives have been identified as crucial for maintaining the European Union's competitive advantage and geopolitical influence in the coming decades.

The process of digitalizing the economy, like to every newly researched topic, is linked to both significant potential and difficulties. These issues include environmental concerns and changes in the structure of the ecological imprint. European scientists predict that if present trends continue the ICT sector's contribution to global CO2 emissions might raise from the current 2% to 14% by 2020. Conversely, the intended purpose of "green" ICTs is to decrease greenhouse gas emissions by 15%, therefore lessening the human impact on the global environment and attaining carbon neutrality in the ICT sector. Furthermore, the widening "digital divide" between technologically advanced nations and less developed economies is causing the preservation of obsolete and environmentally harmful technological systems. This situation positions the latter as providers of raw materials and recipients of hazardous waste. An undeniable manifestation of the "institutional-environment trap" may be seen in the e-waste emigration map.

The diagram illustrates the movement of e-waste and reveals distinct patterns in the geopolitical distribution of global value chain connections. Countries that are environmentally conscious and economically prosperous, with stringent environmental regulations and high costs for legal disposal of electronic waste, tend to import their e-waste to less developed regions. These regions have a more lenient approach towards environmentally hazardous economic activities and offer cheap manual labor. China stands out as the foremost manufacturer of digital items and a significant hub for the buildup of electronic trash. The relationship between ecology and digitalization is evident in the fact that stringent environmental standards in developed countries have hindered the widespread use of digital technology. Standardizing the environmental aspects of a product's life cycle leads to higher expenditures for quality control, production, working conditions, and environmentally responsible disposal of electronic items and associated infrastructure when they are sold.

Noncompliance with established quality standards, whether due to technical or financial reasons, is a prevalent obstacle in both international and local markets. Powerful environmental interest groups in both central and local government, along with protests organized by environmental organizations, contribute to a negative perception of developers of potentially hazardous innovations. This hampers economic growth and slows down research and development progress, while also raising investment risks and imposing a heavier tax burden on businesses. Simultaneously, accurately forecasting the environmental repercussions of digital innovation might prove to be very challenging. Increasing the intensity of wave radiation due to the advancement of digital communications leads to a higher occurrence of congenital genetic mutations in various species such as birds, fish, and insects. This radiation also causes changes in their fundamental behavioral responses, particularly in species that have a social way of life like ants, wasps, bees, termites, and bumblebees. Additionally, it disrupts their migration routes and habitats, resulting in the disturbance of established food chains in ecosystems. Consequently, this leads to a decrease in biodiversity and, in some instances, the collapse of ecosystems. The bee population's mass extinction leads to a decline in the pollination of fruit crops and some plant species, resulting in a potentially devastating impact on the availability and abundance of food.

The European experience has shown that integrating the demands of business 4.0 with the demands of addressing climate and environmental crises necessitates significant changes in the transportation and energy sectors of the business, along with substantial financial expenditures. Preliminary estimates indicate that the European Union need an expenditure of around EUR 3 trillion in order to attain the lofty objectives of being a climate-neutral leader in the digital sector. During the period spanning from 2021 to 2027, the primary financial responsibility is projected to be divided among several entities. The European Investment Bank is planned to contribute around EUR 600 billion, the private sector around EUR 300 billion, the governments of EU member states approximately EUR 100 billion, and the EU budget approximately EUR 7.5 billion. As a result, this program has faced criticism for its perceived unnecessary tax rise and the alleged arbitrary allocation of budget resources by authorities, all under the premise of environmental objectives.

Sustainable Development and Biotechnology

Utilizing living things for certain tasks is known as biotechnology. The methods employed are diverse and may be used to bacteria, plants, and animals. They can entail the manipulation of whole organisms, tissue cells, or individual cells. The field of biotechnology is not new. It has been used for millennia in fermentation activities, including as brewing and bread making, which continue to constitute the foundation of many contemporary food companies.

Since these applications and those in medical don't directly relate to the environment, they won't be covered here. Conventional breeding plans for plants and animals are likewise a kind of biotechnology (Bao, Z. et al. 2023), and recent advancements have fundamentally changed these programs, particularly with regard to agricultural plants.

The capacity of plant cells to grow whole plants, known as totipotency, is exploited by tissue culture, which is now commonly utilized to produce vast numbers of agricultural plants with certain benefits, including disease resistance. Similar to this, somaclonal variation—the genetic diversity that arises during clone production—can be used to enhance crop types, such as potato (Solarium tuberosum). Another method for improving many species is somatic hybridization. To do this, protoplasts—that is, cells without cell walls—must fuse together to form a single, distinct cell that has a new chromosomal arrangement or other features that provide favorable properties.

The latest advancements in biotechnology pertain to "genetic engineering," which is sometimes referred to as in vivo genetic modification or recombinant DNA technology. This involves introducing foreign DNA into a host organism and modifying the basic chromosomal units of cells. The genetic information required to produce desired features is present in the inserted DNA. Thus, the hosts will be 'designed' to generate new tissue and/or progeny with beneficial traits. The majority of genetic engineering's uses in environmental contexts are found in agriculture, particularly in the creation of better agricultural plants. Genetic engineering (Kumar, K. et al. 2023) has promise for improving environmental quality as well.

The primary life support systems of Earth are biogeochemical cycles and energy fluxes, which are the focus of these applications. Additionally, as opposed to the conventional agricultural method of tailoring crops for the environment, biotechnology offers a fresh chance to customize crops for the environment. It is paradoxical that a significant amount of this untapped resource is vanishing as plants and animals are becoming extinct at a pace never seen before, just as human civilization is starting to realize the potential of gene components as a resource. Furthermore, it is critical that modified organisms do not now or in the future endanger the health of people, animals, or plants. Of course, this cannot be guaranteed, but prudent precautions need to be taken to make sure transgenic organisms don't ruin the environment.

Sustainable Development and Electrical Energy

The most significant and promising renewable energy sources for addressing future energy needs are biomass, solar, wind, and hydropower. A nation's sustainable growth should be ensured by renewable energy sources because of the extensive use of fossil fuels, their growing global cost, and their decreased environmental effect. Utilizing nuclear energy (Omri, E. et al. 2023) to generate electricity is one way to lower resource needs to a level that is more sustainable. It matters how much these technologies have been industrialized and made available for purchase. Since the industrial size and rate of development of that technology are higher in developed than in developing nations, the quantity of materials used to produce electricity is determined by how much fossil fuel-producing technology is consumed and how industrialized it is. Modern energy offers many advantages, but guaranteeing access to it can only be possible if it is reasonably priced. For instance, evaluating the choices made in the energy industry may be done by contrasting coal and geothermal energy as the two primary power generating technologies with emerging alternatives like wind and solar power. Given the expenses each power supply choice places on the system as a whole, it's critical to consider how reasonably priced each alternative is.

The need to think about energy policy in terms of its impact on energy security, energy efficiency, and environmental sustainability is necessary given the rapidly increasing global demand for electricity and sustainable development. Doing so presents an opportunity to accelerate economic growth and create more dependable and reasonably priced energy supply options. The establishment of unified electrical markets, such as the Eurasian Economic Union's single electricity market, which includes Russia and many post-Soviet nations, is another example. Cross-border power line construction and preservation, as well as the establishment of precise market regulations governing their usage, may contribute to the mutually beneficial economic growth of the member nations of the shared economic space.

It is very important to have the ability to generate enough power to fulfill demand while also meeting supply. It is clear that the circumstances in emerging nations are much more challenging than those in wealthy nations. They may, however, benefit from efforts to reorganize their energy industry and expand upon more eco-friendly and productive technology. Due to resource shortages, a sizeable section of the population would have trouble accessing essential energy services. Although nuclear power is increasingly acknowledged as a vital element in promoting sustainable development, there is a growing understanding that nuclear energy is essential to achieving the Sustainable Development Goals (SDGs) set out by the United Nations. Because of its great efficiency, low operating and maintenance expenses, high dependability, and cheap operating costs, nuclear energy has a strong competitive position. Compared to other energy sources, nuclear energy provides a number of sustainability advantages. This is shown by the fact that nuclear energy is now used in practically all significant studies that outline realistic routes to sustainable energy supply. For instance, in the case of Bangladesh, the government's energy strategy will play a significant role in the growth of the nuclear energy industry and the country's long-term energy security. It is evident that the nuclear industry has chosen to minimize its negative effects on the environment while conserving a variety of resources for future generations. Petrol will still be the primary fuel used to generate power, but a more varied blend will be created, and the nation's reliance on imported oil and other fossil fuels to support economic expansion will lessen. Furthermore, substituting fossil fuels—electricity produced by nuclear, coal, oil, gas, hydropower, and other sources—could assist fulfill expanding energy requirements while simultaneously reducing air pollution. CO2 emissions are the primary cause of global warming and a significant issue facing the electrical industry.

DIRECTIONS FOR INDIA'S MORE SUSTAINABLE ECONOMY

India has five important sectors that are vital to the nation's green economy. Agriculture (Khanh, P. T. et al. 2023), building, energy, manufacturing, transportation, and tourism are some of these industries.

Agribusiness

In recent years, the organic agricultural sector in India has seen a transformation due to the entry of several new companies that have caused a disturbance in the market. This may be attributed to the influx of several new enterprises into the market. This directly results from the notable rise in the quantity of new businesses that have joined the market in recent years. This state of affairs has arisen directly from the significant rise in the number of new businesses entering the market, which has raised competition. This has the immediate effect of motivating the governments of a large number of other nations to take similar actions. The government has implemented many initiatives in the last several years with the goal of raising and enhancing farmers' standards of life, especially those of smaller farms. The goal of these initiatives is to raise farmers' standards of life. These efforts have specifically focused on improving the standard of living for agricultural laborers. Enhancing the quality of life for dairy farmers has been a top priority for the administration, which has taken major steps in this area. A few of ideas include increasing the minimum support prices, broadening the loan market, creating seed varieties that are resistant to climate change, and putting in place technological interventions like giving farmers Soil Health Cards so they can assess the health of their own soils. It entails increasing the minimum support prices and is among the most important things that can be done. Furthermore, by 2020, the government wants to have more than quadrupled farmer earnings. This goal was first declared in 2010. The first steps toward achieving this aim were taken in 2010. The year 2010 saw the first official announcement of this goal.

THE IMPACT OF AGRICULTURE ON GREEN GROWTH ECONOMIC ADVANTAGES

Should the agricultural sector fail to provide enough food, feed, and fiber to support the world's growing population, green growth would be in jeopardy. Even though it only makes up less than 2% of GDP and less than 6% of employment in OECD member nations, agricultural production is vital to the country's and the world's food supply. With thirty percent of GDP (Gyurkovics, É. Et al. 2023) and sixty-three percent of employment coming from it, respectively, agriculture plays a significant role in the economy of many emerging nations. Advances in agricultural technology should lead to gains in agricultural production in most nations; but, for these technologies to be effective, they must be affordable, flexible enough to accommodate different farming methods, and environmentally conscious.

THE ENVIRONMENT'S PART

Many environmental and ecosystem services that are vital to the growth of a sustainable economy are provided by agriculture. One aspect of these services, which also include a reduction in greenhouse gas emissions, is the storage of carbon. Even while it only accounts for 10% to 12% of greenhouse gas (Roy, A. et al. 2023) emissions directly, agriculture still makes a significant contribution. The potential exists that the emissions produced by the agriculture industry might offset the emissions produced by other industries. Since agriculture is in charge of managing land and water resources, maintaining biodiversity, preventing flooding, preserving habitat, and creating and maintaining landscapes, it has an effect on the environment. A vast array of plant and animal species has evolved as a result of agricultural land management techniques. Wetland regions, woods, and ecosystems all spring to mind. There is a growing recognition of the ecological and economic importance of agriculture, as seen by attempts to put a monetary value on the environmental services it provides.

PARTICIPATION IN SOCIETY

Global food security, or the availability of sufficient quantities of food and agricultural products to fulfill the needs of expanding people, is a prerequisite for achieving green growth. There can be no green growth without global food security. Global population growth is expected to rise by 2.3 billion between 2010 and 2050, with emerging countries accounting for the bulk of this growth.

Figure 1. Agricultural GDP in India for the last 4 years
Source: Reddy et al. (2018)

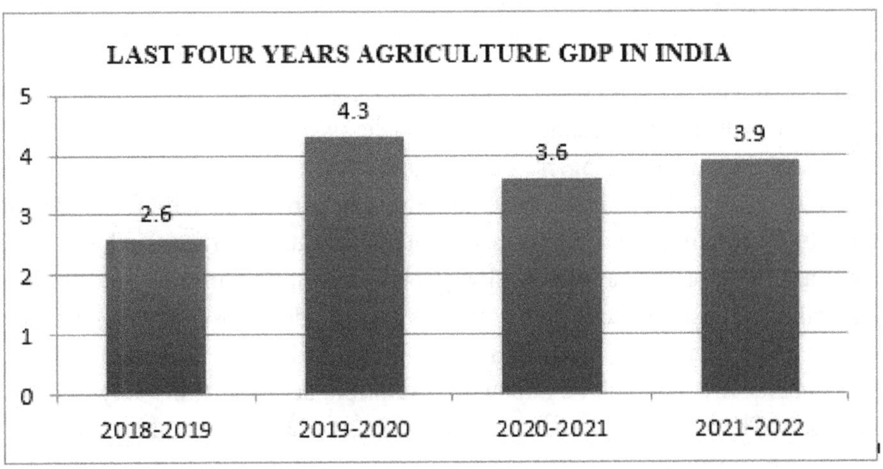

MANUFACTURE

The quantity of resources used by the building sector is disproportionately large. Its substantial material footprint accounts for thirty percent of India's overall power consumption. In terms of "Leadership in Energy and Environmental Design," or LEED, India is now ranked third out of the ten nations in the world. Furthermore, it is projected that the nation's market for eco-friendly structures would grow by 20%. Fly ash consumption has been steadily increasing in the building sector over the last several years. The Model Building Bye-Laws of 2016 stipulate that any building constructed on a plot of land larger than 100 square meters must follow ecologically friendly guidelines.

A CONSTRUCTION'S AID IN GREEN GROWTH ECONOMIC IMPLEMENTATION

Due to their significant financial and economic advantages, green buildings are very relevant to the demands of many building owners and company owners. A sustainable house may save homeowners a lot of money on energy bills, building developers can save money on construction costs and raise the value of their property, and business owners can save money on labor costs and boost staff productivity. Energy and water efficiency may help you reap these financial rewards.

THE ENVIRONMENT'S PART

One of the biggest advantages that green buildings have for our climate and the environment is the efficient reduction of carbon emissions and the removal of direct negative impacts on the ecological system. One of the most significant benefits that green buildings provide is this as well. One of the biggest benefits that environmentally friendly buildings might provide is this. Enough insulation, airtight and waterproof exterior access doors, solar panels, skylights, large window installations, acoustic walls, and other sustainable design elements have made it possible to significantly lower the energy and water consumption of green buildings. Additional instances of these characteristics include adequate insulation, acoustic walls, skylights, and solar panels. These characteristics have allowed us to drastically reduce the amount of energy we consume.

Figure 2. Green economies for the last 4 years
Source: Loiseau et al. (2016)

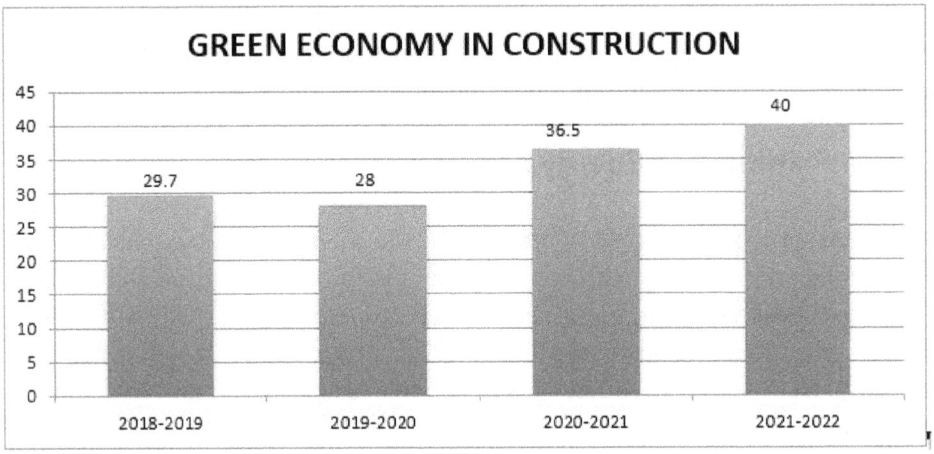

PARTICIPATION IN SOCIETY

Green design benefits not only the environment but also the mental and physical health of those who live in it. A multitude of studies have shown that green buildings have a major positive impact on occupant satisfaction, productivity, well-being, and absenteeism incidence. Highlighting the extra advantages that come with green buildings is a good method to make everyone aware of their importance. All people's lives are generally improved by these psychological advantages, which makes workers happier and businesses more successful.

POWER

India was rated as the ninth best nation in the world for investment in alternative energy sources, according a study released by the United Nations Environment Program (UNEP). This information was provided in relation to the global rankings of nations. The report was gathered and delivered by the United Nations Organization. The goal established by the Ministry of New and Renewable Energy is to build 175 Gigawatts (GW) of renewable energy plants by the year 2022. The goal for building these facilities was set for this date. After it was originally considered in 2017, this goal was made public. Of this amount, it is estimated that wind energy will make up around 60 GW and solar energy will make up about 100 GW. The remaining capacity will be used for hydropower and biofuel production. India's installed capacity for renewable energy sources reached 114.43 Gigawatts (GW) in May 2018. This represents around thirty-three percent of the country's total energy capacity. A significant amount of hydropower construction projects has been included in this calculation. A 648 megawatt (MW) solar plant was built in Tamil Nadu in 2016 and has been there ever since. It is now the most powerful solar plant in the world.

Digital Platforms in Energy and Power

A first crucial choice revolved on determining the appropriate geographical extent. Despite the presence of global energy digital platforms in our database, we have chosen to concentrate on the European Union (EU) due to the following justifications. Initially, given that the objective of this study is to provide policy recommendations, it is advantageous to concentrate on a region that is reasonably uniform and well-integrated, since policies implemented there would have a direct and immediate effect. Furthermore, the EU is actively advocating for a carbon-neutral economy by extensively implementing renewable energy installations, which would need improved system coordination. Consequently, digital platforms may potentially play a role in this endeavor. The EU has been actively pursuing a more comprehensive digital integration via the implementation of the Digital Single Market policy. This approach aims to eliminate any remaining obstacles to digital cross-border transactions.

Another relevant option included selecting between geographical units: nations or regions. The choice to adopt a regional viewpoint arises from two primary considerations. Initially, the inclusion of regional units surpassing nations results in a direct augmentation of the quantity of observations, therefore leading to an increase in the degrees of freedom for our calculations. Furthermore, a theoretical analysis also indicates that due to being in the early stages, digital platforms in the energy sector have a restricted commercial scope that is confined to relatively small regions of impact. This aligns with the anecdotal evidence seen in other industries, where digital platforms first start operations on a limited scale and concentrate on relatively restricted geographical areas before successfully expanding globally. Digital platforms have the ability to expand and possibly attract a large number of users worldwide, but this can only happen if there is a significant number of users from diverse perspectives who join the service. The energy sector has not yet reached this state. Furthermore, with the ongoing shift towards decentralized energy systems, the involvement of local communities is crucial, and a regional approach is more effective in examining these groups. Given that the database contains data on the city where the energy digital platforms have established their main offices, we use this information to assign all of our firms to certain NUTS2 areas. Corporations are not included in the sample, and it is assumed that the location of firms aligns with their respective operational markets.

The third option is to the selection of the econometric model we used for estimation, which is based on assumptions about the dynamics of digital marketplaces. While first-mover advantages in digital industries have significance, their outcome is not necessarily certain. Unlike conventional markets, these benefits result from the interaction of indirect network effects, economies of scale, and switching costs. This issue has significant importance in terms of policy and regulation, since these characteristics have the potential to impede market entrance and foster market concentration. A well-established practice in empirical industrial organization is to examine entrance models, which originated from the works of (Yao, Z., et al. 2023). Nevertheless, the determinations about market access in conventional markets may differ from those made in multi-sided, or platform, markets. The existing empirical research has mostly concentrated on conventional markets, whereas a comprehensive theoretical examination of entrance in multi-sided markets has yet to be formulated. Therefore, any endeavor to calculate an entrance model would inevitably rely on certain theoretical shortcomings, and the outcomes would thereafter be contingent upon the assumptions made. Therefore, we have chosen to concentrate on a simplified econometric model. The objective of the model is to elucidate the quantity of functional digital platforms within the European energy sector.

CONTRIBUTION OF ENERGY FOR GREEN GROWTH FINANCIAL CONTRIBUTION

The phrase "green growth" refers to a hypothetical situation as well as a route of economic expansion that is environmentally sustainable. "Green growth" describes an economic development trajectory that is environmentally sustainable. It is based on the notion that there has to be a separation between the development of the economy and resource consumption and the grave harm that it does to the environment as long as economic growth is the main goal. This understanding serves as the foundation upon which the plan is constructed. Because of this, the ideas of green growth and low-carbon or sustainable development are strongly related to the green economy. The shift to less environmentally hazardous energy sources is one of the main factors driving the growth of the green economy. Those who support green growth policies contend that well carried out green policies may lead to job possibilities in sectors like renewable energy, sustainable forestry, and environmentally friendly agriculture.

THE ENVIRONMENT'S PART

Additionally, the growth of green areas is significantly impacted by carbon emissions. To bolster such a claim, Koondhar et al. examined the effects of carbon emissions and used agricultural output as a stand-in for green development. This was carried out to investigate the effects of carbon emissions. In order to analyze the time-series data, the authors used the ARDL approach. The research indicates that there is a considerable growth retardation of green vegetation with an increase in carbon emissions. Furthermore, there is a straight path from carbon emissions to growth that is ecologically good. Yang and associates, on the other hand, investigated the potential impact of green growth on carbon emissions. When calculating the CO2 emissions, the authors considered the quantity of energy used. They contend that over time, energy use and environmentally friendly economic development have a significant influence on carbon emissions. Furthermore, there is a one-way causal link between long-term carbon emissions and energy consumption and ecologically friendly development. Afterwards, Hao et al. also made the contentious claim that green growth had a significant influence on carbon emissions during the time. This suggests that EAMFP improvements might lead to a possible reduction in carbon emissions. Furthermore, Fernandes and associates proposed that green growth disentangles the ongoing economic development from the depletion of natural resources and adverse environmental impacts.

PARTICIPATION IN SOCIETY

These resources also assist society in other ways, such as better health depending on the consumer's choice, technical breakthroughs, and employment opportunities; yet, there are certain crucial issues that need to be resolved for the sake of all people. These variables include the local climate, educational attainment, quality of life, and urban or rural status, all of which are significant from an agricultural perspective. One must first look at the political and social environment of a country before discussing its economic growth. Utilizing renewable energy sources might lead to greater consumer choice, better employment prospects, better health outcomes for local residents, and the development of new jobs in the community.

Manufacturing: The manufacturing sector's meager 16% GDP contribution is much less than the services sector's 55% GDP contribution. Even if the country's industrial exports are increasing, the manufacturing sector still only accounts for 16% of India's GDP. Manufacturing has the potential to contribute 25–30 percent of the nation's GDP by 2025 and produce 60–90 million new jobs nationwide if given the freedom to operate at full capacity. These estimates are predicated on the idea

Figure 3. Total energy production of green economy in India
Source: Gasparatos et al. (2017)

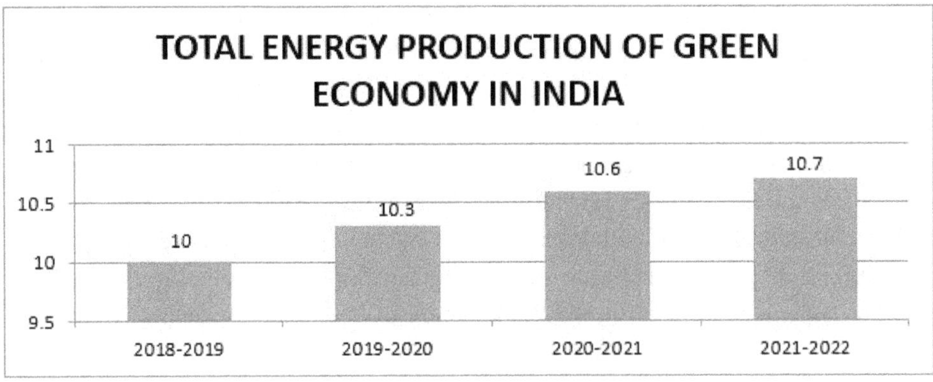

that manufacturing will be given the opportunity to reach its full potential. These projections are based on the assumption that the manufacturing sector will be given the chance to realize its full potential. In India, the production of goods that are less harmful to the environment and hence more ecologically friendly is only getting begun. There is still a great deal of room for improvement on the policy front as well as its acceptance in the fields of green products and green processes, despite the manufacturing sector having made significant strides in the formulation of policies and their acceptance in the field of green energy. This is the case even though the manufacturing sector has made great strides in developing regulations and getting them approved for use in the green energy space.

Manufacturing's Economic Contribution to Green Growth

Efforts that have been emphasized in budgets over the last several years that have highlighted the concept include coal gasification, battery storage, ethanol blending, the PM KUSUM Yojana (Parmar, R. et al. 2023), incentives for solar manufacturing, rooftop solar schemes, and coal gasification. Other initiatives that have received attention include battery storage and coal gasification. There have also been discussions about other possible remedies, such gasifying coal and storing batteries. India has been the world's top country in terms of the pace at which new capacity for renewable energy sources is being added since 2014, when compared to other major economies. Gaining this distinction required growing the overall capacity at a pace far faster than other large economies. The same goal is being approached via a number of other policies and initiatives, including the Gobardhan Yojna for Villages, the PM Pranam Yojna for Farmers, and the Vehicle Scrapping Policy for

Cities, Green Hydrogen, and Wetland Conservation. The aforementioned policies and initiatives are contributing to the same end. All of these many ideas and initiatives are helping to achieve the same overall goal, each in their own unique manner. India has been the largest economy among those with a significant amount of capacity added to renewable energy sources since 2014. This distinction was attained by increasing capacity more quickly than in other large economies.

The contribution of the environment in HUL, Hindustan Among the businesses that took home the 2020–21 IGMC Awards trophy were Coca-Cola, Sun Pharma, UPL, JSW, Borosil, and Schneider. These businesses received recognition for their exceptional contributions to sustainable development, green growth, and the enhancement of industrial processes. A four-phase Green Manufacturing Framework was used to evaluate every individual. Sustainability has become a critical concern, particularly in light of the IPCC's most recent report on climate change. Business executives should follow ecologically responsible procedures and consider the health of the globe while making decisions. This viewpoint contends that a company's customers and staff are the ones pushing it to embrace sustainable policies and environmentally friendly practices. With regard to business, the World Economic Forum notes in its report that "business has the opportunity to dramatically accelerate the transition to a nature-positive economy and collaborate on the advocacy, design, and adoption of policy reforms needed to protect, restore, and sustainably manage nature." The report contains this statement.

SOCIAL CONTRIBUTION

In order for everyone to benefit from and take advantage of the possibilities presented by the shift to an environmentally friendly economy, they should all be given the chance to participate in it. This is due to the fact that everyone will gain from the shift and have the chance to take part in it. It highlights the importance of ecosystems and natural resources to the local population and works to promote respectable employment and long-term sustainable lives in such places.

TRANSPORT AND TOURISM

The Indian Ministry of Road Transport and Highways and Transport for London have partnered to enhance India's public transportation network. By leveraging the expertise of public transport groups, the ministry would act as a facilitator for the states' attempts to enhance public transportation. One emerging trend in India's transportation industry is the growth of carpooling and on-demand transportation

Figure 4. Green manufacturing for the last 4 years
Source: Govindan et al. (2015)

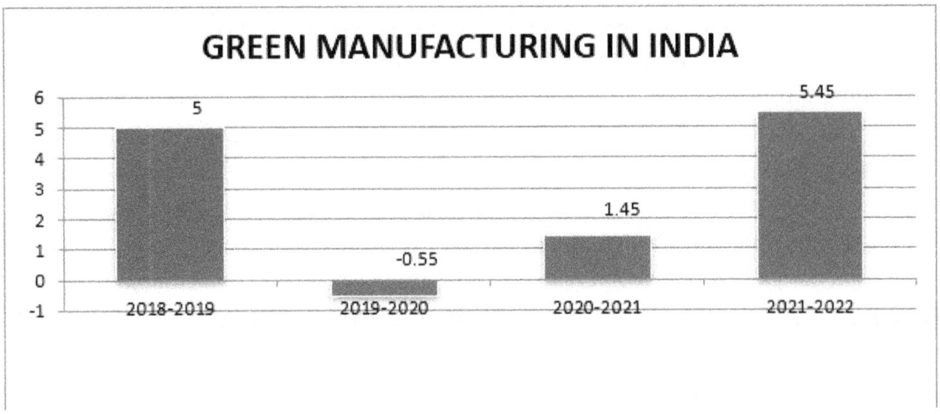

services. They are particularly common in cities, and as more people get access to the Internet, it is predicted that their use would rise exponentially.

THE ROLE OF TOURISM IN GREEN GROWTH: ECONOMIC ROLE

The tourist sector has the ability to significantly contribute to the green economy by supporting ecotourism, lowering the consequences of climate change, and adopting more ecologically responsible practices. This is becoming more generally accepted. The role of the tourist sector will remain significant even under the post-2015 framework for sustainable (Sinha, M. et al. 2021) development. However, there is a lack of consensus regarding how the tourism sector and its associated industries can best contribute to the welfare of people and ensure the sustainability of the environment, while also taking political economy, geographic considerations, and business ethics into account. Within this framework, the book offers a consensus on the nature of the green economy, the potential role that tourism may play in it, early responses from several nations, and ongoing and developing research initiatives that will help the travel industry make the shift to a greener economy.

The Sustainable Development Goals (SDGs) include environmental preservation, social development, and economic development. These are only a few of the numerous objectives that need to be addressed. By finding a balance between these aspects, sustainable tourism seeks to reduce the negative impacts of the sector on travel and tourism's social, economic, cultural, and environmental elements. It tackles the problem of maintaining equilibrium between the consumption of a population that is growing at a fast rate and the available natural resources, which are in finite supply. It specifically addresses the problem of sustaining a level of consumption that is sustainable. The most crucial components of sustainability in the tourism industry are limiting adverse effects on the nearby ecosystems and promoting environmental protection, all while meeting the expectations of both tourists and the communities in which they stay. It is important for the tourism industry and visitors to understand and show respect for the customs, culture, and economics of the people they visit. They should also look into ways that they may contribute to the preservation of the environment.

Consumer Perspective in the Use of Digital Platforms

The research assessed the long-term viability of digital marketing tactics aimed at promoting consumer participation in domestic tourism. The study used a mixed research technique to accomplish its goals and address the following research inquiries: what is the efficacy of digital marketing tactics in promoting consumer participation in domestic tourism? What are the elements that drive tourists to utilize digital marketing tools and platforms? What is the long-term viability of using digital marketing tactics to promote domestic tourism? The study's data was gathered in two distinct phases. For the first phase, occurring from June to July 2021, a total of thirteen comprehensive semi-structured interviews were carried out with tourist marketers hailing from the Free State province. The participants have over five years of experience as tourist marketers. The questionnaire for the second stage of the research was designed by considering the interview data. In September and October 2021, the second phase of the study consisted of conducting a questionnaire survey targeting domestic visitors who visited the Free State province. In order to be classified as domestic tourists, the respondents needed to be visiting the Free State province for the specific aim of leisure and recreation, with a maximum duration of 60 nights. A sample was chosen from five municipalities in the Free State province using a stratified, non-probability and purposive sampling method. Each municipality represents different strata. The Free State province is renowned for its Big Five game animals, which are geographically distributed among its five municipalities: Mangaung, the metropolitan municipality, and four district municipalities - Fezile Dabi, Lejweleputswa, Xhariep, and Thabo Mofutsanyana. The selection of interview participants was based on their availability, accessibility, and willingness to participate. The selection process was based on the individuals' personal attributes, professional activities, and anticipated competence in responding to interview inquiries. The marketers were intentionally chosen based on their affiliation with tourist marketing, marketing expertise, and to ensure representation from all municipalities in the Free State province. They needed to possess familiarity with digital marketing tools and platforms used to impact customer behavior, as well as awareness of their efficacy. The questionnaire survey targeted domestic travelers and was conducted at famous tourist destinations in each municipality. A screening question was used to ascertain that only those residing in South Africa who was travelling for recreational purposes took part in the survey. In 2019, the Free State province received a total of 410,000 domestic visitors, as reported by government data.

SOCIAL CONTRIBUTION

The concept of sustainable tourism development is relatively new, as opposed to mass tourism, which includes large numbers of people and usually takes the shape of planned or pre-packaged holidays. Not only does mass tourism negatively impact the environment and society, but it has also been linked to economic leakage and dependence. As a framing idea, sustainable tourism development has been promoted in a number of ways in opposition to these economic, environmental, and social consequences. Some writers have acknowledged that the concept of sustainable tourism is vague, and this vagueness has been used to support radically diverse approaches to the expansion of tourism. Conflicts between the paradigms of development and conservation may already be exacerbated by these tactics. Sustainable development has benefited greatly from the emergence of alternative tourist models in some nations, including ecotourism, community-based tourism, pro-poor tourism, slow tourism, green tourism, historical tourism, and others. These

Figure 5. Indian tourism and green economy transportation for the last 4 years
Source: Hajam et al. (2023)

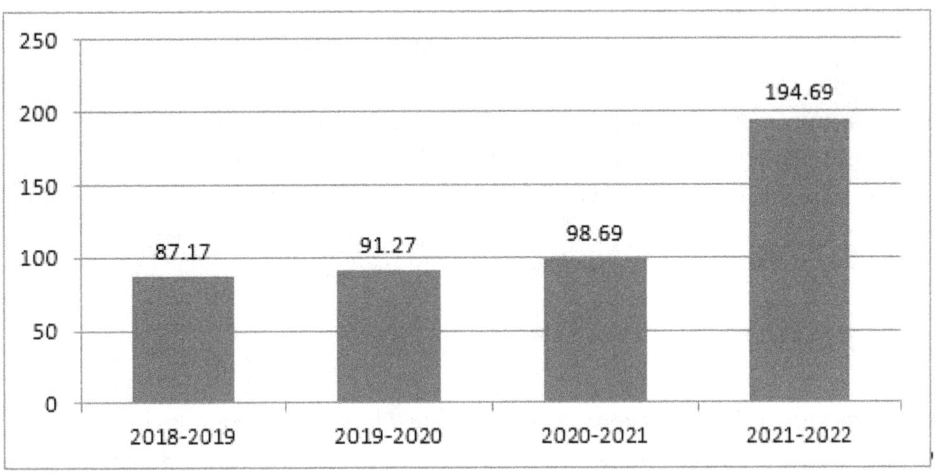

models seek to save the environment, increase local economic development, and enhance people's quality of life. These alternative tourist models have been developed with significant contributions from tourism.

RESULTS AND DISCUSSION

The respondents to the study had knowledge about environmentally friendly products and activities before hand. The great majority of respondents, however, were unaware of the initiatives undertaken by the Indian federal and state governments, non-governmental organizations (NGOs), and private companies to promote ecologically responsible business practices. These methods include using energy-efficient goods and procedures, recycling, and composting proving that these businesses need to communicate more effectively with their consumers about their environmentally friendly business operations and that they need to enhance their marketing communications. They also need to meet the criteria of improving the quality of their marketing communications. Customers said that the most recognizable sources of information they could think of for information about eco-friendly items were television and newspapers. The investigation that was done proved this to be the fact.

THE CURRENT GREEN ECONOMY WORK HAS THREE PRIMARY FOCUSES

1. In order to achieve sustainable economic development at the regional, sub regional and national levels of government and to promote the county's overall economic growth, assistance for a macroeconomic plan is provided.
2. The presentation of many perspectives on the green economy, with a focus primarily on investments, technology, and financing available for the green space.
3. Giving countries support in developing and broadly implementing macroeconomic policies to facilitate the shift to a more environmentally sustainable economic structure.

CONCLUSION

It was observed that consumers were well knowledgeable about environmentally friendly items. Evidence has shown that consumers are very knowledgeable about

Figure 6. Primary focus of green economy

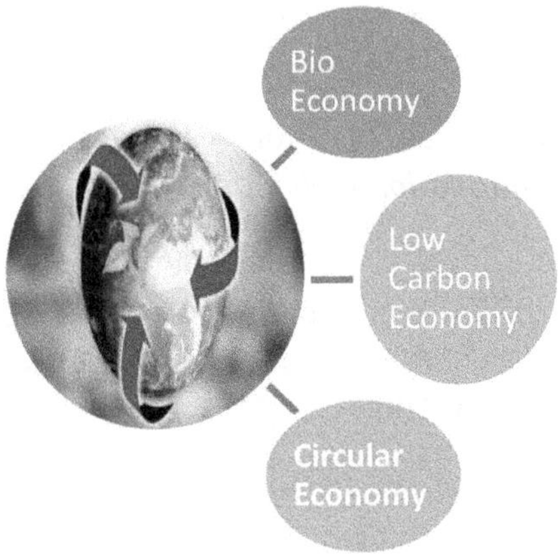

environmentally friendly items. Organizations made up of people or businesses with some connection to this subject matter. Given that the great majority of respondents cite newspapers as their main source of information, it is imperative that this medium be investigated even further in order to enlighten respondents about environmentally friendly goods and practices. To maximize the benefits of the "green" brand positioning they have selected for their goods, markets must be at the forefront of customers' thoughts whenever they consider other comparable markets. Open lines of communication must be maintained by businesses at all times if they want to significantly contribute to creating a unique brand identity using the color green. Customers have shown that they have a favorable attitude toward environmentally friendly items, notwithstanding their concerns regarding the cost and availability of these goods. Consumers have shown that they are eager to buy environmentally friendly products if they are made accessible to them. This means that marketers should provide consumers with easy access to environmentally friendly products so they may decide what to buy. Consumers have shown a willingness to buy eco-friendly products if they are made accessible to them.

REFERENCES

Ahmed, R. R., Streimikiene, D., Qadir, H., & Streimikis, J. (2023). Effect of green marketing mix, green customer value, and attitude on green purchase intention: Evidence from the USA. *Environmental Science and Pollution Research International*, *30*(5), 11473–11495. doi:10.1007/s11356-022-22944-7 PMID:36094715

Bao, Z., Xie, Y., Xu, C., Zhang, Z., & Zhu, D. (2023). Biotechnological production and potential applications of hypocrellins. *Applied Microbiology and Biotechnology, 107*(21), 6421–6438. doi:10.1007/s00253-023-12727-6 PMID:37695342

Carvalho, I., Ramires, A., & Iglesias, M. (2023). Attitudes towards machine translation and languages among travelers. *Information Technology & Tourism, 25*(2), 175–204. doi:10.1007/s40558-023-00253-0

Choi, A., & Schneider, I. E. (2023). Acculturation and tourist stress among US Korean immigrant leisure travelers. *Int. Journal of International Migration and Integration, 24*(3), 1159–1174. doi:10.1007/s12134-022-00997-4

Dal-Ré, R., Becker, S. L., Launay, O., & Pavli, A. (2023). Vaccine certificates for international travelers in future pandemics. *European Journal of Clinical Microbiology & Infectious Diseases, 42*(2), 227–228. doi:10.1007/s10096-022-04544-y PMID:36562922

Dhamodaran, S., Ahamad, S., Ramesh, J. V. N., Muthugurunathan, G., Manikandan, K., Pramanik, S., & Pandey, D. (2023). *Food Quality Assessment using Image Processing Technique. In Thrust Technologies' Effect on Image Processing*. IGI Global.

Dhamodaran, S., Ahamad, S., Ramesh, J. V. N., Sathappan, S., Namdev, A., Kanse, R. R., & Pramanik, S. (2023). *Fire Detection System Utilizing an Aggregate Technique in UAV and Cloud Computing. In Thrust Technologies' Effect on Image Processing*. IGI Global.

Gasparatos, A., Doll, C. N. H., Esteban, M., Ahmed, A., & Olang, T. A. (2017). Renewable energy and biodiversity: Implications for transitioning to a Green Economy. *Renewable and Sustainable Energy Reviews, 70*, 161-184. doi:10.1016/j.rser.2016.08.030

Govindan, K., & Diabat, A. (2015). Analyzing the drivers of green manufacturing with fuzzy approach. *Journal of Cleaner Production, 96*, 182-193. doi:10.1016/j.jclepro.2014.02.054

Gyurkovics, É., & Takács, T. (2023). Estimation of the potential GDP by a new robust filter method. *Central European Journal of Operations Research, 31*(4), 1183–1207. doi:10.1007/s10100-023-00851-7 PMID:37360979

Hajam, A.G., Perween, S., & Malik, M.A. (2023). Re-visiting the causal relationship between tourism and economic growth in India: specific to general modelling approach. *Journal of Hospitality and Tourism Insights*. doi:10.1108/JHTI-09-2022-0459

Ho, C. L., Chen, W. L., & Ou, C. H. (2023). Constructing a personalized travel itinerary recommender system with the Internet of Things. *Wireless Networks*. Advance online publication. doi:10.1007/s11276-023-03453-y

Kaushik, D., & Garg, M. (2022). Application of Machine Learning and Deep Learning in Cyber security: An Innovative Approach. In Cybersecurity and Digital Forensics: Challenges and Future Trends. Wiley. doi:10.1002/9781119795667.ch12

Khanh, P. T., Ngọc, T. H., & Pramanik, S. (2023). Future of Smart Agriculture Techniques and Applications. In A. Khang & I. G. I. Global (Eds.), *Advanced Technologies and AI-Equipped IoT Applications in High Tech Agriculture*. doi:10.4018/978-1-6684-9231-4.ch021

Kumar, K., Shinde, A., Aeron, V., Verma, A., & Arif, N. S. (2023). Genetic engineering of plants for phytoremediation: Advances and challenges. *Journal of Plant Biochemistry and Biotechnology*, *32*(1), 12–30. doi:10.1007/s13562-022-00776-3

Loiseau, E., Saikku, L., Antikainen, R., Droste, N., Hansjürgens, B., Pitkänen, K., Leskinen, P., Kuikman, P., & Thomsen, M. (2016). Green economy and related concepts: An overview. *Journal of Cleaner Production*, *139*, 361-371. doi:10.1016/j.jclepro.2016.08.024

Ngọc, T. H., Khanh, P. T., & Pramanik, S. (2023). Smart Agriculture using a Soil Monitoring System. In A. Khang & I. G. I. Global (Eds.), *Advanced Technologies and AI-Equipped IoT Applications in High Tech Agriculture*. doi:10.4018/978-1-6684-9231-4.ch011

Nguyen, H. (2023). Government-NGO relationship: Regulatory constraints and uncertain policy implementation in Vietnam. *SN Social Sciences*, *3*(6), 100. doi:10.1007/s43545-023-00686-8

Omri, E., & Saadaoui, H. (2023). An empirical investigation of the relationships between nuclear energy, economic growth, trade openness, fossil fuels, and carbon emissions in France: Fresh evidence using asymmetric cointegration. *Environmental Science and Pollution Research International*, *30*(5), 13224–13245. doi:10.1007/s11356-022-22958-1 PMID:36125682

Pandey, B. K., Pandey, D., Nassa, V. K., George, A. S., Pramanik, S., & Dadheech, P. (2023). Applications for the Text Extraction Method of Complex Degraded Images. In *The Impact of Thrust Technologies on Image Processing*. Nova Publishers. doi:10.52305/ATJL4552

Parmar, R. (2023). Challenges in Implementation of the Solar Water Pumps in Rural Agricultural Areas. In A. Rakshit, A. Biswas, D. Sarkar, V. S. Meena, & R. Datta (Eds.), *Handbook of Energy Management in Agriculture*. Springer. doi:10.1007/978-981-19-7736-7_34-1

Pramanik, S., Ghosh, R., Ghonge, M., Narayan, V., Sinha, M., Pandey, D., & Samanta, D. (2020). A Novel Approach using Steganography and Cryptography in Business Intelligence. In A. Azevedo & M. F. Santos (Eds.), *Integration Challenges for Analytics, Business Intelligence and Data Mining* (pp. 192–217). IGI Global.

Reddy, T., & Dutta, M. (2018). Impact of Agricultural Inputs on Agricultural GDP in Indian Economy. *Theoretical Economics Letters*, *8*(10), 1840–1853. doi:10.4236/tel.2018.810121

Roy, A., & Pramanik, S. (2023). A Review of the Hydrogen Fuel Path to Emission Reduction in the Surface Transport Industry. *International Journal of Hydrogen Energy*. Advance online publication. doi:10.1016/j.ijhydene.2023.07.010

Sinha, M., Chacko, E., Makhija, P., & Pramanik, S. (2021). Energy Efficient Smart Cities with Green IoT. In C. Chakrabarty (Ed.), *Green Technological Innovation for Sustainable Smart Societies: Post Pandemic Era*. Springer. doi:10.1007/978-3-030-73295-0_16

Talukdar, V., Kurniullah, A. Z., Keshwani, P., Khan, H., Pramanik, S., Gupta, A., & Pandey, D. (2023). *Load Balancing Techniques in Cloud Computing, Emerging Trends in Cloud Computing. In Analytics, Scalability, and Service Models*. IGI Global.

Trischler, M. F. G., & Li-Ying, J. (2023). Digital business model innovation: Toward construct clarity and future research directions. *Review of Managerial Science*, *17*(1), 3–32. doi:10.1007/s11846-021-00508-2

Vargo, S. L., Peters, L., Kjellberg, H., Koskela-Huotari, K., Nenonen, S., Polese, F., Sarno, D., & Vaughan, C. (2023). Emergence in marketing: An institutional and ecosystem framework. *Journal of the Academy of Marketing Science*, *51*(1), 2–22. doi:10.1007/s11747-022-00849-8

Veeraiah, V., Shiju, D. J., Ramesh, J. V. N., Ganesh Kumar, R., Pramanik, S., Gupta, A., & Pandey, D. (2023). *Healthcare Cloud Services in Image Processing. In Thrust Technologies' Effect on Image Processing*. IGI Global.

Wang, W., Gan, H., Wang, X., Lu, H., & Huang, Y. (2022). Initiatives and challenges in using gamification in transportation: A systematic mapping. *European Transport Research Review*, *14*(1), 41. doi:10.1186/s12544-022-00567-w

Yao, Z., Lum, Y., Johnston, A., Mejia-Mendoza, L. M., Zhou, X., Wen, Y., Aspuru-Guzik, A., Sargent, E. H., & Seh, Z. W. (2023). Machine learning for a sustainable energy future. *Nature Reviews. Materials*, *8*(3), 202–215. doi:10.1038/s41578-022-00490-5 PMID:36277083

Chapter 7
Review of Internet Addiction and Internet Use Habits of Canakkale People

Merve Erdoğan
Çanakkale Onsekiz Mart Üniversitesi, Turkey

ABSTRACT

With technological advancements, the internet, a global communication tool, has become part of our lives. More and more demand has been placed on the internet, which quickly and easily meets people's needs, such as information, entertainment, communications, and so on. But the widespread use of the internet has brought negative consequences. This study will therefore address the concept of internet dependency, one of the negative consequences of the internet. The research was done to determine the internet addiction and internet usage habits of Çanakkale people. Two hundred eleven people aged 18-46 participated in the study using the general scan model. The study using the random sampling technique uses the descriptive statistical technique. The findings found that most participants were using the internet to inform and research and were angry when the internet was disconnected or slowed down. In addition, it has been found that most participants are happy and peaceful when they use the internet, and that using the internet comforts them when they feel anxious or troubled.

1. INTRODUCTION

Internet 20 is one of the most important developments of the century. Since the Internet came into our lives, a new era has begun, societies have evolved, evolved,

DOI: 10.4018/979-8-3693-1182-0.ch007

transformed. This new era, which starts with the Internet, is called the "Age of Information". The Internet, which has become a very short time to be used, has been called the "World Wide Web" (www) and has become an integral part of people's lives. Because the Internet that makes people's lives easier has been an indispensable means of communication for people in order to provide them with different areas of communication, to make it easier to use, to economically and quickly. In particular, people prefer the use of the Internet to access information, to learn about news and developments in their environment or in different places, to surf the Internet, to chat with friends (Solmaz et al., 2013, p. 24; İrge, 2012, p. 77-82; Kılıç & Acar, 2020, p. 8).

The proliferation and increased use of the Internet creates positive situations in people's lives, while also causing negativity. People who want to go online for any reason or reason feel guilty, feel mentally ill and worried. People also think that as they stay away from Internet use, they are unaware of many situations and isolated. This affects their moods in a negative way. In particular, people's constant use of the Internet is due to reduced frequency of face-to-face communication, and the ability to perform social activities in the everyday life in virtual environments. The Internet, which meets people's needs for entertainment, information, making friends, socializing, and so on, ensures that they meet these needs that are mentioned when they go online. The fun, exciting and magical environment that the Internet offers is what drives people to overuse the Internet. But it causes them to lose and even break the bonds they have built with real life (Balcı & Gülnar, 2009, p. 6; Kılıç & Acar, 2020, p. 115).

The Internet that has come into our lives and the increasing use of the Internet, the inability to stop people from wanting to overuse the Internet and spend more time on the Internet, not enough time on the Internet, and people having extreme anger, stress and tension when they can't use the Internet, it causes the environment of friends and family to deteriorate due to excessive Internet access, which causes tension. These behaviors are generally defined as Internet dependency (Weinstein & Lejoyeux, 2010, p. 278). The concept of Internet dependency is defined by individuals dreaming about surfing the Internet, spending more time on the Internet, and going online when they're not on the Internet, even if they don't have any work. Whether people are aware of this situation or not, excessive use of the Internet is causing them to face a number of mental and physical health problems. At the same time, the occurrence of these situations sets the stage for social problems (Goldberg, 1996). People who are addicted to the Internet seem to have a reduced social relationship. They therefore face various problems in their personal relationship with their surroundings. Because the lack of communication and interaction, the lack of time for their families and friends, causes such problems to arise (Batıgün & Hasta, 2010, p. 214).

While people who are addicted to the Internet are more interested in online chatting, playing games, shopping online, it turns out that people who are not addicted to the Internet are often using the Internet to send e-mail and search for information (Yellowlees & Marks, 2007, p. 1449). Some people have their own self-control of their Internet use, while others do not have the ability to do this limitation on their own. Therefore, there are some problems within this topic. Learning these issues is of great importance to prevent Internet dependency (Bozkurt vd., 2016, p. 236). This research is the first study of the Çanakkale people to establish the current situation as part of their Internet usage and Internet dependence. Therefore, it is possible that this study is authentic.

2. INTERNET USE AND INTERNET COMMITMENT

Even if addictions such as alcohol, cigarettes, gambling, chemical substances occur to people who have heard of addiction, it is seen that the concept of addiction indicates a wide area. It is also known that there are also Internet dependencies, television monitoring dependencies, game addiction and non-chemical behavioral dependencies such as this (Bozkurt et al., 2016, p. 236).

There are many indicators of Internet dependency. It's an indication of Internet addiction that people are constantly wanting to use the Internet, and they're thinking about surfing the Internet and doing various activities there. The fact that Internet users enjoy their online participation in all kinds of online visits, their Internet trips, their activities, and their inability to satisfy them, also indicates Internet dependency. It also happens when users later find that the Internet is too much to use and think that the Internet is damaging their own life, they are unable to stop using the Internet. Because they're so used to the Internet and the unreal activities on the Internet that they feel uneasy and unhappy when they don't go online. People whose emotions are affected by this situation also feel nervous, nervous, anxious and helpless if they don't go online. They also turn back to Internet use to prevent these immortality. The people who have been through all of this are both displeased with themselves and their family and friends. People who are addicted to the Internet stay away from their social environment because they go online frequently and excessively. They also turn to lying to other people about the hours they log in and out of the Internet or the time they spend on the Internet. Because they're aware of their negative feelings when they can't go online (Young, 1998, p. 237-240). Young and his friends have mentioned that there are subtypes of Internet addiction. Virtual sex has concluded that relationships with different people online on the Internet through various activities, gambling with virtual roads on the Internet, searching, searching information on excessive and unnecessary sites on the Internet, and being on the computer for various reasons, make people addicted to the Internet (Young et al., 1999, p. 475-479).

Continuous and excessive Internet use causes both cognitive and behavioral disorders. Internet addiction is also caused by behavioral addiction. To do this, people need to see and differentiate the real and unreal situations. In addition, the awareness of people abusing the Internet, the use of the Internet on the place and on time, the increasing of book, newspaper reading habits and social, artistic activities, and the prolonging of time spent with family and friends are measures to prevent Internet addiction. It is important that the Internet is known at certain time intervals and knowingly used, to recognize the dangers of excessive Internet use and to take the necessary measures (Kurniasanti et al., 2019, p. 89-90; Kır & Sulak, 2014, p. 155; Alyanak, 2016, p. 21-22).

3. WORK ON INTERNET ADDICTION AND INTERNET USE HABITS

In order for this work to be carried out by the Scientific Research Ethics Board of the Graduate Education Institute of Çanakkale Onsekiz Mart University, the application with the application protocol number 2022-YÖNP-0315 was determined that the study was in accordance with the principles of the ethical board in 14.04.2022. Once the decision has been made, the work and data are collected.

4. RESEARCH METHOD, IMPLEMENTATION, AND SAMPLE

Based on the descriptive statistical method, a quantitative data analysis, this research was conducted against the people of Çanakkale. If you want to access any information about the research universe, selecting a group, sample, or sample from within this universe is with the general scanning model (Karasar, 2005). For this purpose, the study used the general scan model and found 211 participants of age 18-46 and above. The study data was accessed by taking an online survey to the participants.

5. MEASUREMENT TOOLS AND TESTS USED

In this study to examine the Internet dependence and Internet usage habits of Çanakkale people, a total of 22 questions of three sections have been addressed to participants. The six questions in the first section were asked to identify the demographic characteristics of the participants. The questions in the second section were asked to obtain data on the participants' Internet usage times and Internet usage purposes. The questions of Koçer (2012) in the "Internet use habits Scale" were used to measure the intended use of the Internet. In the last section, 11 questions were taken from Günüç (2009) in the "deprivation" section of "Internet Dependency Scale", which is used in his master's thesis. These questions in the last section have been aimed at uncovering feelings when participants use the Internet or are not using it. In addition, instead of using 5 Likert scales in the questions on the scale mentioned, questions were presented to participants as 3 Likert scale, "Yes", "No", "without decision".

Research Questions

1 - What do participants use the Internet most for?
2 - Do participants feel nervous or uneasy when they are not using the Internet?
3 - Do participants use the Internet to avoid their problems?
4 - Do participants search for Internet connections where they go?

6. FINDINGS

The work has been carried out for the people of Çanakkale. First, the socio-demographic characteristics of the participants have been examined. Also, information about how often they go online, how many minutes a day they spend on the Internet, where they connect to the Internet, and which device they connect more. In addition to this information, questions have been asked about the emotional state of the participants when they used the Internet, did not use the Internet, or used the Internet. The results of the data were based on frequency analysis and the percentage values obtained from the answers.

98.6% of respondents are shown to use the Internet every day. That's proof that the Internet is now an integral part of our lives.

Table 1. Frequency and percent values of gender of participants

		N (Total Number)	Percent (%)
Gender	Female	119	56,4
	Male	92	43,6
	Total	*211*	*100,0*

56,4% of the participants are females (N=119), 43,6% of the participants are males (N=92).

Table 2. Frequency and percent values of participants age range

		N (Total Number)	Percent (%)
Age Range	18-25	32	15,2
	26-35	87	41,2
	36-45	57	27
	Above 46	35	16,6
	Total	*211*	*100,0*

Age range of participants is 15,2% (N=32) 18-25 age, 41,2% (N=87) 26-35 age, 27% (N=57) 36-45 age and 16,6% (N=35) 46 and over.

Table 3. Marital status of participants

		N	Percent (%)
Married Single		123	58,3
		88	41,7
	Total	*211*	*100,0*

Marital status of the participants are; 48,3% (N=123) married, 41,7% (N=88) single.

Table 4. Educational status of participants

		N (Total Number)	Percent (%)
Education Status	Primary Education Graduate	7	3,3
	High School Graduate	34	16,1
	Associate Degree Graduate	20	9,5
	Undergraduate Degree	114	54
	Post Graduate	31	14,7
	Ph.D. Graduate	7	3,3
	Total	*211*	*100,0*

Participants of the research are 54% (N=114) Undergraduate Degree, 16,1% (N=34) High School Graduate, 14,7% (N=31) Post Graduate, 9,5% (N=20) Associate Degree Graduate, 3,3% (N=7) Primary Education Graduate, 3,3% (N=7) Ph.D. Graduate.

Table 5. Occupations of the participants

		N (Total Number)	Percent (%)
Occupations of the participants	Not working	36	17,1
	Private sector	60	28,4
	Public	103	48,8
	Self-employment	7	3,3
	Retired	5	2,4
	Total	*211*	*100,0*

Participants 17,1% (N=36)'i not working, 28,4% (N=60)'ü private sector, 48,8% (N=103)'si public, 3,3% (N=7)'si self-employment, 2,4% (N=5) Retired.

Table 6. Frequency and percent values of participants' income status

		N	Percent (%)
Income Status	0 TL-4000 TL	45	21,3
	4001 TL- 8000 TL	79	37,4
	8001TL -12000 TL	71	33,6
	Above 12000 TL	16	7,6
	Total	*211*	*100,0*

Income status of participants' are; 21,3% (N=45) 0-4000 TL, 37,4% (N=79) 4001 TL-8000 TL, 33,6% (N=71) 8001 TL- 12000TL and 7,6% (N=16) 12000 TL and over.

Figure 1. Participants' internet use frequency

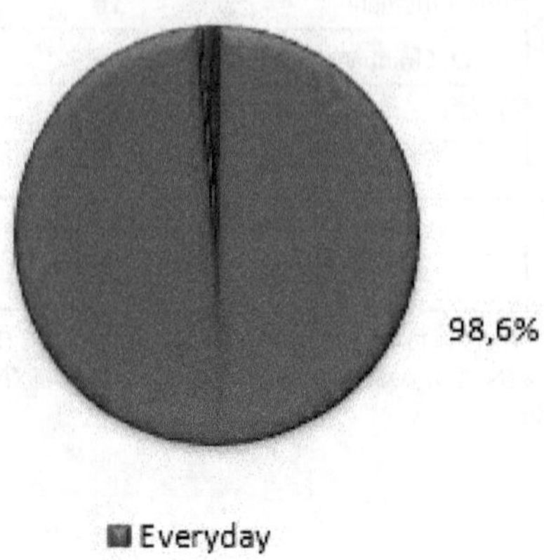

Figure 2. The time participants spend daily on the internet

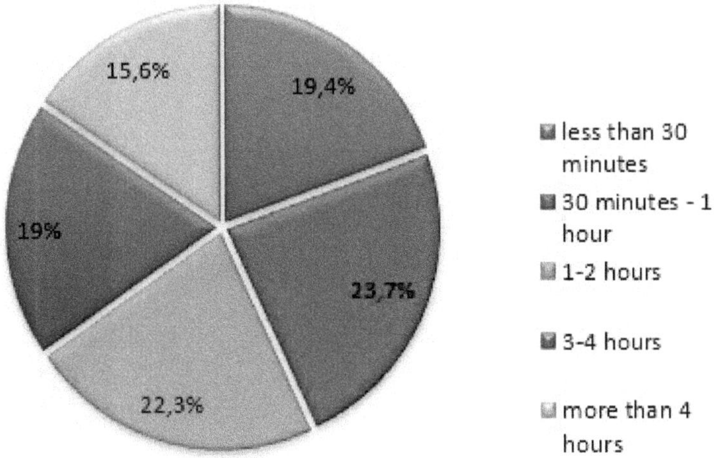

Figure 3. Where participants connect most to the internet

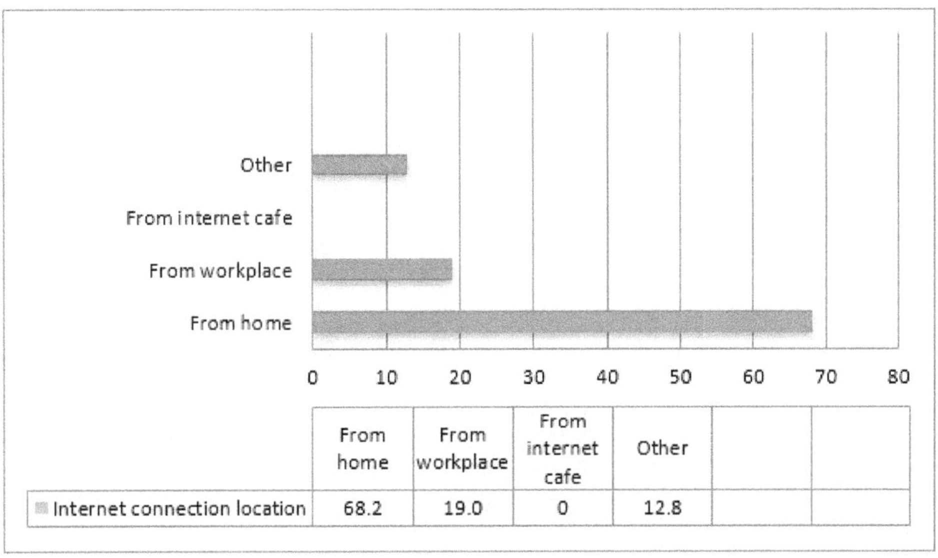

Looking at the time spent on the daily Internet, it is seen that 23.7% spend 30 minutes to 1 hours, 22.3% spend 1-2 hours, 19.4% less than 30 minutes, 19% 3-4 hours, 15.6% more than 4 hours on the Internet.

68.2% of respondents are posted online from home, 19% from work, 12.8% from other locations. There are no participants from the Internet cafe to the Internet.

Figure 4. The device participants connect to the internet most

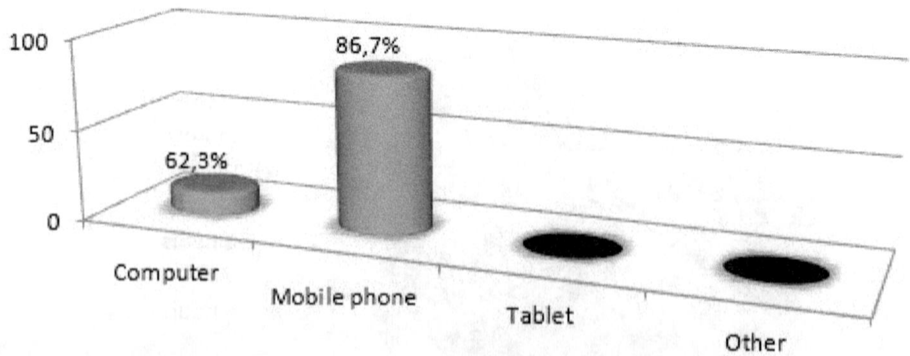

Figure 5. Participants' internet use reasons

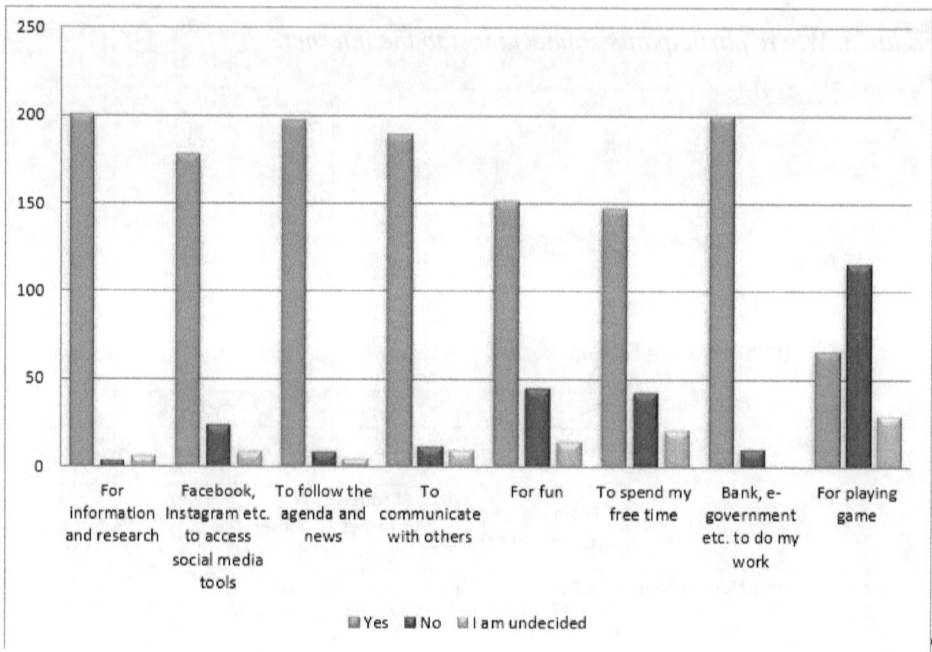

Participants find that at most 86.2% of the Internet is connected to the Internet from their mobile phones and 62.3% of the users are connected to the Internet from their computers. There are no participants connected to the Internet from tablets and other tools.

Figure 6. "Do you feel nervous/uneasy when you are not using the Internet?" A percentage of the answers they gave to their question.

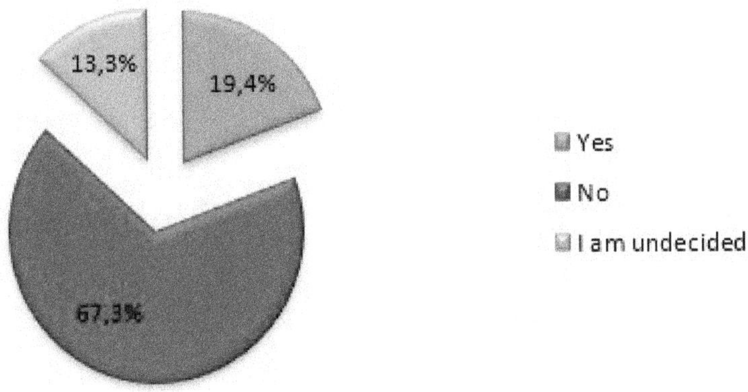

As shown in the graphic above, 200 participants are connected to the Internet for the most information and research. According to this number, the first research question has been answered. 199 participants are banks, e-government, etc. To do their job, 197 participants to follow the agenda, 189 people to communicate with others, 178 people to Facebook, Instagram, etc. to access social media tools, 151 people go online for fun and 147 people go online to spend their free time and 66 people go online to play games.

67.3% of respondents do not feel nervous/uneasy when they are not using the Internet. 19.4% of respondents feel nervous/uneasy when they are not using the Internet. If 13.3% participants have answered this question unambivalent. According to these answers, most participants are seen to be nervous or unrestless when they are not using the Internet, and the second research question is answered.

64% of respondents do not feel angry or angry when they are trying to use the Internet or not. 23.7%' participants feel angry and angry when they want to use the Internet and can't use it. the other participants, 12.3%, answered the question unresolved.

59.2% of respondents are frustrated if the Internet connection is lost or slowed down. at 26.5%, participants are not angry if the Internet connection is lost or slowed down. The remaining 14.2% participants have answered this question unresolved.

42.7% of respondents feel happy and peaceful when using the Internet. 24.2% of respondents do not feel happy and peaceful when using the Internet. The participants are shown to have an indecisive response from 33.2% of this question.

40.3% of respondents are shown to be directed toward Internet use when they feel anxious or troubled. at 38.9%, it turns out that participants do not seek Internet use

Figure 7. "Do you get angry/angry when you want to use the Internet or not?" A percentage of the answers they gave to their question.

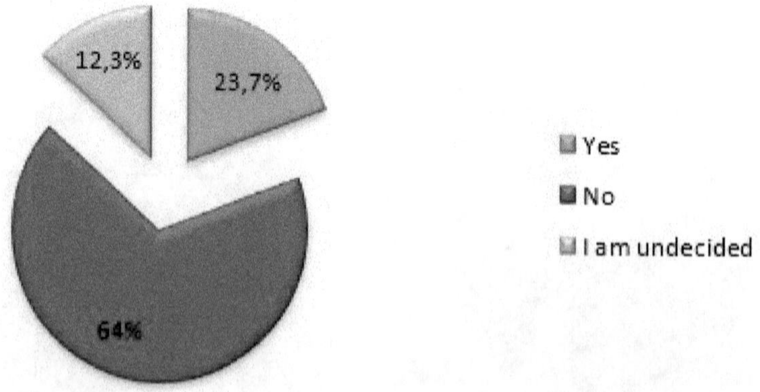

Figure 8. "Would you be angry if the Internet connection is lost or slowed down?" A percentage of the answers they gave to their question.

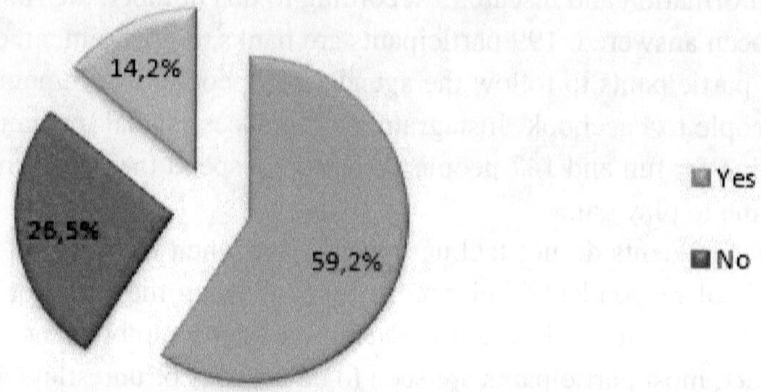

Figure 9. "Do you be happy/peaceful when you use the internet?" A percentage of the answers they gave to their question.

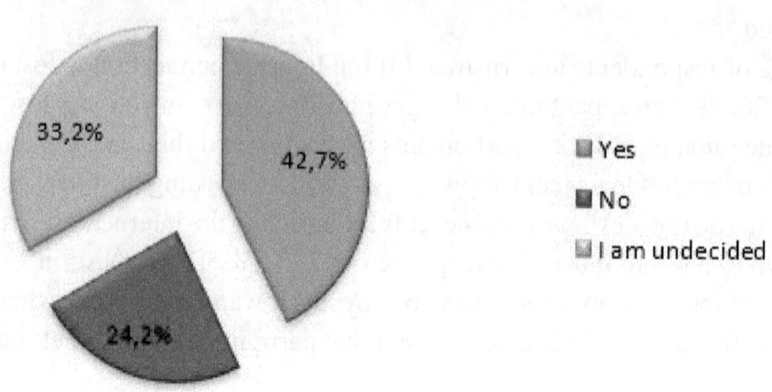

Figure 10. "Do you feel comfortable using the Internet when you feel anxious or troubled?" A percentage of the answers they gave to their question.

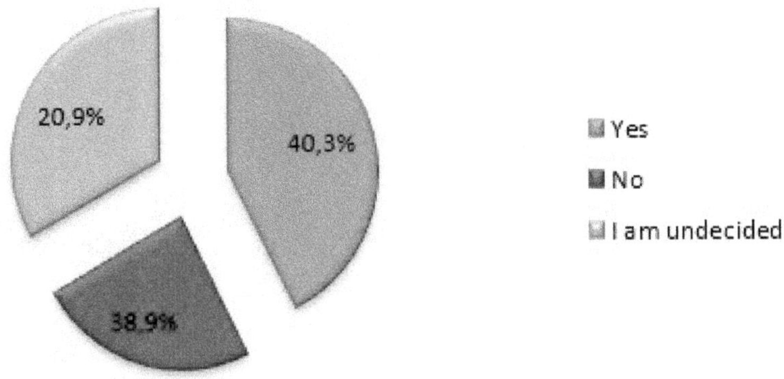

Figure 11. "Would you be angry if someone took you off the internet?" A percentage of the answers they gave to their question.

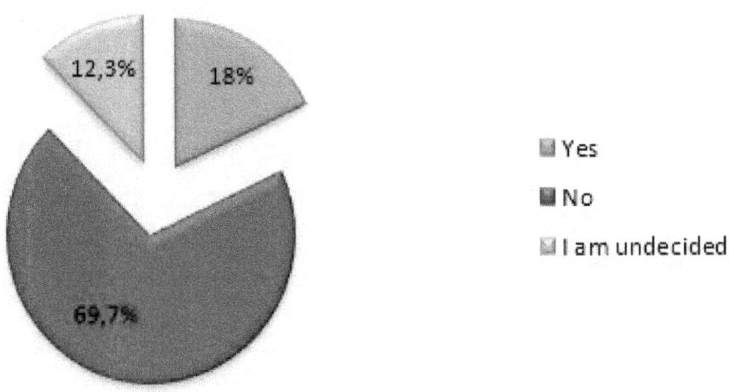

when they feel anxious or troubled. 20.9% of respondents answered this question unresolved.

69.7% of respondents are shown not to be angry with the situation that someone has taken them away from the beginning of the Internet, and 18% are angry at it. The remaining 12.3% of the respondents have found that they have responded to this situation unresolved.

54% of respondents do not use the Internet to avoid their problems. 28.9% respondents responded to their use of the Internet to avoid their problems. at 17.1%, the other participants were hesitant to answer the question. The result of data was

Figure 12. "Would you be willing to use the internet to avoid your problems?" A percentage of the answers they gave to their question.

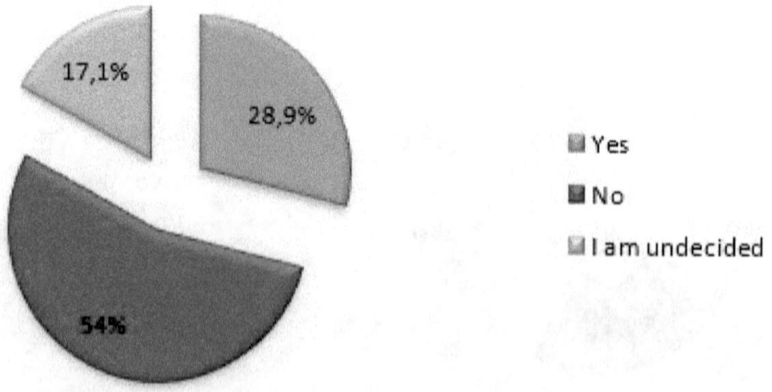

Figure 13. "Would you be angry if you couldn't enter the internet when you plan to?" A percentage of the answers they gave to their question.

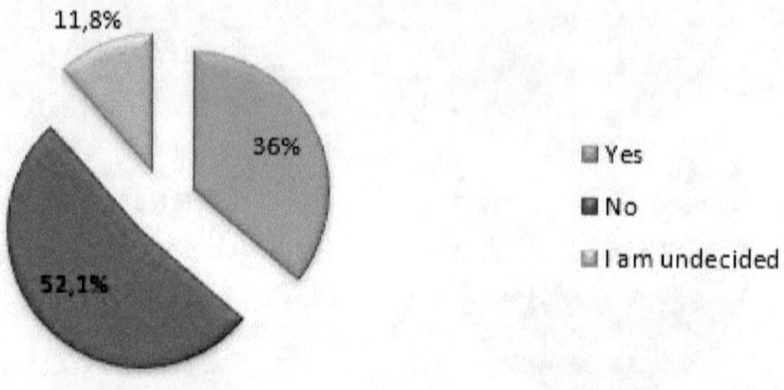

central, as many of the participants did not go online to avoid their problems. The third research question was then answered.

52.1% of respondents are not angry when they are planning to go online and 36% are angry. If 11.8% participants have answered this question unresolved.

19.9% of respondents want to be alone and go online with people around you. 65.4% of them don't want to be alone and go online with people around you. If 14.7% participants have answered this question unresolved.

When not using the Internet, 67.8% of respondents are not impatient to go online, while 19% are impatient. If 13.3% participants are unsure of this question.

Figure 14. "Would you like to be alone and go online with people around you?" A percentage of the answers they gave to their question.

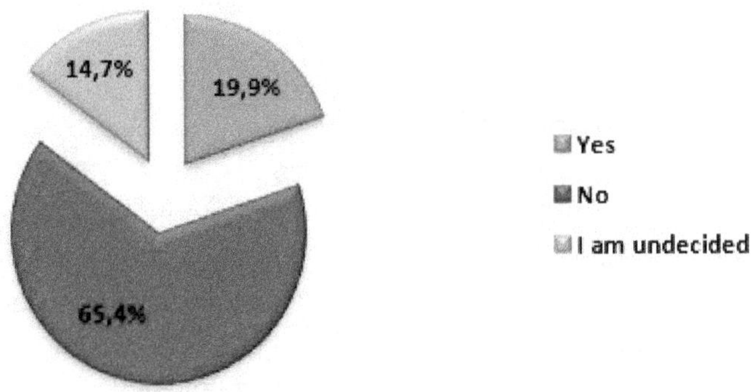

Figure 15. "Can't wait to get online when you're not using the internet?" A percentage of the answers they gave to their question.

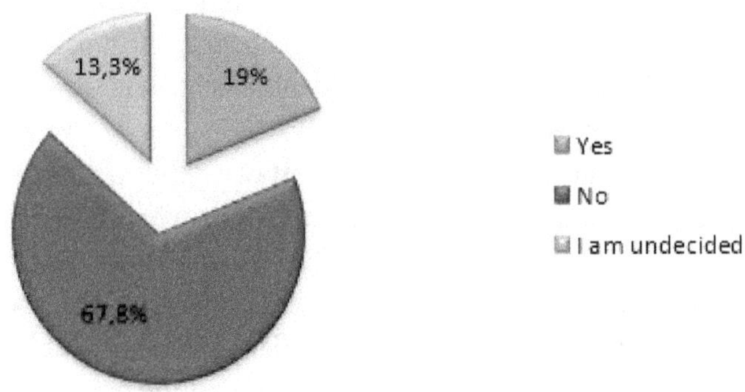

Figure 16. "Would you look for an Internet connection where you are going?" A percentage of the answers they gave to their question.

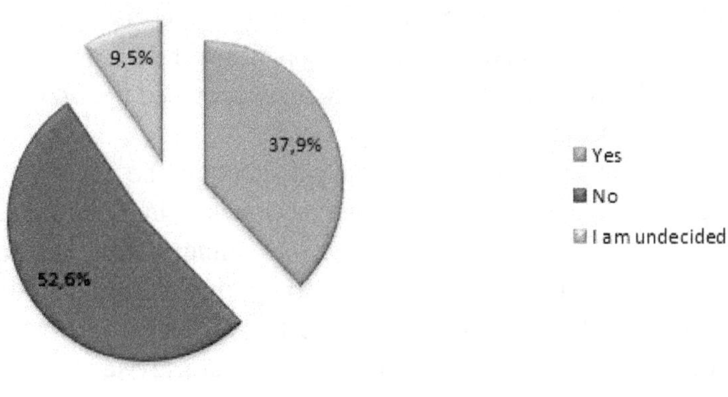

52.6 of the respondents do not search for Internet connections where they go, while 37.9% search for the Internet. 9.5% of respondents responded unresolved to this question. The fourth research question was then answered.

7. RESULTS AND ASSESSMENT

This research has been conducted to determine the Internet addiction and Internet usage habits of Çanakkale people. The study examined the socio-demographic characteristics of the Çanakkale people first. There are also questions about how often Çanakkale people go online, where they go online, which device they use most to access the Internet, how they use the Internet, and how they determine their Internet dependencies.

The research results in many important data. First of all, almost all who participate in the research use the Internet every day. This is an indication that the Internet is essential every moment of our lives and that people need the Internet. Most participants spend time online every day from 30 minutes to 1 hours. Participants often prefer to connect from home and mobile phones to the Internet. Most participants, in turn, are informed of the Internet and researched, bank, e-state, etc. they use it to handle their business, to keep track of the agenda.

Most participants do not feel nervous or unrest when they do not use the Internet. In addition, participants do not feel anger and anger when they want to use the Internet or not. But when they go online, the disconnect or deceleration of the Internet makes most of the respondents angry. The research data shows that most participants tend to use the Internet when they feel happy and peaceful when they use the Internet and feel worried, troubled. So it is said that the participants of Internet use make them feel emotionally good. When a large part of the respondents have a problem with something, they do not seek to use the Internet to avoid their issues. Participants also stated that they were not angry when they couldn't go online when they were planning, and that they were surrounded by people, they were alone, they didn't want to go online, they didn't look for Internet connections where they were going, and they couldn't wait to get online when they weren't using the Internet. In fact, this is an indication that the participants have provided their own self-control of their use of the Internet.

In this study, aimed at revealing the current situation, the further advancement of technology is focused on a number of issues aimed at increasing the use of the Internet and increased Internet dependence of communication technologies. So given that we do everything online, it's safe to say that becoming addicted to the Internet can be inevitable. Therefore, it is important to prevent Internet dependence and take necessary measures. To prevent this, people are advised to be aware of the correct use of the Internet at an early age. In addition, in the changing and evolving technology age, it is thought that the research on these issues should be updated, increased, and their relationship with different variables should be examined, given that new formations will occur through the Internet and the Internet. Because further research is recommended to identify the causes of Internet dependence and to take precautions on Internet dependency to prevent Internet dependency.

REFERENCES

Alyanak, B. (2016). Internet addiction. *Journal of Clinical Medicine Pediatrics, 8*(5), 20–24.

Aviv, W., & Lejoyeux, M. (2010). Internet Addiction or Excessive Internet Use. *The American Journal of Drug and Alcohol Abuse, 36*(5), 277–283. doi:10.3109/00952990.2010.491880 PMID:20545603

Balcı, Ş., & Gülnar, B. (2009). Internet addiction among university students and the profile of Internet addicts. *Journal of Selcuk Communication, 6*(1), 5–22.

Batıgün, A. D., & Hasta, D. (2010). Internet addiction: An evaluation in terms of loneliness and interpersonal relationship styles. *Anatolian Journal of Psychiatry, 11*(3), 213–219.

Bozkurt, H., Şahin, S., & Zoroğlu, S. (2016). Internet addiction: A current review. *Journal of Contemporary Medicine, 6*(3), 235–247.

Goldberg, I. (1996). *Internet Addiction Disorder*. Academic Press.

Günüç, S. (2009). *Development of the Internet addiction scale and examination of the relationships between some demographic variables and the Internet* [Master's thesis]. Yüzüncü Yıl University, Institute of Social Sciences, Faculty of Educational Sciences. Department of Curriculum and Instruction.

İbrahim, K. I. R., & Sulak, Ş. Examination of Internet Addiction Levels of Education Faculty Students. *Electronic Journal of Social Sciences, 13*(51).

İrge, N. F. (2012). In the Process of Information Society and Social Change Social media. *Akdeniz University Faculty of Communication Journal*, (17), 63–86.

Karasar, N. (2005). Scientific research method. Ankara: Nobel Publishing Distribution.

Kılıç, Ü., & Acar, N. (2020). A field research on virtual religious communication motivations: Sivas Cumhuriyet University students. *Journal of Media and Religious Studies, 3*(1), 5–22.

Kılıç, Ü., & Acar, N. (2020). *A Qualitative Research on University Students' Religious Internet Use and Satisfaction. In Art and Communication Studies*. Iksad Publications.

Koçer, M. (2012). Internet and social media usage habits of Erciyes University students. *Akdeniz University Faculty of Communication Journal*, (18), 70–85.

Kurniasanti, K. S., Assandi, P., Ismail, R. I., Nasrun, M. W. S., & Wiguna, T. (2019). Internet addiction: A newaddiction? *Medical Journal of Indonesia*, *28*(1), 82–91. doi:10.13181/mji.v28i1.2752

Solmaz, B., Tekin, G., Herzem, Z., & Demir, M. (2013). An Application on Internet and Social Media Usage. *Journal of Selcuk Communication*, *7*(4), 23–32.

Yellowlees, P. M., & Marks, S. (2007). Problematic Internet use or Internet addiction? *Computers in Human Behavior*, *23*(3), 1447–1453. doi:10.1016/j.chb.2005.05.004

Young, K., Pistner, M., O'mara, J., & Buchanan, J. (1999). Cyber disorders: The mental health concern for the new millennium. *Cyberpsychology & Behavior*, *2*(5), 475–479. doi:10.1089/cpb.1999.2.475 PMID:19178220

Young, K. S. (1998). Internet Addiction: The Emergence of a New Clinical Disorder. *Cyberpsychology & Behavior*, *1*(3), 237–244. doi:10.1089/cpb.1998.1.237

Chapter 8
The Reflections of the Digital Nomad Community on Social Media:
A Case Study on Twitter

Burak Ili
https://orcid.org/0000-0003-2816-101X
Iğdır University, Turkey

ABSTRACT

Digital nomads, who can be defined as individuals capable of conducting all their work digitally and frequently traveling without being tied to a fixed home or workplace, are pursuing a lifestyle characterized by flexibility and freedom. This research aims to uncover how the concept is defined on the Twitter social network, specifically within the context of the #digitalnomad hashtag. Designed as a qualitative study, content analysis was employed as the data analysis strategy. The obtained data were subjected to analysis using the qualitative analysis software MAXQDA. According to the findings, the most frequently used hashtags alongside #digitalnomad were found to be #workfromhome, #remotework, #remotejob, #workanywhere, #workfromanywhere, #freelance, #passiveincome, #entrepreneur, #travel, and #coworking. This indicates that the concept of digital nomadism is predominantly associated with financial freedom and promises individuals a more flexible lifestyle.

DOI: 10.4018/979-8-3693-1182-0.ch008

INTRODUCTION

The widespread adoption of internet technologies and the widespread use of mobile devices have led to profound changes in the lifestyles of individuals and societies. People are pursuing a more liberated and mobile lifestyle facilitated by the opportunities offered by digital technologies. The most prominent and tangible manifestation of this quest is digital nomadism, symbolizing the emergence of a new experience that challenges traditional patterns of work and lifestyle. This experience encompasses the independence, flexibility, and freedom of individuals. The phenomenon of digital nomadism has attracted attention in the academic world and has been extensively researched. In recent years, there has been an increasing interest in and academic studies on the digital nomad community (Müller, 2016; Mancinelli, 2020; Reichenberger, 2018; Cook, 2022; Šímová, 2023). These studies aim to define digital nomadism and address topics related to remote work and lifestyle choices within the community, as well as the working conditions of digital nomads.

With digitization, in addition to working full-time from an office, flexible work models such as remote work and freelancing have become popular. Companies are increasingly collaborating with remote workers or digital nomads, as it is often less costly than hiring a full-time employee Digital nomads can conduct their work from anywhere they choose, such as cafes, beaches, or coworking spaces, outside the confines of their homes. This freedom allows them to set their own working hours and conditions. Many digital nomads embrace a mobile lifestyle driven by a desire to travel and explore new cultures without being tethered to a traditional office. The fundamental tools for digital nomads are remote working tools such as video conferencing, instant messaging, cloud storage, and collaboration software. These tools make it possible to bridge distant locations and different time zones worldwide.

Countries that recognize the potential of digital nomads who contribute economically and culturally to the places they travel to view them as an economic opportunity (Busuttil, 2021). As a result, the number of various regulations such as visa facilitations, shared work and living spaces, and the improvement of wireless internet infrastructure aimed at attracting digital nomads to their cities and countries is increasing day by day. These practices aim to boost the local economy by drawing in digital nomads (Sánchez-Vergara, Orel, & Capdevila, 2023).

As the COVID-19 pandemic led to lockdowns around the world, significant changes emerged on a global scale, and many areas, from education to the economy, transitioned to digital operations. The closure of borders, the halt in transportation, and the inability of businesses to open restricted travel mobility. However, these circumstances also led to the experimentation with potential remote work and new business models (Hermann & Paris, 2020, p. 329). Additionally, COVID-19, out of necessity, made remote and home-based work models popular. It blurred the traditional boundaries between work, home, leisure, and travel, contributing to the rise of digital nomadism (Ehn, Jorge, & Marques-Pita, 2022). This extraordinary process compelled people to work from home or remotely, even when they had no prior experience with these models. Even after the COVID-19 pandemic, businesses continue to offer their employees the opportunity to work from either their homes or any location around the world as a result of the experiences gained during this period. Individuals who have experienced the ability to conduct most of their work digitally are increasingly turning to remote work and the digital nomad lifestyle in pursuit of greater flexibility. Individuals actively use social media for purposes such as communication and acquiring information. In addition to individuals, businesses and organizations also utilize social media with the goals of sustaining their presence, staying competitive, and engaging with users. For digital nomads and businesses alike, social media serves as a practical and effective tool for various functions, including finding potential jobs and customers, conducting advertising and promotional activities, and enhancing brand values and visibility. Social media networks like Instagram, YouTube, and Facebook have become spaces where digital nomads can actively share their experiences and even conduct their businesses directly. It has been observed that tourists, travelers, and digital nomads increasingly take online ideas and recommendations into account when planning their travel itineraries, coinciding with the widespread use of social media (Magnini, Crotts, & Zehrer, 2011).

This research aims to contribute to the literature by identifying and uncovering a series of embedded subthemes within the digital nomad community on Twitter.

DIGITAL NOMAD COMMUNITY

The digital nomad community has emerged as a significant trend in recent years, impacting the business world, digital technologies, and individuals' lifestyles. Digital nomads are characterized by various descriptors, such as a business model, a type of traveler, and a way of life, and they constitute a trend with increasing numbers and popularity each year. Digital nomads, who prefer not to be tied to a traditional office and working hours, can conduct all their work digitally through laptops and other portable devices. Their ability to often set their own working hours and work from the location of their choice plays a significant role in maintaining a travel-focused lifestyle. The fact that many jobs and professions can be performed digitally today suggests that the number of digital nomads is likely to continue increasing in the future.

When examining the literature related to the digital nomad community, it is observed that research predominantly focuses on lifestyle aspects (Bonneau et al.,

2023; Chevtaeva & Denizci-Guillet, 2021; Thompson, 2019; Toivanen, 2023), shared workspaces (Hemsley et al., 2020; Orel, 2019; Pacheco & Azevedo, 2023; Von Zumbusch et al., 2020), the relationship between work and leisure (Cook, 2020; Rainoldi et al., 2022), economy (Sutherland & Jarrahi, 2017; Woldoff & Litchfield, 2021), and tourism (Håkansson & Bejaković, 2023; Prabawa & Pertiwi, 2020; Vagena, 2021). Within this scope, both the absence of a consensus on a clear definition for the concept of digital nomadism and the confusion of digital nomads with closely related terms such as remote workers and freelancers emphasize the necessity of establishing precise definitions and characteristics for the concept.

The concept of digital nomadism was first introduced by Makimoto and Manners (1997) in their book where they expressed the idea that human lives would undergo a radical transformation as a result of new media technologies, new work arrangements, and entrepreneurial practices. They advocated for the idea of a global world. Since then, research on digital nomadism has revealed various classifications of the concept. When examining the research conducted on digital nomadism from that time to the present, it becomes evident that the concept has been defined within different classifications. It has been characterized as a type of backpacker-style travel (MacRae, 2016), a typology of tourists engaged in coworking and communal living (Chevtaeva, 2021), and a new way of life (Thompson, 2019). Individuals who reject settled living and traditional work models in favor of a more flexible and free lifestyle, traveling frequently and conducting all their work remotely through digital means, can be described as digital nomads. The key distinction that sets digital nomads apart from other remote, freelance, and flexible workers is their continuous pursuit of a nomadic lifestyle characterized by constant travel in search of greater freedom and a better life (Schlagwein, 2018, p. 32). Kropp (2018) suggests that all digital nomads can be considered as freelance or remote workers, but not all freelance or remote workers qualify as digital nomads. This distinction arises primarily from the fact that digital nomads choose a mobile lifestyle, in contrast to the settled lifestyle preference of others. Digital nomads who combine remote work with travel are predominantly English-speaking, hailing from North America and Europe, and are often well-educated knowledge workers (Statista, 2023). This situation creates a certain privilege for them compared to other digital nomads. Digital nomads with strong passports and national identities have an advantage over others in terms of traveling more frequently and easily. While digital technologies and the internet enable people to communicate limitlessly and work remotely, the country of birth and citizenship individuals hold remain significant factors affecting the work and living conditions of digital nomads. This highlights the presence of inequality among digital nomads. One of the most powerful motivations behind digital nomadism is the desire for a free lifestyle and work style. In this context, the community traditionally enjoys the opportunity to work from wherever they please (such as cafes, libraries, beachfronts, coworking spaces, etc.) without being tied to a fixed home or workplace (Orel, 2019). Additionally, digital nomads consider criteria such as internet speed and connectivity, climate, monthly average cost of living, accommodation options, visa requirements, and natural and cultural attractions when choosing destinations for their travels. Working from home or remotely instead of a traditional office is more environmentally beneficial. When daily workplace commutes decrease or disappear, air pollution, greenhouse gas emissions, and carbon footprints are reduced. Given the current climate crisis, remote and flexible working is seen as a more eco-friendly approach (Prossack, 2021).

Digital nomads are the new generation of digital workers who can work worldwide, leaving their homes behind. Typically engaged in project-based or short-term work, this community consists of cosmopolitan individuals who embrace the world as their home beyond their national identities and reject national boundaries. Unlike traditional nomadism, digital nomads mostly travel alone and maintain a lifestyle that is based on preference rather than necessity.

DIGITAL NOMADS AND NEW BUSINESS MODELS

The relationship between digital nomads and new and existing economic models has become an increasingly prominent research area. According to David (2016), this community can be categorized in three ways: The first category comprises individuals employed by international companies who work remotely. The second and most common category includes freelancers whose work is often based on the gig economy and flexible arrangements. The third and final category consists of entrepreneurs. Furthermore, digital nomads often gravitate towards digital jobs that are suitable for remote and flexible work, such as web design, software engineering, social media management, digital content creation, graphic design, and digital marketing (Hermann & Paris, 2020, p. 332). Emerging technologies like the Internet of Things, artificial intelligence, virtual and augmented reality, and blockchain have played a significant role in the emergence of new professions and business models in recent years. Digital nomads, who reject the imposed work models and lifestyles of today, have transcended local and national boundaries and identities, becoming an economic opportunity and commodity for companies, institutions, and countries (Busuttil, 2021).

The global mobile workforce has gained significant momentum in recent years (Ameen et al., 2021). This trend has led to a rapid increase in coworking and communal living spaces that cater to digital nomads and remote workers as alternatives to traditional offices. These shared workspaces, often frequented by independent knowledge workers, offer not only cost savings but also new business and socialization opportunities (Spinuzzi, Bodrožić, Scaratti, & Ivaldi, 2019). In recent years, many communal living and working spaces have been established to serve digital nomads and remote workers. These spaces are designed not just as offices but as work environments integrated with social areas (Bilandzic & Foth, 2013). They encourage networking among coworkers and support socialization, making them a preferred choice. While the term "coworking" may imply working together, it also signifies a new working concept that allows individuals with different professional backgrounds to collaborate, share opportunities, and connect with each other (Johns & Gratton, 2013). The connections formed in communal working and living spaces contribute to the well-being of digital nomads, primarily in terms of both economics and socialization (Naz, 2016).

The convergence of the gig economy, characterized by short-term jobs, and digital technologies allows digital nomads to work in their desired destinations without being bound by traditional employment rules. This often leads digital nomads to engage in project-based and temporary work arrangements (De Stefano, 2016). Companies are increasingly collaborating with remote workers and digital nomads because it is often more cost-effective than hiring full-time employees (Frey, 2013, p. 46). The growth in the number of digital nomads has drawn the attention of companies, destinations, and countries, making it inevitable for new regulations to be put in place, such as visa exemptions, shared working and living spaces, and high-speed wireless internet access for this community. In addition to being creative, innovative, and willing to take risks, digital nomads are also conscious and rational consumers. They often utilize and popularize new trends in consumer behavior based on collaboration and collective structures. This attitude can be associated with the sharing economy (Botsman & Rogers, 2010). The sharing economy is an increasingly popular economic model today, allowing people to generate additional income by sharing their resources or services or accessing their needs more economically and sustainably. The sharing economy is based on people sharing, bartering, or renting goods and services. Businesses like Airbnb, Couchsurfing, and Uber are successful examples of the sharing economy.

The flexibility and mobility offered by the digital nomad lifestyle are seen as opportunities for digital workers. However, this lifestyle also presents various challenges for individuals trying to strike a balance between freedom and stability (Richter & Richter, 2020). Common challenges for digital nomads, who often engage in project-based and short-term work, include the absence of regular and stable income, limited visa durations, varying regulations in different countries concerning taxation and healthcare, difficulty in balancing work and personal life, and an inability to form lasting relationships due to frequent travel, resulting in feelings of loneliness. On the flip side, the digital nomad lifestyle offers opportunities such as escaping negative aspects of traditional work models like workplace harassment, pressure to meet deadlines, and pressure from bosses. It also allows for the exploration of new places. These opportunities can be seen as advantages for both existing digital nomads and those aspiring to become digital nomads. Digital nomads have the potential to create new entrepreneurial opportunities in addition to traditional work models. They reject traditional office environments and working for a single company in favor of running their own businesses and setting their own workspaces and hours. Flexible work formats like remote work and freelancing enable digital nomads to carry out their work globally. Moreover, digital nomadism not only changes working patterns but also fosters innovation in business models. Digital nomads are exploring new business opportunities in various sectors, such as the sharing economy and online marketplaces. Platforms like Airbnb, Uber, and Fiverr serve as both sources of income and opportunities to provide services for digital nomads. Additionally, digital nomads who generate additional income through social media networks like Instagram and YouTube are pushing the boundaries of the traditional business world, combining work and travel experiences to open the doors to a more free and flexible lifestyle.

THE ROLE OF SOCIAL MEDIA ON DIGITAL NOMADS

Social media platforms that first emerged in the early 2000s have brought together billions of people worldwide and have fundamentally changed both individual and societal communication methods. While initially introduced as platforms that facilitated communication among friends and family members, over time, social media has brought about a significant transformation used by various sectors such as business, politics, education, and more. Platforms like Facebook, Twitter, YouTube, Instagram, and LinkedIn have enabled individuals to establish personal and professional relationships, access news, and express themselves.

Social media has the potential to reach and engage both existing and potential consumers and create a strong image for a business or product. When used correctly and effectively, it can make positive contributions in various areas, from marketing to commerce, from establishing new business partnerships to enhancing brand image (Infante & Mardikaningsih, 2022, p. 46). Additionally, social media and the internet bring together interpersonal communication, corporate communication, and mass communication, effectively bringing the entire world into homes and workplaces (van Dijk, 2006, p. 241).

In March 2020, when COVID-19 had a widespread impact worldwide and the quarantine period began, it was found that there was a 15-fold increase in the number of tweets related to remote work compared to the pre-pandemic period (Wrycza & Maślankowski, 2020, p. 295). In another study, 60 digital nomads with open profiles on social media were examined, and it was found that many of them shared their experiences with other users, provided advice to those aspiring to become digital nomads, and generated significant income through sponsorships and product promotions (Bonneau & Aroles, 2021). This indicates that digital nomads are commodifying their life experiences through social media. Todd (2022) identifies the reasons why social media platforms are important and effective tools for digital nomads as follows:

- **Networking and Community Building**: Social media platforms allow digital nomads to connect with like-minded individuals, form communities, and share insights, tips, and experiences related to their lifestyle.
- **Self-Promotion and Branding**: Digital nomads can use social media to promote themselves as personal brands, showcase their skills, and attract potential clients or employers.
- **Income Generation**: Many digital nomads leverage their social media presence to secure sponsorships, partnerships, and advertising deals, which can provide a significant source of income.
- **Information and Resource Sharing**: Social media platforms are hubs of information where digital nomads can access valuable resources, such as travel recommendations, accommodation options, and work opportunities.
- **Lifestyle Documentation**: Social media allows digital nomads to document their unique lifestyle, adventures, and travel experiences, which can be both personally fulfilling and appealing to their followers.

Digital nomads actively creating content, generating income, and engaging with users on social media is crucial for their lifestyle. They produce content such as vlogs and travel articles by sharing their lifestyle, and they can also use social media networks like YouTube and Instagram with the intention of directly earning income. Advertisements, sponsorships, and paid content through these platforms serve as significant sources of income for digital nomads. Therefore, it can be said that social media holds critical importance for digital nomads. They use social media actively for various purposes, including socializing, finding work, sharing their lifestyle and experiences, and directly earning income in both their personal and professional lives.

METHODOLOGY

The rise of the World Wide Web (WWW) has provided data in various fields for content analysis research. Previously inaccessible data has become accessible and available to everyone. Through software that can analyze even complex data, researchers have found convenience (Weare & Lin, 2000). Content analysis is one of the methods that facilitates examining and categorizing data in detail. It is a flexible research method applied in many different fields according to various research objectives and purposes (White & Marsh, 2006).

In the study aimed at uncovering the content of digital nomads' social media posts and determining how digital nomadism is positioned on Twitter (Even though it is currently used under the name X, the term "Twitter" is used because it was used as Twitter at the time the work was done), a qualitative research design called a case study was preferred. The intended case to be revealed is what digital nomadism is associated with in the posts of digital nomads or in tweets shared about digital nomadism.

Within this scope, the data were automatically collected between April 16, 2023, and May 14, 2023. Using the Twitter extension of MAXQDA software, 16,991 tweets with the #digitalnomad hashtag were automatically prepared for analysis. Other hashtags used in conjunction with this hashtag were categorized and examined in detail. Additionally, the frequency of hashtag usage and the texts related to digital nomads/nomadism were analyzed. The analysis results were visualized and tabulated using MAXQDA software. The data was obtained through automatic coding, resulting in 19 files, and word frequencies were automatically counted within these files. The total number of words counted was determined to be 422,135. After the process of excluding words such as stop words, combined words (digitalnomad-digitalnomads, etc.), erroneous words, and letters, the total word count obtained was 333,708. When repeated word groups were combined, 29,088 words were identified. Below, the word frequencies and word groups obtained are shared. From the MAXQDA visual tools tab, a word cloud and frequency representing the research were selected, and 20 words are shown in the table. In the word cloud, 100 words are visualized to represent the research, with the most frequently repeated word shown the largest, and the colors are arbitrary. The word frequency in the table is included in the word cloud.

RESULTS FROM #DIGITALNOMAD HASHTAG IN TWITTER

The first finding of the research is the word percentages and frequencies. Word percentages and frequencies provide a general framework of the study's content and offer clues about the research. The most mentioned and prominently featured "https" extension indicates that users tweeting about digital nomads or digital nomads themselves, as well as employers, provide job listings through links.

When the data is examined, many job listings are being updated on Twitter, and particularly the same users post listings almost every day. The high frequency of

Table 1. Word percentages and frequencies for the data

Words	Frequency	Percent
https	13515	4,05
digitalnomad	12120	3,63
English	5420	1,62
workfromhome	5391	1,62
remotework	4398	1,32
Twitter	3300	0,99
remotejobs	2867	0,86
App	2628	0,79
Web	2495	0,75
hiring	2222	0,67
jobsearch	2219	0,66
jobhunt	2188	0,66
Remote	2172	0,65
techjobs	2156	0,65
travel	1830	0,55
DigitalNomad	1753	0,53
jobs	1505	0,45
digital	1436	0,43
makemoneyonline	1367	0,40

Figure 1. Word cloud for the data

the word "digitalnomad" is due to its inclusion in the scope of the study and being a searched word on Twitter. The words "workfromhome," "remotework," and "remotejobs" are words that express the flexible work structure of digital nomadism.

In Figure 1, the most frequently used hashtags along with #digitalnomad are visualized as a word cloud. Accordingly, it is concluded that the concept of digital nomadism is frequently associated with terms and word groups such as working from home, remote work, freelancing, entrepreneurship, travel, and passive income.

Digital nomads have the freedom to work from all around the world, thanks to the global accessibility of the internet and remote work opportunities. This community frequently utilizes online tools such as social media platforms to promote their work, engage with clients, and share their travel experiences. Specifically on Twitter, they use the platform for purposes such as self-promotion of their businesses, networking with other digital nomads, employers, and service providers, staying updated on current trends and developments, and sharing their experiences. Twitter, serving not only their professional endeavors but also their social lives, stands out as a significant tool for digital nomads.

One noteworthy result identified in the analysis is that tweets using the #digitalnomad hashtag on Twitter are often used in conjunction with other hashtags:

"🌟 *Embrace the #freelance life & unleash your true potential!* 🚀 *Break free from the 9-5 & shape your own destiny* 🌈✨ *Be fearless, be bold, be YOU!* 😎🔥 *#Freelancer #DigitalNomad #WorkFromAnywhere #Hustle #DreamBig #RemoteWork #BeYourOwnBoss* 💼🌍✈️🏄🔝 "

Table 2. Frequencies of hashtags

Hashtags	Frequency Σ
#digitalnomad/s	6541
#workfromhome	2413
#remotework	2407
#remotejob/s	1622
#workanywhere/workfromanywhere	837
#freelance/r/ing	459
#passiveincome	373
#entepreneur	365
#travel	281
#coworking	107

Table 3. Hashtags and text mentioned in tweets

Texts Mentioned in Tweets	Hashtags in Tweets
"Anything could happen when you're traveling as a digital nomad."	#digitalnomad #remotework #traveltips
"Looking for a flexible way to earn money? Learn about these 7 online side hustles that can be done from anywhere in the world!"	#digitalnomad #locationindependent #travel
"Being a freelancer is all about being your own boss, setting your own hours, and taking on projects you're truly passionate about. It's not always easy, but the freedom and flexibility make it all worth it."	#freelancing #workfromhome #digitalnomad
"Being a digital nomad isn't just about working from anywhere - it's about building a life on your own terms. Are you ready to take the leap?"	#digitalnomad #remotework #lifestyle #techie #wfa
"Looking for a profitable side hustle? Discover why Airbnb is a great option! Boost your income, meet new people and build valuable skills."	#Airbnb #sidehustle #entrepreneurship #makemoney #hospitality #travel #financialfreedom #passiveincome #investment #digitalnomad
"Need an office where you can work flexibly and without too much financial commitment? Don't worry! We provide open spaces so that you can work in the greatest possible comfort, even with access to a kitchen."	#unoffice #empreendedorismo #business #coworking #digitalnomad
"Taking into account visas, quality of life, and cost - What do you think is the best country for digital nomads in Europe?"	#remotework #europe #digitalnomad #travel
"Choose digital nomad locations wisely consider affordability, reliable wifi, and suitability for your needs. Geo-arbitrage can be an advantage but live within your means. Appreciate your current circumstances while pursuing your goals."	#digitalnomad #yonderpreneur #entrepreneurs
"Freelancing has become a popular way to work in today's digital age. With the freedom to choose your clients and projects, it's no wonder why so many people are taking the leap and becoming their own boss!"	#freelancing #workfromhome #digitalnomad"
"FINANCIAL INDEPENDENCE - Starting a business with Forever gives you the potential to earn a significant income stream, have time and #freedom to build your life according to your #dreams."	#freedomlifestyle #financialfreedom #digitalnomad

"🛫 What are your top packing tips for digital nomads? Share your secrets for traveling light and staying organized on the go! 🎒 #NomadPackingTips #digitalnomad"

"Save your hiring time and budget with Remotebase. Assemble your engineering team of the right remote developers for your company within 24 hours without going through the hassle! 📈 #remotework #futureofwork #workfromhome #digitalnomad #remote https://t.co/YvXMelyzAK"

In the analysis of tweets posted using the #digitalnomad hashtag, it was observed that many of the posts were promotional in nature and directed users to another link or application:

"🛠 Requirements: All you need to start is a computer, internet connection, and a Craftly AI subscription. Explore endless opportunities and grow your side hustle! 💡 🌱 #DigitalNomad #RemoteWork"

"💻 Contribute to a more connected remote working community! 🤝 Take our survey: https://t.co/w5WBCMTeIO 🌐 #DigitalNomad #RemoteWork #Freelancer 🔮 Mystery prize awaits one lucky participant! 🎁 "

"🌱 Our new international health insurance for digital nomads - World Resident covers a wide range of treatments, all sports, all people of any age, and any citizenship. Prices start at €105 per month: https://t.co/Ew0jUe8TNc#healthinsurance #digitalnomad #travelhealth https://t.co/mNRJ2q168M"

Once again, through the analysis, it was observed that many of the tweets posted used emojis multiple times:

"💼💸 Ready to Ditch Your Desk? 😎✈ Explore these 10 Mind-Blowing Ways to Travel and Earn Money on the Road! 🌍💰 Don't miss out on your passport to financial freedom! Click now! 👉 #TravelAndEarn #DigitalNomad #WorkFromAnywhere https://t.co/3VuwO6XtiE"

"💼 Let's make the remote working world more connected! Join our survey at https://t.co/w5WBCMTeIO & share your thoughts 🌍 #DigitalNomad #RemoteWork #Freelancer ⏳ Mystery prize for one lucky participant! 🎁 "

" 💡 Three keys to a digital nomad's paradise: Turbo-speed Internet 🚀 Wallet-friendly living 🏛 Inspiring culture 🎭 Is your 'office' checking these boxes? #business #digitalnomad"

Social media provides a significant opportunity for interaction and awareness. The widespread use of social media plays an important role in reshaping various aspects of society, including social movements and activism activities. This book chapter focuses on the recent phenomenon of digital nomadism while aiming to uncover trends within the community. In this regard, it examines the most frequently used hashtags related to digital nomads on Twitter, one of the most widely used social media platforms. Twitter is known for being one of the platforms where hashtags

Figure 2. Model for digital nomad conceptual framework

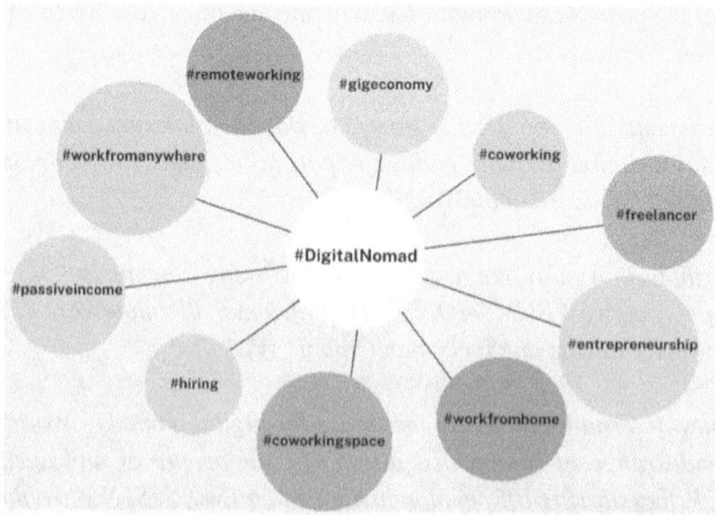

are used extensively. Hashtags on Twitter facilitate the widespread dissemination of information and content on social media (Ofori-Parku & Moscato, 2018). Analyzing how hashtags are used individually and collectively provides important insights into how cultural meanings are shaped on social media (Blaszka et al., 2012).

In order to elucidate the lifestyles, work patterns, and interactions of digital nomads, the above model has been depicted, incorporating various concepts that can define digital nomads. According to Figure 2, characteristics that can be attributed to digital nomads as defining and distinctive features include their pursuit of passive income, desire for entrepreneurship and freelance work, their ability to leverage opportunities for remote, home-based, and location-independent work, as well as their preference for co-working spaces.

CONCLUSION AND DISCUSSION

The pursuit of temporal, spatial, and financial freedom is the fundamental driving force behind the emergence and growing popularity of the digital nomad lifestyle. Digital nomadism is not just seen as a growing trend but is also considered a permanent way of life. Digital nomadism goes beyond being just a lifestyle choice; it also creates new opportunities and business models in the corporate world. Companies are increasingly inclined to collaborate with remote workers or digital nomads because they are often more cost-effective than full-time employees. Therefore, the business world, destinations, and countries need to catch up with this new trend and adjust their workforce strategies accordingly.

Within the scope of this research, the distinctive features of digital nomads are outlined as follows:

- Digital nomads attain geographical flexibility and freedom by conducting their work over the internet, offering the opportunity to work and live outside the traditional office environment.
- The internet, cloud technology, virtual office tools, and other communication technologies are fundamental tools that enable digital nomads to carry out independent work.
- Digital nomads often engage in various global communities, showcase their lives on social networks, and expand their networks with other digital nomads, facilitating the exchange of experiences and knowledge.
- Digital nomads tend to prefer destinations with low living costs and high quality of life, providing the opportunity to live in different locations worldwide.
- By accessing various online educational resources and participating in global projects, digital nomads can enhance their careers. Their entrepreneurial spirit and approach to self-learning and specialization are fundamental aspects of this lifestyle.
- The sense of community brings along various challenges such as interacting with different cultures, working across time zones, and establishing communication. Digital nomads may occasionally face difficulties in balancing their work and personal lives.

Digital nomadism continues to influence more individuals with the evolution of modern work and lifestyle trends. Those who embrace this lifestyle have the opportunity, thanks to technology, to transcend geographical boundaries, pursue their careers, and lead a free life. The trend towards becoming a digital nomad is likely to continue to increase in the coming years. Factors influencing this new trend are directly related to the development of digital tools, visa exemptions, and the transformation of business models. As the digital nomad lifestyle becomes more popular, their unique needs and consumer behaviors will also undergo transformation. Consequently, new projects and business models like the sharing economy and gig economy will emerge. Additionally, companies looking to hire skilled workers will need to reconsider their employment strategies to account for the growing number of digital nomads in the workforce.

RECOMMENDATIONS FOR FUTURE RESEARCH

In the future, research on various topics related to digital nomads, such as their economic, cultural, and social contributions to destinations, the sustainability of digital nomadism, its significance for countries, and proposed solutions to the challenges faced by digital nomads, will play a crucial role in understanding trends within the community and gaining a better appreciation of the importance of digital nomadism. Research into the issues faced by digital nomads and the strategies employed by businesses, destinations, and countries providing services to them will also be instrumental in shaping the future trends of this community.

REFERENCES

Ameen, N., Tarhini, A., Shah, M. H., Madichie, N., Paul, J., & Choudrie, J. (2021). Keeping customers' data secure: A cross-cultural study of cybersecurity compliance among the Gen-Mobile workforce. Computers *in Human Behavior, 114, 1065*31. *d*oi:10.1016/j.chb.2020.106531

Bilandzic, M., & Foth, M. (2013). Libraries as coworking spaces: Understanding user motivations and perceived barriers to social learning. Library *Hi Tech, 31(2), 254*–273. doi:10.1108/07378831311329040

Blaszka, M., Burch, L. M., Frederick, E. L., Clavio, G., & Walsh, P. (2012). #WorldSeries: An empirical examination of a Twitter hashtag during a major sporting event. Inter*national Journal of Sport Communication, 5(4*), 435–453. doi:10.1123/ijsc.5.4.435

Bonneau, C., & Aroles, J. (2021). Digital nomads: A new form of leisure class? In J. *Aroles, F. X. De Vaujany, & K. Dale, Experiencing the new world of work.* Cambridge University Press. doi:10.1017/9781108865814.011

Bonneau, C., Aroles, J., & Estagnasié, C. (2023). Romanticisation and monetisation of the digital nomad lifestyle: The role played by online narratives in shaping professional identity work. *Organization*, *30*(1), 65–88. doi:10.1177/13505084221131638

Botsman, R., & Rogers, R. (2010). *What's mine is yours: The rise of collaborative consumption*. Collins.

Busuttil, S. (2021). *The rise of the digital nomad.* https://pursuit.unimelb.edu.au/articles/the-rise-of-the-digital-nomad

Busuttil, S. (2021, August 31). *The rise of the digital nomad*. Retrieved 23 August 2023, from The University of Melbourne: https://pursuit.unimelb.edu.au/articles/the-rise-of-the-digital-nomad

Chevtaeva, E. (2021). *Coworking and coliving: The attraction for digital nomad tourists. In Information and Communication Technologies in Tourism 2021*. Springer.

Chevtaeva, E., & Denizci-Guillet, B. (2021). Digital nomads' lifestyles and coworkation. *Journal of Destination Marketing & Management, 21*, 100633. doi:10.1016/j.jdmm.2021.100633

Cook, D. (2020). The freedom trap: Digital nomads and the use of disciplining practices to manage work/leisure boundaries. *Information Technology & Tourism, 22*(3), 355–390. doi:10.1007/s40558-020-00172-4

Cook, D. (2022). Breaking the contract: Digital nomads and the state. *Critique of Anthropology, 42*(3), 304–323. doi:10.1177/0308275X221120172

David, E. (2016, March 26). *Digital nomad careers*. Retrieved 12 July 2023, from Become Nomad: https://becomenomad.com/digital-nomad-careers/

De Stefano, V. (2016). The rise of the just-in-time workforce: On-demand work, crowdwork, and labor protection in the gig-economy. *Comparative Labor Law & Policy Journal, 37*(3), 461–471.

Ehn, K., Jorge, A., & Marques-Pita, M. (2022). Digital nomads and the COVID-19 pandemic: Narratives about relocation in a time of lockdowns and reduced mobility. *Social Media + Society, 8*(1), 1–11. doi:10.1177/20563051221084958

Frey, T. (2013). The great freelancer movement: Eight reasons why your next job will be a project. *Journal of Environmental Health, 76*(5), 46. PMID:24437051

Håkansson, P. G., & Bejaković, P. (2023). Can digital nomads solve the problem of tourist economy? The case of Croatian islands. *Eastern Journal of European Studies, 14*(Special Issue), 116–134. doi:10.47743/ejes-2023-SI07

Hemsley, J., Erickson, I., Jarrahi, M. H., & Karami, A. (2020). Digital nomads, coworking, and other expressions of mobile work on Twitter. *First Monday, 25*(3). Advance online publication. doi:10.5210/fm.v25i3.10246

Hermann, I., & Paris, C. M. (2020). Digital nomadism: The nexus of remote working and travel mobility. *Information Technology & Tourism, 22*(3), 329–334. doi:10.1007/s40558-020-00188-w

Infante, A., & Mardikaningsih, R. (2022). The potential of social media as a means of online business promotion. *Journal of Social Science Studies*, *2*(2), 45–49.

Johns, T., & Gratton, L. (2013). The third wave of virtual work. *Harvard Business Review*, *91*(1), 66–73.

Kropp, R. (2018, January 18). *Digital nomads vs remote workers: Why you need to know the difference*. Retrieved 4 March 2023, from Allwork: https://allwork.space/2018/01/digital-nomads-vs-remote-workers-why-you-need-to-know-the-difference/

MacRae, G. (2016). Community and cosmopolitanism in the new Ubud. *Annals of Tourism Research*, *59*, 16–29. doi:10.1016/j.annals.2016.03.005

Magnini, V. P., Crotts, J. C., & Zehrer, A. (2011). Understanding customer delight: An application of travel blog analysis. *Journal of Travel Research*, *50*(5), 535–545. doi:10.1177/0047287510379162

Makimoto, T., & Manners, D. (1997). *Digital nomad*. Wiley.

Mancinelli, F. (2020). Digital nomads: Freedom, responsibility and the neoliberal order. *Information Technology & Tourism*, *22*(3), 417–437. doi:10.1007/s40558-020-00174-2

Müller, A. (2016). The digital nomad: Buzzword or research category? *Transnational Social Review*, *6*(3), 344–348. doi:10.1080/21931674.2016.1229930

Naz, A. (2016). Interactive living space design for neo-nomads: anticipation through spatial articulation. In M. Nadin (Ed.), *Anticipation Across Disciplines* (pp. 393–403). Springer. doi:10.1007/978-3-319-22599-9_23

Ofori-Parku, S. S., & Moscato, D. (2018). Hashtag activism as a form of political action: A qualitative analysis of the #BringBackOurGirls campaign in Nigerian, UK, and US press. *International Journal of Communication*, (12), 2480–2502.

Orel, M. (2019). Coworking environments and digital nomadism: Balancing work and leisure whilst on the move. *World Leisure Journal*, *61*(3), 215–227. doi:10.1080/16078055.2019.1639275

Pacheco, C., & Azevedo, A. (2023). Mapping the journey of the CoLiving experience of digital nomads, using verbal and visual narratives. *World Leisure Journal*, *65*(2), 192–217. doi:10.1080/16078055.2022.2156593

Prabawa, I. W. S. W., & Pertiwi, P. R. (2020). The digital nomad tourist motivation in Bali: Exploratory research based on push and pull theory. *Athens Journal of Tourism, 7*(3), 161–174. doi:10.30958/ajt.7-3-3

Prossack, A. (2021, April 25). *Office not required – why remote work is here to stay*. Retrieved 28 August 2023, from Forbes: https://www.forbes.com/sites/ashiraprossack1/2021/04/25/office-not-required--why- remote-work-is-here-to-stay/?sh=75f550ff6ab4

Rainoldi, M., Ladkin, A., & Buhalis, D. (2022). Blending work and leisure: A future digital worker hybrid lifestyle perspective. *Annals of Leisure Research*, 1–21. doi:10.1080/11745398.2022.2070513

Reichenberger, I. (2018). Digital nomads–a quest for holistic freedom in work and leisure. *Annals of Leisure Research, 21*(3), 364–380. doi:10.1080/11745398.2017.1358098

Richter, S., & Richter, A. (2020). Digital nomads. *Business & Information Systems Engineering, 62*(1), 77–81. doi:10.1007/s12599-019-00615-1

Sánchez-Vergara, J. I., Orel, M., & Capdevila, I. (2023). Digital nomad visa systems and remote work-focused leisure policies. *World Leisure Journal, 65*(2), 236–255. doi:10.1080/16078055.2023.2165142

Schlagwein, D. (2018). Escaping the rat race: Justifications in digital nomadism. In *European Conference on Information Systems (ECIS)* (pp. 31-39). AIS Electronic Library.

Šímová, T. (2023). A research framework for digital nomadism: A bibliometric study. *World Leisure Journal, 65*(2), 175–191. doi:10.1080/16078055.2022.2134200

Spinuzzi, C., Bodrožić, Z., Scaratti, G., & Ivaldi, S. (2019). "Coworking is about community": But what is "community" in coworking? *Journal of Business and Technical Communication, 33*(2), 112–140. doi:10.1177/1050651918816357

Statista. (2023, January 2). *Digital nomads - statistics & facts*. Retrieved from Statista: https://www.statista.com/topics/9259/digital-nomads/#topicOverview

Sutherland, W., & Jarrahi, M. H. (2017). The gig economy and information infrastructure: The case of the digital nomad community. *Proceedings of the ACM on Human-Computer Interaction (CSCW)*, 1-24. 10.1145/3134732

Thompson, B. Y. (2019). The digital nomad lifestyle: (Remote) work/leisure balance, privilege, and constructed community. *International Journal of the Sociology of Leisure, 2*(1-2), 27–42. doi:10.1007/s41978-018-00030-y

Todd, S. (2022). *Why social media is a valuable tool for digital nomads*. Retrieved 17 August 2023, from Open Sourced Workplace: https://opensourcedworkplace.com/news/why-social-media-is-a-valuable-tool-for-digital-nomads

Toivanen, M. (2023). Countercultural lifestyle no more? Digital nomadism and the commodification of neo-nomadic mobilities. *Mobility Humanities*, *2*(2), 70–89.

Vagena, A. (2021). Digital nomads and tourism industry. *Academia Letters*, Article 765.

van Dijk, J. A. (2006). *The network society*. Sage Publications.

von Zumbusch, J. S. H., & Lalicic, L. (2020). The role of co-living spaces in digital nomads' well-being. *Information Technology & Tourism*, *22*(3), 439–453. doi:10.1007/s40558-020-00182-2

Weare, C., & Lin, W.-Y. (2000). Content Analysis of the World Wide Web: Opportunities and Challenges. *Social Science Computer Review*, *18*(3), 272–292. doi:10.1177/089443930001800304

White, M. D., & Marsh, E. E. (2006). Content Analysis: A Flexible Methodology. *Library Trends*, *55*(1), 22–45. doi:10.1353/lib.2006.0053

Woldoff, R. A., & Litchfield, R. C. (2021). *Digital nomads: In search of freedom, community, and meaningful work in the new economy*. Oxford University Press. doi:10.1093/oso/9780190931780.001.0001

Wrycza, S., & Maślankowski, J. (2020). Social media users' opinions on remote work during the COVID-19 pandemic. Thematic and sentiment analysis. *Information Systems Management*, *37*(4), 288–297. doi:10.1080/10580530.2020.1820631

Chapter 9
Unveiling Gender Dynamics in Digital Capitalism:
Navigating the Path to Social Gender Equality

Surjit Singha
https://orcid.org/0000-0002-5730-8677
Kristu Jayanti College (Autonomous), India

ABSTRACT

In the intricate domain of digital capitalism, we are at a crossroads where promise and complexity intersect. This transition into the digital era necessitates a comprehensive comprehension of the difficulties and opportunities presented by new media technologies. The insights shared in this chapter provide a foundation for envisioning policies, strategies, and collaborations that can propel us toward a future where digital capitalism catalyzes profound social transformation. This envisioned future is one in which the digital landscape becomes a powerful instrument for dismantling profoundly ingrained gender biases, fostering inclusivity, and making gender equality a concrete reality. It represents a world in which the digital domain is not just a place to fantasize about equality but a platform where equality thrives. We can utilize the potential of technology to dismantle existing gender biases, thereby creating a digital world that fosters equality. This promises endless chances and gender equality for everybody.

DOI: 10.4018/979-8-3693-1182-0.ch009

1. INTRODUCTION

The accelerated development of digital technologies has ushered in a period of unprecedented connectivity, innovation, and Transformation. These digital tools have fundamentally altered the functioning of society, breaking down geographical barriers and redefining how we communicate, transact business, and interact with the global community. While technological advancements have created numerous opportunities and advantages, they have also revealed and exacerbated underlying complexities and disparities, especially in gender equality. Within the context of the new media era, this chapter explores the intricate interplay between digital capitalism and gender dynamics. The digital landscape, characterized by the proliferation of online platforms, data-driven decision-making, and global interconnectivity, has profound implications for how gender is understood, experienced, and acted upon in our contemporary world (Ding & Chai, 2022). This chapter provides an original contribution to the ongoing dialogue surrounding the convergence of technology, economics, and gender within the dynamic realm of digital capitalism. As society explores the intricacies of the new media age, there is a clear emphasis on elucidating the gender dynamics inherent in digital capitalism (Nicklich & Pfeiffer, 2023; Ding & Chai, 2022). Through a comprehensive analysis of the multifaceted nature of this intricate connection, our objective is to illuminate the obstacles, prospects, and routes that lead to the realization of social-gender parity in the digital domain. This investigation not only highlights the significance of comprehending the reciprocal influence between gender norms and digital capitalism but also offers valuable perspectives on cultivating a digital future that is inclusive and equitable for all. Contemporary digital communication platforms offer extensive and rapid accessibility (Erdoğan & Topçu, 2022). Although modern digital communication platforms provide widespread accessibility, it is crucial to acknowledge the difficulties associated with excessive information, exhaustion from digital interactions, and issues around privacy. The continual consideration of maintaining a balance between connectivity and well-being is crucial in the rapidly developing realm of digital communication.

This chapter examines the ever-changing terrain of digital capitalism, analyzing its multifaceted effects on economic, social, and cultural structures. It investigates how digital capitalism interacts with gender issues, reflecting and influencing societal norms and power structures. The objective is to shed light on the intricate relationships between technology, economics, and gender, recognizing that they are not unidirectional but dynamic and interactive. The influence of digital capitalism on social gender equality is one of the central questions we aim to address. It examines gender disparities in digital labour markets, the representation and visibility of diverse genders in digital media, and the role of algorithms and data-driven technologies in perpetuating or mitigating gender inequalities as we venture deeper into this inquiry

(Bannykh, 2021; Belingheri et al., 2021). It aims to provide insights and strategies for leveraging technology as a force to promote a more equitable future. By analyzing policy initiatives, corporate practices, grassroots movements, and illuminating case studies, we hope to equip individuals, organizations, and policymakers with the tools necessary to navigate the path toward social gender equality in the digital age. This chapter guides us through the uncharted waters of digital capitalism and gender dynamics. It fosters critical reflection, stimulates constructive dialogue, and inspires informed action to guide our society towards a future where digital capitalism drives positive social change, eradicating gender disparities and establishing equality and empowerment as paramount (Peng, 2022). As we embark on this voyage, let us collectively navigate the complexities of our digital world, striving to make it a place where everyone, regardless of gender identity or expression, can flourish. It aims to investigate and analyze the complex relationship between digital capitalism and gender dynamics in the context of the new media era. It aims to illuminate the complex relationships between technology, economics, and gender, addressing the challenges and opportunities at their intersection.

It explores the fundamental concepts of digital capitalism, including its evolution, characteristics, and consequences. It lays the groundwork for understanding how digital technologies have altered economic, social, and cultural structures. It investigates how gender is conceptualized, experienced, and acted upon in the digital age. It examines the intricate relationships between digital capitalism and gender issues, including how digital platforms reflect and influence societal norms and power. This chapter investigates gender disparities in digital labour markets and assesses their impact on economic opportunities and outcomes. It evaluates the representation and visibility of diverse genders in digital media, addressing the role of technology in reinforcing or confronting traditional gender norms and stereotypes. Analyzing how algorithms and data-driven technologies influence gender equality is a crucial aspect of the scope. It will entail investigating instances of algorithmic bias and investigating efforts to reduce bias and promote fairness in algorithmic decision-making. In addition to identifying obstacles, this chapter provides insights and strategies for leveraging technology as a force to advance gender equality in the digital age. It includes analyzing policy initiatives, corporate practices, grassroots movements, and inspiring case studies that empower individuals, organizations, and policymakers to act. The scope encompasses promoting critical reflection, facilitating constructive dialogue, and encouraging informed action. It aims to inspire positive change by cultivating a vision in which digital capitalism propels social progress, eradicates gender disparities, and realizes a future of equality and empowerment. It aims to equip readers with the knowledge and tools necessary to actively contribute to a more equitable and inclusive digital future where gender identity and expression do not impede the success of any individual. To investigate the intricate relationship between digital capitalism and gender dynamics in the context of the new media era, it establishes the theoretical framework and context that underlie this inquiry.

This chapter is based on the concept of digital capitalism, which acknowledges that the digital era has altered the fundamental structures of capitalism. Traditional economic systems have transitioned into a digital economy characterized by online platforms, data-driven decision-making, and global interconnectivity. This concept provides the framework for the examination of gender dynamics. Gender theory provides a lens for examining how individuals and societies conceptualize and construct gender. It recognizes that gender is a social construct, not a biological fact, and investigates how it affects identity, roles, and power dynamics (Risman, 2018; Osmond & Thorne, 2008). Mainly, feminist theories aid in comprehending gender disparities and the struggle for gender equality. Intersectionality is a crucial theoretical framework acknowledging that individuals possess multiple intersecting identities, including gender, race, socioeconomic status, and sexual orientation. It highlights how these identities can combine and interact to produce unique privilege and oppression experiences. Understanding intersectionality is essential for analyzing how gender disparities are experienced differently by different demographic groups (Robinson, 2018; Dey & Orton, 2016; Shields, 2008; Weldon, 2008). The digital divide refers to disparities in access to digital technologies and the internet. This gap can exacerbate gender-based disparities (Vassilakopoulou & Hustad, 2021; Acilar & Sæbø, 2021). For example, women may need help accessing digital resources, limiting their participation in the digital economy. A central concept within the context of digital capitalism is algorithmic bias. It refers to the inherent prejudices that may be present in algorithms and machine learning models, which frequently reflect and perpetuate societal biases, such as those related to gender. The effects of algorithmic bias on fairness, discrimination, and inequality are profound (Crespo, 2023; Prodnik, 2021). It is crucial to comprehend the role of policy initiatives, corporate practices, and grassroots movements in promoting gender equality in digital capitalism. This background information illuminates potential change avenues and empowers individuals and organizations to advocate for more inclusive practices and policies. As we navigate the complex terrain of digital capitalism and gender dynamics, these theoretical frameworks and background concepts will help us critically analyze the issues at hand, identify opportunities for positive change, and ultimately contribute to a more equitable and inclusive digital future (Bannykh, 2021; Acilar & Sæbø, 2021; Sinha, 2018).

The theoretical framework elucidates the dynamic interrelationships between gender theories, digital capitalism, and the pursuit of social equality in modern society in a comprehensive and unified manner. By incorporating critical perspectives grounded in sociology, economics, and gender studies, the framework endeavours to reconcile theoretical understandings and shed light on the complex interplay among technology, economics, and gender dynamics. Within the domain of digital capitalism, the structural analysis investigates the system's fundamental structures, assessing how digital technologies and platforms impact the creation, utilization, and dissemination of the virtual environment (Ding & Chai, 2022). At the same time, looking at how technological determinism affects cultural norms, economic models, and social structures shows how significant digital progress is for power dynamics, access, and participation in the digital world. The framework acknowledges and analyzes the interdependence of diverse social identities—including gender, race, class, and sexual orientation—through the lens of intersectionality, which is firmly rooted in feminist theory (Robinson, 2018; Harris & Bartlow, 2015). This aspect highlights how these interrelated elements influence the digital experiences of individuals, thereby affecting their access, representation, and opportunities. By adopting a poststructuralist stance, the analysis questions fundamentalist conceptions of gender. It investigates how discourse, language, and representation form and maintain gender-based standards in digital environments.

To achieve social equality, the theoretical framework incorporates the capability approach to evaluate how individuals can freely and autonomously participate in the digital realm. This analysis scrutinizes the potential of digital capitalism to either augment or hinder these capacities, with a particular focus on allocating resources, opportunities, and entry. Furthermore, this approach integrates critical pedagogy, emphasizing the importance of education and consciousness in cultivating a discerning comprehension of gender dynamics in digital capitalism. It also investigates the potential of disseminating knowledge to challenge and dismantle prejudices, preconceived notions, and disparities. Combining these three parts gives the framework a solid foundation for analysis. It encourages a thorough look beyond a simple reliance on technological determinism. It acknowledges the complicated and always-changing link between digital capitalism, gender relations, and the search for social justice. At the heart of this study is a profound exploration of how digital capitalism exerts a profound and nuanced influence on gender dynamics. The intricate interplay between these two fundamentals is not merely coincidental but deeply rooted in the systemic structures and transformative forces inherent in the digital realm. Digital capitalism, with its structural foundations and technological advancements, serves as a dynamic catalyst that shapes the very fabric of societal norms, economic models, and cultural paradigms (Ding & Chai, 2022; Pace, 2018). It acts as an amplifier, both magnifying and reshaping existing gender dynamics.

By looking at digital capitalism through a structural lens, we can see how platforms and technologies become the ones who decide who has power, changing the way that production, consumption, and distribution have always worked. This restructuring is not impartial; it carries profound implications for gender relations. Existing gender norms are reinforced or challenged digitally, impacting individuals' opportunities, representation, and access. Moreover, the application of technological determinism unveils a transformative narrative. Advancements in digital technologies do more than streamline processes—they redefine societal structures, economic hierarchies, and cultural norms. The digital arena becomes a crucible where power dynamics are reshaped and access to resources is redefined. This transformative impact is inherently linked to gender dynamics, influencing how individuals navigate and negotiate their roles within the digital ecosystem(Ding & Chai, 2022). This study underscores that digital capitalism is not a neutral force in the gender equation. It actively participates in constructing and perpetuating gender norms within the digital space. Through the lenses of structural analysis and technological determinism, we can uncover how digital capitalism actively shapes and is shaped by gender dynamics. This nuanced understanding is pivotal for comprehending the intricate interplay between these two fundamentals and navigating the path towards a more equitable digital future.

2. GENDERED DIGITAL SPACES: UNPACKING THE LANDSCAPE

Gender representation in digital spaces is essential for comprehending how technology interacts with societal norms and inequalities on a broader scale. Digital environments include numerous online platforms, such as social media, forums, virtual worlds, and online gaming communities (Andreevskikh & Muravyeva, 2020). Historically, men have frequently dominated these spaces, perpetuating stereotypes and discouraging women and gender-diverse individuals from participating fully, especially in computer science and gaming (Scarcelli et al., 2020; Green & Singleton, 2013). While we have progressed, gender-based antagonism and hostility persist, discouraging many individuals from expressing themselves freely. In addition, online gender representation is influenced by intersecting factors such as race, ethnicity, sexual orientation, and socioeconomic status, highlighting the diversity of experiences (Majumdar et al., 2022). Digital spaces serve as platforms for feminist activism, the challenge of stereotypes, and the promotion of inclusivity. Improving gender representation requires an inclusive design, content moderation, and promoting positive role models. Ongoing research and data collection assist in informing policy changes and initiatives, fostering more equitable online environments (Santoniccolo et al., 2023; Patnaik, 2020). Due to their potential to perpetuate societal inequalities, gender biases in algorithms and AI systems are garnering attention. Biased training data can result in discriminatory outcomes such as skewed suggestions or content filtering. Artificial intelligence-generated text may normalize detrimental gender beliefs by reinforcing stereotypes. Diversity in AI development teams is essential for effectively identifying and addressing biases. Due to the intricacy of AI models, achieving transparency and accountability is complex and requires robust ethical guidelines. Researchers develop mitigation strategies, such as debiasing techniques and models retrained with diverse data. Defeating gender biases in AI is a multidimensional challenge that requires ethical considerations, transparency, diverse representation, and ongoing research so that AI can contribute to gender equality regardless of gender identity (Franzoni, 2023; O'Connor & Liu, 2023; Hall & Ellis, 2023). Comprehending and accepting diversity is crucial for constructing inclusive settings and cultivating robust relationships in our personal and professional spheres (Singha & Singha, 2023).

In recent years, gender biases in algorithms and artificial intelligence (AI) systems have received considerable attention due to their potential to perpetuate and exacerbate societal inequalities. These biases can manifest in various ways, from the biased data used to train AI models to their design and decision-making processes. Understanding gender bias in AI and algorithms is crucial for addressing and mitigating their adverse effects. Biased training data is one of the primary sources of gender bias in AI systems. Machine learning models learn from historical data, and if this data reflects existing gender biases, machine learning models may incorporate and perpetuate these biases in their predictions and decisions. For instance, if previous hiring decisions were biased against women, an AI recruitment tool trained on this data could discriminate against female job applicants (Carlisle et al., 2023; Leavy et al., 2020). Gender bias in artificial intelligence can reinforce detrimental stereotypes. For example, language models trained on biased text data may generate text that reinforces gender stereotypes and discriminatory language. It can normalize and perpetuate damaging gender-based beliefs and attitudes. AI systems are utilized in various applications, including search engines, recommendation systems, and advertisement ABCs. These systems' gender biases may result in biased recommendations and content. For instance, a recommendation algorithm that prioritizes male-centric content may not give women equal access to information and opportunities.

In some cases, AI systems can discriminate against individuals based on gender. It can occur during the employment, lending, and other decision-making processes. When AI models are not meticulously designed and audited, they may inadvertently favour one gender over another, resulting in unjust outcomes (O'Connor & Liu, 2023; Belloso, 2022). An absence of diversity in AI system development teams can contribute to gender bias. Diverse groups are more likely to identify and address potential biases during development. To reduce these biases, it is crucial to ensure that AI development teams contain members with diverse gender identities and backgrounds. Because the inner workings of many AI models are opaque and complex, detecting and addressing gender biases in AI can be challenging (Hall & Ellis, 2023; O'Connor & Liu, 2023). It is essential to ensure transparency and accountability in

AI development and deployment. It includes documenting data sources, auditing algorithms for biases, and providing explicit reporting and resolution mechanisms. Ethical principles and guidelines must govern the development and implementation of artificial intelligence systems. Organizations and researchers working in AI should prioritize ethical considerations, such as fairness, equity, and inclusivity, to prevent gender biases and their detrimental effects. Researchers and practitioners are devising techniques to reduce gender bias in artificial intelligence, such as debiasing techniques and retraining models with more diverse and representative data (Novelli et al., 2023; FoschVillaronga & Poulsen, 2022).

These strategies seek to make artificial intelligence systems more equitable and less likely to reinforce harmful stereotypes. A multifaceted challenge, addressing gender biases in algorithms and AI requires ethical guidelines, diverse representation in AI development teams, transparency, and ongoing research. By recognizing these biases and actively working to eliminate them, we can employ the power of AI to promote gender equality and ensure fair and equitable outcomes for all individuals, regardless of their gender identity. The digital gender divide, also known as the digital gender gap or digital gender inequality, is a pervasive issue characterized by gender-based disparities in access to and use of digital technologies, especially the internet and digital tools. This divide highlights the unequal distribution of opportunities and benefits that technology provides, which has multifaceted effects on individuals, communities, and societies (Acilar & Sæbø, 2021). Access to technology is fundamental, with women and girls in many regions and communities around the globe having less access to computers, smartphones, and the internet than their male counterparts, often due to economic disparities, cultural norms, and inadequate infrastructure. Even when access is available, women's participation in the digital economy and online activities is hampered by digital literacy and abilities disparities. Moreover, the digital gender divide extends beyond access and encompasses active engagement, with women less likely to partake in online spaces due to concerns about harassment, privacy, and cultural expectations. The underrepresentation of women in online work, e-commerce, and digital entrepreneurship perpetuates economic disparities (Sinha, 2018). It affects education, health, and political participation, depriving women of transformative learning opportunities, vital health resources, and opportunities for political participation. Significantly, the digital gender gap intersects with other factors such as race, ethnicity, socioeconomic status, and geographic location, resulting in heightened obstacles for women with intersecting identities. Governments, civil society organizations, the private sector, and communities must collaborate to bridge this divide. Initiatives must prioritize the improvement of digital infrastructure, the promotion of digital literacy among women and girls, the rise of a secure online environment, and the challenge of gender norms that limit access and participation. By addressing the digital gender gap, societies can unlock the full potential of technology to promote gender equality and empower women and girls in all spheres (Campos & Scherer, 2023; Acilar & Sæbø, 2021).

3. REINFORCING STEREOTYPES: MEDIA, ADVERTISING, AND REPRESENTATION

The persistence of gender stereotypes in digital media remains a pervasive and troubling issue, significantly impacting society's perception and interpretation of gender roles and identities. Digital media, encompassing television, movies, online content, and advertising, consistently reinforces these stereotypes, resulting in far-reaching consequences. These enduring stereotypes, portraying men as powerful and dominant while depicting women as submissive and nurturing, continue to shape perceptions and limit individual aspirations. The strong emphasis on physical appearance, particularly for women, perpetuates unattainable beauty standards and reduces the value of women to their appearance. Biased portrayals of gender in specific professions and occupations, like the association of technology fields with men and caregiving roles with women, reinforce traditional gender norms and further constrict opportunities. Stereotypes regarding emotional expression and relationship dynamics discourage emotional authenticity and agency for all genders. The lack of representation for gender-variant and non-binary individuals marginalizes these communities further and reinforces the binary concept of gender. Even humour in digital media can sometimes be a vehicle for perpetuating stereotypes if used without consideration (Santoniccolo et al., 2023; Meier et al., 2020; Scharrer, 2013). These representations and biases in digital media have real-world implications, contributing to gender-based discrimination and inequality. Diverse stakeholders, including content creators, media channels, and consumers, can take proactive measures to combat these issues. Promoting media literacy programs can assist individuals in analyzing and questioning gender representations in digital media, thereby cultivating a more discriminating audience. Changing societal perceptions requires encouraging content creators and media outlets to adopt diverse and authentic expressions of gender identities and roles (Patnaik, 2020; Scharer, 2013). Advocating for responsible and inclusive representation and holding media outlets and advertisers accountable for perpetuating stereotypes is essential. Engaging in debates and campaigns that challenge traditional gender norms propagated by digital media can facilitate change. Lastly, by amplifying the voices and narratives of gender-diverse and non-binary individuals, visibility can be increased, and gender diversity can be better understood. Addressing the perpetuation of gender stereotypes in digital media is a complex challenge with far-reaching consequences. We can work towards a media landscape that accurately reflects the diverse realities of gender and promotes greater equality and understanding in society by actively challenging these stereotypes and advocating for more inclusive and authentic portrayals of gender (Santoniccolo et al., 2023; Meier et al., 2020).

Online gendered marketing strategies are advertising and promotional approaches that target specific genders and frequently reinforce traditional gender roles and stereotypes. Businesses and marketers often employ these strategies to appeal to specific demographics based on their perceptions of gender norms and interests. Some gender-based marketing may be innocuous or beneficial in certain situations, but it can also perpetuate harmful stereotypes and contribute to gender inequality. Frequently, gender-targeted marketing entails positioning products and brands following traditional gender roles and expectations. For instance, certain products may be marketed as "for men" or "for women," with packaging, colours, and copy tailored to appeal to these specific demographics. It can restrict consumer options and reinforce gender-based stereotypes regarding the suitability of various products. Bohmer & Griese (2020) Gendered marketing frequently employs stereotypical messaging based on traditional gender norms. For instance, advertisements may depict women as caregivers and homemakers while portraying men as breadwinners and decision-makers. These messages can be restrictive and contribute to a restricted understanding of gender roles. Marketers frequently use colour and design to target specific genders. Marketers frequently link products aimed at women with pastel colours and floral arrangements, while they employ darker colours and bold graphics for products targeted at males. These design decisions can reinforce gender stereotypes and restrict personal expression. Some products and services, such as clothing, fragrances, and personal care items, are categorical about gender. This categorization can limit the options available to consumers and reinforce the notion that certain products are exclusively for one gender. Typically, gendered marketing associates products with stereotypical pastimes and passions (Ng et al., 2020; Paswan, 2012). For example, toys relating to construction or technology are marketed to males, while dolls and domestic toys target girls. These divisions can limit the exposure of children to diverse interests and abilities. By reinforcing traditional gender norms, expectations, and roles, gendered marketing can contribute to gender inequality. It can discourage people from investigating interests and products that do not align with their perceived gender, limiting personal development and reinforcing harmful biases. There has been a growing consumer backlash against gendered marketing in recent years. Numerous individuals and advocacy organizations have demanded more inclusive and gender-neutral marketing strategies, compelling businesses to reconsider their approach. Some companies and brands employ more inclusive and gender-neutral marketing strategies (Bohmer & Griese, 2020; Stavrianea et al., 2020).

They acknowledge that consumers are diverse and that marketing should reflect this. Individuals can educate themselves on the effects of gendered marketing on society. Individuals can make more conscientious decisions about the products and brands they support if they are informed consumers. Individuals and advocacy organizations can advocate for inclusive and gender-neutral marketing practices. They can raise awareness of the adverse effects of gendered advertising and advocate for change. Companies and brands should evaluate their marketing strategies critically and consider the potential harm of reinforcing gender stereotypes. They can employ more inclusive marketing practices and reflect the diversity of their customer base. Online gendered marketing strategies can perpetuate traditional gender stereotypes and restrict individual options and choices. Recognizing the impact of these strategies and advocating for more inclusive and gender-neutral marketing practices can lead to greater gender equality and a more diverse and tolerant society (Stavrianea et al., 2020). Representation of underrepresented genders in new media is essential to fostering diversity, inclusion, and social progress in the digital age. New media platforms, including social media networks and online content creation, enable individuals from marginalized gender groups, such as transgender, non-binary, and genderqueer individuals, to share their unique stories, experiences, and points of view. This newfound visibility not only educates the general public about the diversity of gender identities but also amplifies the voices of marginalized gender individuals, enabling them to advocate for their rights and recognition. Online communities offer marginalized genders vital spaces to find support, share resources, and engage with like-minded individuals, fostering a sense of belonging and promoting collective advocacy and empowerment. Content creators in new media have the creative freedom to represent marginalized gender identities authentically and inclusively, producing narratives, art, and media that challenge stereotypes and promote greater understanding. These platforms also provide educational resources for learning about gender diversity and the experiences of marginalized genders (Santoniccolo et al., 2023; Patnaik, 2020).

New media has been instrumental in mobilizing marginalized gender communities for advocacy and activism, championing crucial issues such as gender discrimination and gender-based violence, and pursuing legal protections. Nonetheless, it is essential to recognize the challenges and risks associated with representation in new media, such as online harassment, doxxing, and privacy concerns, which disproportionately affect individuals of marginalized genders. To effectively support the presentation of marginalized genders, it is essential to encourage inclusive representation in content creation, advocate for more robust measures against online harassment, amplify the voices of marginalized groups, and promote ongoing education and awareness about gender diversity and intersectionality (Scharrer, 2013). By doing so, we can actively contribute to a more equitable, informed, and accepting digital landscape.

4. FROM ACCESS TO EMPOWERMENT: WOMEN AND TECHNOLOGY

In our technology-driven world, confronting gender disparities and promoting equality depend on women's digital skills and empowerment. By providing women with access to comprehensive digital training, we enable them to maximize the potential of technology for their own personal and professional development. To bridge the digital gender gap, it is necessary to ensure equal access to technology, reduce infrastructure disparities, and reduce technology costs. Providing women with digital skills opens doors to economic opportunities, enabling them to engage in online work, freelancing, e-commerce, and tech entrepreneurship, thereby enhancing their financial well-being. It is essential to encourage women to pursue STEM education and careers, as these disciplines offer numerous opportunities in the technology sector. In addition, digital empowerment fosters digital literacy, online safety, and cybersecurity awareness to safeguard women from online harassment and cyberbullying. It is essential to ensure that digital tools and content are accessible to all individuals, regardless of their abilities. Mentorship and role models in the tech industry provide women with guidance and assistance as they navigate the tech landscape. Government policies and initiatives are pivotal in promoting digital skills and empowerment by investing in infrastructure and supporting educational programs targeting women and girls. Evaluating a program's impact is essential, noting outcomes such as increased employment and income in the technology industry. Recognizing the intersectionality of women's experiences and resolving their unique needs based on race, ethnicity, disability, and socioeconomic status are crucial for ensuring the inclusiveness of digital empowerment initiatives. Digital skills and empowerment for women ultimately unleash their potential and contribute to more equitable and inclusive digital spaces (Christou & Parmaxi, 2021).

Tech entrepreneurship is a dynamic and innovative industry, but persistent gender disparities impede the achievement of gender equality in the technology startup ecosystem. Women remain underrepresented among startup entrepreneurs, especially in male-dominated fields such as software development, artificial intelligence, and hardware technology. This underrepresentation reduces the industry's diversity of thought and experience, potentially impeding creativity and innovation. The stark inequality in access to funding for women-led enterprises is one of the most glaring gender disparities in tech entrepreneurship. Extensive research indicates that women-led businesses receive significantly less venture capital funding than those led by men. This funding disparity presents significant obstacles, limiting the development and scalability of women-led companies and preventing them from realizing their full potential. Building robust professional networks and gaining access to mentorship and advice are crucial to the success of a tech entrepreneur.

However, gender disparities frequently limit women entrepreneurs' access to these vital support systems. The absence of female role models and mentors can discourage women from pursuing entrepreneurial endeavours, further exacerbating the gender disparity (Raina, 2016).

In the tech startup ecosystem, gender bias and profoundly ingrained stereotypes persist, subjecting women entrepreneurs to scepticism, unconscious bias, and discrimination when seeking funding, partners, or customers. These preconceived notions about women's abilities in technical and leadership positions can be detrimental to their advancement. In addition, the demands of juggling entrepreneurship with family obligations present a formidable obstacle for many women. The unrelenting efforts to develop and scale a startup frequently conflict with traditional gender roles and societal caregiving expectations. Access to resources such as co-working spaces, incubators, accelerators, and educational programs can be unequally distributed, with women-led startups frequently confronting growth and development obstacles. When intersecting with other factors such as race, ethnicity, sexual orientation, and socioeconomic status, gender disparities in tech entrepreneurship become even more pronounced. Women from marginalized backgrounds face even more significant barriers and discrimination, which exacerbates the difficulties they experience (Kleinert & Mochkabadi, 2021; Bullough et al., 2021). Concerted efforts are required to combat these disparities and advance gender equality in tech entrepreneurship. Promoting diversity in entrepreneurship and creating environments where all genders are supported and welcomed is essential. Initiatives designed to increase funding opportunities for women-led startups, such as venture capital firms and funding programs geared toward women, can help close the financing divide. Women entrepreneurs must have access to mentorship and networking opportunities to provide the necessary guidance and support. Customized education and training programs for women interested in entrepreneurship can improve their skills and boost their confidence. Combating gender bias and dismantling stereotypes within the tech industry are essential measures to create a more equitable ecosystem. In addition, government policies and regulations advocating for gender equality in entrepreneurship and advocacy efforts can help reduce these disparities. Correcting gender disparities in tech entrepreneurship is a matter of fairness and a strategic necessity. In the startup ecosystem, embracing diverse perspectives and nurturing inclusive teams are known to foster innovation and resiliency. By actively reducing these disparities, we can pave the way for a more inclusive, prosperous, and equitable landscape for tech entrepreneurship across all genders.

5. CASE STUDIES OF SUCCESSFUL WOMEN-LED TECH INITIATIVES

Sara Chipps co-founded Girl Develop It (GDI). GDI was founded in 2010 to provide women interested in learning software development and programming with affordable and accessible learning opportunities. The organization offers coding classes and workshops, establishing a supportive community for women to thrive in the tech industry. GDI has enabled thousands of women to enter the technology industry by equipping them with essential computing skills. It has expanded its reach to numerous cities across the United States, providing a platform for women to excel in technology-related professions.

Katrina Lake established Stitch Fix. It is an online personal styling service that utilizes data science and algorithms to select apparel items for clients based on their preferences and sense of style. The company was founded by Katrina Lake in 2011 and went public in 2017. Katrina Lake has pioneered the technology industry as one of the few female-led tech companies to go public. Stitch Fix has disrupted the fashion retail industry by combining data-driven algorithms with personalized styling to provide a novel shopping experience for consumers.

Melanie Perkins established the company Canva. Canva is a platform for graphic design that allows users to create various visual content, including social media graphics, presentations, and posters. Melanie Perkins co-founded Canva, which has since become one of the most valuable privately held technology companies. Under Melanie Perkins's direction, Canva has become a global design powerhouse with millions of consumers worldwide. The user-friendly design tools on the platform have made graphic design accessible to individuals and enterprises of all sizes.

Kimberly Bryant founded Black Girls CODE in 2011 to address the underrepresentation of Black girls and women in technology. The organization provides young Black females with coding and technology education, empowering them with digital skills. Kimberly Bryant's initiative has reached tens of thousands of young women and provided them with opportunities to investigate computer programming, robotics, and other fields of technology. Black Girls CODE promotes diversity and inclusion in the technology industry.

Clara Shih founded the Hearsay System. Hearsay Systems is a software company that provides financial services with consumer engagement solutions. In 2009, Clara Shih co-founded the company and became a prominent figure in the finance industry. Hearsay Systems has become a well-known provider of digital solutions for financial advisors and institutions under the direction of Clara Shih. The company's technology has revolutionized how financial services professionals interact with clients in the digital age.

These case studies emphasize the significant contributions of women-led technology initiatives to the tech industry and society. They demonstrate women's potential for success in technology and entrepreneurship while confronting gender disparities.

6. ONLINE ACTIVISM AND FEMINIST MOVEMENTS IN THE DIGITAL AGE

Digital platforms have transformed feminist organizing, heralding a new advocacy, mobilization, and global solidarity era. These platforms, mainly social media, have offered feminist movements an unprecedented international stage. With hashtags like #MeToo and #TimesUp spreading like wildfire, activists can now rapidly share their messages, stories, and campaigns with global audiences, connecting survivors and supporters across borders and cultures. This rapid dissemination of information has accelerated feminist movements, allowing for prompt responses to emergent concerns. In addition, digital platforms have provided marginalized and underrepresented feminist groups with a potent megaphone.

Women of colour, LGBTQ+ individuals, individuals with disabilities, and others historically marginalized now have accessible platforms to share their unique experiences and perspectives, enhancing feminist discourse and fostering inclusivity (Mendes et al., 2019). These platforms also provide a plethora of organizational tools which streamline feminist efforts and make it simpler to coordinate protests, fundraisers, and advocacy initiatives. They have become indispensable storytelling tools, enabling feminists to share personal narratives and testimonies, humanizing issues such as sexual harassment, assault, and discrimination, fostering empathy and promoting social change. Crowdfunding and online fundraising platforms have enabled feminist organizations and activists to pursue their missions without relying on traditional funding sources (Pyun, 2022).

Online spaces have fostered thriving feminist communities that offer support and solidarity to those who face gender-based discrimination and violence. In highlighting the intersectionality of gender with other forms of discrimination, such as racism, homophobia, and ableism, these platforms have also contributed to a more comprehensive comprehension of the challenges diverse groups of women face. Digital media resonate strongly with young activists, engaging a new generation in feminist causes, including youth-led movements that intersect with feminist objectives, such as "March for Our Lives" and climate activism. Despite these remarkable benefits, digital platforms also present challenges, such as online harassment, privacy concerns, and the digital divide, which require concerted efforts to address if the digital age is to continue to be a potent force for advancing gender equality and feminist goals.

Cyberfeminism, a term coined in the 1990s, represents the intersection of feminism and technology and seeks to investigate and challenge the impact of digital technologies and online spaces on gender equality and the feminist movement. Cyberfeminism has contributed significantly to advancing feminist discourse in the digital era but also faces unique challenges. The digital divide is one of cyberfeminism's primary obstacles. Not all women have equal access to technology and the internet. Economic disparities, limited infrastructure in certain regions, and cultural obstacles can impede marginalized women's full participation in digital spaces. Cyberfeminism must address these disparities to ensure that all women have a voice in the digital sphere. Cyberfeminists are frequently subjected to online harassment and abuse, such as threats, doxxing, and hate speech. This results in the silencing of women's voices and a hostile online environment. Cyberfeminists face a significant challenge in addressing online harassment, as it requires legal and technological solutions and a shift in online culture and norms. As digital technologies progress, surveillance and privacy concerns become more imperative. Women activists are susceptible to management and administration by state and non-state actors. Protecting cyberfeminists' privacy and security is crucial to ensuring their safety and the continued efficacy of their work.

Algorithms and AI systems can perpetuate gender biases and discrimination, affecting women's online experiences and opportunities in various fields. Cyberfeminism must confront the complex problem of addressing prejudice in digital technologies and advocating for ethical AI. Intersectionality is a fundamental tenet of feminism, recognizing that gender inequality intersects with other forms of oppression, such as ethnicity, class, and sexual orientation. Cyberfeminism confronts the challenge of ensuring its work is inclusive and considers women's experiences with diverse identities. The commercialization of the internet and digital spaces can restrict cyberfeminists' autonomy. Large tech corporations exert considerable influence over online platforms, and their policies can affect free speech and feminist activism. Finding methods to challenge corporate management while using digital media for advocacy is a delicate balancing act. Online activism can be temporary, with hashtags and fads appearing and disappearing rapidly. Cyberfeminists struggle to maintain momentum and translate online actions into real-world change and policy reform. Cyberfeminism is a global phenomenon, which necessitates that strategies and communications be culturally sensitive and adaptable to various contexts. Balancing a global perspective with cultural nuances and local activism can be difficult. Cyberfeminism has made significant strides in utilizing digital technologies to advance feminist objectives and increase awareness of gender inequality. However, it confronts several obstacles, including bridging the digital divide and combating online harassment, algorithmic bias and corporate control. Overcoming these obstacles requires collaboration, advocacy, and a determination to make the digital age a more inclusive and equitable space for women and underrepresented gender groups.

To establish safe and inclusive digital spaces, it is essential to combat online harassment and abuse, particularly for women and marginalized gender individuals who frequently endure the brunt of online abuse. This pervasive problem incorporates a variety of harmful behaviours, including cyberbullying, trolling, doxxing, hate speech, and threats of violence. Effectively combating online harassment and abuse requires a multifaceted approach that includes individuals, online platforms, legal systems, and civil society. Raising public awareness to help individuals recognize and comprehend the harm caused by online abuse, enacting and enforcing robust legal measures to hold perpetrators accountable, establishing user-friendly reporting mechanisms on online platforms, implementing community moderation policies, empowering users with tools for online safety, offering digital literacy programs, creating support networks for victims, and fostering collaboration are critical strategies in this effort. By committing collectively to these strategies, we can establish a digital culture of respect and responsibility in which everyone, regardless of gender or identity, can participate in online spaces without fear of harassment or abuse (Vilk, 2020).

7. POLICY IMPLICATIONS FOR A GENDER-INCLUSIVE DIGITAL FUTURE

Governmental and organizational initiatives for gender equality are crucial for confronting systemic disparities and fostering inclusive environments that empower both sexes. These initiatives aim to level the playing field in the workplace, the public sphere, and society. The strategies vary from ensuring equal pay for equal work through policy enforcement and regular audits to establishing diversity and inclusion programs that recognize intersectionality and go beyond gender. Mentoring and leadership development opportunities promote career advancement, while parental leave policies and flexible work arrangements promote work-life balance. Anti-discrimination laws and policies safeguard against gender-based discrimination, while gender-responsive budgeting addresses disparities in public expenditure. Campaigns promoting education raise awareness about gender equality and workplace harassment, and quotas encouraging diverse leadership promote representation. Supporting research initiatives and fostering collaboration among various stakeholders drive progress, all while assuring legal protections for gender identity and expression and establishing mechanisms for reporting and accountability.

These efforts aim to eliminate systemic barriers and nurture a world where all genders have equal rights and opportunities.

In the digital age, privacy, data protection, and gender considerations are intertwined, and resolving them collectively is essential for protecting individual rights and advancing gender equality. Privacy protection is fundamental, with informed and voluntary consent required for data acquisition and information sharing, especially considering the disproportionate impact of privacy breaches on women and marginalized genders. To prevent the perpetuation of gender biases, algorithms and data-driven technologies must be scrutinized, and legal frameworks and platform policies should address gender-based online harassment and doxxing to protect personal information. Transparency in data practices, particularly data sharing, is crucial for gaining users' trust, especially those from marginalized groups. Regarding data security and privacy safeguards, transgender and gender-nonconforming individuals require special consideration.

Moreover, governments and organizations should collect and analyze gender-sensitive data to inform anti-discrimination policies. Legal protections for gender identity and expression are essential, as are increasing cybersecurity awareness, empowering individuals with digital security expertise, and addressing consent-related issues. Comprehensive data protection policies are ensured by recognizing the intersectionality of gender with other factors, such as race and ability. The proper equilibrium between technological advancements and individual rights is essential for a digital society to be equitable. Policies, legal frameworks, and technical practices should evolve to address new challenges and safeguard the privacy and rights of all genders, fostering inclusion, security, and respect for the autonomy and identities of individuals.

Regulations to combat online gender-based violence are paramount for fostering a safer and more inclusive digital environment, particularly for women and marginalized gender groups who often bear the brunt of online abuse. These regulations should take a comprehensive approach, addressing multiple crucial facets of this problem. Governments should enact and enforce laws specifically addressing online gender-based violence, with clear definitions of forms of abuse, such as cyberbullying, harassment, doxxing, and revenge porn, and legal repercussions for perpetrators. Online platforms and service providers must develop accessible reporting mechanisms that prioritize the privacy and safety of victims and ensure prompt action in response to reported incidents. Law enforcement agencies should be trained to recognize and effectively respond to online gender-based violence, considering its unique nature and the damage it causes. As online abuse frequently crosses international boundaries, cooperation and information sharing among governments and law enforcement agencies are essential for tracking and prosecuting transnational offenders. In addition, legal systems ought to provide protection orders comparable to those for physical violence, empowering victims to seek restraining orders against their abusers.

Comprehensive support services, including legal aid and counselling, should help victims contend with online abuse's emotional and psychological effects. Individuals can be educated about the consequences of online gender-based violence and encouraged to behave respectfully online through public awareness campaigns, integrated digital literacy education, and school cyberbullying prevention programs (Mittal & Singh, 2020). To effectively identify and eradicate abusive content, online platforms should invest in technological solutions such as automated content moderation systems and AI algorithms. In addition, regulations should prioritize protecting victims' privacy throughout legal proceedings, preventing further damage to their personal information. It is essential to collect and analyze online gender-based violence data to comprehend its scope, monitor trends, and inform policy decisions. Civil society organizations and advocacy groups are crucial in holding governments and online platforms accountable, promoting policy changes, and driving legal reforms.

Ongoing research and evaluation are indispensable for refining strategies and adapting to new forms of online harassment. Regulations aimed at curbing online gender-based violence are essential for cultivating a digital space that is secure and welcoming for all. It is essential to combat this pervasive issue by combining legal measures, technological innovations, support services, educational initiatives, and advocacy efforts to ensure that individuals of any gender can participate in online communities without fear of harassment or abuse (Parker, 2011).

8. DISCUSSION

This chapter emphasizes the necessity of thoroughly examining the complexities of digital capitalism and recognizing the presence of obstacles and prospects. Notwithstanding its intricacy, it exhibits encouraging prospects for constructive Transformation. The knowledge and understandings offered establish a solid basis for creating policies, advancing strategies, and cooperative endeavours, guiding us towards a future in which digital capitalism instigates significant societal change. With an eye toward the future, the central objective is to employ the digital domain to eliminate pervasive gender prejudices. The appeal for action reflects the shared obligation to utilize technology to pursue equality, envisioning a digital realm where all individuals, irrespective of gender, flourish without encountering discrimination. The chapter argues that establishing a just and all-encompassing community is a duty inextricably linked to the transition to the digital era. It urges us to acknowledge and leverage the revolutionary potential of digital capitalism in support of the indisputable truth of gender equality.

The profound and diverse consequences of gender disparities in digital labour markets extend to economic opportunities for individuals of all genders. Prejudices and stereotypes perpetuate occupational segregation within the digital domain, restricting the economic opportunities of people of various genders by preventing them from entering particular sectors and assuming specific roles. Wage disparities are another aspect of this segregation; women and gender minorities frequently face pay discrepancies even in equivalent positions, which serves to sustain systemic inequities and impede the accumulation of resources and financial security. Non-dominant gender groups face obstacles to economic empowerment due to restricted mentorship and networking opportunities in the absence of visibility. Systemic barriers, such as gendered work environments and biased recruitment practices, hinder the participation of individuals of disparate genders in digital occupations. The influence of traditional gender roles on work structures impedes economic prospects and complicates work-life balance. In digital entrepreneurship, gender disparities stem from inequitable access to networks and funding. A comprehensive approach is essential for addressing biases and nurturing an inclusive digital labour environment that promotes empowerment and equal opportunities to rectify inequalities. A comprehensive examination of the design of a prominent social media platform reveals how colour schemes and emoticons inadvertently perpetuate conventional gender norms. While initially intended to promote inclusivity, default avatars unintentionally reinforce stereotypes, influencing user perceptions. The chapter emphasizes design's critical role in influencing societal norms and urges deliberate decisions to confront biases. Recognizing the existence of favourable and unfavourable consequences, it urges designers, policymakers, and users to actively participate critically to promote fair and just digital environments. Customizable avatars on social media platforms, intended to promote inclusivity, unintentionally perpetuate gender stereotypes, as revealed by an analysis of their design intricacies. The importance of ongoing evaluation necessitates designers reevaluating, testing, and soliciting user feedback to prevent bias perpetuation. Continual endeavours in inclusive design necessitate the refinement of avatar algorithms and the comprehension of user responses for a more equitable digital future; this underscores the significance of collaborative critical analysis.

9. CONCLUSION

As we journey deeper into the intricate domain of digital capitalism, we find ourselves at a crossroads where promise and complexity converge. This path forward necessitates a comprehensive comprehension of the potential challenges and opportunities presented by the emergence of new media technologies. This chapter lays the groundwork for imagining policies, strategies, and collaborations that will propel us toward a future in which digital capitalism catalyzes profound social Transformation. This imagined future is where the digital landscape becomes a potent instrument for dismantling entrenched gender biases, promoting inclusivity, and making gender equality tangible. It is a future in which the digital domain is not only a place to fantasize about equality but also a platform where equality flourishes. Together, we can harness the potential of technology to dismantle existing gender biases, thereby creating a digital world that fosters equity. In doing so, we create a world where everyone, regardless of gender, can anticipate a future filled with limitless possibilities and enduring equality.

REFERENCES

Acilar, A., & Sæbø, Ø. (2021). Towards understanding the gender digital divide: A systematic literature review. *Global Knowledge. Memory and Communication*, *72*(3), 233–249. doi:10.1108/GKMC-09-2021-0147

Andreevskikh, O., & Muravyeva, M. (2020). Doing Gender Online: Digital Spaces for Identity Politics. In Springer eBooks (pp. 205–219). doi:10.1007/978-3-030-42855-6_12

Bannykh, G. (2021). Gender Digital Inequality: Conceptualization and Practices. In Lecture notes in information systems and organization (pp. 167–181). doi:10.1007/978-3-030-71397-3_13

Belingheri, P., Chiarello, F., Colladon, A. F., & Rovelli, P. (2021). Twenty years of gender equality research: A scoping review based on a new semantic indicator. *PLoS One*, *16*(9), e0256474. doi:10.1371/journal.pone.0256474 PMID:34547029

Belloso, M. L. (2022). Women's Rights Under AI Regulation: Fighting AI gender bias through a feminist and intersectional approach. In T.M.C. Asser Press eBooks (pp. 87–107). doi:10.1007/978-94-6265-523-2_5

Böhmer, N., & Griese, K. M. (2020). Developing Gender Equality Marketing Beyond 2025: A Systematic Literature Review. In Springer eBooks (pp. 715–741). doi:10.1007/978-3-030-42412-1_36

Bullough, A., Guelich, U., Manolova, T. S., & Schjoedt, L. (2021). Women's entrepreneurship and culture: Gender role expectations, identities, societal culture, and entrepreneurial environment. *Small Business Economics*, *58*(2), 985–996. doi:10.1007/s11187-020-00429-6

Campos, D., & Scherer, R. (2023). Digital gender gaps in Students' knowledge, attitudes and skills: An integrative data analysis across 32 Countries. *Education and Information Technologies*. Advance online publication. doi:10.1007/s10639-023-12272-9

Carlisle, B. G., Coffman, D. L., Egleston, B. L., & Salholz-Hillel, M. (2023). Training Artificial Intelligence in a Gender-Biased Virtual World Can Result in Biased Conclusions. *Annals of Surgical Oncology*, *30*(8), 5282–5283. doi:10.1245/s10434-023-13557-6 PMID:37140747

Christou, E., & Parmaxi, A. (2022). Gender-sensitive tools and materials for women empowerment in STEM: A systematic review with industrial and instructional recommendations and implications. *Universal Access in the Information Society*, *22*(3), 699–714. doi:10.1007/s10209-022-00881-z

Crespo, R. F. (2023). Moderating the effects of "surveillance capitalism": An Aristotelian perspective. *AI and Ethics*. Advance online publication. doi:10.1007/s43681-023-00334-0

Dey, A., & Orton, B. (2016). Gender and caste intersectionality in India: An analysis of the Nirbhaya Case, December 16 2012. In Advances in gender research (pp. 87–105). doi:10.1108/S1529-212620160000021006

Ding, X., & Chai, Q. (2022). *The rise of digital capitalism and the social changes it caused: how to develop the digital economy in socialist China*. China Political Economy. doi:10.1108/CPE-10-2022-0017

Erdoğan, M., & Topçu, Ç. (2022). Yeni Medya Okuryazarlığı Üzerine Bir Araştırma: Çanakkale Onsekiz Mart Üniversitesi Örneği. *Akdeniz Üniversitesi İletişim Fakültesi Dergisi*, (37), 252–272. doi:10.31123/akil.1077886

Fosch-Villaronga, E., & Poulsen, A. (2022). Diversity and inclusion in artificial intelligence. In T.M.C. Asser Press eBooks (pp. 109–134). doi:10.1007/978-94-6265-523-2_6

Franzoni, V. (2023). Gender differences and bias in artificial intelligence. In Intelligent Systems Reference Library (pp. 27–43). doi:10.1007/978-3-031-21606-0_2

Green, E., & Singleton, C. (2013). 'Gendering the Digital': The Impact of Gender and Technology Perspectives on the Sociological Imagination. In K. Orton-Johnson & N. Prior (Eds.), *Digital Sociology*. Palgrave Macmillan. doi:10.1057/9781137297792_3

Hall, P., & Ellis, D. J. (2023). A systematic review of socio-technical gender bias in AI algorithms. *Online Information Review*, *47*(7), 1264–1279. Advance online publication. doi:10.1108/OIR-08-2021-0452

Harris, A., & Bartlow, S. (2015). Intersectionality: race, gender, sexuality, and class. In Handbooks of sociology and social research (pp. 261–271). doi:10.1007/978-3-319-17341-2_15

Kleinert, S., & Mochkabadi, K. (2021). Gender stereotypes in equity crowdfunding: The effect of gender bias on interpreting quality signals. *The Journal of Technology Transfer*, *47*(6), 1640–1661. doi:10.1007/s10961-021-09892-z

Leavy, S., Meaney, G., Wade, K., & Greene, D. (2020). Mitigating gender bias in machine learning data sets. In Communications in computer and information science (pp. 12–26). doi:10.1007/978-3-030-52485-2_2

Majumdar, S., Tewatia, M., Jamkhedkar, D., & Bhatia, K. (2022). "You do not know me, so do not try to judge me": Gender and identity performance on social media among young Indian users. *Frontiers in Psychology*, *13*, 855947. Advance online publication. doi:10.3389/fpsyg.2022.855947 PMID:35783737

Meier, T., Boyd, R. L., Mehl, M. R., Milek, A., Pennebaker, J. W., Martin, M., Wolf, M., & Horn, A. B. (2020). Stereotyping in the digital age: Male language is "ingenious", female language is "beautiful" – and popular. *PLoS One*, *15*(12), e0243637. doi:10.1371/journal.pone.0243637 PMID:33326456

Mendes, K., Ringrose, J., & Keller, J. (2019). Digital Feminist activism. In Oxford University Press eBooks. doi:10.1093/oso/9780190697846.001.0001

Mittal, S., & Singh, T. (2020). Gender-Based Violence During COVID-19 Pandemic: A Mini-Review. Frontiers in Global Women's Health, 1. doi:10.3389/fgwh.2020.00004

Ng, S., Bharti, M., & Faust, N. T. (2020). The Cambridge Handbook of the International Psychology of Women. In Cambridge University Press eBooks. doi:10.1017/9781108561716

Nicklich, M., & Pfeiffer, S. (2023). Digitalization and self-perpetuation: Dynamics, drivers and temporalities of the Transformation of working worlds. *Work Organisation, Labour & Globalisation*, *17*(1), 7–11. doi:10.13169/workorgalaboglob.17.1.0007

Novelli, C., Taddeo, M., & Floridi, L. (2023). Accountability in artificial intelligence: What it is and how it works. *AI & Society*. Advance online publication. doi:10.1007/s00146-023-01635-y

O'Connor, S., & Liu, H. (2023). Gender bias perpetuation and mitigation in AI technologies: Challenges and opportunities. *AI & Society*. Advance online publication. doi:10.1007/s00146-023-01675-4

Osmond, M. W., & Thorne, B. (2008). Feminist theories. In Springer eBooks (pp. 591–625). doi:10.1007/978-0-387-85764-0_23

Pace, J. (2018). The concept of digital capitalism. *Communication Theory*, *28*(3), 254–269. doi:10.1093/ct/qtx009

Parker, R. (2011). *Grassroots activism, civil society mobilization, and the politics of the global HIV/AIDS epidemic on JSTOR*. https://www.jstor.org/stable/24590789

Paswan, A. K. (2012). Gender, Design and Marketing20122Gloria Moss. Gender, Design and Marketing. Gower Applied Business Research, 2009. 245 pp. $60.00. *Journal of Consumer Marketing*, *29*(6), 456–457. doi:10.1108/07363761211259278

Patnaik, P. P. (2020). Gendered representations in media. In Encyclopedia of the UN sustainable development goals (pp. 1–11). doi:10.1007/978-3-319-70060-1_125-1

Peng, Y. (2022). Gendered division of digital labour in parenting: A qualitative study in Urban China. *Sex Roles*, *86*(5–6), 283–304. doi:10.1007/s11199-021-01267-w PMID:35043029

Prodnik, J. A. (2021). Algorithmic Logic in Digital Capitalism. In AI for Everyone? Critical Perspectives, University of Westminster Press. doi:10.16997/book55.l

Pyun, K. (2022). Introduction: Artists for Political Engagement: A table for women and gender non-conforming artists. In Springer eBooks (pp. 3–26). doi:10.1007/978-3-031-09378-4_1

Raina, S. (2016). *Research: The gender gap in startup success disappears when women fund women*. Harvard Business Review. https://hbr.org/2016/07/research-the-gender-gap-in-startup-success-disappears-when-women-fund-women

Risman, B. J. (2018). Gender as a social structure. In Handbooks of Sociology and Social Research (pp. 19–43). doi:10.1007/978-3-319-76333-0_2

Robinson, Z. F. (2018). Intersectionality and gender theory. In Handbooks of Sociology and Social Research (pp. 69–80). doi:10.1007/978-3-319-76333-0_5

Santoniccolo, F., Trombetta, T., Paradiso, M. N., & Rollè, L. (2023). Gender and Media Representations: A literature review on gender stereotypes, objectification and sexualization. *International Journal of Environmental Research and Public Health, 20*(10), 5770. doi:10.3390/ijerph20105770 PMID:37239498

Scarcelli, C. M., Krijnen, T., & Nixon, P. (2020). Sexuality, gender, media. Identity articulations in the contemporary media landscape. *Information Communication and Society, 24*(8), 1063–1072. doi:10.1080/1369118X.2020.1804603

Scharrer, E. (2013). Representations of gender in the media. In Oxford University Press eBooks (pp. 267–284). doi:10.1093/oxfordhb/9780195398809.013.0015

Shields, S. A. (2008b). Gender: An Intersectionality Perspective. *Sex Roles, 59*(5–6), 301–311. doi:10.1007/s11199-008-9501-8

Singha, S., & Singha, R. (2023). Understanding diversity: The power of differences. In A. M. Even & B. Christiansen (Eds.), *Enhancing Employee Engagement and Productivity in the Post-Pandemic Multigenerational Workforce* (pp. 297–313). IGI Global. doi:10.4018/978-1-6684-9172-0.ch015

Sinha, S. (2018). Gender Digital divide in India: Impacting women's participation in the labour market. In Springer eBooks (pp. 293–310). doi:10.1007/978-981-13-1414-8_14

Stavrianea, A., Theodosis, A., & Kamenidou, I. (2020). Consumers' Perceptions of Gender-Neutral Advertising: An Empirical study. In Springer eBooks (pp. 799–804). doi:10.1007/978-3-030-36126-6_88

Vassilakopoulou, P., & Hustad, E. (2021). Bridging Digital Divides: A Literature Review and Research Agenda for Information Systems Research. *Information Systems Frontiers, 25*(3), 955–969. doi:10.1007/s10796-020-10096-3 PMID:33424421

Vilk, V. (2020, June 3). *You are Not Powerless in the Face of Online Harassment.* Harvard Business Review. https://hbr.org/2020/06/youre-not-powerless-in-the-face-of-online-harassment

Weldon, S. L. (2008). Intersectionality. In *Cambridge University Press eBooks* (pp. 193–218).

KEY TERMS AND DEFINITIONS

Digital Capitalism: Is an economic framework characterized by the preponderance of digital technologies in producing, distributing, and consuming products and services, with the internet and information technology serving as critical components.

Gender Dynamics: Encompass the interplay, responsibilities, and associations among individuals, influenced by their perceived or designated gender. It includes cultural norms, power dynamics, and societal expectations.

New Media Era: An epoch distinguished by the advent and prevalence of interactive and digital communication technologies, fundamentally transformed information generation, distribution, and consumption processes.

Policy Implications: Governmental or organizational entities should consider the outcomes, factors, and suggested actions derived from examining policies and their potential repercussions on communities, individuals, or larger systems.

Social Gender Equality: Endeavours to attain equitable treatment, rights, and opportunities for all individuals of every gender within society while simultaneously confronting and deconstructing systemic prejudices and discrimination predicated on gender.

Societal Transformation: Encompasses extensive and profound alterations to a given society's frameworks, conventions, and principles; technological, cultural, or political developments and results in a distinct social environment frequently instigated it.

Technological Interventions: Refer to deliberate implementations of technology to resolve, enhance, or revolutionize diverse facets of human existence, sectors, or communal concerns.

Chapter 10
Biographical Documentaries on Digital Platforms as a Self-Presentation:
What Happened, Miss Simone? Performance and Pain in the Documentary

Azime Cantaş
https://orcid.org/0000-0002-9356-3050
Afyon Kocatepe University, Turkey

ABSTRACT

The aim of this study is to examine Netflix's film What Happened, Miss Simone, which is an example of a biographical documentary, with sociologist Erving Goffman's concept of self-presentation and performance, and to reveal the roles in the star's life. The details of individual identity, group relations, the impact of the environment, and the action and interactive meaning of information, which Goffman deals with with a micro-sociological analysis, constitute the scope of the study. The documentary tells the life of civil rights activist and American singer Nina Simone during the turmoil of the 1960s. Goffman's approach to the mode of presentation used by the actor and its meaning in the wider social context appears to offer a new perspective on the nature of social interaction and the psychology of the individual in documentary film.

DOI: 10.4018/979-8-3693-1182-0.ch010

INTRODUCTION

With the rise of digitalization, viewing habits have changed, further fueling the debate surrounding documentary cinema. The main issue related to these debates is whether the knowledge of reality about social events and periods that the documentary presents manipulates people. As a result of digitalization, the emergence of on-demand viewing platforms and the enrichment of documentary content in line with the preferences of their viewers has become inevitable in order to attract more viewers. For this reason, digital platforms are focused on commercial strategies that prioritize popularization and producing popular content. As an example of a digital platform, Netflix has undoubtedly revolutionized the digital media industry by providing viewers with more convenient and personalized services. Ultimately, the documentary genre has also become a matter of debate as it embraces the potential of new technologies and techniques to enrich its visual language, while maintaining its primary purpose of providing factual information about life.

The new concept of documentary cinema adopted in the digital age emerges as a commercial popular culture product, beyond the production of content as a product of social memory and social heritage. When examining the most watched documentary films, the transformation of viewers' preferences will also be seen. The most watched content from Netflix; biographical documentaries, scientific documentaries, crime documentaries and socio-cultural documentaries. Documentary is a genre primarily concerned with scientific content and social consequences. Internal goals should be taken into account in documentary filmmaking, including reflecting reality, informing, questioning, and creating social memory (Vaughan, 2019, p. 22). It is important to research the content of popular documentaries and reveal their effects on the audience level. This creates a more ethical approach to documentary filmmaking and ensures that documentary cinema continues to be a valuable tool in creating social memory. "True life" documentaries tend to focus on individual stories rather than social issues. These types of documentaries are typically associated with a specific period or society and are less interested in establishing a social following. While the study discusses debates about reality and objectivity as a backdrop to Netflix's biographical documentaries, individual It aims to reveal the roles in the star's life by examining the film *What Happened, Miss Simone?* (Liz Garbus, 2015), which is thought to reveal a performance ranging from stories to social events, with sociologist Erving Goffman's concept of self-presentation and performance.

In his most important work, The Presentation of the Daily Self in Life, Goffman basically examines the transcultural and almost bio-socially based structure of self-construction and socialization. At the same time, he is considered an early representative of the postmodern perspective, saying that all societies and cultures are characterized by discursive and performative social reality/self (Featherstone, 1995, p. 6). The concepts in which Goffman discusses the details of individual identity, group relations, environmental impact, movement and interactive meaning of information with a micro-sociological analysis constitute the scope of the study (2020, p. 27). *What Happened, Miss Simone?* The biographical documentary tells the life of civil rights activist and American singer Nina Simone. Nina Simone's life necessarily takes us on a journey into collective memory. In the case of biographical documentaries, analysis of the ways in which subjects display their identities and what impact these films have on an audience in an increasingly performance-based society has been used to explore the ways in which members of various cultures and subcultures understand who they are and how they fit into the world they live in.

PRESENTATION OF SELF AND PERFORMANCE IN DAILY LIFE

The self is a multidimensional reality where the individual and the social are intertwined. Although it is mostly defined as centered on "person and self", sociality has an intense impact on the formation and development process of the self (Kağıtçıbaşı, 2009, p. 97). In his 1959 book The Presentation of Self in Everyday Life, Erving Goffman establishes a discursive connection between the theatrical stage and the techniques used by the theater actor and the way the individual presents himself to others during various types of social interaction. In this respect, both the individual and the others he interacts with are aware that a certain performance has occurred. This is communication in the traditional and narrow sense. In his "self theory", Goffman focuses on the close bond of the self with society. He explains this bond with the metaphor of a theater where the individual is the actor and the society is the audience (2020, p. 76). According to Goffman, the individual exhibits his/her self in the social field through four performances: dramatic enactment, idealization, mystification, reality and fiction. However, if we can apply these theories to film, and especially to biographical documentaries, we can see the complex interrelationship of performance in everyday life and the constructive framework of the documentary camera. It is stated that due to the perceived purpose of documentary to record an aspect of the world or an argument, it appears to be the cinematic equivalent of social drama (Vaughan, 2019, p. 30).

Goffman was influenced by C. H. Mead's concept of "self" and advanced his observations through it. However, in his work, he drew frameworks for other concepts based on the concept of "performance". Goffman often uses theater terms when constructing his concepts in his work. However, at the end of his book, Goffman states that the purpose of the terms used is not to promote theatre, they are for social life. First of all, two basic aspects are mentioned in social life. These;

It is called "actor and audience" and while the actor corresponds to the person who performs roles, the audience serves as the person opposite the actor and watching his performance. While the actor's presentation within the framework of his roles is called "performance", the appearance created by this performance is "showcase". Showcase can be defined as "standard equipment of expression" and is conceptualized as "subjectivities that follow the individual wherever he goes" (Goffman, 2020, p. 33). These are not only the features, but also the expression, walking style, sitting style that are easily seen by the audience; age, height, gender, etc. What is meant by showcase here can also be determined as the external features that can only be observed of the external appearance. Dramatic animation is one of the first conceptualizations put forward by Goffman. The actor underlines some confirmatory facts that will remain vague about him and equips these meanings with his performance. Idealization, on the other hand, is the staging of the performance, which is the expectation of the audience, which allows it to create abstract effects on the audience through the showcase while the routine is staged. There is a point in these performances called "expressive harmony". When there is no harmony, the so-called "misrepresentation" occurs. One of the methods we frequently experience in daily life is the so-called "mystification" or "mystification" that the actor uses during the presentation, in which some points in the performance are revealed while others are deliberately hidden. At this point, it would not be wrong to say that the teams resemble a secret society. Regions and regional behaviors refer to the characteristics of the sections that will be called the front of the stage and the backstage. Discrete roles complicate the relationship between function, knowledge, and place. The chapter that Goffman refers to and which contains the most unifying part of the book is "The Art of Impression Control", which means avoiding art performance disruptions (2020, p. 196).

G. Herbert Mead, in his work titled Mind, Self and Society, states that the self is formed as a result of the individual's social experience process as a whole and his relationships with other individuals participating in this process (1972, p. 135). This explains that social life is a mutual interaction and the self is a product of this interaction. Therefore, according to Mead, the self should not be analyzed as a one-way process in which society pours its characteristics onto the individual. The individual creates his/her self through the communication and interaction he/she establishes with other people, individually or in groups. This communication and interaction also makes it possible to understand and receive the behavior and thought patterns observed in others. What is understood and received also includes a process that is exhibited in society. For this reason, the individual-society relationship creates an area where not only the self is formed but also where the self is exhibited or, in Goffman's words, presented. Goffman analyzes society through relationships between people rather than grand theories. Therefore, society is a field of interaction. Individual humans are active and intelligent beings (Wallace & Wolf, 1995, p. 219). However, based on his observations, he thinks that in the relationship between the individual and society, the individual acts by taking into account the elements in the social sphere. In this context, he based the Self-Presentation Theory on the expectations of the society from the individual and the individual's effort to meet the expectations. The etiquette that ensures daily functioning is central to this expectation (Goffman, 1966, p. 24).

The individual meets the expectation to the extent that he reflects the rules of etiquette in his behavior. Accordingly, the individual is the actor, while the audience is the society. A role is a predetermined pattern of action by the actor that can be exhibited or played in other situations (Goffman, 2020, p. 28). In other words, status draws the boundary of actions in the social sphere and it is up to the individual to play the role required by that status. For example, a judge to be prudent and cautious while doing his job, a pilot in the flight cabin to be cool, and an accountant to be sensitive are the roles required by their status (Goffman, 1972, p. 77). At this point, the impression created by the role played on the audience becomes important. Goffman divides the impression into given and radiated. The former involves the verbal parts of role-based performance, while the latter involves actions (2020, p. 31). If the actor's performance is inadequate in the verbal and/or operational parts, the impression of the audience will be negative. However, if the opposite is the case, the actor has successfully fulfilled his role and will receive acceptance and approval from the audience such as love, support, respect and reputation. Therefore, the audience, whose expectations are fulfilled, will not refrain from applauding the actor. It is possible to see this as the final point of the role expectation and the relationship between the role, the audience and the actor. The point reached also constitutes the nature of the individual-society relationship. In this relationship, the individual will develop and present his/her self, but the important thing is to present a self that is compatible with the social field. In other words, the self will be revealed as a behavior in accordance with the determined rules (Poloma, 1979, p. 158). The rewards obtained by the individual who presents himself by playing his role in the social sphere also stimulate his conscious or unconscious effort to create a positive self-perception. Goffman calls this impression management. According to him, the individual uses many tools to give the best possible impression of himself. Personal showcase of position or rank, clothing, gender, age, racial characteristics, size, posture, speech patterns, facial expressions and body movements; Furniture, items and accessories are also the tools that make up the set. The individual directs society's impression of himself by using these in accordance with the environment he is in.

Biographical Documentaries on Digital Platforms as a Self-Presentation

As influential as Goffman's theories were in understanding how people behave in everyday life, the way we communicate has changed significantly since 1959, when his ideas were first published. For example, the assumption underlying nearly all of Goffman's social event studies is that these interactions occur face-to-face; two or more individuals are in direct contact in the same physical and temporal space. Since then, technological advances such as the birth of the internet and the proliferation of digital production processes have had a profound impact on how we communicate with each other. These factors and others have led to increased globalization, in which "the peoples of the world are incorporated into a single world society" (Albrow, 1990, p. 9). In some way, these developments have led to changes in our social performance, which in turn has affected the types of documentaries we watch.

Biographical documentary films draw attention to how performance functions in constructing individual identity and can be interpreted as an invitation for viewers to reflect on their own sense of self. Broadly speaking, Nigel Hamilton defines biography as "our creative nonfictional output dedicated to recording and interpreting real lives" (2007, p. 1). To this he adds that, as has plagued documentary criticism, the recent increasing popularity of biography has intensified the debate about the form's notions of "reality and imagination". According to Hamilton, the ongoing tension for biography is the tug of war between idealization (the tendency of biographers, especially in ancient times, to offer complimentary things) on the other. Where does truth end and interpretation begin? Is biography essentially a chronicle of an individual's life journey or is it an art form of human portraiture that must capture essence and distinctiveness for socially and psychologically constructive reasons? (Hamilton, 2007, p. 15). Although its factual basis may precede any of its recordings or representations, the film itself is necessarily performative, since the interplay between performance and reality gives it meaning (Bruzzi, 2013, p. 186). The performance techniques or stylistic devices historically associated with fictional film, then, are instrumental to the structure and aesthetics of the performative documentary. These can include reconstruction, artificial lighting, non-narrative music, makeup, costumes, animation, or any other number of stylistic choices. Documentary film has a very important role to play in the representation of our cultures. However, rather than assessing how authentic this representation is in contemporary biographical documentaries, it is clear that it would be more fruitful to analyze how these films fully negotiate meaning through performativity and engage the viewer with performance and performative elements to reflect on their own identity.

It is recognized that the ways in which documentary filmmakers represent the "real world" correspond to the social and cultural contexts that determine how subjectivity is shaped and understood. The function of the documentary is implied from the outset by John Grierson's approach to the "creative handling of reality" in reference to the work of Robert Flaherty (Rotha, 1952, p. 70). Over the following decades, however, critical debate has argued that the performative potential inherent in Grierson's depiction is firmly associated with "fact" and "phenomenon" in the documentary. It is noteworthy how numerous feature-length documentary films published in the twenty-first century respond to the perceptions and debates of "truth" and "fact" in our contemporary society transformed by Web 2.0 and 3.0, virtual reality technologies and digital media. This leads us to think about how we see ourselves, how we construct ourselves, and how we become our selves through social changes, a deliberate performance aesthetic (Taylor, 2001). Contemporary documentary can play a powerful role in the construction of identity, both for the individuals in the films and for the audiences who watch them in the wider social sphere. According to Goffman (2020, p. 77), if the whole world is not a stage, it remains an important space for us to identify, experience, and exhibit our various "selves" and a rich source of personal stories for the documentary filmmaker to capture. The current era of digital publishing has led to a worldwide increase in the number of users and view rates (Koluaçık, 2023, p. 211). When it comes to digital media, the future of the Netflix platform instantly comes to everyone's mind as a unique reality. Netflix, a digital streaming platform founded in 1997 in Los Gatos, California, has gained a lot of attention and popularity around the world in a relatively short period of time (Artillery, 2023, p. 133). By expanding its services to different countries and partnering with technology companies to stream on all devices, Netflix has become a global phenomenon.

Documentary cinema is a unique type of cinema that transforms viewing into a witnessing experience and gives the viewer a sense of moral responsibility. Documentary cinema sheds light on society and social qualities as a memory space, making it a collective work. However, in recent years, it has been observed that collective memory is ignored in new documentary cinema products available on digital platforms. Instead, biographical documentaries of popular people have become the focus, embracing individuality rather than collective memory as a tool of popular culture. The new concept of documentary cinema adopted in the digital age is the production of content as a product of social memory and emerges as a commercial popular culture product beyond being a product of social heritage. Any discussion of a revolution in documentary filmmaking must consider its inherent goals, including reflecting reality, informing, questioning, and creating social memory. Recent examples of documentary films and original productions on platforms such as Netflix show that the genre is moving away from these basic aims. "True life" documentaries tend to focus on individual stories rather than social issues. Documentary film can be considered the intersection of Goffman's social acting/theatre acting hypothesis due to its historical and critical ties to the representation of the "real" world. There are social interaction and various performance tools available to an individual. Managing this situation is included in the narrative of the documentary film. In any case, the on-screen actions of a person captured by documentary filmmakers will reveal some aspect of that person's identity. These features; film director, editor, cinematographer, etc. The way it is framed by will affect how the movie audience responds to the person being filmed. This means that the identity of the documentary subject is not fixed and is more or less out of his or her control. One of Goffman's conclusions was (2020, p. 77): "The ordinary social relationship itself is brought together in creating a scene through the exchange of dramatically exaggerated actions, counterreactions, and terminating responses. Even in the hands of inexperienced actors, scenarios can come to life because life itself is a dramatically animated thing. The whole world is not a stage, of course, but it is not easy to determine in what important ways it is not."

WHAT HAPPENED, MISS SIMONE? PERFORMANCE AND PAIN IN THE DOCUMENTARY

"Do you know what freedom means to me?

Don't be afraid! "I wish half my life was spent without fear."

What Happened, Miss Simone? It is an American biographical documentary film about Nina Simone, directed by Liz Garbus. The film was released on Netflix on June 26, 2015, after its premiere at the 2015 Sundance Film Festival. The film takes an intimate look at the legendary life of Nina Simone, a classically trained pianist who became a chart-topping chanteuse and dedicated civil rights activist. Amidst the violent, haunting, and senseless daily life of the civil rights era in 1960s America, Simone struggled to reconcile her artistic identity and ambition with her commitment to a movement. Compiled from hours of autobiographical tapes, the film reveals the life of a great artist and the absurdities of his time. At the height of her fame, Simone estranged herself from her family, country, career and fans and gave up performing. Establishing a relationship between Erving Goffman's concept of performance and Nina Simone's biographical documentary offers an interesting approach to understanding the artist's life and performance on stage from a social interaction and dramaturgical perspective. According to Goffman, people enact social roles in their daily lives and perform on a kind of stage. These performances are shaped according to the audience's perceptions and society's expectations. When Nina Simone's biographical documentary is considered in this context, Simone's periodic performances in her life seem to be shaped in response to social changes and her own internal struggles. For example, the performances of Simone, who is also known as an activist as well as her musical career, can be considered not only as a musical event, but also as a struggle and performance for social change. When a person enacts a role, he implicitly demands that his observers take seriously the impressions unfolding before their eyes. They are asked to believe that the character they are watching really has the qualities they pretend to have, that the work they are doing will actually lead to the results it is implied to have, and that, in general, everything is as it seems. When considering performance, it would be appropriate to turn the question around and start with the question of whether the person himself believes in the impression of reality he is trying to create in others. Goffman, who follows this inverted question throughout the book, emphasizes believing in the role one plays in daily life and being absorbed in this role. According to him, a person does this sometimes for his personal interests, sometimes for the interests of a group, and sometimes for the society. The transformations in Nina Simone's life reveal that she performs for society. Goffman mentions two extremes (2020, p. 31): "I mentioned two extremes: One can believe in one's own game or take a cynical approach."

Erving Goffman defines the intentional or unintentional expressions we make during performances as showcases. The stimuli that make up the personal showcase are divided into two as appearance and attitude, according to the function of the information they carry. Nina Simone is an iconic performer who has a strong presence on stage with her African-American appearance. His presence on stage reflects his strong and independent personality. There is a distinct presence in facial expressions and body language that conveys the strength and resilience of African-American culture. Her clothing style reflects Simone's commitment to her African-American heritage. She usually preferred stylish and original clothes. Her Afro hair style, curly and natural hair texture, and clothing choices made with colorful fabrics show her deep commitment to African-American culture and aesthetics. Simone's African-American appearance includes not only an external aesthetic but also a combative stance. His stance against racial discrimination and social injustice in 1960s America is a call for the strengthening of the African-American community. This stance is not only a part of his art, but also an expression of a social message. Nina Simone's appearance, stage performances, clothing style and stance enable an artist to express her cultural and social identity beyond just music. This view, which reflects the beauty, difficulties and resilience of African-American culture, makes his art more profound and impressive.

Dramatic Enactment: Art as Part of Social Change

Goffman's concept is about individuals playing their role in society, but also emphasizes social change. Nina Simone's documentary illustrates Goffman's concept of dramatic animation by explaining how her art contributes to social change and how she creates a social impact through her music. Dramatic enactment is a performance undertaken by an individual assuming the characteristics he or she carries or claims to have. From time to time, artists wanted to appear as individuals who carried/reflected the general tendencies of the period they lived in, and they reflected these motivations on their scenes, which were the most personal form of self-presentation. The culmination of all the accumulations such as biography, iconography and symbolic and imaginary meanings needed in the interpretation of some songs is the effect of dramaturgy on the formation of the self (Grant & Sloniowski, 2013, p. xxiv).

Simone is not just a singer; she is also a songwriter and a classically trained pianist. His repertoire includes jazz, folk and American music standards, as well as original compositions about racial and social injustice. As critic Stanley Crouch stated in the film, "Once you hear Simone's voice, you will not forget her." This documentary demonstrates dramatic reenactment with numerous examples of Simone's compositions and interpretations. These include "Mississippi Goddam", "Backlash Blues", "Strange Fruit", "I Loves You Porgy", "Ain't Got No/I Got Life", "My Baby Just". Using archival photographs and film, including performances by Simone over three decades, excerpts from the singer's diaries, and interviews with family members, friends, and musical colleagues, director Liz Garbus not only traces Simone's life and career, but also her career. It also serves as a reminder of the history that shaped his perspective and the course of his life. Among the interviewees is Lisa Simone Kelly, Simone's only child, who worked closely on this account of her mother's life. It also describes how Schackman, Simone's longtime guitarist and music director, gave clear-sighted accounts of Simone's many problems, while also describing his devotion to her for more than forty years.

Nina Simone, whose real name is Eunice Waymon, was born in 1933 in the town of Tryon, North Carolina, USA. He was introduced to music at the age of 4 by playing the piano at the church where his mother served as a preacher, when he attended services (Garbus, 2015). Later, she also took part in events organized by the church choir. At one of these events, music teacher Ms. Mazzanovich, one of the two white women in the audience, decided to give lessons to Nina Simone, and Nina Simone began her classical piano training, which would last for 5 years. At a time when black people lived in separate residential areas, could not sit in the same seats on buses, and black women were servants of white people, a white woman's desire to teach a talented black girl is also an example of female solidarity. During this period when the railways separated the residential areas of blacks and whites, Simone would cross the railway and go to Miss Mazzovich every weekend for music education. In these classes, Mrs. Mazzanovich and Simone Bach studied the works of classical music geniuses such as Beethoven and Brahms. Nina Simone gave many concerts during this period, and the income from the concert was accumulated in the "Eunice Waymon" fund created by Mrs. Mazzanovich. Nina Simone continued her music education through this fund (Simone, 2023). In an interview, he mentioned that during these periods, it was forbidden to talk about racial segregation at home, and that it was forbidden to talk about different residential areas of blacks and whites, so he could not consciously realize the discrimination. After graduating from high school, he was shocked when he realized that the reason why his scholarship application to the Curtis Institute of Music was rejected was because he was black (Garbus, 2015).

After this date, he wanted to become America's first black classical music artist, but due to financial difficulties, he had to start playing the piano in a bar in Atlantic City and singing after the bar owner stated that he had to sing if he wanted to continue working. Simone, who started singing for the first time in her life because she needed money, changed her name from Eunice Waymon to Nina Simone so that her family would not learn about this action, which they would consider a sin. Simone, who performed all kinds of music at first, later made only Blues music. The act of singing, which Nina Simone started as a necessity, hence music; Due to her gender and race, she has become the only tool through which she can express herself while struggling with the difficulties brought by the masculine and social gaze. At the age of 25, Nina Simone released her debut album, Little Girl Blue, in 1958 (Simone, 2023). Since then, he has become a blues artist with many fans. At that time, black women were last in the hierarchy of rights in America after black men. So much so that black women identified themselves as other others (Krolokke & Sorenson, 2012). However, women like Nina Simone, who have been able to create a space of expression for themselves through music, have been able to exist in the public sphere and reflect this in their behavior. Despite all this, Simone accepted the request of Andrew Stroud, whom she fell in love with, who wanted to quit her job as a police officer and become her manager after marriage, and gave her husband the right to have a say in his career. Andrew Stroud fulfilled Nina Simone's dream of performing at the Carnegie Halida. After this concert, which took place in one of the most famous concert halls in the world, Nina Simone became a well-known name all over the world and fascinated many people.

The African American civil rights movement is the most active period of the social justice struggle that took place throughout the 1950s and 1960s for black Americans to obtain equal rights before the law in the United States and to prevent prejudice and violence against blacks (Gürocak, 2023, p. 144). It is not a coincidence that during such a period, Nina Simone developed an activist attitude by joining the black movement (Civil Rights Movement) and reflected this in her music. After these dates, the stage and music; He used it as a tool to stand against racial discrimination, which he wanted to ignore before, and to support the black struggle. He called the protest music he performed during this period as Civil Rights Music (Garbus, 2015). Backlash Blues, Mississippi Goddam, Four Women, Lorraine Hansberry's play To Be Young, Gifted and Black, Marthin Luther King's posthumous Why? (The King of Love is Dead). After the bomb attack on the church in Birmingham on September 15, 1963, in which 4 little girls were killed and 20 black people were injured, he wrote the most angry song in his history, Mississippi Goddam (Garbus, 2015). Stage artist and activist Dick Gregory said about Mississippi Goddam, "There is something different about women. If you look at what black people have suffered over the years, not a single black man has had the courage to say 'Damn Mississippi'. Then how happy they were when that little woman talked about the problems. We all wanted to say it, but he said it: "Damn Mississippi!" (Garbus, 2015). The reason why such harsh words were written by a woman was the pressure and violence she experienced in every field, from all segments of society, but most of all from the man she married, Andrew Stroud. With these harsh words, Nina Simone was expressing her anger against male violence, which she tried to convince herself was not a bad thing for a long time, and against racial discrimination, which she could not accept for a long time. As a result of male violence, Simone; She decided to express herself through the songs she wrote and performed and the music she played, and she was quite successful. Nina Simone often expressed race and gender issues in her works. Simone said that her close friend, playwright and activist and feminist Lorraine Hansberry, initiated her political education and saw herself as a black person in a white country and as a woman in a world ruled by men (Perry, 2018). In other words, in the 60s, she became politicized about race and gender, and expressed the problems she could not solve and express about male violence in her private life with her songs.

Retaining Control of Expression

After some time after their marriage, Nina Simone mentions that Andrew Stroud made her work so much that she could not spare enough time for her daughter Lisa and that she was very tired. Moreover, she has been exposed to physical/psychological and sexual violence almost from the first days of her marriage, including her pregnancy. In these years after 1960, even though women gained their rights such as participating in business life and political life, they were still exposed to many discriminations in their social and private lives. Especially black women; They have been subjected to various types of violence from white men because they are women and black, from white women because they are black, and from black men because they are women. Moreover, they had difficulty in participating in the women's struggle due to racial discrimination, and as a result, they internalized sexist conditioning and were exposed to a great and irreparable degree of sexism (Hooks, 2012, p. 77). Almost all of them have been subjected to psychological/physical/sexual violence by their spouses or lovers and other men. Years later, Nina Simone described this violence in an interview in which she said that Andrew protected her from everyone except herself and that she was very afraid of him. In the interview shared in the documentary, "What is freedom?" "For me, being free means not being afraid!" answered (Garbus, 2015). The song Brown Baby, which he sang in 1962, the date his daughter Lisa was born, emphasizes freedom, racial discrimination and male violence: *"As you grow up I want you to drink from the plenty cup... I want you to stand up tall and proud ...And I want you to speak up clear and loud...Brown Baby..."* (Nina Simone, Brown Baby, 1962). Simone, who gives the impression that she is talking to her baby Lisa, asks her not to assume the roles that society expects from women and to stand against all kinds of discrimination. In this case, since black people were advised to stand up against inequality, Simone, in a way, tried to express that she herself stood up. The song emphasizes freedom and talks about the evils of men who dominate the masculine system created in the world. The meaning of the songs sung and written by Nina Simone showed a parallel attitude with her life, that is, they became a means of communication for her.

After joining the Civil Rights Movement, Nina Simone focused on political songs and began to fight for a common political goal with the leading names of the black movement such as Malcolm X, Betty Shabaz, Martin Luther King, and Lorraine Hansberry. However, as the days went by, he became more and more angry during this struggle, said that he was not anti-violence, and even started to advocate violence. Due to his protest songs and violent statements, he could not take part in many television programs and could not perform in many venues. Nina Simone about violence in an interview: "If it were up to me, I would be a murderer. I would buy a bunch of guns, go to the South, and fight violence with violence, guns with guns. But my husband said, 'You don't know anything about guns' and refused to teach. All I had was music, so I listened to it" (Garbus, 2015). She felt the need to express her anger to the extent that she accepted not to perform in many venues or appear on television programs anymore. In this way, she used her music as a message tool to express the anger within her. In fact, he has tried to tell something with this anger throughout his life, with all his songs. Her anger in her songs is, in a way, Simone's cries for help. His answer to the question of whether the artist's real role is to draw attention to the need for change is remarkable. Simone: "It's something I chose to do and I felt an obligation to do it. So, that's my role. But sometimes, I wish it wasn't like that. Artists who don't try to give a message are probably happier. But I have to live with Nina, and it's a very difficult thing" (Garbus, 2015). During this time, which corresponds to the end of the 1960s, Nina Simone was also struggling with tantrums and depression. Of these cries for help, he wrote in his diary, "Every night I was worn out for years in these filthy places called dressing rooms. I pretended to be happy when I was sad. I'm screaming 'someone help me' but my voice can't be heard, it's like a silent scream..." He also mentioned it in his sentences. Nina Simone's anger and the way she expresses it, the screams and crises, the fact that people are discriminated against because of their race, as well as the fact that people are exposed to discrimination, oppression and violence because they are women and that she is one of those women, can be understood from the following sentences she wrote in her diary: "I hate her." "I do, I intend to leave him, if the beatings continue, I can't stand the beatings – it's killing me inside."

Mystification

This concept includes the idea of how people can present themselves by consciously playing a role in social interactions, and in this way arouse the curiosity of the other party. Nina Simone's documentary deals with the difficulties in the artist's personal life, emotional struggles and personal triumphs. Within the framework of Goffman's concept, the documentary attracts the curiosity of the audience by mystifying Simone's private life. Special memories, personal triumphs and hardships are used as an element of mystery in the documentary. Nina Simone's social activism and struggles are mysteriously presented in the documentary, allowing viewers to gain a deeper understanding of the artist's social interactions. The documentary explored the emotional depths and inner conflicts behind Nina Simone's art, adding an element of mystery to viewers about how she interacted with the artist's music.

In the song Four Women, which he wrote in 1966, he told the story of 4 women in their language. In the first part of the song, the difficulties of black-skinned Aunt Sarah are mentioned. The suffering of black women is expressed using the example of Aunt Sarah, and in fact, these sentences seem to be written for all black women. In the second part of the song, Saffrona, who was born as a result of a white man sexually assaulting her black mother, is mentioned. This part of the song describes the plea of a girl born as a result of rape. The situation of women and girls, who do not feel like they belong anywhere due to social pressures and have been exposed to many similar situations, has been conveyed to the whole world through this song. In the third part of the song, a prostitute is mentioned. Making sentences as if she was a prostitute for such a period is a very brave move and, in a way, a criticism of the order. In the last part of the song, the story of a child born as a slave is told. As can be understood from the sentences used, Simone, who expressed the experiences of a young child with empathy, wanted to express how difficult it can be to be a slave child. In this song, Nina Simone tells the story of four women who have different lives but have common pain. Contrary to the songs that draw attention to the beauty and delicacy of women, the song, which tells about women who are forced to face various kinds of difficulties under racial discrimination and male domination, is one of Nina Simone's contributions to women's solidarity (Dalaylı & Ünlü, 2022, p. 84).

By the 70s, Nina Simone decided that she did not want to live in America and, saying that she never wanted to return, divorced her husband Andrew and went to Liberia in Africa, a country founded by former American slaves. When she was leaving, she wrote the following sentences to her husband Andrew: "I have nothing left to give, Andrew. I'm too tired to talk. You go your way, I go mine. If possible, somewhere where I won't have much to do with people. "I am strangely at peace." Nina Simone, who said that she had the happiest days of her life in Africa, did not sing, did not go on stage or play the piano in Liberia, and even said that she hated the piano. The reason behind this attitude of Nina Simone, who has been playing the piano since the age of four, is that she feels truly free: "I remember thinking that America was something I had seen in my dreams and that it had disappeared as if it had never existed. It was just a dream I had before and I woke up with my own efforts. Because I worked there, in that prison, for a very long time. But now I was home, I was free now, and I wasn't going back" (Garbus, 2015). These sentences he uttered in an interview prove that he felt truly free after leaving America, where people were discriminated against only because of their skin color and did not feel free because of the violence they experienced in their relationships. Simone also mentioned in an interview that she felt free several times while singing on stage. After a while, she settled in France because she had to earn money. The following sentences he made at the Montreux Jazz Festival, where he took the stage again after a long break, prove that he expressed himself through music:

It's very nice, you haven't forgotten me. I didn't think you'd forgotten, but I'm tired. You don't understand what I mean. A lot of people in the show business say; 'He used to be a star. It's already hit rock bottom.' Things like that that don't mean anything to me. I hope you will soon see me or my soul in another space, on another plane. I don't want to disappoint you, but that's how I feel. I think the only way to describe what kind of person I am right now would be to sing a song by Janislan. (Garbus, 2015)

Nina Simone sang the song Stars after these sentences. With the lyrics in the song, it is understood that despite everything, he cannot leave his disappointments behind and that he carries the tiredness of the pain of the scars of past traumas. Despite all the feeling of freedom away from America, traces of the bad days and traumas of the past remained, and in the following years, Nina Simone was diagnosed with manic depressive and bipolar disorder. At this stage of her life, Nina Simone gained strength from music as well as medications, and music was a major factor in her recovery phase. His daughter, Lisa Simone, said: "He was very happy making music. I think music saved him" (Garbus, 2015). In the film, Stroud expresses that he became impatient with Simone's interest in civil rights and political issues and warned her that it threatened her career. It has also been pointed out that their relationship has become violent and abusive at times.

CONCLUSION

Nina Simone, on the one hand, as a restless impression maker engaged in the very human business of staging performances; On the other hand, he is a character, a symbol, a subject with the courage, strength and other superior qualities that the performance aims to convey. The concept of idealization gives the opportunity to think about Simone's place in her life, regarding how well she complies with social norms or how she resists these norms. Simone's performance on stage reflects her sensitivity and struggle for social issues through her music. This performance is seen by the audience as a reaction against social injustices and an expression of activism. During the artist's lifetime, the mass anti-Vietnam War movement grew, and was soon followed by a wave of strikes by the American working class. Meanwhile, the assassinations of Malcolm. Simone increasingly rejected the reformism and pacifism of the official protests, but embraced cultural black nationalism and an increasingly hardline outlook. The second half of the documentary focuses on Simone's personal difficulties and mental illness, but something important has been overlooked in the process. Although the singer's psychological problems cannot be ignored, it seems that they could not be contextualized with the enormous changes that took place in American political life during this period. As the old civil rights institution gradually merged with the Democratic Party, "black power" and nationalist demagogues such as former Student Nonviolent Coordinating Committee (SNCC) leader Stokely Carmichael emerged with a pseudo-revolutionary message that was openly hostile to the working class. Friends and colleagues eventually found out that Simone was living in terrible conditions in Paris, stealing $300 a night in a small café. Schackman and others helped the troubled singer get medical treatment. He was able to continue performing from time to time both in Europe and occasionally in the USA. She died at her home in Carry-le-Rouet, near Marseille, France, in April 2003, after several years of treatment for breast cancer. With someone as caring and sensitive as Simone, it would certainly be a mistake to view her emotional traumas as purely personal traumas. Given her level of intellectual and moral commitment, and the expectations aroused by the great struggles of the 1960s, how can Simone's ultimate disappointment, confusion, and helplessness, which find painful spiritual expression, be fully grasped without taking into account the betrayals of these struggles? (Hayes & Mazelis, 2015, p. 2).

Simone's activist attitude, which argued that black people should have equal rights at a time when white people were claimed to be superior, turned into an idealized representation for black people. The social significance of Simone's music should be sought in the revolutionary structures of Africans who have created their own aesthetics. Because his style is actually a revolution of Africans. For this reason, Simone's performance is a form of endurance that black people have created to revive their own culture, and it also carries deep meanings. Although aesthetic and moral standards are dictated by the dominant white culture, Nina Simone has not given up on being herself even in the existing social order and has recreated her true self. At a time when the perception of women, and especially black women, was to serve, to look beautiful to men, to entertain them, and to keep silent as much as possible, she used her music as an effective means of communication by drawing attention to their not rosy lives. The fact that it is a raw and original expression of instinctive emotions such as pain, love, pleasure and anger has made his music powerful. For Simone, who suffered great difficulties in her early years, music has always existed as both a way of life and communication.

REFERENCES

Albrow, M. (1990). *'Introduction' in Globalization, Knowledge and Society: Readings from International Sociology.* London: Sage in association with the International Sociological Association.

Bruzzi, S. (2013). *'Introduction' in New Documentary* (2nd ed.). Routledge.

Dalaylı, F. Ü., & Ünlü, E. (2022). İletişim, Kadın ve Blues Müzik. *International Journal of Interdisciplinary and Intercultural Art, 7*(14), 72–88. doi:10.29228/ijiia.181

Featherstone, M. (1995). *'Introduction: Globalizing Cultural Complexity' in Undoing Culture: Globalization, Postmodernism and Identity*. SAGE.

Garbus, L. (2015). *What Happened, Miss Simone? Belgeseli* [Sinema Filmi].

Goffman, E. (1966). *Behavior in Public Places: Notes on The Social Organization of Gatherings*. The Free Press.

Goffman, E. (1972). *Encounters: Two Studies in The Sociology of Interaction.* Penguin University Books.

Goffman, E. (2020). *Günlük Yaşamda Benliğin Sunumu.* Metis Yayınları.

Grant, B. K., & Sloniowski, J. (2013). *Introduction' in Documenting the Documentary: Close Readings of Documentary Film and Video New Edition.* Wayne State University Press.

Gürocak, T. (2023). Queer Mücadele ve Erken Dönem Queer Video Aktivizmi. In I. E. Er (Ed.), *Medya ve Kültür Odağında İletişim* (pp. 143–162). Akademisyen Yayınevi Kitabevi.

Hamilton, N. (2007). *'Prologue' in Biography: A Brief History.* Harvard University Press. doi:10.4159/9780674038226

Hayes, H., & Mazelis, F. (2015, July 22). *What Happened, Miss Simone?: The life of African-American singer, pianist and civil rights activist Nina Simone.* World Socialist Web Site: wsws.org/contact

Hooks, B. (2012). *Feminizm Herkes İçindir* (Z. Demirsu & O. Günay, Trans.). BGST Yayıncılık.

Kağıtçıbaşı, Ç. (2009). *Family, Self and Human Development Across Cultures: Theoιy and Applications (2nd ed.).* Psychology Press.

Koluaçık, İ. (2023). Dijital Platformlar ve Türk Filmi İçerikleri Bağlamında "Disney+" ve "Netflix" Karşılaştırması. In T. Söğütlüler (Ed.), *Ekran ve Toplum -Sinema, Televizyon ve Dijital Platformlar Üzerine Tartışmalar* (pp. 211–238). Nobel Akademik Yayıncılık.

Krolokke, C., & Sorenson, S. (2012). Gender Communication Theories, Analyses: From Silence to Performance. Londan: Sage.

Mead, G. H. (1972). *Mind, Self & Society: From The Standpoint of A Social Behaviorist. Eighteenth Impression.* The University of Chicago Press.

Perry, I. (2018). *How the Great Lorraine Hansberry Tried To Make Sense of it All.* https://lithub.com/how-the-great-lorraine-hansberry-tried-to-make-sense-of-it-all/

Poloma, M. (1979). *Contemporary Sociological Theory.* Macmillan Publishing Co. Inc.

Rotha, P. (1952). *The Documentary Film* (2nd ed.). Faber.

Simone, N. (2023). *Nina Simone Biyografi.* Retrieved from Nina Simone: http://www.ninasimone.com/bio/

Taylor, C. (2001). *Sources of Self: The Making of The Modern Identity (10th ed.).* Harvard University Press.

Topçu, Ç. (2023). Akademik Çalışmalarda Netflix Durumu: Sistematik Bir Okuma. In T. Söğütlüler (Ed.), *Ekran ve Toplum: Sinema, Televizyon ve Dijital Platformlar Üzerine Tartışmalar* (pp. 133–153). Nobel Yayıncılık.

Vaughan, A. J. (2019). Performing Identity in Contemporary Biographical Documentary. *Faculty of Arts and Humanities Thesis for the degree of Doctor of Philosophy.* University of Southampton.

Wallace, R., & Wolf, A. (1995). *Contemporary Sociological Theory: Continuing The Classical Tradition (4th ed.).* Prentice-Hall Inc.

Compilation of References

Acilar, A., & Sæbø, Ø. (2021). Towards understanding the gender digital divide: A systematic literature review. *Global Knowledge. Memory and Communication, 72*(3), 233–249. doi:10.1108/GKMC-09-2021-0147

Adi, A. (2018). *Protest Public Relations: Communicating dissent and activism.* Routledge. doi:10.4324/9781351173605

Ahamad, S., Veeraiah, V., Ramesh, J. V. N., Rajadevi, R., Reeja, S. R., Pramanik, S., & Gupta, A. (2023). *Deep Learning based Cancer Detection Technique, Thrust Technologies' Effect on Image Processing*. IGI Global.

Ahmed, R. R., Streimikiene, D., Qadir, H., & Streimikis, J. (2023). Effect of green marketing mix, green customer value, and attitude on green purchase intention: Evidence from the USA. *Environmental Science and Pollution Research International, 30*(5), 11473–11495. doi:10.1007/s11356-022-22944-7 PMID:36094715

Aktan, C. C., & Tunç, M. (1998). Bilgi Toplumu ve Türkiye. *Yeni Türkiye Dergisi, 4*(19), 118–133.

Albrow, M. (1990). *'Introduction' in Globalization, Knowledge and Society: Readings from International Sociology.* London: Sage in association with the International Sociological Association.

Ali, H. M., Boddy, J., O'Leary, P., & Ewart, J. (2016). *Exploring the use of public relations in organising activism: Implications for addressing gender-based violence in the developing world.* Academic Press.

Alkon, A., & Norgaard, K. M. (2009). Breaking the food chains: An investigation of food justice activism. *Sociological Inquiry, 79*(3), 289–305. doi:10.1111/j.1475-682X.2009.00291.x

Allagui, I., & Breslow, H. (2016). Social media for public relations: Lessons from four effective cases. *Public Relations Review, 42*(1), 20–30. doi:10.1016/j.pubrev.2015.12.001

Al-Sarawi, S., Anbar, M., Alieyan, K., & Alzubaidi, M. (2017). Internet of Things (IoT) communication protocols: Review. *Proceedings of the ICIT 2017—8th International Conference on Information Technology*, 685–690.

Alyanak, B. (2016). Internet addiction. *Journal of Clinical Medicine Pediatrics, 8*(5), 20–24.

Ameen, N., Tarhini, A., Shah, M. H., Madichie, N., Paul, J., & Choudrie, J. (2021). Keeping customers' data secure: A cross-cultural study of cybersecurity compliance among the Gen-Mobile workforce. *Computers in Human Behavior, 114*, 106531. doi:10.1016/j.chb.2020.106531

Anderson, D. S. (1992). Identifying and responding to activist publics: A case study. *Journal of Public Relations Research, 4*(3), 151–165. doi:10.1207/s1532754xjprr0403_02

Anderson, W. B. (2017). Social movements and public relations in the early twentieth century: How one group used public relations to curtail venereal disease rates. *Journal of Public Relations Research, 29*(1), 3–15. doi:10.1080/1062726X.2017.1281135

Anderson, W. B. (2019). How to keep Rosie the riveter from contracting VD: A case study of how U.S. social reformers used public relations during World War II. *Public Relations Review, 45*(5), 101787. doi:10.1016/j.pubrev.2019.05.008

Andreevskikh, O., & Muravyeva, M. (2020). Doing Gender Online: Digital Spaces for Identity Politics. In Springer eBooks (pp. 205–219). doi:10.1007/978-3-030-42855-6_12

Aronczyk, M. (2018). Public relations, issue management, and the transformation of american environmentalism, 1948–1992. *Enterprise and Society, 19*(4), 836–863. doi:10.1017/eso.2017.69

Askew, K., & Wilk, R. (Eds.). (2002). *The Anthropology of Media: A Reader*. Blackwell.

Asuman, M. K. A., & Subeshini, M. (2023). 17 Women's Participation in Indigenous Language Media An Analysis of Five Community Radio Stations in Northern Ghana. *African Language Media*, 12.

Atton, C. (Ed.). (2015). *The Routledge companion to alternative and community media*. Routledge. doi:10.4324/9781315717241

Avenell, S. (2016). Antinuclear radicals: Scientific experts and antinuclear activism in Japan. *Science, Technology & Society, 21*(1), 88–109. doi:10.1177/0971721815622742

Aviv, W., & Lejoyeux, M. (2010). Internet Addiction or Excessive Internet Use. *The American Journal of Drug and Alcohol Abuse, 36*(5), 277–283. doi:10.3109/00952990.2010.491880 PMID:20545603

Aydın, İ. H., & Değirmenci, C. H. (2018). *Yapay Zeka*. Girdap Kitap.

Bacon, J. (2012). *The art of community: Building the new age of participation*. O'Reilly Media, Inc.

Balcı, Ş., & Gülnar, B. (2009). Internet addiction among university students and the profile of Internet addicts. *Journal of Selcuk Communication, 6*(1), 5–22.

Baldini, G. (2011). A Cognitive Framework for Realizing and Exploiting the Internet of Things Concept. In *27th WWRF Meeting*, Dusseldorf, Germany

Bannykh, G. (2021). Gender Digital Inequality: Conceptualization and Practices. In Lecture notes in information systems and organization (pp. 167–181). doi:10.1007/978-3-030-71397-3_13

Bao, Z., Xie, Y., Xu, C., Zhang, Z., & Zhu, D. (2023). Biotechnological production and potential applications of hypocrellins. *Applied Microbiology and Biotechnology*, *107*(21), 6421–6438. doi:10.1007/s00253-023-12727-6 PMID:37695342

Barassi, V. (2015). *Activism on the web: Everyday struggles against digital capitalism*. Routledge. doi:10.4324/9781315870991

Batıgün, A. D., & Hasta, D. (2010). Internet addiction: An evaluation in terms of loneliness and interpersonal relationship styles. *Anatolian Journal of Psychiatry*, *11*(3), 213–219.

Bayçu, S. (2013). Halkla İlişkilerde Medya İlişkileri ve Uygulamaları. In Anadolu Üniversitesi Açıköğretim Fakültesi Yayınları. Eskişehir.

Belingheri, P., Chiarello, F., Colladon, A. F., & Rovelli, P. (2021). Twenty years of gender equality research: A scoping review based on a new semantic indicator. *PLoS One*, *16*(9), e0256474. doi:10.1371/journal.pone.0256474 PMID:34547029

Belloso, M. L. (2022). Women's Rights Under AI Regulation: Fighting AI gender bias through a feminist and intersectional approach. In T.M.C. Asser Press eBooks (pp. 87–107). doi:10.1007/978-94-6265-523-2_5

Benecke, D. R., & Oksiutycz, A. (2015). Changing conversation and dialogue through LeadSA: An example of public relations activism in South Africa. *Public Relations Review*, *41*(5), 816–824. doi:10.1016/j.pubrev.2015.06.003

Berger, B. K. (2005). Power Over, Power With, and Power to Relations: Critical Reflections on Public Relations, the Dominant Coalition, and Activism. *Journal of Public Relations Research*, *17*(1), 5–28. doi:10.1207/s1532754xjprr1701_3

Betancourt, M. (2015). *The critique of digital capitalism: An analysis of the political economy of digital culture and technology*. Punctum Books.

Bilandzic, M., & Foth, M. (2013). Libraries as coworking spaces: Understanding user motivations and perceived barriers to social learning. *Library Hi Tech*, *31*(2), 254–273. doi:10.1108/07378831311329040

Blaszka, M., Burch, L. M., Frederick, E. L., Clavio, G., & Walsh, P. (2012). #WorldSeries: An empirical examination of a Twitter hashtag during a major sporting event. *International Journal of Sport Communication*, *5*(4), 435–453. doi:10.1123/ijsc.5.4.435

Bodkin, C. D., Amato, L. H., & Amato, C. H. (2015). The influence of green advertising during a corporate disaster. *Corporate Communications*, *20*(3), 256–275. doi:10.1108/CCIJ-08-2014-0055

Böhmer, N., & Griese, K. M. (2020). Developing Gender Equality Marketing Beyond 2025: A Systematic Literature Review. In Springer eBooks (pp. 715–741). doi:10.1007/978-3-030-42412-1_36

Bonneau, C., & Aroles, J. (2021). Digital nomads: A new form of leisure class? In *J. Aroles, F. X. De Vaujany, & K. Dale, Experiencing the new world of work.* Cambridge University Press. doi:10.1017/9781108865814.011

Bonneau, C., Aroles, J., & Estagnasié, C. (2023). Romanticisation and monetisation of the digital nomad lifestyle: The role played by online narratives in shaping professional identity work. *Organization, 30*(1), 65–88. doi:10.1177/13505084221131638

Botsman, R., & Rogers, R. (2010). *What's mine is yours: The rise of collaborative consumption.* Collins.

Bozkurt, H., Şahin, S., & Zoroğlu, S. (2016). Internet addiction: A current review. *Journal of Contemporary Medicine, 6*(3), 235–247.

Brooks, K. J., Wakefield, R. I., & Plowman, K. D. (2018). Activism, prosocial public relations and negotiation: The case of St Vincent de Paul. *Corporate Communications, 23*(1), 139–150. doi:10.1108/CCIJ-10-2016-0072

Brotman, S., Ferrer, I., & Koehn, S. (2019). Situating the life story narratives of aging immigrants within a structural context: The intersectional life course perspective as research praxis. *Qualitative Research, 20*(4), 465–484. doi:10.1177/1468794119880746

Bruzzi, S. (2013). *'Introduction' in New Documentary* (2nd ed.). Routledge.

Bullert, B. J. (2000). Progressive Public Relations, Sweatshops, and the Net. *Political Communication, 17*(4), 403–407. doi:10.1080/10584600050179022

Bullough, A., Guelich, U., Manolova, T. S., & Schjoedt, L. (2021). Women's entrepreneurship and culture: Gender role expectations, identities, societal culture, and entrepreneurial environment. *Small Business Economics, 58*(2), 985–996. doi:10.1007/s11187-020-00429-6

Burns, J. P., Green, C. D., & Nolan, J. (2018). New genealogies and the courage of truth: Toward an ethics of adversarial public educational scholarship and policy activism. *Education Policy Analysis Archives, 26*, 151–151. doi:10.14507/epaa.26.3397

Busuttil, S. (2021). *The rise of the digital nomad.* https://pursuit.unimelb.edu.au/articles/the-rise-of-the-digital-nomad

Busuttil, S. (2021, August 31). *The rise of the digital nomad.* Retrieved 23 August 2023, from The University of Melbourne: https://pursuit.unimelb.edu.au/articles/the-rise-of-the-digital-nomad

Campos, D., & Scherer, R. (2023). Digital gender gaps in Students' knowledge, attitudes and skills: An integrative data analysis across 32 Countries. *Education and Information Technologies.* Advance online publication. doi:10.1007/s10639-023-12272-9

Carlisle, B. G., Coffman, D. L., Egleston, B. L., & Salholz-Hillel, M. (2023). Training Artificial Intelligence in a Gender-Biased Virtual World Can Result in Biased Conclusions. *Annals of Surgical Oncology, 30*(8), 5282–5283. doi:10.1245/s10434-023-13557-6 PMID:37140747

Carpentier, N. (2011). *Media and participation: A site of ideological-democratic struggle.* Intellect. doi:10.26530/OAPEN_606390

Carvalho, I., Ramires, A., & Iglesias, M. (2023). Attitudes towards machine translation and languages among travelers. *Information Technology & Tourism*, *25*(2), 175–204. doi:10.1007/s40558-023-00253-0

Castells, M. (2013). *Communication Power.* OUP Oxford.

Chalmers, I., & Altman, D. G. (1995). *Systematic reviews.* BMJ Publishing.

Chandan, R. R., Soni, S., Raj, A., Veeraiah, V., Dhabliya, D., Pramanik, S., & Gupta, A. (2023). Genetic Algorithm and Machine Learning. In Advanced Bioinspiration Methods for Healthcare Standards, Policies, and Reform. IGI Global. doi:10.4018/978-1-6684-5656-9

Chatterji, A. K., & Toffel, M. W. (2017). Can CEO Activism Spark Sustainability Transitions? Evidence from a Field Experiment. Harvard Business School.

Chetty, K., Aneja, U., Mishra, V., Gcora, N., & Josie, J. (2018). Bridging the digital divide in the G20: Skills for the new age. *Economics*, *12*(1), 20180024. doi:10.5018/economics-ejournal.ja.2018-24

Chevtaeva, E. (2021). *Coworking and coliving: The attraction for digital nomad tourists. In Information and Communication Technologies in Tourism 2021.* Springer.

Chevtaeva, E., & Denizci-Guillet, B. (2021). Digital nomads' lifestyles and coworkation. *Journal of Destination Marketing & Management*, *21*, 100633. doi:10.1016/j.jdmm.2021.100633

Choi, A., & Schneider, I. E. (2023). Acculturation and tourist stress among US Korean immigrant leisure travelers. *Int. Journal of International Migration and Integration*, *24*(3), 1159–1174. doi:10.1007/s12134-022-00997-4

Christou, E., & Parmaxi, A. (2022). Gender-sensitive tools and materials for women empowerment in STEM: A systematic review with industrial and instructional recommendations and implications. *Universal Access in the Information Society*, *22*(3), 699–714. doi:10.1007/s10209-022-00881-z

Ciszek, E. L. (2015). Bridging the gap: Mapping the relationship between activism and public relations. *Public Relations Review*, *41*(4), 447–455. doi:10.1016/j.pubrev.2015.05.016

Ciszek, E. L. (2016). Digital activism: How social media and dissensus inform theory and practice. *Public Relations Review*, *42*(2), 314–321. doi:10.1016/j.pubrev.2016.02.002

Ciszek, E. L. (2017a). Activist Strategic Communication for Social Change: A Transnational Case Study of Lesbian, Gay, Bisexual, and Transgender Activism. *Journal of Communication*, *67*(5), 702–718. doi:10.1111/jcom.12319

Ciszek, E. L. (2017b). Public relations, activism and identity: A cultural-economic examination of contemporary LGBT activism. *Public Relations Review*, *43*(4), 809–816. doi:10.1016/j.pubrev.2017.01.005

Ciszek, E. L. (2018). Queering PR: Directions in theory and research for public relations scholarship. *Journal of Public Relations Research, 30*(4), 134–145. doi:10.1080/1062726X.2018.1440354

Clarke, J., Castro, R., Sharma, A., Lopez, J., & Suri, N. (2012). Trust & security RTD in the internet of things: Opportunities for international cooperation. *Proc. 1st Int. Conf. Security of Internet of Things*, 172-178. 10.1145/2490428.2490452

Cook, D. (2020). The freedom trap: Digital nomads and the use of disciplining practices to manage work/leisure boundaries. *Information Technology & Tourism, 22*(3), 355–390. doi:10.1007/s40558-020-00172-4

Cook, D. (2022). Breaking the contract: Digital nomads and the state. *Critique of Anthropology, 42*(3), 304–323. doi:10.1177/0308275X221120172

Coombs, W. T., & Holladay, S. J. (2012a). Fringe public relations: How activism moves critical pr toward the mainstream. *Public Relations Review, 38*(5), 880–887. doi:10.1016/j.pubrev.2012.02.008

Coombs, W. T., & Holladay, S. J. (2012b). Privileging an activist vs. A corporate view of public relations history in the U.S. *Public Relations Review, 38*(3), 347–353. doi:10.1016/j.pubrev.2011.11.010

Crespo, R. F. (2023). Moderating the effects of "surveillance capitalism": An Aristotelian perspective. *AI and Ethics*. Advance online publication. doi:10.1007/s43681-023-00334-0

Curtin, P. A. (2016). Exploring articulation in internal activism and public relations theory: A case study. *Journal of Public Relations Research, 28*(1), 19–34. doi:10.1080/1062726X.2015.1131696

Dalaylı, F. Ü., & Ünlü, E. (2022). İletişim, Kadın ve Blues Müzik. *International Journal of Interdisciplinary and Intercultural Art, 7*(14), 72–88. doi:10.29228/ijiia.181

Dal-Ré, R., Becker, S. L., Launay, O., & Pavli, A. (2023). Vaccine certificates for international travelers in future pandemics. *European Journal of Clinical Microbiology & Infectious Diseases, 42*(2), 227–228. doi:10.1007/s10096-022-04544-y PMID:36562922

David, E. (2016, March 26). *Digital nomad careers.* Retrieved 12 July 2023, from Become Nomad: https://becomenomad.com/digital-nomad-careers/

De Moya, M., & Bravo, V. (2016). The role of public relations in ethnic advocacy and activism: A proposed research agenda. *Public Relations Inquiry, 5*(3), 233–251. doi:10.1177/2046147X16635225

de Souza, J. T., de Francisco, A. C., Piekarski, C. M., & do Prado, G. F. (2019). Data mining and machine learning to promote smart cities: A systematic review from 2000 to 2018. *Sustainability (Basel), 11*(4), 1077. doi:10.3390/su11041077

De Stefano, V. (2016). The rise of the just-in-time workforce: On-demand work, crowdwork, and labor protection in the gig-economy. *Comparative Labor Law & Policy Journal, 37*(3), 461–471.

Demetrious, K. (2008). Corporate social responsibility, new activism and public relations. *Social Responsibility Journal*, *4*(1/2), 104–119. doi:10.1108/17471110810856875

Denisova, A., & O'Brien, M. (2019). From High Visibility to High Vulnerability: Feminist, Postcolonial and Anti-Gentrification Activism at Risk. *Westminster Papers in Communication and Culture*, *14*(1), 1. Advance online publication. doi:10.16997/wpcc.323

Dey, A., & Orton, B. (2016). Gender and caste intersectionality in India: An analysis of the Nirbhaya Case, December 16 2012. In Advances in gender research (pp. 87–105). doi:10.1108/S1529-212620160000021006

Dhamodaran, S., Ahamad, S., Ramesh, J. V. N., Muthugurunathan, G., Manikandan, K., Pramanik, S., & Pandey, D. (2023). *Food Quality Assessment using Image Processing Technique. In Thrust Technologies' Effect on Image Processing*. IGI Global.

Dhamodaran, S., Ahamad, S., Ramesh, J. V. N., Sathappan, S., Namdev, A., Kanse, R. R., & Pramanik, S. (2023). *Fire Detection System Utilizing an Aggregate Technique in UAV and Cloud Computing. In Thrust Technologies' Effect on Image Processing*. IGI Global.

Dhir, K. S. (2007). Stakeholder activism through nonviolence. *Corporate Communications*, *12*(1), 75–93. doi:10.1108/13563280710723769

Dimitrov, R. (2008). Gender violence, fan activism and public relations in sport: The case of "Footy Fans Against Sexual Assault.". *Public Relations Review*, *34*(2), 90–98. doi:10.1016/j.pubrev.2008.03.002

Ding, X., & Chai, Q. (2022). *The rise of digital capitalism and the social changes it caused: how to develop the digital economy in socialist China*. China Political Economy. doi:10.1108/CPE-10-2022-0017

Doan, M. A., & Toledano, M. (2018). Beyond organization-centred public relations: Collective action through a civic crowdfunding campaign. *Public Relations Review*, *44*(1), 37–46. doi:10.1016/j.pubrev.2017.10.001

Drucker, P. F. (1994). Kapitalist Ötesi Toplum. İnkılap Kitapevi.

Edwards, L. (2018). Public relations, voice and recognition: A case study. *Media Culture & Society*, *40*(3), 317–332. doi:10.1177/0163443717705000

Ehn, K., Jorge, A., & Marques-Pita, M. (2022). Digital nomads and the COVID-19 pandemic: Narratives about relocation in a time of lockdowns and reduced mobility. *Social Media + Society*, *8*(1), 1–11. doi:10.1177/20563051221084958

Ellis, J., & Hall, N. (2019). Introduction: What is hands on media history? In Hands on Media History (pp. 1-8). Routledge.

Elms, H. (2006). Corporate (and stakeholder) responsibility in Central and Eastern Europe. *International Journal of Emerging Markets*, *1*(3), 203–211. doi:10.1108/17468800610674435

Erdoğan, M., & Topçu, Ç. (2022). Yeni Medya Okuryazarlığı Üzerine Bir Araştırma: Çanakkale Onsekiz Mart Üniversitesi Örneği. *Akdeniz Üniversitesi İletişim Fakültesi Dergisi*, (37), 252–272. doi:10.31123/akil.1077886

Fan, J., Fang, L., Wu, J., Guo, Y., & Dai, Q. (2020). From Brain Science to Artificial Intelligence. *Engineering (Beijing)*, *6*(3), 248–252. doi:10.1016/j.eng.2019.11.012

Featherstone, M. (1995). *'Introduction: Globalizing Cultural Complexity' in Undoing Culture: Globalization, Postmodernism and Identity*. SAGE.

Fosch-Villaronga, E., & Poulsen, A. (2022). Diversity and inclusion in artificial intelligence. In T.M.C. Asser Press eBooks (pp. 109–134). doi:10.1007/978-94-6265-523-2_6

Franzoni, V. (2023). Gender differences and bias in artificial intelligence. In Intelligent Systems Reference Library (pp. 27–43). doi:10.1007/978-3-031-21606-0_2

Fraser, C., & Estrada, S. R. (2001). *Community radio handbook*. Unesco.

Frey, T. (2013). The great freelancer movement: Eight reasons why your next job will be a project. *Journal of Environmental Health*, *76*(5), 46. PMID:24437051

Fuchs, C. (2016). Sosyal Medya: Eleştirel Bir Giriş. NotaBene Yayınları.

Fuchs, C., & Mosco, V. (2016). Introduction: Marx is back–the importance of Marxist theory and research for critical communication studies today. In Marx in the age of digital capitalism (pp. 1-21). Brill.

Fuchs, C. (2015). *Dijital Emek ve Karl Marx*. Notabene Yayınları.

Fukuyama, F. (2000). Büyük Çözülme: İnsanın Doğası ve Toplumsal Düzenin Yeniden Oluşması. Sabah Kitapları.

Garbus, L. (2015). *What Happened, Miss Simone? Belgeseli* [Sinema Filmi].

Gasparatos, A., Doll, C. N. H., Esteban, M., Ahmed, A., & Olang, T. A. (2017). Renewable energy and biodiversity: Implications for transitioning to a Green Economy. *Renewable and Sustainable Energy Reviews, 70,* 161-184. doi:10.1016/j.rser.2016.08.030

Gavaldà, J., & Ribera-Fumaz, R. (2012). Barcelona 5.0: from knowledge to smartness? *IN3 Working Paper Series.*

Gillespie, T. (2018). *Custodians of the Internet: Platforms, content moderation, and the hidden decisions that shape social media.* Yale University Press.

Goffman, E. (1966). *Behavior in Public Places: Notes on The Social Organization of Gatherings.* The Free Press.

Goffman, E. (1972). *Encounters: Two Studies in The Sociology of Interaction.* Penguin University Books.

Goffman, E. (2020). *Günlük Yaşamda Benliğin Sunumu.* Metis Yayınları.

Goldberg, I. (1996). *Internet Addiction Disorder*. Academic Press.

Govindan, K., & Diabat, A. (2015). Analyzing the drivers of green manufacturing with fuzzy approach. *Journal of Cleaner Production, 96*, 182-193. doi:10.1016/j.jclepro.2014.02.054

Grant, B. K., & Sloniowski, J. (2013). *Introduction' in Documenting the Documentary: Close Readings of Documentary Film and Video New Edition*. Wayne State University Press.

Green, E., & Singleton, C. (2013). 'Gendering the Digital': The Impact of Gender and Technology Perspectives on the Sociological Imagination. In K. Orton-Johnson & N. Prior (Eds.), *Digital Sociology*. Palgrave Macmillan. doi:10.1057/9781137297792_3

Guedes, B. O., Bart, C., & Nico, C. (2008). *Understanding Alternative Media*. Open University Press.

Guiniven, J. E. (2002). Dealing with activism in Canada: An ideal cultural fit for the two-way symmetrical public relations model. *Public Relations Review, 28*(4), 393–402. doi:10.1016/S0363-8111(02)00162-5

Günüç, S. (2009). *Development of the Internet addiction scale and examination of the relationships between some demographic variables and the Internet* [Master's thesis]. Yüzüncü Yıl University, Institute of Social Sciences, Faculty of Educational Sciences. Department of Curriculum and Instruction.

Gupta, S., Kumar, V., & Karam, E. (2020). New-age technologies-driven social innovation: What, how, where, and why? *Industrial Marketing Management, 89*, 499–516. doi:10.1016/j.indmarman.2019.09.009

Gürocak, T. (2023). Queer Mücadele ve Erken Dönem Queer Video Aktivizmi. In I. E. Er (Ed.), *Medya ve Kültür Odağında İletişim* (pp. 143–162). Akademisyen Yayınevi Kitabevi.

Gyurkovics, É., & Takács, T. (2023). Estimation of the potential GDP by a new robust filter method. *Central European Journal of Operations Research, 31*(4), 1183–1207. doi:10.1007/s10100-023-00851-7 PMID:37360979

Haggart, B. (2019). The age of surveillance capitalism: The fight for a human future at the new frontier of power. *Journal of Digital Media & Policy, 10*(2), 229-243.

Hajam, A.G., Perween, S., & Malik, M.A. (2023). Re-visiting the causal relationship between tourism and economic growth in India: specific to general modelling approach. *Journal of Hospitality and Tourism Insights*. doi:10.1108/JHTI-09-2022-0459

Håkansson, P. G., & Bejaković, P. (2023). Can digital nomads solve the problem of tourist economy? The case of Croatian islands. *Eastern Journal of European Studies, 14*(Special Issue), 116–134. doi:10.47743/ejes-2023-SI07

Hallahan, K. (2001). The Dynamics of Issues Activation and Response: An Issues Processes Model. *Journal of Public Relations Research, 13*(1), 27–59. doi:10.1207/S1532754XJPRR1301_3

Hall, N., & Ellis, J. (2020). *Hands on media history: A new methodology in the humanities and social sciences*. Taylor & Francis.

Hall, P., & Ellis, D. J. (2023). A systematic review of socio-technical gender bias in AI algorithms. *Online Information Review*, *47*(7), 1264–1279. Advance online publication. doi:10.1108/OIR-08-2021-0452

Hamilton, N. (2007). *'Prologue' in Biography: A Brief History*. Harvard University Press. doi:10.4159/9780674038226

Hammi, B., Khatoun, R., Zeadally, S., Fayad, A., & Khoukhi, L. (2018). IoT technologies for smart cities. *IET Networks*, *2018*(7), 1–13. doi:10.1049/iet-net.2017.0163

Han, G., & Zhang, A. (2009). Starbucks is forbidden in the Forbidden City: Blog, circuit of culture and informal public relations campaign in China. *Public Relations Review*, *35*(4), 395–401. doi:10.1016/j.pubrev.2009.07.004

Harris, A., & Bartlow, S. (2015). Intersectionality: race, gender, sexuality, and class. In Handbooks of sociology and social research (pp. 261–271). doi:10.1007/978-3-319-17341-2_15

Harrison, A., & Scorse, J. (2006). Improving the conditions of workers? Minimum wage legislation and anti-sweatshop activism. *California Management Review*, *48*(2), 144–160. doi:10.2307/41166342

Harrison, F. V. (2004). Global Apartheid, Environmental Degradation, And Women's Activism For Sustainable Well-Being: A Conceptual And Theoretical Overview. *Urban Anthropology and Studies of Cultural Systems and World Economic Development*, *33*(1), 1–35.

Hart, E., Kuijpers, G., Laverack, G., & Scheele, F. (2021). The Process Leading to Physician Activism for Sustainable Change. *Sustainability (Basel)*, *13*(18), 18. Advance online publication. doi:10.3390/su131810003

Harvey, B., Burns, D., & Oswald, K. (2012). Linking community, radio, and action research on climate change: Reflections on a systemic approach. *IDS Bulletin*, *43*(3), 101–117. doi:10.1111/j.1759-5436.2012.00326.x

Hayes, H., & Mazelis, F. (2015, July 22). *What Happened, Miss Simone?: The life of African-American singer, pianist and civil rights activist Nina Simone*. World Socialist Web Site: wsws.org/contact

Hemsley, J., Erickson, I., Jarrahi, M. H., & Karami, A. (2020). Digital nomads, coworking, and other expressions of mobile work on Twitter. *First Monday*, *25*(3). Advance online publication. doi:10.5210/fm.v25i3.10246

Henderson, A. (2005). Activism in "Paradise": Identity Management in a Public Relations Campaign Against Genetic Engineering. *Journal of Public Relations Research*, *17*(2), 117–137. doi:10.1207/s1532754xjprr1702_4

Hermann, I., & Paris, C. M. (2020). Digital nomadism: The nexus of remote working and travel mobility. *Information Technology & Tourism*, *22*(3), 329–334. doi:10.1007/s40558-020-00188-w

Hertz, G., & Parikka, J. (2012). Zombie Media: Circuit Bending Media Archaeology into an Art Method. *Leonardo*, *45*(5), 424–420. doi:10.1162/LEON_a_00438

Ho, C. L., Chen, W. L., & Ou, C. H. (2023). Constructing a personalized travel itinerary recommender system with the Internet of Things. *Wireless Networks*. Advance online publication. doi:10.1007/s11276-023-03453-y

Hockenberry, M., & LaRiviere, J. (Eds.). (2020). Hands on media history: A new methodology in the humanities and social sciences. Taylor & Francis.

Holtzhausen, D. R., & Voto, R. (2002). Resistance From the Margins: The Postmodern Public Relations Practitioner as Organizational Activist. *Journal of Public Relations Research*, *14*(1), 57–84. doi:10.1207/S1532754XJPRR1401_3

Honda, L. P. (2016). Motivations for activists' participation in the 'It Gets Better Project.'. *Public Relations Inquiry*, *5*(3), 253–276. doi:10.1177/2046147X15625710

Hooks, B. (2012). *Feminizm Herkes İçindir* (Z. Demirsu & O. Günay, Trans.). BGST Yayıncılık.

Horrigan, J. B., & Schement, J. R. (2021). *Broadband as civic infrastructure: community empowerment, equity, and a Digital New Deal*. German Marshall Fund of the United States.

Hou, J. Z. (2021). The articulation of 'agency': How can public relations scholarship and institutional theory enrich each other? *Public Relations Inquiry*, *10*(1), 97–117. doi:10.1177/2046147X20932136

Huhtamo, E., & Parikka, J. (2011). *Media Archaeologies: Approaches, Applications, and Implications*. University of California Press. doi:10.1525/9780520948518

Hung, C. F. (2003). Relationship building, activism, and conflict resolution—A case study on the termination of licensed prostitution in Taipei City. *Asian Journal of Communication*, *13*(2), 21–49. doi:10.1080/01292980309364837

Iarovyi, P. (2016). *From artificial cognitive systems and open architectures to cognitive manufacturing systems*. Academic Press.

İbrahim, K. I. R., & Sulak, Ş. Examination of Internet Addiction Levels of Education Faculty Students. *Electronic Journal of Social Sciences*, *13*(51).

Ihsan & Kabir Hassan. (2002). Technical, scale and allocative efficiencies of Turkish banking industry. *Journal of Banking & Finance*, *26*(4), 719-766. doi:10.1016/S0378-4266(01)00167-4

Infante, A., & Mardikaningsih, R. (2022). The potential of social media as a means of online business promotion. *Journal of Social Science Studies*, *2*(2), 45–49.

İrge, N. F. (2012). In the Process of Information Society and Social Change Social media. *Akdeniz University Faculty of Communication Journal*, (17), 63–86.

Işık, V. (2013). Holografik Sanat. *Elektronik Sosyal Bilimler Dergisi, 12*(47), 212–231.

Jabareen, Y. (2008). A New Conceptual Framework for Sustainable Development. *Environment, Development and Sustainability, 10*(2), 179–192. doi:10.1007/s10668-006-9058-z

Jackson, V. (Ed.). (2020). Hands on media history: A new methodology in the humanities and social sciences. Taylor & Francis.

Jackson, S. J., & Foucault Welles, B. (2015). Hijacking #MYNYPD: Social Media Dissent and Networked Counterpublics. *Journal of Communication, 65*(6), 932–952. doi:10.1111/jcom.12185

Jayasingh, R., & Kumar, J. (2022). Speckle noise removal by SORAMA segmentation in Digital Image Processing to facilitate precise robotic surgery. *International Journal of Reliable and Quality E-Healthcare, 11*(1), 1–19. Advance online publication. doi:10.4018/IJRQEH.295083

Jenkins, H. (2006). *Convergence culture: Where old and new media collide.* NYU Press.

Johns, T., & Gratton, L. (2013). The third wave of virtual work. *Harvard Business Review, 91*(1), 66–73.

Kağıtçıbaşı, Ç. (2009). *Family, Self and Human Development Across Cultures: Theoıy and Applications (2nd ed.).* Psychology Press.

Karaman, Özen, & Yildirim. (2006). Structure and Operation of AtaNesA Object Warehouse. *Education and Science, 31*(140). http://213.14.10.181/index.php/EB/article/view/5005

Karaman, İ. (1998). Bilgi Toplumu Olmaya Süratle Yönelmeliyiz. *Yeni Türkiye Dergisi, 4*(19), 239–250.

Karasar, N. (2005). Scientific research method. Ankara: Nobel Publishing Distribution.

Kaushik, D., & Garg, M. (2022). Application of Machine Learning and Deep Learning in Cyber security: An Innovative Approach. In Cybersecurity and Digital Forensics: Challenges and Future Trends. Wiley. doi:10.1002/9781119795667.ch12

Kılıç, N. P. (2017). *Artırılmış Gerçeklik Uygulamalarının Halkla İlişkiler Açısından Olanak ve Sınırlılıkları. İletişim Araştırmaları, 14*(2), 87–118.

Kılıç, Ü., & Acar, N. (2020). A field research on virtual religious communication motivations: Sivas Cumhuriyet University students. *Journal of Media and Religious Studies, 3*(1), 5–22.

Kılıç, Ü., & Acar, N. (2020). *A Qualitative Research on University Students' Religious Internet Use and Satisfaction. In Art and Communication Studies.* Iksad Publications.

Kitchenham, B. (2004). *Procedures for performing systematic reviews* [Technical Report TR/SE-0401]. Keele University.

Kiyan, Z. (2019). İletişim Teknolojileri ve Toplumsal Hareketler: Sistematik Bir Literatür İncelemesi. *Gaziantep University Journal of Social Sciences, 18*(2), Article 2.

Kleinert, S., & Mochkabadi, K. (2021). Gender stereotypes in equity crowdfunding: The effect of gender bias on interpreting quality signals. *The Journal of Technology Transfer*, *47*(6), 1640–1661. doi:10.1007/s10961-021-09892-z

Knight, G., & Greenberg, J. (2002). Promotionalism and Subpolitics: Nike and Its Labor Critics. *Management Communication Quarterly*, *15*(4), 541–570. doi:10.1177/0893318902154002

Koçer, M. (2012). Internet and social media usage habits of Erciyes University students. *Akdeniz University Faculty of Communication Journal*, (18), 70–85.

Koluaçık, İ. (2023). Dijital Platformlar ve Türk Filmi İçerikleri Bağlamında "Disney+" ve "Netflix" Karşılaştırması. In T. Söğütlüler (Ed.), *Ekran ve Toplum -Sinema, Televizyon ve Dijital Platformlar Üzerine Tartışmalar* (pp. 211–238). Nobel Akademik Yayıncılık.

Kovacs, R. (2001). Relationship building as integral to British activism: Its impact on accountability in broadcasting. *Public Relations Review*, *27*(4), 421–436. doi:10.1016/S0363-8111(01)00098-4

Krolokke, C., & Sorenson, S. (2012). Gender Communication Theories, Analyses: From Silence to Performance. Londan: Sage.

Kropp, R. (2018, January 18). *Digital nomads vs remote workers: Why you need to know the difference*. Retrieved 4 March 2023, from Allwork: https://allwork.space/2018/01/digital-nomads-vs-remote-workers-why-you-need-to-know-the-difference/

Kumar, K., Shinde, A., Aeron, V., Verma, A., & Arif, N. S. (2023). Genetic engineering of plants for phytoremediation: Advances and challenges. *Journal of Plant Biochemistry and Biotechnology*, *32*(1), 12–30. doi:10.1007/s13562-022-00776-3

Kuppusamy, P., Muthuraj, S., & Gopinath, S. (2016). Survey and challenges of Li-Fi with comparison of Wi-Fi. *Proceedings of the 2016 International Conference on Wireless Communications, Signal Processing and Networking (WiSPNET)*, 896–899. 10.1109/WiSPNET.2016.7566262

Kurniasanti, K. S., Assandi, P., Ismail, R. I., Nasrun, M. W. S., & Wiguna, T. (2019). Internet addiction: A newaddiction? *Medical Journal of Indonesia*, *28*(1), 82–91. doi:10.13181/mji.v28i1.2752

Kutoglu Kuruç, U., & Opiyo, B. (2019). Social media usage and activism by non-western budding PR professionals during crisis communication. *Corporate Communications*, *25*(1), 98–112. doi:10.1108/CCIJ-07-2019-0082

Kuzlu, M., & Pipattanasomporn, M. (2013). Assessment of communication technologies and network requirements for different smart grid applications. *Proceedings of the 2013 IEEE PES Innovative Smart Grid Technologies Conference, ISGT 2013*, 1–6. 10.1109/ISGT.2013.6497873

Kwak, N. H. (2018). Anti-gentrification Campaigns and the Fight for Local Control in California Cities. *New Global Studies*, *12*(1), 9–20. doi:10.1515/ngs-2018-0008

Lan, X., Tarasevich, S., Proverbs, P., Myslik, B., & Kiousis, S. (2020). President Trump vs. CEOs: A comparison of presidential and corporate agenda building. *Journal of Public Relations Research, 32*(1-2), 1–17. doi:10.1080/1062726X.2020.1719494

Latour, B. (1999). *Pandora's Hope: Essays on the Reality of Science Studies*. Harvard University Press.

Leavy, S., Meaney, G., Wade, K., & Greene, D. (2020). Mitigating gender bias in machine learning data sets. In Communications in computer and information science (pp. 12–26). doi:10.1007/978-3-030-52485-2_2

Leonidou, C. N., Gruber, V., & Schlegelmilch, B. B. (2022). Consumers' Environmental Sustainability Beliefs and Activism: A Cross-Cultural Examination. *Journal of International Marketing, 30*(4), 78–104. doi:10.1177/1069031X221128786

Levy, S. J. (1988). *Information technologies in universities: An institutional case study*. Northern Arizona University.

Li, F., Jin, C., Jing, Y., Wilamowska-Korsak, M., & Bi, Z. (2013). A rough programming model based on the greatest compatible classes and synthesis effect. *Systems Research and Behavioral Science, 30*(3), 229–243. doi:10.1002/sres.2175

Loiseau, E., Saikku, L., Antikainen, R., Droste, N., Hansjürgens, B., Pitkänen, K., Leskinen, P., Kuikman, P., & Thomsen, M. (2016). Green economy and related concepts: An overview. *Journal of Cleaner Production, 139*, 361-371. doi:10.1016/j.jclepro.2016.08.024

MacRae, G. (2016). Community and cosmopolitanism in the new Ubud. *Annals of Tourism Research, 59*, 16–29. doi:10.1016/j.annals.2016.03.005

Madden, S., Janoske, M., Winkler, R. B., & Harpole, Z. (2018). Who loves consent? Social media and the culture jamming of Victoria's Secret. *Public Relations Inquiry, 7*(2), 171–186. doi:10.1177/2046147X18764216

Magnini, V. P., Crotts, J. C., & Zehrer, A. (2011). Understanding customer delight: An application of travel blog analysis. *Journal of Travel Research, 50*(5), 535–545. doi:10.1177/0047287510379162

Majumdar, S., Tewatia, M., Jamkhedkar, D., & Bhatia, K. (2022). "You do not know me, so do not try to judge me": Gender and identity performance on social media among young Indian users. *Frontiers in Psychology, 13*, 855947. Advance online publication. doi:10.3389/fpsyg.2022.855947 PMID:35783737

Mäkelä, M., & Olkkonen, L. (2021). Sustainability activism: A review of the state of the art. Research Handbook of Sustainability Agency, 140–154.

Makimoto, T., & Manners, D. (1997). *Digital nomad*. Wiley.

Mäkinen, M. (2006). Digital empowerment as a process for enhancing citizens' participation. *E-Learning and Digital Media, 3*(3), 381–395. doi:10.2304/elea.2006.3.3.381

Malafouris, L. (2013). *How Things Shape the Mind: A Theory of Material Engagement*. MIT Press. doi:10.7551/mitpress/9476.001.0001

Mancinelli, F. (2020). Digital nomads: Freedom, responsibility and the neoliberal order. *Information Technology & Tourism*, *22*(3), 417–437. doi:10.1007/s40558-020-00174-2

Manovich, L. (2001). Post-media aesthetics. *Transmedia frictions, the digital, the arts, and the humanities, 416.*

Manovich, L. (2001). What is new media. *The Language of New Media, 6*, 1-15.

Mansell, R. (2015). Futures of knowledge societies–destabilization in whose interest? *Information Communication and Society*, *18*(6), 627–643. doi:10.1080/1369118X.2014.979215

Maudos, J., & Pastor, J. M. (2003). Cost and profit efficiency in the Spanish banking sector (1985–1996): A non-parametric approach. *Applied Financial Economics*, *13*(1), 1–12. doi:10.1080/09603100110086087

Maxwell, R., & Miller, T. (2016). The Propaganda Machine Behind the Controversy Over Climate Science: Can You Spot the Lie in This Title? *The American Behavioral Scientist*, *60*(3), 288–304. doi:10.1177/0002764215613405

Mead, G. H. (1972). *Mind, Self & Society: From The Standpoint of A Social Behaviorist. Eighteenth Impression*. The University of Chicago Press.

Meier, T., Boyd, R. L., Mehl, M. R., Milek, A., Pennebaker, J. W., Martin, M., Wolf, M., & Horn, A. B. (2020). Stereotyping in the digital age: Male language is "ingenious", female language is "beautiful" – and popular. *PLoS One*, *15*(12), e0243637. doi:10.1371/journal.pone.0243637 PMID:33326456

Mekki, K., Bajic, E., Chaxel, F., & Meyer, F. (2019). A comparative study of LPWAN technologies for large-scale IoT deployment. *ICT Express*, *5*(1), 1–7. doi:10.1016/j.icte.2017.12.005

Mendes, K., Ringrose, J., & Keller, J. (2019). Digital Feminist activism. In Oxford University Press eBooks. doi:10.1093/oso/9780190697846.001.0001

Methods of Nonviolent Action. (2014). Einstein Institute. https://www.aeinstein.org/wp-content/uploads/2014/12/198-Methods.pdf

Milan, S. (2009). Four steps to community media as a development tool. *Development in Practice*, *19*(4-5), 598–609. doi:10.1080/09614520902866421

Miles, J. (2013). *YouTube marketing power: How to use video to find more prospects, launch your products, and reach a massive audience*. McGraw-Hill.

Miller, K. (2012). *Playing along: Digital games, YouTube, and virtual performance*. Oxford University Press. doi:10.1093/acprof:oso/9780199753451.001.0001

Mittal, S., & Singh, T. (2020). Gender-Based Violence During COVID-19 Pandemic: A Mini-Review. Frontiers in Global Women's Health, 1. doi:10.3389/fgwh.2020.00004

Mohamed, A. R. I. F. F., & Luc, C. A. N. (2008). Cost and profit efficiency of Chinese banks: A non-parametric analysis. *China Economic Review, 19*(2), 260-273. doi:10.1016/j.chieco.2007.04.001

Moloney, K., McQueen, D., Surowiec, P., & Yaxley, H. (2013). *Dissent and Protest Public Relations*. Public Relations Research Group.

Mondal, D., Ratnaparkhi, A., Deshpande, A., Deshpande, V., Kshirsagar, A. P., & Pramanik, S. (2023). Applications, Modern Trends and Challenges of Multiscale Modelling in Smart Cities. In *Data-Driven Mathematical Modeling in Smart Cities*. IGI Global. doi:10.4018/978-1-6684-6408-3.ch001

Moscato, D. (2019). The metanarrative of rural environmentalism: Rhetorical activism in Bold Nebraska's Harvest the Hope. *Public Relations Inquiry, 8*(1), 23–47. doi:10.1177/2046147X18810733

Mosco, V., & McKercher, C. (2009). *The laboring of communication: Will knowledge workers of the world unite?* Rowman & Littlefield.

Müller, N. (2021). *Corporate activism trends and public relations strategies for the UN sustainable development goals*. Academic Press.

Müller, A. (2016). The digital nomad: Buzzword or research category? *Transnational Social Review, 6*(3), 344–348. doi:10.1080/21931674.2016.1229930

Myers, M. (2008). *Radio and development in Africa*. A concept paper prepared for the International Development Research Centre (IDRC) of Canada.

Nagorny, K., Lima-Monteiro, P., Barata, J., & Colombo, A. W. (2017). "Big Data Analysis in Smart Manufacturing": A Review. *International Journal of Communications, Network and Systems Sciences, 10*(3), 31–58. doi:10.4236/ijcns.2017.103003

Nassani, A. M., Khader, J. A., Moemen, M. A., & Ali, I. (2013). Consumer environmental activism, sustainable consumption behavior and satisfaction with life. *Life Science Journal, 10*(2), 1000–1006.

Naz, A. (2016). Interactive living space design for neo-nomads: anticipation through spatial articulation. In M. Nadin (Ed.), *Anticipation Across Disciplines* (pp. 393–403). Springer. doi:10.1007/978-3-319-22599-9_23

Ng, S., Bharti, M., & Faust, N. T. (2020). The Cambridge Handbook of the International Psychology of Women. In Cambridge University Press eBooks. doi:10.1017/9781108561716

Nguyen, H. (2023). Government-NGO relationship: Regulatory constraints and uncertain policy implementation in Vietnam. *SN Social Sciences, 3*(6), 100. doi:10.1007/s43545-023-00686-8

Nicklich, M., & Pfeiffer, S. (2023). Digitalization and self-perpetuation: Dynamics, drivers and temporalities of the Transformation of working worlds. *Work Organisation, Labour & Globalisation, 17*(1), 7–11. doi:10.13169/workorgalaboglob.17.1.0007

Niesen, M. (2015). From Gray Panther to National Nanny: The Kidvid Crusade and the Eclipse of the U.S. Federal Trade Commission, 1977–1980. *Communication, Culture & Critique*, *8*(4), 576–593. doi:10.1111/cccr.12100

Novelli, C., Taddeo, M., & Floridi, L. (2023). Accountability in artificial intelligence: What it is and how it works. *AI & Society*. Advance online publication. doi:10.1007/s00146-023-01635-y

O'Brien, K., Selboe, E., & Hayward, B. M. (2018). Exploring youth activism on climate change: Dutiful, disruptive, and dangerous dissent. *Ecology and Society*, *23*(3), art42. doi:10.5751/ES-10287-230342

O'Connor, S., & Liu, H. (2023). Gender bias perpetuation and mitigation in AI technologies: Challenges and opportunities. *AI & Society*. Advance online publication. doi:10.1007/s00146-023-01675-4

Offor, J. O. (2002). *Community radio and its influence in the society. The case of the Enugu State, Nigeria.* IKO-Verlag fur Interkulturelle Kommunikation.

Ofori-Parku, S. S., & Moscato, D. (2018). Hashtag activism as a form of political action: A qualitative analysis of the #BringBackOurGirls campaign in Nigerian, UK, and US press. *International Journal of Communication*, (12), 2480–2502.

Omrani, H., Shamsi, M., & Emrouznejad, A. (2023). Evaluating sustainable efficiency of decision-making units considering undesirable outputs: An application to airline using integrated multi-objective DEA-TOPSIS. *Environment, Development and Sustainability*, *25*(7), 5899–5930. doi:10.1007/s10668-022-02285-8 PMID:35370449

Omri, E., & Saadaoui, H. (2023). An empirical investigation of the relationships between nuclear energy, economic growth, trade openness, fossil fuels, and carbon emissions in France: Fresh evidence using asymmetric cointegration. *Environmental Science and Pollution Research International*, *30*(5), 13224–13245. doi:10.1007/s11356-022-22958-1 PMID:36125682

Orel, M. (2019). Coworking environments and digital nomadism: Balancing work and leisure whilst on the move. *World Leisure Journal*, *61*(3), 215–227. doi:10.1080/16078055.2019.1639275

Ortiz Juarez-Paz, A. V. (2017). Undocumented identity storytelling:(Re) framing public relations. *International Journal of Media and Cultural Politics*, *13*(1–2), 165–178. doi:10.1386/macp.13.1-2.165_1

Osmond, M. W., & Thorne, B. (2008). Feminist theories. In Springer eBooks (pp. 591–625). doi:10.1007/978-0-387-85764-0_23

Özkaya, B. (2013). *Yeni Medy'da Demokrasi: Sosyal Medya'ya Dair Araştırmalar*. Literatürk Yayınları.

Pace, J. (2018). The concept of digital capitalism. *Communication Theory*, *28*(3), 254–269. doi:10.1093/ct/qtx009

Pacheco, C., & Azevedo, A. (2023). Mapping the journey of the CoLiving experience of digital nomads, using verbal and visual narratives. *World Leisure Journal*, *65*(2), 192–217. doi:10.1080/16078055.2022.2156593

Pandey, D., Ogunmola, G. A., Enbeyle, W., Abdullahi, M., Pandey, B. K., & Pramanik, S. (2021). *Covid-19: A Framework for Effective Delivering of Online Classes during Lockdown.* Human Arenas. doi:10.1007/s42087-020-00175-x

Pandey, B. K., Pandey, D., Nassa, V. K., George, A. S., Pramanik, S., & Dadheech, P. (2023). Applications for the Text Extraction Method of Complex Degraded Images. In *The Impact of Thrust Technologies on Image Processing*. Nova Publishers. doi:10.52305/ATJL4552

Parker, R. (2011). *Grassroots activism, civil society mobilization, and the politics of the global HIV/AIDS epidemic on JSTOR.* https://www.jstor.org/stable/24590789

Parmar, R. (2023). Challenges in Implementation of the Solar Water Pumps in Rural Agricultural Areas. In A. Rakshit, A. Biswas, D. Sarkar, V. S. Meena, & R. Datta (Eds.), *Handbook of Energy Management in Agriculture*. Springer. doi:10.1007/978-981-19-7736-7_34-1

Paswan, A. K. (2012). Gender, Design and Marketing20122Gloria Moss. Gender, Design and Marketing. Gower Applied Business Research, 2009. 245 pp. $60.00. *Journal of Consumer Marketing*, *29*(6), 456–457. doi:10.1108/07363761211259278

Patnaik, P. P. (2020). Gendered representations in media. In Encyclopedia of the UN sustainable development goals (pp. 1–11). doi:10.1007/978-3-319-70060-1_125-1

Peng, Y. (2022). Gendered division of digital labour in parenting: A qualitative study in Urban China. *Sex Roles*, *86*(5–6), 283–304. doi:10.1007/s11199-021-01267-w PMID:35043029

Perry, I. (2018). *How the Great Lorraine Hansberry Tried To Make Sense of it All.* https://lithub.com/how-the-great-lorraine-hansberry-tried-to-make-sense-of-it-all/

Petit, E., Ferrari, S., Mekni, M. M., & Rouillon, S. (2010). Citizen participation in the steps for emisssion permits: economic efficiency and ethical questions. *VertigO-La Revue Electronique en Sciences de l'Environment, 10*(1).

Pink, S. (2015). Ethnography, co-design and emergence: Slow activism for sustainable design. Global Media Journal: Australian Edition, 9(2), 1–10.

Poloma, M. (1979). *Contemporary Sociological Theory*. Macmillan Publishing Co. Inc.

Prabawa, I. W. S. W., & Pertiwi, P. R. (2020). The digital nomad tourist motivation in Bali: Exploratory research based on push and pull theory. *Athens Journal of Tourism*, *7*(3), 161–174. doi:10.30958/ajt.7-3-3

Pramanik, S. (2022). Carpooling Solutions using Machine Learning Tools. In *Handbook of Research on Evolving Designs and Innovation in ICT and Intelligent Systems for Real-World Applications*. IGI Global. doi:10.4018/978-1-7998-9795-8.ch002

Pramanik, S. (2023). A Novel Data Hiding Locating Approach in Image Steganography. *Multimedia Tools and Applications*. Advance online publication. doi:10.1007/s11042-023-16762-3

Pramanik, S., Ghosh, R., Ghonge, M., Narayan, V., Sinha, M., Pandey, D., & Samanta, D. (2020). A Novel Approach using Steganography and Cryptography in Business Intelligence. In A. Azevedo & M. F. Santos (Eds.), *Integration Challenges for Analytics, Business Intelligence and Data Mining* (pp. 192–217). IGI Global.

Prescott, H. M. (2019). We Must Not Allow a Contraception Gap: Planned Parenthood's Campaign for New Birth Control and Feminist Health Activism in the 1990s. *Technology and Culture*, *60*(3), 816–832. doi:10.1353/tech.2019.0074 PMID:31422967

Prodnik, J. A. (2021). Algorithmic Logic in Digital Capitalism. In AI for Everyone? Critical Perspectives, University of Westminster Press. doi:10.16997/book55.1

Prossack, A. (2021, April 25). *Office not required – why remote work is here to stay*. Retrieved 28 August 2023, from Forbes: https://www.forbes.com/sites/ashiraprossack1/2021/04/25/office-not-required--why- remote-work-is-here-to-stay/?sh=75f550ff6ab4

Pyun, K. (2022). Introduction: Artists for Political Engagement: A table for women and gender non-conforming artists. In Springer eBooks (pp. 3–26). doi:10.1007/978-3-031-09378-4_1

Ragas, M. W. (2013). Agenda building during activist shareholder campaigns. *Public Relations Review*, *39*(3), 219–221. doi:10.1016/j.pubrev.2013.03.007

Raina, S. (2016). *Research: The gender gap in startup success disappears when women fund women*. Harvard Business Review. https://hbr.org/2016/07/research-the-gender-gap-in-startup-success-disappears-when-women-fund-women

Rainoldi, M., Ladkin, A., & Buhalis, D. (2022). Blending work and leisure: A future digital worker hybrid lifestyle perspective. *Annals of Leisure Research*, 1–21. doi:10.1080/11745398.2022.2070513

Ray, A. M., Pramanik, S., Das, B., Khanna, A. (2023). Hybrid Cryptography and Steganography Method to Provide Safe Data Transmission in IoT. *ICDAM 2023*.

Reber, B. H., & Berger, B. K. (2005). Framing analysis of activist rhetoric: How the Sierra Club succeeds or fails at creating salient messages. *Public Relations Review*, *31*(2), 185–195. doi:10.1016/j.pubrev.2005.02.020

Reber, B. H., Pētersone, B., & Berger, B. K. (2010). Managing from the middle: The role of mid-level gatekeepers in mobilizing grassroots activism and encouraging facilitative relationships. *Journal of Communication Management (London)*, *14*(1), 32–46. doi:10.1108/13632541011017799

Reddy, T., & Dutta, M. (2018). Impact of Agricultural Inputs on Agricultural GDP in Indian Economy. *Theoretical Economics Letters*, *8*(10), 1840–1853. doi:10.4236/tel.2018.810121

Reichenberger, I. (2018). Digital nomads–a quest for holistic freedom in work and leisure. *Annals of Leisure Research*, *21*(3), 364–380. doi:10.1080/11745398.2017.1358098

Rentschler, C. A. (2015). Distributed Activism: Domestic Violence and Feminist Media Infrastructure in the Fax Age. *Communication, Culture & Critique*, *8*(2), 182–198. doi:10.1111/cccr.12079

Richter, S., & Richter, A. (2020). Digital nomads. *Business & Information Systems Engineering*, *62*(1), 77–81. doi:10.1007/s12599-019-00615-1

Riessman, C., & Quinney, L. (2005). Narrative in social work. *Qualitative Social Work: Research and Practice*, *4*(4), 391–412. doi:10.1177/1473325005058643

Ripp, M., & Hauer, S. (2017). Communication model for built heritage assets going from knowing to identification. *Built Heritage*, *1*(4), 1–10. doi:10.1186/BF03545653

Risman, B. J. (2018). Gender as a social structure. In Handbooks of Sociology and Social Research (pp. 19–43). doi:10.1007/978-3-319-76333-0_2

Roberson, T. (2020). On social change, agency, and public interest: What can science communication learn from public relations? *JCOM, Journal of Science Communication*, *19*(2), Y01. doi:10.22323/2.19020401

Robertson, K. (2011). Capitalist Cocktails and Moscow Mules: The Art World and Alter-globalization Protest. *Globalizations*, *8*(4), 473–486. doi:10.1080/14747731.2011.585849

Robinson, Z. F. (2018). Intersectionality and gender theory. In Handbooks of Sociology and Social Research (pp. 69–80). doi:10.1007/978-3-319-76333-0_5

Rodriguez, C. (2001). *Fissures in the mediascape: An international study of citizens' media*. No Title.

Rodriguez-Labajos, B. (2022). Artistic activism promotes three major forms of sustainability transformation. *Current Opinion in Environmental Sustainability*, *57*, 101199. doi:10.1016/j.cosust.2022.101199

Rome, A. (2019). DuPont and the Limits of Corporate Environmentalism. *Business History Review*, *93*(1), 75–99. doi:10.1017/S0007680519000345

Roper, J. (2012). Environmental risk, sustainability discourses, and public relations. *Public Relations Inquiry*, *1*(1), 69–87. doi:10.1177/2046147X11422147

Ross, A. (2008). The quandaries of consumer-based labor activism: A low-wage case study. *Cultural Studies*, *22*(5), 770–787. doi:10.1080/09502380802246017

Rotha, P. (1952). *The Documentary Film* (2nd ed.). Faber.

Roy, A., & Pramanik, S. (2023). A Review of the Hydrogen Fuel Path to Emission Reduction in the Surface Transport Industry. *International Journal of Hydrogen Energy*. Advance online publication. doi:10.1016/j.ijhydene.2023.07.010

Sadowski, J. (2020). The internet of landlords: Digital platforms and new mechanisms of rentier capitalism. *Antipode*, *52*(2), 562–580. doi:10.1111/anti.12595

Salgues, B. (2018). *Society 5.0: industry of the future, technologies, methods and tools*. John Wiley & Sons. doi:10.1002/9781119507314

Samanta, D., Dutta, S., Galety, M. G., & Pramanik, S. (2021). A Novel Approach for Web Mining Taxonomy for High-Performance Computing. *The 4th International Conference of Computer Science and Renewable Energies (ICCSRE'2021)*. 10.1051/e3sconf/202129701073

Samuel, S. S. I. (2016). A review of connectivity challenges in IoT-smart home. *Proceedings of the 2016 3rd MEC International Conference on Big Data and Smart City, ICBDSC 2016*, 364–367. 10.1109/ICBDSC.2016.7460395

Sancar, G. A. (2017). Aktivist Halkla İlişkiler Bağlamında WWF Dünya Saati Kampanya Örneği. *Erciyes İletişim Dergisi*, *5*(1), 2–18. doi:10.17680/erciyesakademia.291883

Sánchez-Vergara, J. I., Orel, M., & Capdevila, I. (2023). Digital nomad visa systems and remote work-focused leisure policies. *World Leisure Journal*, *65*(2), 236–255. doi:10.1080/16078055.2023.2165142

Santoniccolo, F., Trombetta, T., Paradiso, M. N., & Rollè, L. (2023). Gender and Media Representations: A literature review on gender stereotypes, objectification and sexualization. *International Journal of Environmental Research and Public Health*, *20*(10), 5770. doi:10.3390/ijerph20105770 PMID:37239498

Scarcelli, C. M., Krijnen, T., & Nixon, P. (2020). Sexuality, gender, media. Identity articulations in the contemporary media landscape. *Information Communication and Society*, *24*(8), 1063–1072. doi:10.1080/1369118X.2020.1804603

Scharrer, E. (2013). Representations of gender in the media. In Oxford University Press eBooks (pp. 267–284). doi:10.1093/oxfordhb/9780195398809.013.0015

Schlagwein, D. (2018). Escaping the rat race: Justifications in digital nomadism. In *European Conference on Information Systems (ECIS)* (pp. 31-39). AIS Electronic Library.

Sejrup, J. (2014). Awakening the sufferers: Reflections on public relations, activism, and subalternity in postcolonial controversies between Taiwan and Japan. *Public Relations Inquiry*, *3*(1), 51–68. doi:10.1177/2046147X13519637

Semih Yildirim, H., & Philippatos, G. C. (2007). Efficiency of Banks: Recent Evidence from the Transition Economies of Europe, 1993–2000. *European Journal of Finance*, *13*(2), 123–143. doi:10.1080/13518470600763687

Seo, H., Kim, J. Y., & Yang, S.-U. (2009). Global activism and new media: A study of transnational NGOs' online public relations. *Public Relations Review*, *35*(2), 123–126. doi:10.1016/j.pubrev.2009.02.002

Sharma, G. D., Yadav, A., & Chopra, R. (2020). Artificial Intellegence and Effective Governance: A Review, Critique and Research Agenda. *Sustainable Futures : An Applied Journal of Technology, Environment and Society*, 1–6.

Shaw, J., Ferrer, I., & Lorenzetti, L. (2021). Ethical Storytelling and Digital Narratives: Lessons Learned in Student-led Podcasts and Community Radio Partnerships. *International Journal of Social Work Values & Ethics, 18*(1).

Shayan, N. (2015). A survey on Internet of Things: applications and challenges. *Second International Congress on Technology, Communication and Knowledge)- Mashhad Branch, Islamic Azad University, Mashhad, Iran,* 165-169.

Shields, S. A. (2008b). Gender: An Intersectionality Perspective. *Sex Roles, 59*(5–6), 301–311. doi:10.1007/s11199-008-9501-8

Simone, N. (2023). *Nina Simone Biyografi.* Retrieved from Nina Simone: http://www.ninasimone.com/bio/

Šímová, T. (2023). A research framework for digital nomadism: A bibliometric study. *World Leisure Journal, 65*(2), 175–191. doi:10.1080/16078055.2022.2134200

Singha, S., & Singha, R. (2023). Understanding diversity: The power of differences. In A. M. Even & B. Christiansen (Eds.), *Enhancing Employee Engagement and Productivity in the Post-Pandemic Multigenerational Workforce* (pp. 297–313). IGI Global. doi:10.4018/978-1-6684-9172-0.ch015

Sinha, S. (2018). Gender Digital divide in India: Impacting women's participation in the labour market. In Springer eBooks (pp. 293–310). doi:10.1007/978-981-13-1414-8_14

Sinha, M., Chacko, E., Makhija, P., & Pramanik, S. (2021). Energy Efficient Smart Cities with Green IoT. In C. Chakrabarty (Ed.), *Green Technological Innovation for Sustainable Smart Societies: Post Pandemic Era.* Springer. doi:10.1007/978-3-030-73295-0_16

Smith, A. D. (1995). *Toplumsal Değişme Anlayışı (İşlevselci Toplumsal Değişme Kuramının Bir Eleştirisi)* (Ü. Oskay, Trans.). Gündoğan Yayınları.

Snelson, C. (2011). YouTube across the disciplines: A review of the literature. *Journal of Online Learning and Teaching.*

Snickars, P., & Vondereau, P. (2009). *The YouTube reader.* National Library of Sweden.

Solmaz, B., Tekin, G., Herzem, Z., & Demir, M. (2013). An Application on Internet and Social Media Usage. *Journal of Selcuk Communication, 7*(4), 23–32.

Sommerfeldt, E. (2011). Activist online resource mobilization: Relationship building features that fulfill resource dependencies. *Public Relations Review, 37*(4), 429–431. doi:10.1016/j.pubrev.2011.03.003

Sommerfeldt, E. J., Kent, M. L., & Taylor, M. (2012). Activist practitioner perspectives of website public relations: Why aren't activist websites fulfilling the dialogic promise? *Public Relations Review, 38*(2), 303–312. doi:10.1016/j.pubrev.2012.01.001

Sommerfeldt, E. J., & Yang, A. (2017). Relationship networks as strategic issues management: An issue-stage framework of social movement organization network strategies. *Public Relations Review*, *43*(4), 829–839. doi:10.1016/j.pubrev.2017.06.012

Spinuzzi, C., Bodrožić, Z., Scaratti, G., & Ivaldi, S. (2019). "Coworking is about community": But what is "community" in coworking? *Journal of Business and Technical Communication*, *33*(2), 112–140. doi:10.1177/1050651918816357

Statista. (2023, January 2). *Digital nomads - statistics & facts.* Retrieved from Statista: https://www.statista.com/topics/9259/digital-nomads/#topicOverview

Stavrianea, A., Theodosis, A., & Kamenidou, I. (2020). Consumers' Perceptions of Gender-Neutral Advertising: An Empirical study. In Springer eBooks (pp. 799–804). doi:10.1007/978-3-030-36126-6_88

Sterne, J. (2015). Compression: A Loose History. In L. Parks & N. Starosielski (Eds.), *Signal Traffic: Critical Studies of Media Infrastructures*. University of Illinois Press.

Stokes, A. Q., & Atkins-Sayre, W. (2018). PETA, rhetorical fracture, and the power of digital activism. *Public Relations Inquiry*, *7*(2), 149–170. doi:10.1177/2046147X18770216

Stokes, A. Q., & Rubin, D. (2010). Activism and the Limits of Symmetry: The Public Relations Battle Between Colorado GASP and Philip Morris. *Journal of Public Relations Research*, *22*(1), 26–48. doi:10.1080/10627260903150268

Stückelberger, C. (2009). Dialogue Ethics: Ethical Criteria and Conditions for a Successful Dialogue Between Companies and Societal Actors. *Journal of Business Ethics*, *84*(3), 329–339. doi:10.1007/s10551-009-0201-2

Sutherland, W., & Jarrahi, M. H. (2017). The gig economy and information infrastructure: The case of the digital nomad community. *Proceedings of the ACM on Human-Computer Interaction (CSCW),* 1-24. 10.1145/3134732

Talukdar, V., Kurniullah, A. Z., Keshwani, P., Khan, H., Pramanik, S., Gupta, A., & Pandey, D. (2023). *Load Balancing Techniques in Cloud Computing, Emerging Trends in Cloud Computing. In Analytics, Scalability, and Service Models*. IGI Global.

Taylor, C. (2001). *Sources of Self: The Making of The Modern Identity (10th ed.).* Harvard University Press.

Tecuci, G. (2012). Artificial Intelligence. *Wiley Interdisciplinary Reviews: Computational Statistics*, *4*(2), 168–180. doi:10.1002/wics.200

Thompson, B. Y. (2019). The digital nomad lifestyle: (Remote) work/leisure balance, privilege, and constructed community. *International Journal of the Sociology of Leisure*, *2*(1-2), 27–42. doi:10.1007/s41978-018-00030-y

Thompson, G. (2016). Towards a theory of rent-seeking in activist public relations. *Public Relations Inquiry*, *5*(3), 213–231. doi:10.1177/2046147X16644005

Thompson, G. (2018). Social gains from the public relations voice of activist investors: The case of Herbalife and Pershing Square Capital Management. *Public Relations Review*, *44*(4), 481–489. doi:10.1016/j.pubrev.2018.04.003

Tilley, E. (2011). *New Culture/Old Ethics: What Technological Determinism Can Teach Us About New Media. In The Ethics of Emerging Media: Information, Social Norms and New Media Technology*. The Continuum International Publishing Group.

Todd, S. (2022). *Why social media is a valuable tool for digital nomads*. Retrieved 17 August 2023, from Open Sourced Workplace: https://opensourcedworkplace.com/news/why-social-media-is-a-valuable-tool-for-digital-nomads

Toffler, A. (1980). The third wave. Morrow.

Toivanen, M. (2023). Countercultural lifestyle no more? Digital nomadism and the commodification of neo-nomadic mobilities. *Mobility Humanities*, *2*(2), 70–89.

Toledano, M. (2016). Advocating for reconciliation: Public relations, activism, advocacy and dialogue. *Public Relations Inquiry*, *5*(3), 277–294. doi:10.1177/2046147X16666595

Tombleson, B., & Wolf, K. (2017). Rethinking the circuit of culture: How participatory culture has transformed cross-cultural communication. *Public Relations Review*, *43*(1), 14–25. doi:10.1016/j.pubrev.2016.10.017

Topçu, Ç. (2023). Akademik Çalışmalarda Netflix Durumu: Sistematik Bir Okuma. In T. Söğütlüler (Ed.), *Ekran ve Toplum: Sinema, Televizyon ve Dijital Platformlar Üzerine Tartışmalar* (pp. 133–153). Nobel Yayıncılık.

Tranfield, D., Denyer, D., & Smart, P. (2003). Content analysis and thematic analysis: Implications for conducting a qualitative descriptive study. *British Journal of Management*, *14*, 207–222. doi:10.1111/1467-8551.00375

Trischler, M. F. G., & Li-Ying, J. (2023). Digital business model innovation: Toward construct clarity and future research directions. *Review of Managerial Science*, *17*(1), 3–32. doi:10.1007/s11846-021-00508-2

Tsiatsis, V., Karnouskos, S., Holler, J., Boyle, D., & Mulligan, C. (2018). *Internet of Things: technologies and applications for a new age of intelligence*. Academic Press.

Uysal, N., & Yang, A. (2013). The power of activist networks in the mass self-communication era: A triangulation study of the impact of WikiLeaks on the stock value of Bank of America. *Public Relations Review*, *39*(5), 459–469. doi:10.1016/j.pubrev.2013.09.007

Vagena, A. (2021). Digital nomads and tourism industry. *Academia Letters*, Article 765.

Vaismoradi, M., Turunen, H., & Bondas, T. (2013). *Content analysis and thematic analysis: Implications for conducting a qualitative descriptive study*. Academic Press.

van Dijk, J. A. (2006). *The network society*. Sage Publications.

Vargo, S. L., Peters, L., Kjellberg, H., Koskela-Huotari, K., Nenonen, S., Polese, F., Sarno, D., & Vaughan, C. (2023). Emergence in marketing: An institutional and ecosystem framework. *Journal of the Academy of Marketing Science*, *51*(1), 2–22. doi:10.1007/s11747-022-00849-8

Vassilakopoulou, P., & Hustad, E. (2021). Bridging Digital Divides: A Literature Review and Research Agenda for Information Systems Research. *Information Systems Frontiers*, *25*(3), 955–969. doi:10.1007/s10796-020-10096-3 PMID:33424421

Vaughan, A. J. (2019). Performing Identity in Contemporary Biographical Documentary. *Faculty of Arts and Humanities Thesis for the degree of Doctor of Philosophy*. University of Southampton.

Veeraiah, V., Shiju, D. J., Ramesh, J. V. N., Ganesh Kumar, R., Pramanik, S., Gupta, A., & Pandey, D. (2023). *Healthcare Cloud Services in Image Processing. In Thrust Technologies' Effect on Image Processing*. IGI Global.

Veil, S. R., Reno, J., Freihaut, R., & Oldham, J. (2015). Online activists vs. Kraft foods: A case of social media hijacking. *Public Relations Review*, *41*(1), 103–108. doi:10.1016/j.pubrev.2014.11.017

Verhoeven, P., Zerfass, A., Verčič, D., Tench, R., & Moreno, A. (2018). Public relations and the rise of hypermodern values: Exploring the profession in Europe. *Public Relations Review*, *44*(4), 471–480. doi:10.1016/j.pubrev.2018.06.001

Vilk, V. (2020, June 3). *You are Not Powerless in the Face of Online Harassment*. Harvard Business Review. https://hbr.org/2020/06/youre-not-powerless-in-the-face-of-online-harassment

von Zumbusch, J. S. H., & Lalicic, L. (2020). The role of co-living spaces in digital nomads' well-being. *Information Technology & Tourism*, *22*(3), 439–453. doi:10.1007/s40558-020-00182-2

Wakefield, R. I. (2007). Theory of International Public Relations, the Internet, and Activism: A Personal Reflection. *Journal of Public Relations Research*, *20*(1), 138–157. doi:10.1080/10627260701727069

Wallace, R., & Wolf, A. (1995). *Contemporary Sociological Theory: Continuing The Classical Tradition (4th ed.)*. Prentice-Hall Inc.

Waltz, M. (2005). *Alternative and activist media*. Edinburgh University Press. doi:10.1515/9780748626229

Wang, W., Gan, H., Wang, X., Lu, H., & Huang, Y. (2022). Initiatives and challenges in using gamification in transportation: A systematic mapping. *European Transport Research Review*, *14*(1), 41. doi:10.1186/s12544-022-00567-w

Weare, C., & Lin, W.-Y. (2000). Content Analysis of the World Wide Web: Opportunities and Challenges. *Social Science Computer Review*, *18*(3), 272–292. doi:10.1177/089443930001800304

Weaver, C. K. (2010). Carnivalesque activism as a public relations genre: A case study of the New Zealand group Mothers Against Genetic Engineering. *Public Relations Review*, *36*(1), 35–41. doi:10.1016/j.pubrev.2009.09.001

Wehbi, S., Cowell, A., Perreault-Laird, J., El-Lahib, Y., & Straka, S. (2017). Intersecting interests: Qualitative research synthesis on art in the social work classroom. *The Canadian Journal for the Scholarship of Teaching and Learning*, *8*(3), 1–15. doi:10.5206/cjsotl-rcacea.2017.3.6

Wehbi, S., El-Lahib, Y., Perreault-Laird, J., & Zakharova, G. (2018). Oasis in a concrete jungle: Arts-informed methods in social work classrooms. *Social Work Education*, *37*(5), 617–632. doi:10.1080/02615479.2018.1450372

Weldon, S. L. (2008). Intersectionality. In *Cambridge University Press eBooks* (pp. 193–218).

White, C. (2012). Activist efforts of the Center for Media and Democracy to affect FCC policy for video news releases. *Public Relations Review*, *38*(1), 76–82. doi:10.1016/j.pubrev.2011.12.001

Whitehead, C. A. (1987). Southampton versus Out-of-Town Shopping Centres. *Property Management*, *5*(4), 350–354. doi:10.1108/eb006672

White, M. D., & Marsh, E. E. (2006). Content Analysis: A Flexible Methodology. *Library Trends*, *55*(1), 22–45. doi:10.1353/lib.2006.0053

Woldoff, R. A., & Litchfield, R. C. (2021). *Digital nomads: In search of freedom, community, and meaningful work in the new economy*. Oxford University Press. doi:10.1093/oso/9780190931780.001.0001

Wolf, K. (2019). PRi special edition: The intersections between public relations and neoliberalism – The road to nowhere: Re-examining activists' role in civil societies. Public Relations Inquiry, 8(2), 167–188. doi:10.1177/2046147X19846578

Wolf, K. (2018). Power struggles: A sociological approach to activist communication. *Public Relations Review*, *44*(2), 308–316. doi:10.1016/j.pubrev.2018.03.004

Woods, C. L. (2019). From an "outside group" to a catalyst for corporate change: Examining activists' legitimation strategies. *Public Relations Review*, *45*(2), 332–347. doi:10.1016/j.pubrev.2019.02.001

Wrycza, S., & Maślankowski, J. (2020). Social media users' opinions on remote work during the COVID-19 pandemic. Thematic and sentiment analysis. *Information Systems Management*, *37*(4), 288–297. doi:10.1080/10580530.2020.1820631

Wuest, T. (2016). Machine learning in manufacturing: advantages, challenges, and application. *Production & Manufacturing Research: An Open Access Journal*, *4*(1), 23-45. http://dx.doi.org/doi:10.1080/21693277.2016.119251

Wu, H. (2014). Developing Vehicular Data Cloud Services in the IoT Environment. *IEEE Transactions on Industrial Informatics*, *10*(2), 1587–1595. doi:10.1109/TII.2014.2299233

Xu, L. (2013). Introduction: Systems science in industrial sectors. *Systems Research and Behavioral Science*, *30*(3), 211–213. doi:10.1002/sres.2186

Yao, Z., Lum, Y., Johnston, A., Mejia-Mendoza, L. M., Zhou, X., Wen, Y., Aspuru-Guzik, A., Sargent, E. H., & Seh, Z. W. (2023). Machine learning for a sustainable energy future. *Nature Reviews. Materials*, *8*(3), 202–215. doi:10.1038/s41578-022-00490-5 PMID:36277083

Yellowlees, P. M., & Marks, S. (2007). Problematic Internet use or Internet addiction? *Computers in Human Behavior*, *23*(3), 1447–1453. doi:10.1016/j.chb.2005.05.004

Yengin, D., & Bayrak, T. (2017). Sosyal Medyada Dijital Kamuoyu. *The Turkish Online Journal of Design, Art and Communication*, *7*(2), 376–386.

Young, K. S. (1998). Internet Addiction: The Emergence of a New Clinical Disorder. *Cyberpsychology & Behavior*, *1*(3), 237–244. doi:10.1089/cpb.1998.1.237

Young, K., Pistner, M., O'mara, J., & Buchanan, J. (1999). Cyber disorders: The mental health concern for the new millennium. *Cyberpsychology & Behavior*, *2*(5), 475–479. doi:10.1089/cpb.1999.2.475 PMID:19178220

Zoller, H. M., & Tener, M. (2010). Corporate Proactivity as a Discursive Fiction: Managing Environmental Health Activism and Regulation. *Management Communication Quarterly*, *24*(3), 391–418. doi:10.1177/0893318909354116

Related References

To continue our tradition of advancing information science and technology research, we have compiled a list of recommended IGI Global readings. These references will provide additional information and guidance to further enrich your knowledge and assist you with your own research and future publications.

Abdul Razak, R., & Mansor, N. A. (2021). Instagram Influencers in Social Media-Induced Tourism: Rethinking Tourist Trust Towards Tourism Destination. In M. Dinis, L. Bonixe, S. Lamy, & Z. Breda (Eds.), *Impact of New Media in Tourism* (pp. 135-144). IGI Global. https://doi.org/10.4018/978-1-7998-7095-1.ch009

Abir, T., & Khan, M. Y. (2022). Importance of ICT Advancement and Culture of Adaptation in the Tourism and Hospitality Industry for Developing Countries. In C. Ramos, S. Quinteiro, & A. Gonçalves (Eds.), *ICT as Innovator Between Tourism and Culture* (pp. 30–41). IGI Global. https://doi.org/10.4018/978-1-7998-8165-0.ch003

Abir, T., & Khan, M. Y. (2022). Importance of ICT Advancement and Culture of Adaptation in the Tourism and Hospitality Industry for Developing Countries. In C. Ramos, S. Quinteiro, & A. Gonçalves (Eds.), *ICT as Innovator Between Tourism and Culture* (pp. 30–41). IGI Global. https://doi.org/10.4018/978-1-7998-8165-0.ch003

Abtahi, M. S., Behboudi, L., & Hasanabad, H. M. (2017). Factors Affecting Internet Advertising Adoption in Ad Agencies. *International Journal of Innovation in the Digital Economy, 8*(4), 18–29. doi:10.4018/IJIDE.2017100102

Afenyo-Agbe, E., & Mensah, I. (2022). Principles, Benefits, and Barriers to Community-Based Tourism: Implications for Management. In I. Mensah & E. Afenyo-Agbe (Eds.), *Prospects and Challenges of Community-Based Tourism and Changing Demographics* (pp. 1–29). IGI Global. doi:10.4018/978-1-7998-7335-8.ch001

Agbo, V. M. (2022). Distributive Justice Issues in Community-Based Tourism. In I. Mensah & E. Afenyo-Agbe (Eds.), *Prospects and Challenges of Community-Based Tourism and Changing Demographics* (pp. 107–129). IGI Global. https://doi.org/10.4018/978-1-7998-7335-8.ch005

Agrawal, S. (2017). The Impact of Emerging Technologies and Social Media on Different Business(es): Marketing and Management. In O. Rishi & A. Sharma (Eds.), *Maximizing Business Performance and Efficiency Through Intelligent Systems* (pp. 37–49). Hershey, PA: IGI Global. doi:10.4018/978-1-5225-2234-8.ch002

Ahmad, A., & Johari, S. (2022). Georgetown as a Gastronomy Tourism Destination: Visitor Awareness Towards Revisit Intention of Nasi Kandar Restaurant. In M. Valeri (Ed.), *New Governance and Management in Touristic Destinations* (pp. 71–83). IGI Global. https://doi.org/10.4018/978-1-6684-3889-3.ch005

Alkhatib, G., & Bayouq, S. T. (2021). A TAM-Based Model of Technological Factors Affecting Use of E-Tourism. *International Journal of Tourism and Hospitality Management in the Digital Age*, *5*(2), 50–67. https://doi.org/10.4018/IJTHMDA.20210701.oa1

Altinay Ozdemir, M. (2021). Virtual Reality (VR) and Augmented Reality (AR) Technologies for Accessibility and Marketing in the Tourism Industry. In C. Eusébio, L. Teixeira, & M. Carneiro (Eds.), *ICT Tools and Applications for Accessible Tourism* (pp. 277-301). IGI Global. https://doi.org/10.4018/978-1-7998-6428-8.ch013

Anantharaman, R. N., Rajeswari, K. S., Angusamy, A., & Kuppusamy, J. (2017). Role of Self-Efficacy and Collective Efficacy as Moderators of Occupational Stress Among Software Development Professionals. *International Journal of Human Capital and Information Technology Professionals*, *8*(2), 45–58. doi:10.4018/IJHCITP.2017040103

Aninze, F., El-Gohary, H., & Hussain, J. (2018). The Role of Microfinance to Empower Women: The Case of Developing Countries. *International Journal of Customer Relationship Marketing and Management*, *9*(1), 54–78. doi:10.4018/IJCRMM.2018010104

Antosova, G., Sabogal-Salamanca, M., & Krizova, E. (2021). Human Capital in Tourism: A Practical Model of Endogenous and Exogenous Territorial Tourism Planning in Bahía Solano, Colombia. In V. Costa, A. Moura, & M. Mira (Eds.), *Handbook of Research on Human Capital and People Management in the Tourism Industry* (pp. 282–302). IGI Global. https://doi.org/10.4018/978-1-7998-4318-4.ch014

Arsenijević, O. M., Orčić, D., & Kastratović, E. (2017). Development of an Optimization Tool for Intangibles in SMEs: A Case Study from Serbia with a Pilot Research in the Prestige by Milka Company. In M. Vemić (Ed.), *Optimal Management Strategies in Small and Medium Enterprises* (pp. 320–347). Hershey, PA: IGI Global. doi:10.4018/978-1-5225-1949-2.ch015

Aryanto, V. D., Wismantoro, Y., & Widyatmoko, K. (2018). Implementing Eco-Innovation by Utilizing the Internet to Enhance Firm's Marketing Performance: Study of Green Batik Small and Medium Enterprises in Indonesia. *International Journal of E-Business Research, 14*(1), 21–36. doi:10.4018/IJEBR.2018010102

Asero, V., & Billi, S. (2022). New Perspective of Networking in the DMO Model. In M. Valeri (Ed.), *New Governance and Management in Touristic Destinations* (pp. 105–118). IGI Global. https://doi.org/10.4018/978-1-6684-3889-3.ch007

Atiku, S. O., & Fields, Z. (2017). Multicultural Orientations for 21st Century Global Leadership. In N. Baporikar (Ed.), *Management Education for Global Leadership* (pp. 28–51). Hershey, PA: IGI Global. doi:10.4018/978-1-5225-1013-0.ch002

Atiku, S. O., & Fields, Z. (2018). Organisational Learning Dimensions and Talent Retention Strategies for the Service Industries. In N. Baporikar (Ed.), *Global Practices in Knowledge Management for Societal and Organizational Development* (pp. 358–381). Hershey, PA: IGI Global. doi:10.4018/978-1-5225-3009-1.ch017

Atsa'am, D. D., & Kuset Bodur, E. (2021). Pattern Mining on How Organizational Tenure Affects the Psychological Capital of Employees Within the Hospitality and Tourism Industry: Linking Employees' Organizational Tenure With PsyCap. *International Journal of Tourism and Hospitality Management in the Digital Age, 5*(2), 17–28. https://doi.org/10.4018/IJTHMDA.2021070102

Ávila, L., & Teixeira, L. (2018). The Main Concepts Behind the Dematerialization of Business Processes. In M. Khosrow-Pour, D.B.A. (Ed.), Encyclopedia of Information Science and Technology, Fourth Edition (pp. 888-898). Hershey, PA: IGI Global. https://doi.org/ doi:10.4018/978-1-5225-2255-3.ch076

Ayorekire, J., Mugizi, F., Obua, J., & Ampaire, G. (2022). Community-Based Tourism and Local People's Perceptions Towards Conservation: The Case of Queen Elizabeth Conservation Area, Uganda. In I. Mensah & E. Afenyo-Agbe (Eds.), *Prospects and Challenges of Community-Based Tourism and Changing Demographics* (pp. 56–82). IGI Global. https://doi.org/10.4018/978-1-7998-7335-8.ch003

Baleiro, R. (2022). Tourist Literature and the Architecture of Travel in Olga Tokarczuk and Patti Smith. In R. Baleiro & R. Pereira (Eds.), *Global Perspectives on Literary Tourism and Film-Induced Tourism* (pp. 202-216). IGI Global. https://doi.org/10.4018/978-1-7998-8262-6.ch011

Barat, S. (2021). Looking at the Future of Medical Tourism in Asia. *International Journal of Tourism and Hospitality Management in the Digital Age*, *5*(1), 19–33. https://doi.org/10.4018/IJTHMDA.2021010102

Barbosa, C. A., Magalhães, M., & Nunes, M. R. (2021). Travel Instagramability: A Way of Choosing a Destination? In M. Dinis, L. Bonixe, S. Lamy, & Z. Breda (Eds.), *Impact of New Media in Tourism* (pp. 173-190). IGI Global. https://doi.org/10.4018/978-1-7998-7095-1.ch011

Bari, M. W., & Khan, Q. (2021). Pakistan as a Destination of Religious Tourism. In E. Alaverdov & M. Bari (Eds.), *Global Development of Religious Tourism* (pp. 1-10). IGI Global. https://doi.org/10.4018/978-1-7998-5792-1.ch001

Bartens, Y., Chunpir, H. I., Schulte, F., & Voß, S. (2017). Business/IT Alignment in Two-Sided Markets: A COBIT 5 Analysis for Media Streaming Business Models. In S. De Haes & W. Van Grembergen (Eds.), *Strategic IT Governance and Alignment in Business Settings* (pp. 82–111). Hershey, PA: IGI Global. doi:10.4018/978-1-5225-0861-8.ch004

Bashayreh, A. M. (2018). Organizational Culture and Organizational Performance. In W. Lee & F. Sabetzadeh (Eds.), *Contemporary Knowledge and Systems Science* (pp. 50–69). Hershey, PA: IGI Global. doi:10.4018/978-1-5225-5655-8.ch003

Bechthold, L., Lude, M., & Prügl, R. (2021). Crisis Favors the Prepared Firm: How Organizational Ambidexterity Relates to Perceptions of Organizational Resilience. In A. Zehrer, G. Glowka, K. Schwaiger, & V. Ranacher-Lackner (Eds.), *Resiliency Models and Addressing Future Risks for Family Firms in the Tourism Industry* (pp. 178–205). IGI Global. https://doi.org/10.4018/978-1-7998-7352-5.ch008

Bedford, D. A. (2018). Sustainable Knowledge Management Strategies: Aligning Business Capabilities and Knowledge Management Goals. In N. Baporikar (Ed.), *Global Practices in Knowledge Management for Societal and Organizational Development* (pp. 46–73). Hershey, PA: IGI Global. doi:10.4018/978-1-5225-3009-1.ch003

Bekjanov, D., & Matyusupov, B. (2021). Influence of Innovative Processes in the Competitiveness of Tourist Destination. In J. Soares (Ed.), *Innovation and Entrepreneurial Opportunities in Community Tourism* (pp. 243–263). IGI Global. https://doi.org/10.4018/978-1-7998-4855-4.ch014

Bharwani, S., & Musunuri, D. (2018). Reflection as a Process From Theory to Practice. In M. Khosrow-Pour, D.B.A. (Ed.), Encyclopedia of Information Science and Technology, Fourth Edition (pp. 1529-1539). Hershey, PA: IGI Global. doi:10.4018/978-1-5225-2255-3.ch132

Bhatt, G. D., Wang, Z., & Rodger, J. A. (2017). Information Systems Capabilities and Their Effects on Competitive Advantages: A Study of Chinese Companies. *Information Resources Management Journal*, *30*(3), 41–57. doi:10.4018/IRMJ.2017070103

Bhushan, M., & Yadav, A. (2017). Concept of Cloud Computing in ESB. In R. Bhadoria, N. Chaudhari, G. Tomar, & S. Singh (Eds.), *Exploring Enterprise Service Bus in the Service-Oriented Architecture Paradigm* (pp. 116–127). Hershey, PA: IGI Global. doi:10.4018/978-1-5225-2157-0.ch008

Bhushan, S. (2017). System Dynamics Base-Model of Humanitarian Supply Chain (HSCM) in Disaster Prone Eco-Communities of India: A Discussion on Simulation and Scenario Results. *International Journal of System Dynamics Applications*, *6*(3), 20–37. doi:10.4018/IJSDA.2017070102

Binder, D., & Miller, J. W. (2021). A Generations' Perspective on Employer Branding in Tourism. In V. Costa, A. Moura, & M. Mira (Eds.), *Handbook of Research on Human Capital and People Management in the Tourism Industry* (pp. 152–174). IGI Global. https://doi.org/10.4018/978-1-7998-4318-4.ch008

Birch Freeman, A. A., Mensah, I., & Antwi, K. B. (2022). Smiling vs. Frowning Faces: Community Participation for Sustainable Tourism in Ghanaian Communities. In I. Mensah & E. Afenyo-Agbe (Eds.), *Prospects and Challenges of Community-Based Tourism and Changing Demographics* (pp. 83–106). IGI Global. https://doi.org/10.4018/978-1-7998-7335-8.ch004

Biswas, A., & De, A. K. (2017). On Development of a Fuzzy Stochastic Programming Model with Its Application to Business Management. In S. Trivedi, S. Dey, A. Kumar, & T. Panda (Eds.), *Handbook of Research on Advanced Data Mining Techniques and Applications for Business Intelligence* (pp. 353–378). Hershey, PA: IGI Global. doi:10.4018/978-1-5225-2031-3.ch021

Boragnio, A., & Faracce Macia, C. (2021). "Taking Care of Yourself at Home": Use of E-Commerce About Food and Care During the COVID-19 Pandemic in the City of Buenos Aires. In M. Korstanje (Ed.), *Socio-Economic Effects and Recovery Efforts for the Rental Industry: Post-COVID-19 Strategies* (pp. 45–71). IGI Global. https://doi.org/10.4018/978-1-7998-7287-0.ch003

Borges, V. D. (2021). Happiness: The Basis for Public Policy in Tourism. In A. Perinotto, V. Mayer, & J. Soares (Eds.), *Rebuilding and Restructuring the Tourism Industry: Infusion of Happiness and Quality of Life* (pp. 1–25). IGI Global. https://doi.org/10.4018/978-1-7998-7239-9.ch001

Bücker, J., & Ernste, K. (2018). Use of Brand Heroes in Strategic Reputation Management: The Case of Bacardi, Adidas, and Daimler. In A. Erdemir (Ed.), *Reputation Management Techniques in Public Relations* (pp. 126–150). Hershey, PA: IGI Global. doi:10.4018/978-1-5225-3619-2.ch007

Buluk Eşitti, B. (2021). COVID-19 and Alternative Tourism: New Destinations and New Tourism Products. In M. Demir, A. Dalgıç, & F. Ergen (Eds.), *Handbook of Research on the Impacts and Implications of COVID-19 on the Tourism Industry* (pp. 786–805). IGI Global. https://doi.org/10.4018/978-1-7998-8231-2.ch038

Bureš, V. (2018). Industry 4.0 From the Systems Engineering Perspective: Alternative Holistic Framework Development. In R. Brunet-Thornton & F. Martinez (Eds.), *Analyzing the Impacts of Industry 4.0 in Modern Business Environments* (pp. 199–223). Hershey, PA: IGI Global. doi:10.4018/978-1-5225-3468-6.ch011

Buzady, Z. (2017). Resolving the Magic Cube of Effective Case Teaching: Benchmarking Case Teaching Practices in Emerging Markets – Insights from the Central European University Business School, Hungary. In D. Latusek (Ed.), *Case Studies as a Teaching Tool in Management Education* (pp. 79–103). Hershey, PA: IGI Global. doi:10.4018/978-1-5225-0770-3.ch005

Camillo, A. (2021). *Legal Matters, Risk Management, and Risk Prevention: From Forming a Business to Legal Representation.* IGI Global. doi:10.4018/978-1-7998-4342-9.ch004

Căpusneanu, S., & Topor, D. I. (2018). Business Ethics and Cost Management in SMEs: Theories of Business Ethics and Cost Management Ethos. In I. Oncioiu (Ed.), *Ethics and Decision-Making for Sustainable Business Practices* (pp. 109–127). Hershey, PA: IGI Global. doi:10.4018/978-1-5225-3773-1.ch007

Chan, R. L., Mo, P. L., & Moon, K. K. (2018). Strategic and Tactical Measures in Managing Enterprise Risks: A Study of the Textile and Apparel Industry. In K. Strang, M. Korstanje, & N. Vajjhala (Eds.), *Research, Practices, and Innovations in Global Risk and Contingency Management* (pp. 1–19). Hershey, PA: IGI Global. doi:10.4018/978-1-5225-4754-9.ch001

Charlier, S. D., Burke-Smalley, L. A., & Fisher, S. L. (2018). Undergraduate Programs in the U.S: A Contextual and Content-Based Analysis. In J. Mendy (Ed.), *Teaching Human Resources and Organizational Behavior at the College Level* (pp. 26–57). Hershey, PA: IGI Global. doi:10.4018/978-1-5225-2820-3.ch002

Chumillas, J., Güell, M., & Quer, P. (2022). The Use of ICT in Tourist and Educational Literary Routes: The Role of the Guide. In C. Ramos, S. Quinteiro, & A. Gonçalves (Eds.), *ICT as Innovator Between Tourism and Culture* (pp. 15–29). IGI Global. https://doi.org/10.4018/978-1-7998-8165-0.ch002

Dahlberg, T., Kivijärvi, H., & Saarinen, T. (2017). IT Investment Consistency and Other Factors Influencing the Success of IT Performance. In S. De Haes & W. Van Grembergen (Eds.), *Strategic IT Governance and Alignment in Business Settings* (pp. 176–208). Hershey, PA: IGI Global. doi:10.4018/978-1-5225-0861-8.ch007

Damnjanović, A. M. (2017). Knowledge Management Optimization through IT and E-Business Utilization: A Qualitative Study on Serbian SMEs. In M. Vemić (Ed.), *Optimal Management Strategies in Small and Medium Enterprises* (pp. 249–267). Hershey, PA: IGI Global. doi:10.4018/978-1-5225-1949-2.ch012

Daneshpour, H. (2017). Integrating Sustainable Development into Project Portfolio Management through Application of Open Innovation. In M. Vemić (Ed.), *Optimal Management Strategies in Small and Medium Enterprises* (pp. 370–387). Hershey, PA: IGI Global. doi:10.4018/978-1-5225-1949-2.ch017

Daniel, A. D., & Reis de Castro, V. (2018). Entrepreneurship Education: How to Measure the Impact on Nascent Entrepreneurs. In A. Carrizo Moreira, J. Guilherme Leitão Dantas, & F. Manuel Valente (Eds.), *Nascent Entrepreneurship and Successful New Venture Creation* (pp. 85–110). Hershey, PA: IGI Global. doi:10.4018/978-1-5225-2936-1.ch004

David, R., Swami, B. N., & Tangirala, S. (2018). Ethics Impact on Knowledge Management in Organizational Development: A Case Study. In N. Baporikar (Ed.), *Global Practices in Knowledge Management for Societal and Organizational Development* (pp. 19–45). Hershey, PA: IGI Global. doi:10.4018/978-1-5225-3009-1.ch002

De Uña-Álvarez, E., & Villarino-Pérez, M. (2022). Fostering Ecocultural Resources, Identity, and Tourism in Inland Territories (Galicia, NW Spain). In G. Fernandes (Ed.), *Challenges and New Opportunities for Tourism in Inland Territories: Ecocultural Resources and Sustainable Initiatives* (pp. 1-16). IGI Global. https://doi.org/10.4018/978-1-7998-7339-6.ch001

Delias, P., & Lakiotaki, K. (2018). Discovering Process Horizontal Boundaries to Facilitate Process Comprehension. *International Journal of Operations Research and Information Systems*, *9*(2), 1–31. doi:10.4018/IJORIS.2018040101

Denholm, J., & Lee-Davies, L. (2018). Success Factors for Games in Business and Project Management. In *Enhancing Education and Training Initiatives Through Serious Games* (pp. 34–68). Hershey, PA: IGI Global. doi:10.4018/978-1-5225-3689-5.ch002

Deshpande, M. (2017). Best Practices in Management Institutions for Global Leadership: Policy Aspects. In N. Baporikar (Ed.), *Management Education for Global Leadership* (pp. 1–27). Hershey, PA: IGI Global. doi:10.4018/978-1-5225-1013-0.ch001

Deshpande, M. (2018). Policy Perspectives for SMEs Knowledge Management. In N. Baporikar (Ed.), *Knowledge Integration Strategies for Entrepreneurship and Sustainability* (pp. 23–46). Hershey, PA: IGI Global. doi:10.4018/978-1-5225-5115-7.ch002

Dezdar, S. (2017). ERP Implementation Projects in Asian Countries: A Comparative Study on Iran and China. *International Journal of Information Technology Project Management*, *8*(3), 52–68. doi:10.4018/IJITPM.2017070104

Domingos, D., Respício, A., & Martinho, R. (2017). Reliability of IoT-Aware BPMN Healthcare Processes. In C. Reis & M. Maximiano (Eds.), *Internet of Things and Advanced Application in Healthcare* (pp. 214–248). Hershey, PA: IGI Global. doi:10.4018/978-1-5225-1820-4.ch008

Dosumu, O., Hussain, J., & El-Gohary, H. (2017). An Exploratory Study of the Impact of Government Policies on the Development of Small and Medium Enterprises in Developing Countries: The Case of Nigeria. *International Journal of Customer Relationship Marketing and Management*, *8*(4), 51–62. doi:10.4018/IJCRMM.2017100104

Durst, S., Bruns, G., & Edvardsson, I. R. (2017). Retaining Knowledge in Smaller Building and Construction Firms. *International Journal of Knowledge and Systems Science*, *8*(3), 1–12. doi:10.4018/IJKSS.2017070101

Edvardsson, I. R., & Durst, S. (2017). Outsourcing, Knowledge, and Learning: A Critical Review. *International Journal of Knowledge-Based Organizations*, *7*(2), 13–26. doi:10.4018/IJKBO.2017040102

Edwards, J. S. (2018). Integrating Knowledge Management and Business Processes. In M. Khosrow-Pour, D.B.A. (Ed.), Encyclopedia of Information Science and Technology, Fourth Edition (pp. 5046-5055). Hershey, PA: IGI Global. doi:10.4018/978-1-5225-2255-3.ch437

Eichelberger, S., & Peters, M. (2021). Family Firm Management in Turbulent Times: Opportunities for Responsible Tourism. In A. Zehrer, G. Glowka, K. Schwaiger, & V. Ranacher-Lackner (Eds.), *Resiliency Models and Addressing Future Risks for Family Firms in the Tourism Industry* (pp. 103–124). IGI Global. https://doi.org/10.4018/978-1-7998-7352-5.ch005

Eide, D., Hjalager, A., & Hansen, M. (2022). Innovative Certifications in Adventure Tourism: Attributes and Diffusion. In R. Augusto Costa, F. Brandão, Z. Breda, & C. Costa (Eds.), *Planning and Managing the Experience Economy in Tourism* (pp. 161-175). IGI Global. https://doi.org/10.4018/978-1-7998-8775-1.ch009

Ejiogu, A. O. (2018). Economics of Farm Management. In *Agricultural Finance and Opportunities for Investment and Expansion* (pp. 56–72). Hershey, PA: IGI Global. doi:10.4018/978-1-5225-3059-6.ch003

Ekanem, I., & Abiade, G. E. (2018). Factors Influencing the Use of E-Commerce by Small Enterprises in Nigeria. *International Journal of ICT Research in Africa and the Middle East*, *7*(1), 37–53. doi:10.4018/IJICTRAME.2018010103

Ekanem, I., & Alrossais, L. A. (2017). Succession Challenges Facing Family Businesses in Saudi Arabia. In P. Zgheib (Ed.), *Entrepreneurship and Business Innovation in the Middle East* (pp. 122–146). Hershey, PA: IGI Global. doi:10.4018/978-1-5225-2066-5.ch007

El Faquih, L., & Fredj, M. (2017). Ontology-Based Framework for Quality in Configurable Process Models. *Journal of Electronic Commerce in Organizations*, *15*(2), 48–60. doi:10.4018/JECO.2017040104

Faisal, M. N., & Talib, F. (2017). Building Ambidextrous Supply Chains in SMEs: How to Tackle the Barriers? *International Journal of Information Systems and Supply Chain Management*, *10*(4), 80–100. doi:10.4018/IJISSCM.2017100105

Fernandes, T. M., Gomes, J., & Romão, M. (2017). Investments in E-Government: A Benefit Management Case Study. *International Journal of Electronic Government Research*, *13*(3), 1–17. doi:10.4018/IJEGR.2017070101

Figueira, L. M., Honrado, G. R., & Dionísio, M. S. (2021). Human Capital Management in the Tourism Industry in Portugal. In V. Costa, A. Moura, & M. Mira (Eds.), *Handbook of Research on Human Capital and People Management in the Tourism Industry* (pp. 1–19). IGI Global. doi:10.4018/978-1-7998-4318-4.ch001

Gao, S. S., Oreal, S., & Zhang, J. (2018). Contemporary Financial Risk Management Perceptions and Practices of Small-Sized Chinese Businesses. In I. Management Association (Ed.), Global Business Expansion: Concepts, Methodologies, Tools, and Applications (pp. 917-931). Hershey, PA: IGI Global. doi:10.4018/978-1-5225-5481-3.ch041

Garg, R., & Berning, S. C. (2017). Indigenous Chinese Management Philosophies: Key Concepts and Relevance for Modern Chinese Firms. In B. Christiansen & G. Koc (Eds.), *Transcontinental Strategies for Industrial Development and Economic Growth* (pp. 43–57). Hershey, PA: IGI Global. doi:10.4018/978-1-5225-2160-0.ch003

Gencer, Y. G. (2017). Supply Chain Management in Retailing Business. In U. Akkucuk (Ed.), *Ethics and Sustainability in Global Supply Chain Management* (pp. 197–210). Hershey, PA: IGI Global. doi:10.4018/978-1-5225-2036-8.ch011

Gera, R., Arora, S., & Malik, S. (2021). Emotional Labor in the Tourism Industry: Strategies, Antecedents, and Outcomes. In V. Costa, A. Moura, & M. Mira (Eds.), *Handbook of Research on Human Capital and People Management in the Tourism Industry* (pp. 73–91). IGI Global. https://doi.org/10.4018/978-1-7998-4318-4.ch004

Giacosa, E. (2018). The Increasing of the Regional Development Thanks to the Luxury Business Innovation. In L. Carvalho (Ed.), *Handbook of Research on Entrepreneurial Ecosystems and Social Dynamics in a Globalized World* (pp. 260–273). Hershey, PA: IGI Global. doi:10.4018/978-1-5225-3525-6.ch011

Glowka, G., Tusch, M., & Zehrer, A. (2021). The Risk Perception of Family Business Owner-Manager in the Tourism Industry: A Qualitative Comparison of the Intra-Firm Senior and Junior Generation. In A. Zehrer, G. Glowka, K. Schwaiger, & V. Ranacher-Lackner (Eds.), *Resiliency Models and Addressing Future Risks for Family Firms in the Tourism Industry* (pp. 126–153). IGI Global. https://doi.org/10.4018/978-1-7998-7352-5.ch006

Glykas, M., & George, J. (2017). Quality and Process Management Systems in the UAE Maritime Industry. *International Journal of Productivity Management and Assessment Technologies*, *5*(1), 20–39. doi:10.4018/IJPMAT.2017010102

Glykas, M., Valiris, G., Kokkinaki, A., & Koutsoukou, Z. (2018). Banking Business Process Management Implementation. *International Journal of Productivity Management and Assessment Technologies, 6*(1), 50–69. doi:10.4018/IJPMAT.2018010104

Gomes, J., & Romão, M. (2017). The Balanced Scorecard: Keeping Updated and Aligned with Today's Business Trends. *International Journal of Productivity Management and Assessment Technologies, 5*(2), 1–15. doi:10.4018/IJPMAT.2017070101

Gomes, J., & Romão, M. (2017). Aligning Information Systems and Technology with Benefit Management and Balanced Scorecard. In S. De Haes & W. Van Grembergen (Eds.), *Strategic IT Governance and Alignment in Business Settings* (pp. 112–131). Hershey, PA: IGI Global. doi:10.4018/978-1-5225-0861-8.ch005

Goyal, A. (2021). Communicating and Building Destination Brands With New Media. In M. Dinis, L. Bonixe, S. Lamy, & Z. Breda (Eds.), *Impact of New Media in Tourism* (pp. 1-20). IGI Global. https://doi.org/10.4018/978-1-7998-7095-1.ch001

Grefen, P., & Turetken, O. (2017). Advanced Business Process Management in Networked E-Business Scenarios. *International Journal of E-Business Research, 13*(4), 70–104. doi:10.4018/IJEBR.2017100105

Guasca, M., Van Broeck, A. M., & Vanneste, D. (2021). Tourism and the Social Reintegration of Colombian Ex-Combatants. In J. da Silva, Z. Breda, & F. Carbone (Eds.), *Role and Impact of Tourism in Peacebuilding and Conflict Transformation* (pp. 66-86). IGI Global. https://doi.org/10.4018/978-1-7998-5053-3.ch005

Haider, A., & Saetang, S. (2017). Strategic IT Alignment in Service Sector. In S. Rozenes & Y. Cohen (Eds.), *Handbook of Research on Strategic Alliances and Value Co-Creation in the Service Industry* (pp. 231–258). Hershey, PA: IGI Global. doi:10.4018/978-1-5225-2084-9.ch012

Hajilari, A. B., Ghadaksaz, M., & Fasghandis, G. S. (2017). Assessing Organizational Readiness for Implementing ERP System Using Fuzzy Expert System Approach. *International Journal of Enterprise Information Systems, 13*(1), 67–85. doi:10.4018/IJEIS.2017010105

Haldorai, A., Ramu, A., & Murugan, S. (2018). Social Aware Cognitive Radio Networks: Effectiveness of Social Networks as a Strategic Tool for Organizational Business Management. In H. Bansal, G. Shrivastava, G. Nguyen, & L. Stanciu (Eds.), *Social Network Analytics for Contemporary Business Organizations* (pp. 188–202). Hershey, PA: IGI Global. doi:10.4018/978-1-5225-5097-6.ch010

Hall, O. P. Jr. (2017). Social Media Driven Management Education. *International Journal of Knowledge-Based Organizations*, *7*(2), 43–59. doi:10.4018/IJKBO.2017040104

Hanifah, H., Halim, H. A., Ahmad, N. H., & Vafaei-Zadeh, A. (2017). Innovation Culture as a Mediator Between Specific Human Capital and Innovation Performance Among Bumiputera SMEs in Malaysia. In N. Ahmad, T. Ramayah, H. Halim, & S. Rahman (Eds.), *Handbook of Research on Small and Medium Enterprises in Developing Countries* (pp. 261–279). Hershey, PA: IGI Global. doi:10.4018/978-1-5225-2165-5.ch012

Hartlieb, S., & Silvius, G. (2017). Handling Uncertainty in Project Management and Business Development: Similarities and Differences. In Y. Raydugin (Ed.), *Handbook of Research on Leveraging Risk and Uncertainties for Effective Project Management* (pp. 337–362). Hershey, PA: IGI Global. doi:10.4018/978-1-5225-1790-0.ch016

Hass, K. B. (2017). Living on the Edge: Managing Project Complexity. In Y. Raydugin (Ed.), *Handbook of Research on Leveraging Risk and Uncertainties for Effective Project Management* (pp. 177–201). Hershey, PA: IGI Global. doi:10.4018/978-1-5225-1790-0.ch009

Hawking, P., & Carmine Sellitto, C. (2017). Developing an Effective Strategy for Organizational Business Intelligence. In M. Tavana (Ed.), *Enterprise Information Systems and the Digitalization of Business Functions* (pp. 222–237). Hershey, PA: IGI Global. doi:10.4018/978-1-5225-2382-6.ch010

Hawking, P., & Sellitto, C. (2017). A Fast-Moving Consumer Goods Company and Business Intelligence Strategy Development. *International Journal of Enterprise Information Systems*, *13*(2), 22–33. doi:10.4018/IJEIS.2017040102

Hawking, P., & Sellitto, C. (2017). Business Intelligence Strategy: Two Case Studies. *International Journal of Business Intelligence Research*, *8*(2), 17–30. doi:10.4018/IJBIR.2017070102

Hee, W. J., Jalleh, G., Lai, H., & Lin, C. (2017). E-Commerce and IT Projects: Evaluation and Management Issues in Australian and Taiwanese Hospitals. *International Journal of Public Health Management and Ethics*, *2*(1), 69–90. doi:10.4018/IJPHME.2017010104

Hernandez, A. A. (2018). Exploring the Factors to Green IT Adoption of SMEs in the Philippines. *Journal of Cases on Information Technology*, *20*(2), 49–66. doi:10.4018/JCIT.2018040104

Hollman, A., Bickford, S., & Hollman, T. (2017). Cyber InSecurity: A Post-Mortem Attempt to Assess Cyber Problems from IT and Business Management Perspectives. *Journal of Cases on Information Technology, 19*(3), 42–70. doi:10.4018/JCIT.2017070104

Ibrahim, F., & Zainin, N. M. (2021). Exploring the Technological Impacts: The Case of Museums in Brunei Darussalam. *International Journal of Tourism and Hospitality Management in the Digital Age, 5*(1), 1–18. https://doi.org/10.4018/IJTHMDA.2021010101

Igbinakhase, I. (2017). Responsible and Sustainable Management Practices in Developing and Developed Business Environments. In Z. Fields (Ed.), *Collective Creativity for Responsible and Sustainable Business Practice* (pp. 180–207). Hershey, PA: IGI Global. doi:10.4018/978-1-5225-1823-5.ch010

Iwata, J. J., & Hoskins, R. G. (2017). Managing Indigenous Knowledge in Tanzania: A Business Perspective. In P. Jain & N. Mnjama (Eds.), *Managing Knowledge Resources and Records in Modern Organizations* (pp. 198–214). Hershey, PA: IGI Global. doi:10.4018/978-1-5225-1965-2.ch012

Jain, P. (2017). Ethical and Legal Issues in Knowledge Management Life-Cycle in Business. In P. Jain & N. Mnjama (Eds.), *Managing Knowledge Resources and Records in Modern Organizations* (pp. 82–101). Hershey, PA: IGI Global. doi:10.4018/978-1-5225-1965-2.ch006

James, S., & Hauli, E. (2017). Holistic Management Education at Tanzanian Rural Development Planning Institute. In N. Baporikar (Ed.), *Management Education for Global Leadership* (pp. 112–136). Hershey, PA: IGI Global. doi:10.4018/978-1-5225-1013-0.ch006

Janošková, M., Csikósová, A., & Čulková, K. (2018). Measurement of Company Performance as Part of Its Strategic Management. In R. Leon (Ed.), *Managerial Strategies for Business Sustainability During Turbulent Times* (pp. 309–335). Hershey, PA: IGI Global. doi:10.4018/978-1-5225-2716-9.ch017

Jean-Vasile, A., & Alecu, A. (2017). Theoretical and Practical Approaches in Understanding the Influences of Cost-Productivity-Profit Trinomial in Contemporary Enterprises. In A. Jean Vasile & D. Nicolò (Eds.), *Sustainable Entrepreneurship and Investments in the Green Economy* (pp. 28–62). Hershey, PA: IGI Global. doi:10.4018/978-1-5225-2075-7.ch002

Joia, L. A., & Correia, J. C. (2018). CIO Competencies From the IT Professional Perspective: Insights From Brazil. *Journal of Global Information Management, 26*(2), 74–103. doi:10.4018/JGIM.2018040104

Juma, A., & Mzera, N. (2017). Knowledge Management and Records Management and Competitive Advantage in Business. In P. Jain & N. Mnjama (Eds.), *Managing Knowledge Resources and Records in Modern Organizations* (pp. 15–28). Hershey, PA: IGI Global. doi:10.4018/978-1-5225-1965-2.ch002

K., I., & A, V. (2018). Monitoring and Auditing in the Cloud. In K. Munir (Ed.), *Cloud Computing Technologies for Green Enterprises* (pp. 318-350). Hershey, PA: IGI Global. https://doi.org/ doi:10.4018/978-1-5225-3038-1.ch013

Kabra, G., Ghosh, V., & Ramesh, A. (2018). Enterprise Integrated Business Process Management and Business Intelligence Framework for Business Process Sustainability. In A. Paul, D. Bhattacharyya, & S. Anand (Eds.), *Green Initiatives for Business Sustainability and Value Creation* (pp. 228–238). Hershey, PA: IGI Global. doi:10.4018/978-1-5225-2662-9.ch010

Kaoud, M. (2017). Investigation of Customer Knowledge Management: A Case Study Research. *International Journal of Service Science, Management, Engineering, and Technology, 8*(2), 12–22. doi:10.4018/IJSSMET.2017040102

Katuu, S. (2018). A Comparative Assessment of Enterprise Content Management Maturity Models. In N. Gwangwava & M. Mutingi (Eds.), *E-Manufacturing and E-Service Strategies in Contemporary Organizations* (pp. 93–118). Hershey, PA: IGI Global. doi:10.4018/978-1-5225-3628-4.ch005

Khan, M. Y., & Abir, T. (2022). The Role of Social Media Marketing in the Tourism and Hospitality Industry: A Conceptual Study on Bangladesh. In C. Ramos, S. Quinteiro, & A. Gonçalves (Eds.), *ICT as Innovator Between Tourism and Culture* (pp. 213–229). IGI Global. https://doi.org/10.4018/978-1-7998-8165-0.ch013

Kinnunen, S., Ylä-Kujala, A., Marttonen-Arola, S., Kärri, T., & Baglee, D. (2018). Internet of Things in Asset Management: Insights from Industrial Professionals and Academia. *International Journal of Service Science, Management, Engineering, and Technology, 9*(2), 104–119. doi:10.4018/IJSSMET.2018040105

Klein, A. Z., Sabino de Freitas, A., Machado, L., Freitas, J. C. Jr, Graziola, P. G. Jr, & Schlemmer, E. (2017). Virtual Worlds Applications for Management Education. In L. Tomei (Ed.), *Exploring the New Era of Technology-Infused Education* (pp. 279–299). Hershey, PA: IGI Global. doi:10.4018/978-1-5225-1709-2.ch017

Kővári, E., Saleh, M., & Steinbachné Hajmásy, G. (2022). The Impact of Corporate Digital Responsibility (CDR) on Internal Stakeholders' Satisfaction in Hungarian Upscale Hotels. In M. Valeri (Ed.), *New Governance and Management in Touristic Destinations* (pp. 35–51). IGI Global. https://doi.org/10.4018/978-1-6684-3889-3.ch003

Kożuch, B., & Jabłoński, A. (2017). Adopting the Concept of Business Models in Public Management. In M. Lewandowski & B. Kożuch (Eds.), *Public Sector Entrepreneurship and the Integration of Innovative Business Models* (pp. 10–46). Hershey, PA: IGI Global. doi:10.4018/978-1-5225-2215-7.ch002

Kumar, J., Adhikary, A., & Jha, A. (2017). Small Active Investors' Perceptions and Preferences Towards Tax Saving Mutual Fund Schemes in Eastern India: An Empirical Note. *International Journal of Asian Business and Information Management, 8*(2), 35–45. doi:10.4018/IJABIM.2017040103

Latusi, S., & Fissore, M. (2021). Pilgrimage Routes to Happiness: Comparing the Camino de Santiago and Via Francigena. In A. Perinotto, V. Mayer, & J. Soares (Eds.), *Rebuilding and Restructuring the Tourism Industry: Infusion of Happiness and Quality of Life* (pp. 157–182). IGI Global. https://doi.org/10.4018/978-1-7998-7239-9.ch008

Lavassani, K. M., & Movahedi, B. (2017). Applications Driven Information Systems: Beyond Networks toward Business Ecosystems. *International Journal of Innovation in the Digital Economy, 8*(1), 61–75. doi:10.4018/IJIDE.2017010104

Lazzareschi, V. H., & Brito, M. S. (2017). Strategic Information Management: Proposal of Business Project Model. In G. Jamil, A. Soares, & C. Pessoa (Eds.), *Handbook of Research on Information Management for Effective Logistics and Supply Chains* (pp. 59–88). Hershey, PA: IGI Global. doi:10.4018/978-1-5225-0973-8.ch004

Lechuga Sancho, M. P., & Martín Navarro, A. (2022). Evolution of the Literature on Social Responsibility in the Tourism Sector: A Systematic Literature Review. In G. Fernandes (Ed.), *Challenges and New Opportunities for Tourism in Inland Territories: Ecocultural Resources and Sustainable Initiatives* (pp. 169–186). IGI Global. https://doi.org/10.4018/978-1-7998-7339-6.ch010

Lederer, M., Kurz, M., & Lazarov, P. (2017). Usage and Suitability of Methods for Strategic Business Process Initiatives: A Multi Case Study Research. *International Journal of Productivity Management and Assessment Technologies, 5*(1), 40–51. doi:10.4018/IJPMAT.2017010103

Lee, I. (2017). A Social Enterprise Business Model and a Case Study of Pacific Community Ventures (PCV). In V. Potocan, M. Üngan, & Z. Nedelko (Eds.), *Handbook of Research on Managerial Solutions in Non-Profit Organizations* (pp. 182–204). Hershey, PA: IGI Global. doi:10.4018/978-1-5225-0731-4.ch009

Leon, L. A., Seal, K. C., Przasnyski, Z. H., & Wiedenman, I. (2017). Skills and Competencies Required for Jobs in Business Analytics: A Content Analysis of Job Advertisements Using Text Mining. *International Journal of Business Intelligence Research, 8*(1), 1–25. doi:10.4018/IJBIR.2017010101

Levy, C. L., & Elias, N. I. (2017). SOHO Users' Perceptions of Reliability and Continuity of Cloud-Based Services. In M. Moore (Ed.), *Cybersecurity Breaches and Issues Surrounding Online Threat Protection* (pp. 248–287). Hershey, PA: IGI Global. doi:10.4018/978-1-5225-1941-6.ch011

Levy, M. (2018). Change Management Serving Knowledge Management and Organizational Development: Reflections and Review. In N. Baporikar (Ed.), *Global Practices in Knowledge Management for Societal and Organizational Development* (pp. 256–270). Hershey, PA: IGI Global. doi:10.4018/978-1-5225-3009-1.ch012

Lewandowski, M. (2017). Public Organizations and Business Model Innovation: The Role of Public Service Design. In M. Lewandowski & B. Kożuch (Eds.), *Public Sector Entrepreneurship and the Integration of Innovative Business Models* (pp. 47–72). Hershey, PA: IGI Global. doi:10.4018/978-1-5225-2215-7.ch003

Lhannaoui, H., Kabbaj, M. I., & Bakkoury, Z. (2017). A Survey of Risk-Aware Business Process Modelling. *International Journal of Risk and Contingency Management, 6*(3), 14–26. doi:10.4018/IJRCM.2017070102

Li, J., Sun, W., Jiang, W., Yang, H., & Zhang, L. (2017). How the Nature of Exogenous Shocks and Crises Impact Company Performance?: The Effects of Industry Characteristics. *International Journal of Risk and Contingency Management, 6*(4), 40–55. doi:10.4018/IJRCM.2017100103

Lopez-Fernandez, M., Perez-Perez, M., Serrano-Bedia, A., & Cobo-Gonzalez, A. (2021). Small and Medium Tourism Enterprise Survival in Times of Crisis: "El Capricho de Gaudí. In D. Toubes & N. Araújo-Vila (Eds.), *Risk, Crisis, and Disaster Management in Small and Medium-Sized Tourism Enterprises* (pp. 103–129). IGI Global. doi:10.4018/978-1-7998-6996-2.ch005

Mahajan, A., Maidullah, S., & Hossain, M. R. (2022). Experience Toward Smart Tour Guide Apps in Travelling: An Analysis of Users' Reviews on Audio Odigos and Trip My Way. In R. Augusto Costa, F. Brandão, Z. Breda, & C. Costa (Eds.), *Planning and Managing the Experience Economy in Tourism* (pp. 255-273). IGI Global. https://doi.org/10.4018/978-1-7998-8775-1.ch014

Malega, P. (2017). Small and Medium Enterprises in the Slovak Republic: Status and Competitiveness of SMEs in the Global Markets and Possibilities of Optimization. In M. Vemić (Ed.), *Optimal Management Strategies in Small and Medium Enterprises* (pp. 102–124). Hershey, PA: IGI Global. doi:10.4018/978-1-5225-1949-2.ch006

Malewska, K. M. (2017). Intuition in Decision-Making on the Example of a Non-Profit Organization. In V. Potocan, M. Üngan, & Z. Nedelko (Eds.), *Handbook of Research on Managerial Solutions in Non-Profit Organizations* (pp. 378–399). Hershey, PA: IGI Global. doi:10.4018/978-1-5225-0731-4.ch018

Maroofi, F. (2017). Entrepreneurial Orientation and Organizational Learning Ability Analysis for Innovation and Firm Performance. In N. Baporikar (Ed.), *Innovation and Shifting Perspectives in Management Education* (pp. 144–165). Hershey, PA: IGI Global. doi:10.4018/978-1-5225-1019-2.ch007

Marques, M., Moleiro, D., Brito, T. M., & Marques, T. (2021). Customer Relationship Management as an Important Relationship Marketing Tool: The Case of the Hospitality Industry in Estoril Coast. In M. Dinis, L. Bonixe, S. Lamy, & Z. Breda (Eds.), Impact of New Media in Tourism (pp. 39-56). IGI Global. https://doi.org/doi:10.4018/978-1-7998-7095-1.ch003

Martins, P. V., & Zacarias, M. (2017). A Web-based Tool for Business Process Improvement. *International Journal of Web Portals*, *9*(2), 68–84. doi:10.4018/IJWP.2017070104

Matthies, B., & Coners, A. (2017). Exploring the Conceptual Nature of e-Business Projects. *Journal of Electronic Commerce in Organizations*, *15*(3), 33–63. doi:10.4018/JECO.2017070103

Mayer, V. F., Fraga, C. C., & Silva, L. C. (2021). Contributions of Neurosciences to Studies of Well-Being in Tourism. In A. Perinotto, V. Mayer, & J. Soares (Eds.), *Rebuilding and Restructuring the Tourism Industry: Infusion of Happiness and Quality of Life* (pp. 108–128). IGI Global. https://doi.org/10.4018/978-1-7998-7239-9.ch006

McKee, J. (2018). Architecture as a Tool to Solve Business Planning Problems. In M. Khosrow-Pour, D.B.A. (Ed.), Encyclopedia of Information Science and Technology, Fourth Edition (pp. 573-586). Hershey, PA: IGI Global. doi:10.4018/978-1-5225-2255-3.ch050

McMurray, A. J., Cross, J., & Caponecchia, C. (2018). The Risk Management Profession in Australia: Business Continuity Plan Practices. In N. Bajgoric (Ed.), *Always-On Enterprise Information Systems for Modern Organizations* (pp. 112–129). Hershey, PA: IGI Global. doi:10.4018/978-1-5225-3704-5.ch006

Meddah, I. H., & Belkadi, K. (2018). Mining Patterns Using Business Process Management. In R. Hamou (Ed.), *Handbook of Research on Biomimicry in Information Retrieval and Knowledge Management* (pp. 78–89). Hershey, PA: IGI Global. doi:10.4018/978-1-5225-3004-6.ch005

Melian, A. G., & Camprubí, R. (2021). The Accessibility of Museum Websites: The Case of Barcelona. In C. Eusébio, L. Teixeira, & M. Carneiro (Eds.), *ICT Tools and Applications for Accessible Tourism* (pp. 234–255). IGI Global. https://doi.org/10.4018/978-1-7998-6428-8.ch011

Mendes, L. (2017). TQM and Knowledge Management: An Integrated Approach Towards Tacit Knowledge Management. In D. Jaziri-Bouagina & G. Jamil (Eds.), *Handbook of Research on Tacit Knowledge Management for Organizational Success* (pp. 236–263). Hershey, PA: IGI Global. doi:10.4018/978-1-5225-2394-9.ch009

Menezes, V. D., & Cavagnaro, E. (2021). Communicating Sustainable Initiatives in the Hotel Industry: The Case of the Hotel Jakarta Amsterdam. In F. Brandão, Z. Breda, R. Costa, & C. Costa (Eds.), *Handbook of Research on the Role of Tourism in Achieving Sustainable Development Goals* (pp. 224-234). IGI Global. https://doi.org/10.4018/978-1-7998-5691-7.ch013

Menezes, V. D., & Cavagnaro, E. (2021). Communicating Sustainable Initiatives in the Hotel Industry: The Case of the Hotel Jakarta Amsterdam. In F. Brandão, Z. Breda, R. Costa, & C. Costa (Eds.), *Handbook of Research on the Role of Tourism in Achieving Sustainable Development Goals* (pp. 224-234). IGI Global. https://doi.org/10.4018/978-1-7998-5691-7.ch013

Mitas, O., Bastiaansen, M., & Boode, W. (2022). If You're Happy, I'm Happy: Emotion Contagion at a Tourist Information Center. In R. Augusto Costa, F. Brandão, Z. Breda, & C. Costa (Eds.), *Planning and Managing the Experience Economy in Tourism* (pp. 122-140). IGI Global. https://doi.org/10.4018/978-1-7998-8775-1.ch007

Mnjama, N. M. (2017). Preservation of Recorded Information in Public and Private Sector Organizations. In P. Jain & N. Mnjama (Eds.), *Managing Knowledge Resources and Records in Modern Organizations* (pp. 149–167). Hershey, PA: IGI Global. doi:10.4018/978-1-5225-1965-2.ch009

Mokoqama, M., & Fields, Z. (2017). Principles of Responsible Management Education (PRME): Call for Responsible Management Education. In Z. Fields (Ed.), *Collective Creativity for Responsible and Sustainable Business Practice* (pp. 229–241). Hershey, PA: IGI Global. doi:10.4018/978-1-5225-1823-5.ch012

Monteiro, A., Lopes, S., & Carbone, F. (2021). Academic Mobility: Bridging Tourism and Peace Education. In J. da Silva, Z. Breda, & F. Carbone (Eds.), *Role and Impact of Tourism in Peacebuilding and Conflict Transformation* (pp. 275-301). IGI Global. https://doi.org/10.4018/978-1-7998-5053-3.ch016

Muniapan, B. (2017). Philosophy and Management: The Relevance of Vedanta in Management. In P. Ordóñez de Pablos (Ed.), *Managerial Strategies and Solutions for Business Success in Asia* (pp. 124–139). Hershey, PA: IGI Global. doi:10.4018/978-1-5225-1886-0.ch007

Murad, S. E., & Dowaji, S. (2017). Using Value-Based Approach for Managing Cloud-Based Services. In A. Turuk, B. Sahoo, & S. Addya (Eds.), *Resource Management and Efficiency in Cloud Computing Environments* (pp. 33–60). Hershey, PA: IGI Global. doi:10.4018/978-1-5225-1721-4.ch002

Mutahar, A. M., Daud, N. M., Thurasamy, R., Isaac, O., & Abdulsalam, R. (2018). The Mediating of Perceived Usefulness and Perceived Ease of Use: The Case of Mobile Banking in Yemen. *International Journal of Technology Diffusion*, *9*(2), 21–40. doi:10.4018/IJTD.2018040102

Naidoo, V. (2017). E-Learning and Management Education at African Universities. In N. Baporikar (Ed.), *Management Education for Global Leadership* (pp. 181–201). Hershey, PA: IGI Global. doi:10.4018/978-1-5225-1013-0.ch009

Naidoo, V., & Igbinakhase, I. (2018). Opportunities and Challenges of Knowledge Retention in SMEs. In N. Baporikar (Ed.), *Knowledge Integration Strategies for Entrepreneurship and Sustainability* (pp. 70–94). Hershey, PA: IGI Global. doi:10.4018/978-1-5225-5115-7.ch004

Naumov, N., & Costandachi, G. (2021). Creativity and Entrepreneurship: Gastronomic Tourism in Mexico. In J. Soares (Ed.), *Innovation and Entrepreneurial Opportunities in Community Tourism* (pp. 90–108). IGI Global. https://doi.org/10.4018/978-1-7998-4855-4.ch006

Nayak, S., & Prabhu, N. (2017). Paradigm Shift in Management Education: Need for a Cross Functional Perspective. In N. Baporikar (Ed.), *Management Education for Global Leadership* (pp. 241–255). Hershey, PA: IGI Global. doi:10.4018/978-1-5225-1013-0.ch012

Nedelko, Z., & Potocan, V. (2017). Management Solutions in Non-Profit Organizations: Case of Slovenia. In V. Potocan, M. Üngan, & Z. Nedelko (Eds.), *Handbook of Research on Managerial Solutions in Non-Profit Organizations* (pp. 1–22). Hershey, PA: IGI Global. doi:10.4018/978-1-5225-0731-4.ch001

Nedelko, Z., & Potocan, V. (2017). Priority of Management Tools Utilization among Managers: International Comparison. In V. Wang (Ed.), *Encyclopedia of Strategic Leadership and Management* (pp. 1083–1094). Hershey, PA: IGI Global. doi:10.4018/978-1-5225-1049-9.ch075

Nedelko, Z., Raudeliūnienė, J., & Črešnar, R. (2018). Knowledge Dynamics in Supply Chain Management. In N. Baporikar (Ed.), *Knowledge Integration Strategies for Entrepreneurship and Sustainability* (pp. 150–166). Hershey, PA: IGI Global. doi:10.4018/978-1-5225-5115-7.ch008

Nguyen, H. T., & Hipsher, S. A. (2018). Innovation and Creativity Used by Private Sector Firms in a Resources-Constrained Environment. In S. Hipsher (Ed.), *Examining the Private Sector's Role in Wealth Creation and Poverty Reduction* (pp. 219–238). Hershey, PA: IGI Global. doi:10.4018/978-1-5225-3117-3.ch010

Obicci, P. A. (2017). Risk Sharing in a Partnership. In *Risk Management Strategies in Public-Private Partnerships* (pp. 115–152). Hershey, PA: IGI Global. doi:10.4018/978-1-5225-2503-5.ch004

Obidallah, W. J., & Raahemi, B. (2017). Managing Changes in Service Oriented Virtual Organizations: A Structural and Procedural Framework to Facilitate the Process of Change. *Journal of Electronic Commerce in Organizations*, *15*(1), 59–83. doi:10.4018/JECO.2017010104

Ojo, O. (2017). Impact of Innovation on the Entrepreneurial Success in Selected Business Enterprises in South-West Nigeria. *International Journal of Innovation in the Digital Economy*, *8*(2), 29–38. doi:10.4018/IJIDE.2017040103

Okdinawati, L., Simatupang, T. M., & Sunitiyoso, Y. (2017). Multi-Agent Reinforcement Learning for Value Co-Creation of Collaborative Transportation Management (CTM). *International Journal of Information Systems and Supply Chain Management*, *10*(3), 84–95. doi:10.4018/IJISSCM.2017070105

Olivera, V. A., & Carrillo, I. M. (2021). Organizational Culture: A Key Element for the Development of Mexican Micro and Small Tourist Companies. In J. Soares (Ed.), *Innovation and Entrepreneurial Opportunities in Community Tourism* (pp. 227–242). IGI Global. doi:10.4018/978-1-7998-4855-4.ch013

Ossorio, M. (2022). Corporate Museum Experiences in Enogastronomic Tourism. In R. Augusto Costa, F. Brandão, Z. Breda, & C. Costa (Eds.), Planning and Managing the Experience Economy in Tourism (pp. 107-121). IGI Global. https://doi.org/ doi:10.4018/978-1-7998-8775-1.ch006

Ossorio, M. (2022). Enogastronomic Tourism in Times of Pandemic. In G. Fernandes (Ed.), *Challenges and New Opportunities for Tourism in Inland Territories: Ecocultural Resources and Sustainable Initiatives* (pp. 241–255). IGI Global. https://doi.org/10.4018/978-1-7998-7339-6.ch014

Özekici, Y. K. (2022). ICT as an Acculturative Agent and Its Role in the Tourism Context: Introduction, Acculturation Theory, Progress of the Acculturation Theory in Extant Literature. In C. Ramos, S. Quinteiro, & A. Gonçalves (Eds.), *ICT as Innovator Between Tourism and Culture* (pp. 42–66). IGI Global. https://doi.org/10.4018/978-1-7998-8165-0.ch004

Pal, K. (2018). Building High Quality Big Data-Based Applications in Supply Chains. In A. Kumar & S. Saurav (Eds.), *Supply Chain Management Strategies and Risk Assessment in Retail Environments* (pp. 1–24). Hershey, PA: IGI Global. doi:10.4018/978-1-5225-3056-5.ch001

Palos-Sanchez, P. R., & Correia, M. B. (2018). Perspectives of the Adoption of Cloud Computing in the Tourism Sector. In J. Rodrigues, C. Ramos, P. Cardoso, & C. Henriques (Eds.), *Handbook of Research on Technological Developments for Cultural Heritage and eTourism Applications* (pp. 377–400). Hershey, PA: IGI Global. doi:10.4018/978-1-5225-2927-9.ch018

Papadopoulou, G. (2021). Promoting Gender Equality and Women Empowerment in the Tourism Sector. In F. Brandão, Z. Breda, R. Costa, & C. Costa (Eds.), Handbook of Research on the Role of Tourism in Achieving Sustainable Development Goals (pp. 152-174). IGI Global. https://doi.org/ doi:10.4018/978-1-7998-5691-7.ch009

Papp-Váry, Á. F., & Tóth, T. Z. (2022). Analysis of Budapest as a Film Tourism Destination. In R. Baleiro & R. Pereira (Eds.), *Global Perspectives on Literary Tourism and Film-Induced Tourism* (pp. 257-279). IGI Global. https://doi.org/10.4018/978-1-7998-8262-6.ch014

Patiño, B. E. (2017). New Generation Management by Convergence and Individual Identity: A Systemic and Human-Oriented Approach. In N. Baporikar (Ed.), *Innovation and Shifting Perspectives in Management Education* (pp. 119–143). Hershey, PA: IGI Global. doi:10.4018/978-1-5225-1019-2.ch006

Patro, C. S. (2021). Digital Tourism: Influence of E-Marketing Technology. In M. Dinis, L. Bonixe, S. Lamy, & Z. Breda (Eds.), *Impact of New Media in Tourism* (pp. 234-254). IGI Global. https://doi.org/10.4018/978-1-7998-7095-1.ch014

Pawliczek, A., & Rössler, M. (2017). Knowledge of Management Tools and Systems in SMEs: Knowledge Transfer in Management. In A. Bencsik (Ed.), *Knowledge Management Initiatives and Strategies in Small and Medium Enterprises* (pp. 180–203). Hershey, PA: IGI Global. doi:10.4018/978-1-5225-1642-2.ch009

Pejic-Bach, M., Omazic, M. A., Aleksic, A., & Zoroja, J. (2018). Knowledge-Based Decision Making: A Multi-Case Analysis. In R. Leon (Ed.), *Managerial Strategies for Business Sustainability During Turbulent Times* (pp. 160–184). Hershey, PA: IGI Global. doi:10.4018/978-1-5225-2716-9.ch009

Perano, M., Hysa, X., & Calabrese, M. (2018). Strategic Planning, Cultural Context, and Business Continuity Management: Business Cases in the City of Shkoder. In A. Presenza & L. Sheehan (Eds.), *Geopolitics and Strategic Management in the Global Economy* (pp. 57–77). Hershey, PA: IGI Global. doi:10.4018/978-1-5225-2673-5.ch004

Pereira, R., Mira da Silva, M., & Lapão, L. V. (2017). IT Governance Maturity Patterns in Portuguese Healthcare. In S. De Haes & W. Van Grembergen (Eds.), *Strategic IT Governance and Alignment in Business Settings* (pp. 24–52). Hershey, PA: IGI Global. doi:10.4018/978-1-5225-0861-8.ch002

Pérez-Uribe, R. I., Torres, D. A., Jurado, S. P., & Prada, D. M. (2018). Cloud Tools for the Development of Project Management in SMEs. In R. Perez-Uribe, C. Salcedo-Perez, & D. Ocampo-Guzman (Eds.), *Handbook of Research on Intrapreneurship and Organizational Sustainability in SMEs* (pp. 95–120). Hershey, PA: IGI Global. doi:10.4018/978-1-5225-3543-0.ch005

Petrisor, I., & Cozmiuc, D. (2017). Global Supply Chain Management Organization at Siemens in the Advent of Industry 4.0. In L. Saglietto & C. Cezanne (Eds.), *Global Intermediation and Logistics Service Providers* (pp. 123–142). Hershey, PA: IGI Global. doi:10.4018/978-1-5225-2133-4.ch007

Pierce, J. M., Velliaris, D. M., & Edwards, J. (2017). A Living Case Study: A Journey Not a Destination. In N. Silton (Ed.), *Exploring the Benefits of Creativity in Education, Media, and the Arts* (pp. 158–178). Hershey, PA: IGI Global. doi:10.4018/978-1-5225-0504-4.ch008

Pipia, S., & Pipia, S. (2021). Challenges of Religious Tourism in the Conflict Region: An Example of Jerusalem. In E. Alaverdov & M. Bari (Eds.), *Global Development of Religious Tourism* (pp. 135-148). IGI Global. https://doi.org/10.4018/978-1-7998-5792-1.ch009

Poulaki, P., Kritikos, A., Vasilakis, N., & Valeri, M. (2022). The Contribution of Female Creativity to the Development of Gastronomic Tourism in Greece: The Case of the Island of Naxos in the South Aegean Region. In M. Valeri (Ed.), *New Governance and Management in Touristic Destinations* (pp. 246–258). IGI Global. https://doi.org/10.4018/978-1-6684-3889-3.ch015

Radosavljevic, M., & Andjelkovic, A. (2017). Multi-Criteria Decision Making Approach for Choosing Business Process for the Improvement: Upgrading of the Six Sigma Methodology. In J. Stanković, P. Delias, S. Marinković, & S. Rochhia (Eds.), *Tools and Techniques for Economic Decision Analysis* (pp. 225–247). Hershey, PA: IGI Global. doi:10.4018/978-1-5225-0959-2.ch011

Radovic, V. M. (2017). Corporate Sustainability and Responsibility and Disaster Risk Reduction: A Serbian Overview. In M. Camilleri (Ed.), *CSR 2.0 and the New Era of Corporate Citizenship* (pp. 147–164). Hershey, PA: IGI Global. doi:10.4018/978-1-5225-1842-6.ch008

Raghunath, K. M., Devi, S. L., & Patro, C. S. (2018). Impact of Risk Assessment Models on Risk Factors: A Holistic Outlook. In K. Strang, M. Korstanje, & N. Vajjhala (Eds.), *Research, Practices, and Innovations in Global Risk and Contingency Management* (pp. 134–153). Hershey, PA: IGI Global. doi:10.4018/978-1-5225-4754-9.ch008

Raman, A., & Goyal, D. P. (2017). Extending IMPLEMENT Framework for Enterprise Information Systems Implementation to Information System Innovation. In M. Tavana (Ed.), *Enterprise Information Systems and the Digitalization of Business Functions* (pp. 137–177). Hershey, PA: IGI Global. doi:10.4018/978-1-5225-2382-6.ch007

Rao, Y., & Zhang, Y. (2017). The Construction and Development of Academic Library Digital Special Subject Databases. In L. Ruan, Q. Zhu, & Y. Ye (Eds.), *Academic Library Development and Administration in China* (pp. 163–183). Hershey, PA: IGI Global. doi:10.4018/978-1-5225-0550-1.ch010

Ravasan, A. Z., Mohammadi, M. M., & Hamidi, H. (2018). An Investigation Into the Critical Success Factors of Implementing Information Technology Service Management Frameworks. In K. Jakobs (Ed.), *Corporate and Global Standardization Initiatives in Contemporary Society* (pp. 200–218). Hershey, PA: IGI Global. doi:10.4018/978-1-5225-5320-5.ch009

Rezaie, S., Mirabedini, S. J., & Abtahi, A. (2018). Designing a Model for Implementation of Business Intelligence in the Banking Industry. *International Journal of Enterprise Information Systems, 14*(1), 77–103. doi:10.4018/IJEIS.2018010105

Richards, V., Matthews, N., Williams, O. J., & Khan, Z. (2021). The Challenges of Accessible Tourism Information Systems for Tourists With Vision Impairment: Sensory Communications Beyond the Screen. In C. Eusébio, L. Teixeira, & M. Carneiro (Eds.), *ICT Tools and Applications for Accessible Tourism* (pp. 26–54). IGI Global. https://doi.org/10.4018/978-1-7998-6428-8.ch002

Rodrigues de Souza Neto, V., & Marques, O. (2021). Rural Tourism Fostering Welfare Through Sustainable Development: A Conceptual Approach. In A. Perinotto, V. Mayer, & J. Soares (Eds.), *Rebuilding and Restructuring the Tourism Industry: Infusion of Happiness and Quality of Life* (pp. 38–57). IGI Global. https://doi.org/10.4018/978-1-7998-7239-9.ch003

Romano, L., Grimaldi, R., & Colasuonno, F. S. (2017). Demand Management as a Success Factor in Project Portfolio Management. In L. Romano (Ed.), *Project Portfolio Management Strategies for Effective Organizational Operations* (pp. 202–219). Hershey, PA: IGI Global. doi:10.4018/978-1-5225-2151-8.ch008

Rubio-Escuderos, L., & García-Andreu, H. (2021). Competitiveness Factors of Accessible Tourism E-Travel Agencies. In C. Eusébio, L. Teixeira, & M. Carneiro (Eds.), *ICT Tools and Applications for Accessible Tourism* (pp. 196–217). IGI Global. https://doi.org/10.4018/978-1-7998-6428-8.ch009

Rucci, A. C., Porto, N., Darcy, S., & Becka, L. (2021). Smart and Accessible Cities?: Not Always – The Case for Accessible Tourism Initiatives in Buenos Aries and Sydney. In C. Eusébio, L. Teixeira, & M. Carneiro (Eds.), *ICT Tools and Applications for Accessible Tourism* (pp. 115–145). IGI Global. https://doi.org/10.4018/978-1-7998-6428-8.ch006

Ruhi, U. (2018). Towards an Interdisciplinary Socio-Technical Definition of Virtual Communities. In M. Khosrow-Pour, D.B.A. (Ed.), Encyclopedia of Information Science and Technology, Fourth Edition (pp. 4278-4295). Hershey, PA: IGI Global. doi:10.4018/978-1-5225-2255-3.ch371

Ryan, L., Catena, M., Ros, P., & Stephens, S. (2021). Designing Entrepreneurial Ecosystems to Support Resource Management in the Tourism Industry. In V. Costa, A. Moura, & M. Mira (Eds.), *Handbook of Research on Human Capital and People Management in the Tourism Industry* (pp. 265–281). IGI Global. https://doi.org/10.4018/978-1-7998-4318-4.ch013

Sabuncu, I. (2021). Understanding Tourist Perceptions and Expectations During Pandemic Through Social Media Big Data. In M. Demir, A. Dalgıç, & F. Ergen (Eds.), *Handbook of Research on the Impacts and Implications of COVID-19 on the Tourism Industry* (pp. 330–350). IGI Global. https://doi.org/10.4018/978-1-7998-8231-2.ch016

Safari, M. R., & Jiang, Q. (2018). The Theory and Practice of IT Governance Maturity and Strategies Alignment: Evidence From Banking Industry. *Journal of Global Information Management*, *26*(2), 127–146. doi:10.4018/JGIM.2018040106

Sahoo, J., Pati, B., & Mohanty, B. (2017). Knowledge Management as an Academic Discipline: An Assessment. In B. Gunjal (Ed.), *Managing Knowledge and Scholarly Assets in Academic Libraries* (pp. 99–126). Hershey, PA: IGI Global. doi:10.4018/978-1-5225-1741-2.ch005

Saini, D. (2017). Relevance of Teaching Values and Ethics in Management Education. In N. Baporikar (Ed.), *Management Education for Global Leadership* (pp. 90–111). Hershey, PA: IGI Global. doi:10.4018/978-1-5225-1013-0.ch005

Sambhanthan, A. (2017). Assessing and Benchmarking Sustainability in Organisations: An Integrated Conceptual Model. *International Journal of Systems and Service-Oriented Engineering*, *7*(4), 22–43. doi:10.4018/IJSSOE.2017100102

Sambhanthan, A., & Potdar, V. (2017). A Study of the Parameters Impacting Sustainability in Information Technology Organizations. *International Journal of Knowledge-Based Organizations*, *7*(3), 27–39. doi:10.4018/IJKBO.2017070103

Sánchez-Fernández, M. D., & Manríquez, M. R. (2018). The Entrepreneurial Spirit Based on Social Values: The Digital Generation. In P. Isaias & L. Carvalho (Eds.), *User Innovation and the Entrepreneurship Phenomenon in the Digital Economy* (pp. 173–193). Hershey, PA: IGI Global. doi:10.4018/978-1-5225-2826-5.ch009

Sanchez-Ruiz, L., & Blanco, B. (2017). Process Management for SMEs: Barriers, Enablers, and Benefits. In M. Vemić (Ed.), *Optimal Management Strategies in Small and Medium Enterprises* (pp. 293–319). Hershey, PA: IGI Global. doi:10.4018/978-1-5225-1949-2.ch014

Sanz, L. F., Gómez-Pérez, J., & Castillo-Martinez, A. (2018). Analysis of the European ICT Competence Frameworks. In V. Ahuja & S. Rathore (Eds.), *Multidisciplinary Perspectives on Human Capital and Information Technology Professionals* (pp. 225–245). Hershey, PA: IGI Global. doi:10.4018/978-1-5225-5297-0.ch012

Sarvepalli, A., & Godin, J. (2017). Business Process Management in the Classroom. *Journal of Cases on Information Technology, 19*(2), 17–28. doi:10.4018/JCIT.2017040102

Saxena, G. G., & Saxena, A. (2021). Host Community Role in Medical Tourism Development. In M. Singh & S. Kumaran (Eds.), *Growth of the Medical Tourism Industry and Its Impact on Society: Emerging Research and Opportunities* (pp. 105–127). IGI Global. https://doi.org/10.4018/978-1-7998-3427-4.ch006

Saygili, E. E., Ozturkoglu, Y., & Kocakulah, M. C. (2017). End Users' Perceptions of Critical Success Factors in ERP Applications. *International Journal of Enterprise Information Systems, 13*(4), 58–75. doi:10.4018/IJEIS.2017100104

Saygili, E. E., & Saygili, A. T. (2017). Contemporary Issues in Enterprise Information Systems: A Critical Review of CSFs in ERP Implementations. In M. Tavana (Ed.), *Enterprise Information Systems and the Digitalization of Business Functions* (pp. 120–136). Hershey, PA: IGI Global. doi:10.4018/978-1-5225-2382-6.ch006

Schwaiger, K. M., & Zehrer, A. (2021). The COVID-19 Pandemic and Organizational Resilience in Hospitality Family Firms: A Qualitative Approach. In A. Zehrer, G. Glowka, K. Schwaiger, & V. Ranacher-Lackner (Eds.), *Resiliency Models and Addressing Future Risks for Family Firms in the Tourism Industry* (pp. 32–49). IGI Global. https://doi.org/10.4018/978-1-7998-7352-5.ch002

Scott, N., & Campos, A. C. (2022). Cognitive Science of Tourism Experiences. In R. Augusto Costa, F. Brandão, Z. Breda, & C. Costa (Eds.), Planning and Managing the Experience Economy in Tourism (pp. 1-21). IGI Global. https://doi.org/ doi:10.4018/978-1-7998-8775-1.ch001

Seidenstricker, S., & Antonino, A. (2018). Business Model Innovation-Oriented Technology Management for Emergent Technologies. In M. Khosrow-Pour, D.B.A. (Ed.), Encyclopedia of Information Science and Technology, Fourth Edition (pp. 4560-4569). Hershey, PA: IGI Global. doi:10.4018/978-1-5225-2255-3.ch396

Selvi, M. S. (2021). Changes in Tourism Sales and Marketing Post COVID-19. In M. Demir, A. Dalgıç, & F. Ergen (Eds.), *Handbook of Research on the Impacts and Implications of COVID-19 on the Tourism Industry* (pp. 437–460). IGI Global. doi:10.4018/978-1-7998-8231-2.ch021

Senaratne, S., & Gunarathne, A. D. (2017). Excellence Perspective for Management Education from a Global Accountants' Hub in Asia. In N. Baporikar (Ed.), *Management Education for Global Leadership* (pp. 158–180). Hershey, PA: IGI Global. doi:10.4018/978-1-5225-1013-0.ch008

Sensuse, D. I., & Cahyaningsih, E. (2018). Knowledge Management Models: A Summative Review. *International Journal of Information Systems in the Service Sector, 10*(1), 71–100. doi:10.4018/IJISSS.2018010105

Seth, M., Goyal, D., & Kiran, R. (2017). Diminution of Impediments in Implementation of Supply Chain Management Information System for Enhancing its Effectiveness in Indian Automobile Industry. *Journal of Global Information Management, 25*(3), 1–20. doi:10.4018/JGIM.2017070101

Seyal, A. H., & Rahman, M. N. (2017). Investigating Impact of Inter-Organizational Factors in Measuring ERP Systems Success: Bruneian Perspectives. In M. Tavana (Ed.), *Enterprise Information Systems and the Digitalization of Business Functions* (pp. 178–204). Hershey, PA: IGI Global. doi:10.4018/978-1-5225-2382-6.ch008

Shaqrah, A. A. (2018). Analyzing Business Intelligence Systems Based on 7s Model of McKinsey. *International Journal of Business Intelligence Research, 9*(1), 53–63. doi:10.4018/IJBIR.2018010104

Sharma, A. J. (2017). Enhancing Sustainability through Experiential Learning in Management Education. In N. Baporikar (Ed.), *Management Education for Global Leadership* (pp. 256–274). Hershey, PA: IGI Global. doi:10.4018/978-1-5225-1013-0.ch013

Shetty, K. P. (2017). Responsible Global Leadership: Ethical Challenges in Management Education. In N. Baporikar (Ed.), *Innovation and Shifting Perspectives in Management Education* (pp. 194–223). Hershey, PA: IGI Global. doi:10.4018/978-1-5225-1019-2.ch009

Sinthupundaja, J., & Kohda, Y. (2017). Effects of Corporate Social Responsibility and Creating Shared Value on Sustainability. *International Journal of Sustainable Entrepreneurship and Corporate Social Responsibility, 2*(1), 27–38. doi:10.4018/IJSECSR.2017010103

Škarica, I., & Hrgović, A. V. (2018). Implementation of Total Quality Management Principles in Public Health Institutes in the Republic of Croatia. *International Journal of Productivity Management and Assessment Technologies, 6*(1), 1–16. doi:10.4018/IJPMAT.2018010101

Skokic, V. (2021). How Small Hotel Owners Practice Resilience: Longitudinal Study Among Small Family Hotels in Croatia. In A. Zehrer, G. Glowka, K. Schwaiger, & V. Ranacher-Lackner (Eds.), *Resiliency Models and Addressing Future Risks for Family Firms in the Tourism Industry* (pp. 50–73). IGI Global. doi:10.4018/978-1-7998-7352-5.ch003

Smuts, H., Kotzé, P., Van der Merwe, A., & Loock, M. (2017). Framework for Managing Shared Knowledge in an Information Systems Outsourcing Context. *International Journal of Knowledge Management, 13*(4), 1–30. doi:10.4018/IJKM.2017100101

Sousa, M. J., Cruz, R., Dias, I., & Caracol, C. (2017). Information Management Systems in the Supply Chain. In G. Jamil, A. Soares, & C. Pessoa (Eds.), *Handbook of Research on Information Management for Effective Logistics and Supply Chains* (pp. 469–485). Hershey, PA: IGI Global. doi:10.4018/978-1-5225-0973-8.ch025

Spremic, M., Turulja, L., & Bajgoric, N. (2018). Two Approaches in Assessing Business Continuity Management Attitudes in the Organizational Context. In N. Bajgoric (Ed.), *Always-On Enterprise Information Systems for Modern Organizations* (pp. 159–183). Hershey, PA: IGI Global. doi:10.4018/978-1-5225-3704-5.ch008

Steenkamp, A. L. (2018). Some Insights in Computer Science and Information Technology. In *Examining the Changing Role of Supervision in Doctoral Research Projects: Emerging Research and Opportunities* (pp. 113–133). Hershey, PA: IGI Global. doi:10.4018/978-1-5225-2610-0.ch005

Stipanović, C., Rudan, E., & Zubović, V. (2022). Reaching the New Tourist Through Creativity: Sustainable Development Challenges in Croatian Coastal Towns. In M. Valeri (Ed.), *New Governance and Management in Touristic Destinations* (pp. 231–245). IGI Global. https://doi.org/10.4018/978-1-6684-3889-3.ch014

Tabach, A., & Croteau, A. (2017). Configurations of Information Technology Governance Practices and Business Unit Performance. *International Journal of IT/Business Alignment and Governance, 8*(2), 1–27. doi:10.4018/IJITBAG.2017070101

Talaue, G. M., & Iqbal, T. (2017). Assessment of e-Business Mode of Selected Private Universities in the Philippines and Pakistan. *International Journal of Online Marketing, 7*(4), 63–77. doi:10.4018/IJOM.2017100105

Tam, G. C. (2017). Project Manager Sustainability Competence. In *Managerial Strategies and Green Solutions for Project Sustainability* (pp. 178–207). Hershey, PA: IGI Global. doi:10.4018/978-1-5225-2371-0.ch008

Tambo, T. (2018). Fashion Retail Innovation: About Context, Antecedents, and Outcome in Technological Change Projects. In I. Management Association (Ed.), Fashion and Textiles: Breakthroughs in Research and Practice (pp. 233-260). Hershey, PA: IGI Global. https://doi.org/ doi:10.4018/978-1-5225-3432-7.ch010

Tantau, A. D., & Frăţilă, L. C. (2018). Information and Management System for Renewable Energy Business. In *Entrepreneurship and Business Development in the Renewable Energy Sector* (pp. 200–244). Hershey, PA: IGI Global. doi:10.4018/978-1-5225-3625-3.ch006

Teixeira, N., Pardal, P. N., & Rafael, B. G. (2018). Internationalization, Financial Performance, and Organizational Challenges: A Success Case in Portugal. In L. Carvalho (Ed.), *Handbook of Research on Entrepreneurial Ecosystems and Social Dynamics in a Globalized World* (pp. 379–423). Hershey, PA: IGI Global. doi:10.4018/978-1-5225-3525-6.ch017

Teixeira, P., Teixeira, L., Eusébio, C., Silva, S., & Teixeira, A. (2021). The Impact of ICTs on Accessible Tourism: Evidence Based on a Systematic Literature Review. In C. Eusébio, L. Teixeira, & M. Carneiro (Eds.), *ICT Tools and Applications for Accessible Tourism* (pp. 1–25). IGI Global. doi:10.4018/978-1-7998-6428-8.ch001

Trad, A., & Kalpić, D. (2018). The Business Transformation Framework, Agile Project and Change Management. In M. Khosrow-Pour, D.B.A. (Ed.), Encyclopedia of Information Science and Technology, Fourth Edition (pp. 620-635). Hershey, PA: IGI Global. https://doi.org/ doi:10.4018/978-1-5225-2255-3.ch054

Trad, A., & Kalpić, D. (2018). The Business Transformation and Enterprise Architecture Framework: The Financial Engineering E-Risk Management and E-Law Integration. In B. Sergi, F. Fidanoski, M. Ziolo, & V. Naumovski (Eds.), *Regaining Global Stability After the Financial Crisis* (pp. 46–65). Hershey, PA: IGI Global. doi:10.4018/978-1-5225-4026-7.ch003

Trengereid, V. (2022). Conditions of Network Engagement: The Quest for a Common Good. In R. Augusto Costa, F. Brandão, Z. Breda, & C. Costa (Eds.), *Planning and Managing the Experience Economy in Tourism* (pp. 69-84). IGI Global. https://doi.org/10.4018/978-1-7998-8775-1.ch004

Turulja, L., & Bajgoric, N. (2018). Business Continuity and Information Systems: A Systematic Literature Review. In N. Bajgoric (Ed.), *Always-On Enterprise Information Systems for Modern Organizations* (pp. 60–87). Hershey, PA: IGI Global. doi:10.4018/978-1-5225-3704-5.ch004

Vargas-Hernández, J. G. (2017). Professional Integrity in Business Management Education. In N. Baporikar (Ed.), *Management Education for Global Leadership* (pp. 70–89). Hershey, PA: IGI Global. doi:10.4018/978-1-5225-1013-0.ch004

Varnacı Uzun, F. (2021). The Destination Preferences of Foreign Tourists During the COVID-19 Pandemic and Attitudes Towards: Marmaris, Turkey. In M. Demir, A. Dalgıç, & F. Ergen (Eds.), *Handbook of Research on the Impacts and Implications of COVID-19 on the Tourism Industry* (pp. 285–306). IGI Global. https://doi.org/10.4018/978-1-7998-8231-2.ch014

Vasista, T. G., & AlAbdullatif, A. M. (2017). Role of Electronic Customer Relationship Management in Demand Chain Management: A Predictive Analytic Approach. *International Journal of Information Systems and Supply Chain Management, 10*(1), 53–67. doi:10.4018/IJISSCM.2017010104

Vieru, D., & Bourdeau, S. (2017). Survival in the Digital Era: A Digital Competence-Based Multi-Case Study in the Canadian SME Clothing Industry. *International Journal of Social and Organizational Dynamics in IT, 6*(1), 17–34. doi:10.4018/IJSODIT.2017010102

Vijayan, G., & Kamarulzaman, N. H. (2017). An Introduction to Sustainable Supply Chain Management and Business Implications. In M. Khan, M. Hussain, & M. Ajmal (Eds.), *Green Supply Chain Management for Sustainable Business Practice* (pp. 27–50). Hershey, PA: IGI Global. doi:10.4018/978-1-5225-0635-5.ch002

Vlachvei, A., & Notta, O. (2017). Firm Competitiveness: Theories, Evidence, and Measurement. In A. Vlachvei, O. Notta, K. Karantininis, & N. Tsounis (Eds.), *Factors Affecting Firm Competitiveness and Performance in the Modern Business World* (pp. 1–42). Hershey, PA: IGI Global. doi:10.4018/978-1-5225-0843-4.ch001

Wang, C., Schofield, M., Li, X., & Ou, X. (2017). Do Chinese Students in Public and Private Higher Education Institutes Perform at Different Level in One of the Leadership Skills: Critical Thinking?: An Exploratory Comparison. In V. Wang (Ed.), *Encyclopedia of Strategic Leadership and Management* (pp. 160–181). Hershey, PA: IGI Global. doi:10.4018/978-1-5225-1049-9.ch013

Wang, J. (2017). Multi-Agent based Production Management Decision System Modelling for the Textile Enterprise. *Journal of Global Information Management, 25*(4), 1–15. doi:10.4018/JGIM.2017100101

Wiedemann, A., & Gewald, H. (2017). Examining Cross-Domain Alignment: The Correlation of Business Strategy, IT Management, and IT Business Value. *International Journal of IT/Business Alignment and Governance, 8*(1), 17–31. doi:10.4018/IJITBAG.2017010102

Wolf, R., & Thiel, M. (2018). Advancing Global Business Ethics in China: Reducing Poverty Through Human and Social Welfare. In S. Hipsher (Ed.), *Examining the Private Sector's Role in Wealth Creation and Poverty Reduction* (pp. 67–84). Hershey, PA: IGI Global. doi:10.4018/978-1-5225-3117-3.ch004

Yablonsky, S. (2018). Innovation Platforms: Data and Analytics Platforms. In *Multi-Sided Platforms (MSPs) and Sharing Strategies in the Digital Economy: Emerging Research and Opportunities* (pp. 72–95). Hershey, PA: IGI Global. doi:10.4018/978-1-5225-5457-8.ch003

Yaşar, B. (2021). The Impact of COVID-19 on Volatility of Tourism Stocks: Evidence From BIST Tourism Index. In M. Demir, A. Dalgıç, & F. Ergen (Eds.), *Handbook of Research on the Impacts and Implications of COVID-19 on the Tourism Industry* (pp. 23–44). IGI Global. https://doi.org/10.4018/978-1-7998-8231-2.ch002

Yusoff, A., Ahmad, N. H., & Halim, H. A. (2017). Agropreneurship among Gen Y in Malaysia: The Role of Academic Institutions. In N. Ahmad, T. Ramayah, H. Halim, & S. Rahman (Eds.), *Handbook of Research on Small and Medium Enterprises in Developing Countries* (pp. 23–47). Hershey, PA: IGI Global. doi:10.4018/978-1-5225-2165-5.ch002

Zacher, D., & Pechlaner, H. (2021). Resilience as an Opportunity Approach: Challenges and Perspectives for Private Sector Participation on a Community Level. In A. Zehrer, G. Glowka, K. Schwaiger, & V. Ranacher-Lackner (Eds.), *Resiliency Models and Addressing Future Risks for Family Firms in the Tourism Industry* (pp. 75–102). IGI Global. https://doi.org/10.4018/978-1-7998-7352-5.ch004

Zanin, F., Comuzzi, E., & Costantini, A. (2018). The Effect of Business Strategy and Stock Market Listing on the Use of Risk Assessment Tools. In *Management Control Systems in Complex Settings: Emerging Research and Opportunities* (pp. 145–168). Hershey, PA: IGI Global. doi:10.4018/978-1-5225-3987-2.ch007

Zgheib, P. W. (2017). Corporate Innovation and Intrapreneurship in the Middle East. In P. Zgheib (Ed.), *Entrepreneurship and Business Innovation in the Middle East* (pp. 37–56). Hershey, PA: IGI Global. doi:10.4018/978-1-5225-2066-5.ch003

About the Contributors

Gülce Dölkeleş was born in Bursa, Turkey. She graduated from Visual Communication Design Department of Kocaeli University. She got master's Degree in Communication Design and Information Technology Department of Kocaeli University. She got master's Degree in Communication Arts of Yalova University. She got Proficiency in Fine Arts in Combined Art Department of Ankara Hacı Bayram Veli University. Gülce worked in the Graphic Design Department of Faruk Saraç Vocational School of Design. She currently works as an academic in the Communication Design Department of Antalya Belek University, Art and Design Faculty. She is recognised for her work on design and advertisement.

Ankur Gupta has received the B.Tech and M.Tech in Computer Science and Engineering from Ganga Institute of Technology and Management, Kablana affiliated with Maharshi Dayanand University, Rohtak in 2015 and 2017. He is an Assistant Professor in the Department of Computer Science and Engineering at Vaish College of Engineering, Rohtak, and has been working there since January 2019. He has many publications in various reputed national/ international conferences, journals, and online book chapter contributions (Indexed by SCIE, Scopus, ESCI, ACM, DBLP, etc.). He is doing research in the field of cloud computing, data security & machine learning. His research work in M.Tech was based on biometric security in cloud computing.

Ebru Güzeloğlu has been a faculty member at Ege University, Faculty of Communication, Department of Public Relations and Publicity since 2017. She conducts academic studies and provides theoretical/practical training in the field of effective communication in the fields of civil initiatives and youth work. She has publications on social awareness, perception, and strategic communication in marketing communication and public relations disciplines. She worked as a coordinator, researcher, and trainer in national and international projects in which various groups from civil society participated.

Burak Ili graduated from the Department of Radio, Television, and Cinema at Marmara University Faculty of Communication. In 2018, they completed their master's degree in the Department of Cinema-TV Main Art at Beykent University Institute of Social Sciences, and in 2023, they completed their Ph.D. in the Department of Radio-TV Cinema at Istanbul University Institute of Social Sciences with a thesis titled "Digital Nomadism in the Age of New Media: A Study on the Travelers of the 21st Century." In 2019, they started working as a lecturer at Iğdır University Technical Sciences Vocational School, Department of Visual-Auditory Techniques and Media Production, and as of 2023, they continue their duties as an Assistant Professor. They are continuing their studies in the fields of digital nomadism and new media.

Bhupendra Kumar is currently associated with Galgotias University, School of Business (Finance). He's professor with a demonstrated history of global exposure in academics/research and administrative positions for 18 years. Blessed with thoroughly excellent academic performance, research supervision, advisory & consultancy services with global lecturing, expert talks, seminars, curriculum development and other industry-academic collaborations. He has worked with for more than 6 years with foreign universities as full-time regular professor, international relation officer actively associated with top management/directorates for different Global projects, cooperation agreements, world ranking agencies (THE/QS etc.), funding organizations like UNESCO/AU etc. for research collaborations and global presence. Some truly global participations and open lecture opportunities such as Ural State University Yekaterinburg Russia, European University Institute (EUI) Italy, Higher School of Economics (HSE) Russia, Ethiopia and middle East countries motivates to explore further. He's gained great experience as being regular foreign Thesis examiner for PH. D for South Africa, Kenya, Rwanda and other Indian universities. Experience 18 years' academic and administrative experience with 6 years international exposure Qualification PhD (Business Management) – March 2009 Awarded M.Phil. (Economics) – Gold Medalist – 2005 MBA – 2002 B.Sc. (PCM) – 2000 Awards & Recognition Gold Medalist – 2005 Dr. APJ Abdul Kalam 2023, DTU Ethiopia -ICERT India Certifications NISM- Equity Derivatives, Credit Research Analyst SEBI/MCA Resource Person Area of Interests Advanced Financial Management Financial Derivatives / Capital Market Security Analysis Portfolio Management Corporate Finance International Business & Foreign Exchange Market Corporate Governance, Banking & Insurance Books Published Fundamentals of Banking. ISBN: 978-93-82249-76-4. Management of Finance services. ISBN: 978-93-51632-52-8. Managerial Economics ISBN: 978-93-82249-04-7. Research Methods in Business Management. ISBN 978-93-82249-48-1. Other Achievements Research Papers published – 53, Patents -3 Global research projects collaborator /

conference convener – 15 International Keynote speakers / Open Lectures – 38 PhD Thesis supervised -4, Foreign PhD Thesis examined -13.

Anshuman Magar (M.B.A. (Fin.), M.com, NET, SET, Ph.D.) is an Assistant Professor (Finance) at the Lexicon Management Institute of Leadership and Excellence, Pune, and a former acting Principal at the University of Mumbai's constituent V.B. Dr. Babasaheb Ambedkar Model Degree College, Maharashtra. He has more than a decade of teaching experience as well as two and a half years of industrial experience. He is an editorial board member of many peer-reviewed research journals and he has also published patents, authored books, research publications in Scopus, and ABDC Research Journals, and presented research papers at various international and national conferences. His core research areas are International Finance, Fintech, and Corporate Finance.

R. Nagarajan received his B.E. in Electrical and Electronics Engineering from Madurai Kamarajar University, Madurai, India, in 1997. He received his M.E. in Power Electronics and Drives from Anna University, Chennai, India, in 2008. He received his Ph.D in Electrical Engineering from Anna University, Chennai, India, in 2014. He has worked in the industry as an Electrical Engineer. He is currently working as Professor of Electrical and Electronics Engineering at Gnanamani College of Technology, Namakkal, and Tamilnadu, India. His current research interest includes Power Electronics, Power System, Soft Computing Techniques and Renewable Energy Sources. He is published more than ninety research papers in various referred international journal.

Sabyasachi Pramanik is a professional IEEE member. He obtained a PhD in Computer Science and Engineering from Sri Satya Sai University of Technology and Medical Sciences, Bhopal, India. Presently, he is an Associate Professor, Department of Computer Science and Engineering, Haldia Institute of Technology, India. He has many publications in various reputed international conferences, journals, and book chapters (Indexed by SCIE, Scopus, ESCI, etc). He is doing research in the fields of Artificial Intelligence, Data Privacy, Cybersecurity, Network Security, and Machine Learning. He also serves on the editorial boards of several international journals. He is a reviewer of journal articles from IEEE, Springer, Elsevier, Inderscience, IET and IGI Global. He has reviewed many conference papers, has been a keynote speaker, session chair, and technical program committee member at many international conferences. He has authored a book on Wireless Sensor Network. He has edited 8 books from IGI Global, CRC Press, Springer and Wiley Publications.

Vishesh Redhu is a doctoral scholar with the media school at Bennett University. His research interests include digital storytelling, mobile storytelling, cultural and rural heritage.

Nitin Nandkumar Sakhare received B. E. Computer degree in Computer Engineering from Vishwakarma Institute of Information Technology, Pune affiliated to Savitribai Phule Pune University, formerly known as Pune University, in 2012 and Master's degree in Computer Engineering from Sinhgad College of Engineering, Pune affiliated to Savitribai Phule Pune University, formerly known as Pune University, in 2012. Nitin Nandkumar He is currently working toward the Ph.D. degree at the Department of Computer Science and Engineering, KL University, Vijaywada, Andhra Pradesh. He is currently working as an assistant professor in the department of Computer Engineering of Vishwakarma Institute of Information Technology, Pune. His research interests include Data Science, Machine Learning, Computer Networking and Internet of Things.

Surjit Singha is a dedicated researcher interested in UN Sustainable Development Goals, Organizational Climate, Workforce Diversity, Organizational Culture, HRM, Marketing, Finance, IB, Global Business, Business, AI, Women Studies, and Cultural Studies. Currently serving as a faculty member in the Department of Commerce at Kristu Jayanti College (Autonomous), Dr. Surjit holds prestigious positions as Editor, reviewer, and author for renowned Global Publications and Journals, including Editorial review board member at Information Resources Management Journal; Reviewer and author at IGI Global. With over 13 years of extensive experience in Administration, Teaching, and Research, both in Industry and Higher Education Institutions (HEIs), Dr. Surjit is committed to imparting knowledge and guiding students in their research pursuits. As a research mentor, Dr. Surjit is vital in nurturing young minds and fostering academic growth. Leading a team of approximately 35 faculty members, Dr. Surjit also heads website management, promotion, and social media publicity efforts. Dedicated to continuous learning, Dr. Surjit boasts certifications as a Life Skill Trainer by RGNYID, a Microsoft Innovative Educator by Microsoft, and a Yoga Volunteer certified by The Yoga Certification Board, Ministry of AYUSH, Gov. of India. A trailblazer in academia, Dr. Surjit has guided and mentored 21 student projects in the academic year 2022-23, resulting in all 21 students publishing papers under Dr. Surjit's astute guidance. As NSS Faculty Mentor, Dr. Surjit has successfully mentored 65 students in the academic year 2022-23, ensuring all students achieve credits and qualifications. Dr. Surjit Singha has made substantial contributions to research with an impressive track record of over 65 publications as articles, including chapters in books, edited books, and various textbooks. Dr. Surjit continues to excel in academia after being granted 2 US Copyrights and receiving two fully funded minor research projects (Completed and Published) from Kristu Jayanti College (Autonomous). With a firm commitment to excellence in education and research, Dr. Surjit Singha elevates the institution's status and fosters an environment of knowledge dissemination and growth.

Elif Üstündağlı Erten has been the faculty member of Ege University, Faculty of Economics and Administrative Sciences, Department of Production Management and Marketing since 2009. Dr. Üstündağlı Erten's research interests span consumer behavior at the macro level, covering consumer acculturation, consumer identity, ethnicity, online shopping, as well as sustainability and green consumption at the micro level.

Index

www.ingramcontent.com/pod-product-compliance
Lightning Source LLC
LaVergne TN
LVHW081328300926
849161LV00008B/1905